A
MARITIME
HISTORY OF
SCOTLAND,
1650–1790

The title page illustration is of
the seal of the High Court of Admiralty of Scotland

A
MARITIME
HISTORY OF
SCOTLAND,
1650–1790

Eric J. Graham

TUCKWELL PRESS

First published in Great Britain in 2002 by
Tuckwell Press
The Mill House
Phantassie
East Linton
East Lothian EH40 3DG
Scotland

© Eric J. Graham, 2002

ISBN 1 86232 100 0

British Library Cataloguing in Publication Data
A catalogue record for this book is available
on request from the British Library

Design by Mark Blackadder

The publishers gratefully
acknowledge subsidy from the
Scotland Inheritance Fund

Printed and bound by Cromwell Press,
Trowbridge, Wiltshire

CONTENTS

FIGURES

TABLES

ACKNOWLEDGEMENTS

I would like to express my gratitude to a host of like-minded individuals whose open-handed generosity has done so much to enrich this work. This circle of colleagues encompasses a spectrum of academics and maritime enthusiasts, many of whom have gifted their indispensable local knowledge to this study.

I am deeply indebted to Professor C. A. Whatley and Dr. G. Jackson for their unstinting support. My thanks also go to Dr. D. Starkey for his constructive comments and to Dr. D. Richardson, K. Beedham and the late M. M. Schofield whose combined work on the Liverpool Plantation Records was made available to me by the ESRC Data Archive. Likewise, to Professor H. C. Johansen for access to the Danish Sound Tolls database.

I am indebted to many libraries: the Aberdeen Public Library, Aberdeen Maritime Museum, Ayrshire Archives, British Library, Carnegie Library at Ayr, Dundee City Archives, Campbeltown Archives at Dunoon Library, Dumbarton Public Library, Hunterian Library of the University of Glasgow, Edinburgh City Library, Exeter University Library, Lloyd's Register of Shipping, Mitchell Library, National Maritime Museum, National Archives of Scotland, National Library of Scotland, North Ayrshire Library, North Ayrshire Museum, Public Record/Office and the Watt Library at Greenock. I am also indebted to the Society of Nautical Research for a grant towards travelling expenses.

On a more personal note I would like to record my gratitude to: David Alston, Sheena Andrew, Tom Barclay, Frank & Rosemary Bigwood, Richard F. Dell, Michael Dun, Alan W. Graham Ian Hustwick, Jane Jamieson, Janet Kinloch, Bill Lane, Sue Mowat, Donald & Mary Petrie and Frances Wilkins for their generous access to their notes and resources. Also to I. L. Mackay and I. Ryland of HM Customs & Excise and Richard Dargie of Moray House for their support.

Lastly, I am indebted, as always, to my wife – Jan Bateman – for her unstinting support and encouragement throughout a period of research and write-up that extended far beyond all expectations.   ERIC J. GRAHAM

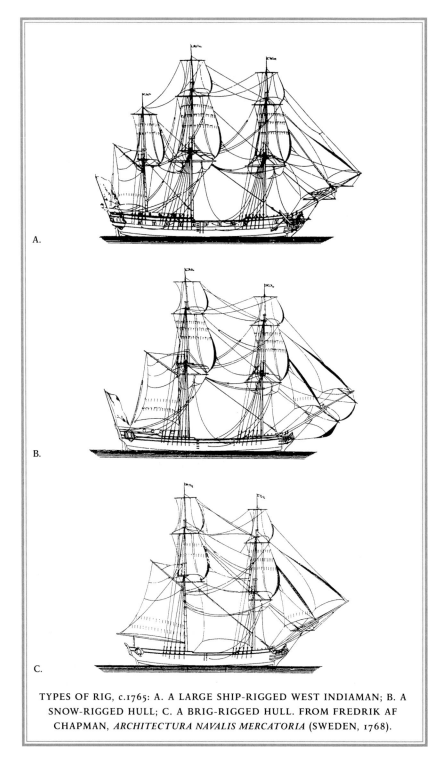

TYPES OF RIG, c.1765: A. A LARGE SHIP-RIGGED WEST INDIAMAN; B. A
SNOW-RIGGED HULL; C. A BRIG-RIGGED HULL. FROM FREDRIK AF
CHAPMAN, *ARCHITECTURA NAVALIS MERCATORIA* (SWEDEN, 1768).

GLOSSARY

Types of seventeenth- and eighteenth-century Scottish vessels

Bark – large open or partially decked seagoing trader, often with leeboards.

Birlin – West Highland oared open boat capable of crossing major channels.

Brig or brigantine – two-masted, square-rigged, wide-decked seagoing vessel of various sizes.

Bucker – the general name for an armed two-masted lugger as first used by the smugglers of Buckie.

Buss – decked fishing boat within 20-80 tons class as prescribed by the bounty rules which included fishing tackle and nets onboard. The larger hulls had a roller set into the bow gunwhale over which fishing tackle and floats were laid and retrieved.

Coble – Small open boat used in inshore fishing and oared by four men – or more if working further out. Capable of stepping a small sail in the right conditions.

Cutter – single-masted vessel, fore and aft rigged, with 'sharp' hull and extended bowsprit.

Doggar – a two-masted Dutch offshore fishing boat.

Fluyt boat – the standardised Dutch medium-sized bulk carrier (up to 600 tons), often flat-bottomed with severe tumble-home and very high narrow stern.

Gabbart – shallow-draft sailing lighter with leeboards suitable for rivers and estuaries.

Galley – A corruption of the term 'galleon' (as in high-sterned, three-masted, oceangoing, armed sailing vessel). This use of this term in Scotland died out by the mid-eighteenth century.

Jager – Dutch supply ship to the grand fisheries. Also used as hospital ship or to run high-priced early-season catches back to market.

Lugger – small two-masted vessel with lug square sails that could be set to work high to windward. Much favoured by smugglers and privateers.

Pink – narrow-decked, round-sterned Dutch bulk carrier with a flat floor interior.

Schooner – two-masted vessel, fore and aft rigged, commonly used in American and West Indian waters.

Shallop – small, fast, two-masted open or partially deck vessel, usually schooner-rigged, used in fishing or dispatches.

Ship – three-masted, all square sail, vessel.

Sixteeren – High-prowed open fishing boat oared by six men used in Shetland and Orkney for offshore line fishing and inter-island communication.

Sloop – general term for single-masted vessels without cutter bow or bowsprit.

Snow – variation of brig where the rear mast had a separate upright from which to set the mizzen sail.

Wherry – broad-decked, shallow-draft hull with lee boards and low freeboard suitable for the deployment of sweeps (large oars).

Yacht – a decked hull with superior passenger accommodation, originally of Dutch design, that was used to convey an important person or persons.

Customs terms

Customs precinct – stretch of shoreline under the supervisor of a Collector.

Head port – the reporting port of the precinct.

Creek – general term used to describe other smaller harbours or anchorages within the precinct.

Collector – Customs officer directly responsible to Edinburgh for the precinct.

Comptroller – second-in-line to Collector and responsible for accounts.

Tidesurveyor – Customs officer in charge of tidewaiters.

Tidewaiter – Customs officer put onboard vessels on entry or departure.

Landsurveyor – Customs officer in charge of landwaiters and landcarriagemen.

Landwaiter – Customs officer deployed onshore.

Landcarriageman – Customs officer deployed at the gateways to a port or major city.

Riding Officer – coastal patrol officer to the precinct.

Blue book – the manifest of cargo kept onboard by the captain that was stamped or witnessed by Customs officers at the point of departure and arrival.

Enumerated goods – those regulated goods listed by the Navigation Acts.

Rummaging – searching the vessel for contraband or undeclared goods.

Prizing – the method of packing of barrels and hogsheads.

ABBREVIATIONS

APS	*Acts of the Parliaments of Scotland*
BL	British Library
CE	Court of Exchequer
CL	Carnegie Library (Ayr)
GCA	Glasgow City Archives
GUL	Glasgow University Library
HCAS	High Court of Admiralty of Scotland
NAS	National Archives of Scotland
OSA	*Old Statistical Account*
PRO	Public Record Office
RPC	*Register of the Privy Council*

MAP 1. EIGHTEENTH-CENTURY MARITIME SCOTLAND

XIV

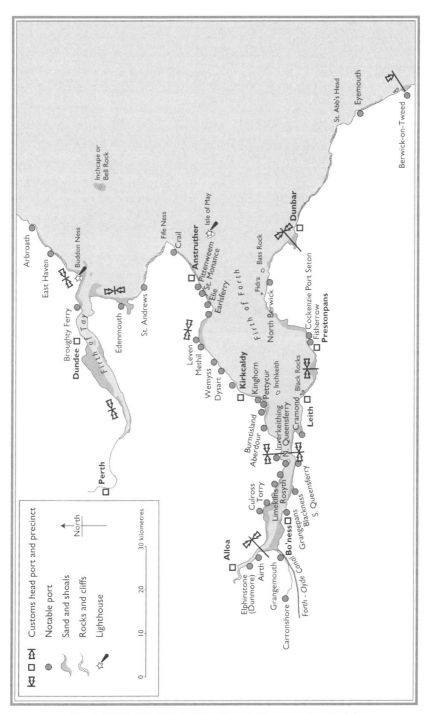

Legend

	Customs head port and precinct
	Notable port
	Sand and shoals
	Rocks and cliffs
	Lighthouse

North

0   10   20   30 kilometres

Map labels

Eyemouth

St. Abb's Head

Berwick-on-Tweed

Inchcape or Bell Rock

Arbroath

East Haven

Buddon Ness

Fife Ness

Crail

Isle of May

Anstruther

Pittenweem

St. Monance

Elie

Earlsferry

Dunbar

Bass Rock

Fidra

North Berwick

Cockenzie Port Seton

Fisherrow

Prestonpans

Broughty Ferry

Dundee

Edenmouth

St. Andrews

Leven

Methil

Wemyss

Dysart

Kirkcaldy

Kinghorn

Pettycur

Inchkeith

Black Rocks

Cramond

Leith

Burntisland

Aberdour

Inverkeithing

N. Queensferry

Perth

Culross

Torry

Rosyth

S. Queensferry

Limekilns

Bo'ness

Grangepans

Blackness

Forth – Clyde Canal

Alloa

Elphinstone (Dunmore)

Airth

Grangemouth

Carronshore

Firth of Tay

Firth of Forth

MAP 2. EIGHTEENTH-CENTURY CUSTOMS PRECINCTS OF
THE FIRTHS OF FORTH AND TAY

XV

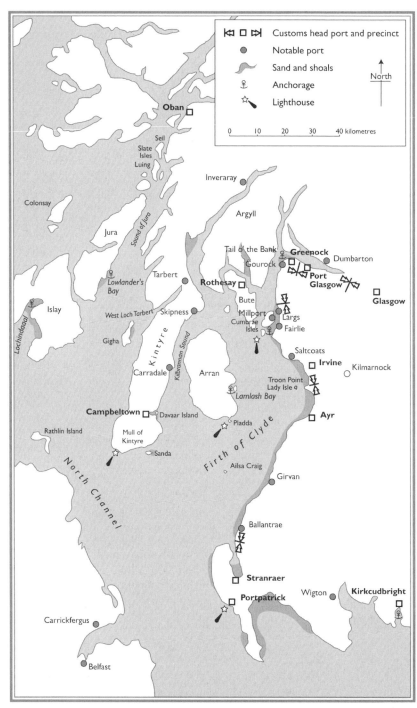

**MAP 3. EIGHTEENTH-CENTURY CUSTOMS PRECINCTS
OF THE FIRTH OF CLYDE**

XVI

INTRODUCTION

This study seeks to demonstrate how state intervention and warfare in the pursuit of mercantilist goals largely determined, intentionally and otherwise, the development of the Scottish marine and its institutions during the period 1650–1790.[1]

'MERCANTILISM' AND 'THE SYSTEM' AS HISTORICAL TERMS

Opinions as to the validity of the term 'mercantilism' vary greatly between schools of history. Those primarily interested in the foreign policy of this period are generally dismissive of what is, in their view, a retrospective invention that parcels a hotchpotch of reactive and restrictive legislation on trade. As Anderson declares:

> Mercantilism, even if it can be spoken about as a unity, was not an inquiry into abstract principles of wealth, in the sense that Adam Smith's *Wealth of Nations*, published in 1776, was ... [it was] a collection of attitudes and assumptions, almost an administrative technology, rather than a science of economics.[2]

On the other hand, while acknowledging this state of affairs during the formative seventeenth century, many economic historians readily apply the term 'mercantilist system' to the administrative regime first introduced in England after 1696. For as Hoon proclaims, the Navigation Act of that year – along with its new regulating agencies – 'marks at once the embarkation

---

1   The term 'mercantilism' has been ascribed to an extensive period of European history: namely, from the advent of the voyages of discovery to the repeal of the British Corn Laws (1492–1846); P .O'Brien, 'Did Europe's mercantilist empires pay?', *History Today*, 46 (1996), p. 32.

2   M.S. Anderson, *Europe in the Eighteenth Century* (London, 1987), p. 114.

upon the mercantilism that is identified with the eighteenth century'.[3]

This Act, together with the protectionist wall of high import tariffs and restrictions raised in the following decade, was largely the work of vested interest. They exploited firstly William's, and latterly Anne's, dependence on the English Parliament to raise the increasingly higher levels of revenue required to maintain their large standing armies. In this manner the mercantilist system synonymous with the eighteenth century came about as much accident as design. As Parry remarks:

> 'System' is perhaps too tidy a description – of rules and
> exceptions, many of which were drafted *ad hoc* to deal with
> particular situations or to still the outcries of particular groups
> of people, rather than to realise consistent economic theories. In
> so far as they dealt with colonial matters, however, they did
> embody certain clear administrative principles. [4]

It is, therefore, with due regard to the limitations highlighted by these quotations that this study employs the term 'mercantilism' to encompass those assumptions and attitudes towards seaborne trade that were part of the wider agenda on international relations. The term 'mercantilist system', however, is used to describe the post-1696 regime of elaborate controls, restrictions and duties imposed on the foreign-going trade and shipping of the nation and her colonies.

THE ASSUMPTIONS BEHIND MERCANTILISM

The main assumption driving the mercantilist mindset in ruling circles was that political and military power was ultimately derived from wealth (initially perceived as bullion). This widely held stance gained international credence as the Spanish monopoly of the influx of new bullion from the New World was seen to finance the alliances and mercenary armies that threatening the continuing independence, if not the very existence, of many smaller European states.

By the early seventeenth century the spectre of a Spanish 'universal monarchy' was a preoccupation of court politicians and the 'bullionist'

---

3   E.E. Hoon, *The Organisation of the English Customs System, 1696–1786* (Newton Abbot, 1968), p. 3.
4   J.H. Parry, *Trade and Dominion* (London, 1971), pp. 51–2.

school of political economists. Shifts in the distribution of wealth between the nations were increasingly perceived in terms of potential shifts in the 'balance of power' in Europe. This, in turn, largely dictated foreign policy and alliances in the dynastic wars of Europe for the next hundred years.[5]

By the mid-seventeenth century the debate had advanced to focus on the question: what constituted national wealth and how should a nation state protect and extend its share of the available wealth? Thomas Munn, the leading light of the more sophisticated 'protectionist' school, promoted the argument (1664) that 'the ordinary means therefore to encrease our wealth and treasure is by foraign trade, wherein wee must ever observe this rule; to sell more to strangers yearly than wee consume of theirs in value'.[6] He singled out the Dutch who, without most natural advantages or an indigenous source of bullion, thrived by dominating the 'north-south' trade of Europe and the Far East. So much so that they were on the verge of assuming the mantle of universal monarchy from the more dissolute Spanish. Colbert, the French Minister of Finance, deftly explained this simple chain of logic to his nephew serving at Rochefort (in 1666): 'Trade is the source of finance, and finance is the vital nerve of war.'

It was, perhaps, inevitable that as an island nation, England (with a forcibly united Scotland in association) should be the first to seek to enhance her maritime power and hence security against the Spanish and Dutch Empires. This was by embracing the exclusive *mare clausum* stance on maritime sovereignty over her colonial and home waters (including Scottish when it suited). It was but a short step for the supporters of this ideology to actively promote practical measures – principally by Navigation Acts – to exclude the marines of rivals from the nation's seaborne trade and fisheries.

WAR AS AN INSTRUMENT OF POLICY

Where England led, others closely followed. Scotland, France, the United Provinces, and later Sweden, Denmark and Prussia, created their own systems that increased competition for wealth and, ultimately, the risk of armed confrontation. As the available global wealth was then considered essentially finite, any increase in one nation's share was assumed to be at

5   J. Black, *A System of Ambition? British Foreign Policy, 1660–1793* (London, 1991)
6   Thomas Munn, *England's Treasure by Foraign Trade. Or, the ballance of our Foraign Trade is the Rule of our Treasure* (1664), reprinted by the Economic History Society (London, 1928), p. 6.

A. Gedaente vant Noordtlyckste van Engelandt
daer beneffens 2 eijlende

Dunstabourg   Bambourg   Barwijck

Angliæ maximæ Septentrion. vultus, dien præternaugatur

S C O

Barnbugel
Edenburg   Liet   Brand e
Kijng
Inskig
Heijn
Mußelbroch
Sethon
Tamtasson
Bass
Dunbar
Maen
S. Abberhuet
Barwijck
Chijruside
MERIDIES

Goßwick
Bambourg
nstabourg
Theijlich landt
Gout steen
De Ploech
Farnel landt
Schasen

Beschrijuinge van een deel vann
Schottlandt van Bambourg tot Aberdein
daer Edenburg de princepaele Coepstat in is, So
hem tlant daer-bihoont beneffens 2 eijlende.
Oræ maritimæ Scotiæ a Bamburgo
ad Aberdinum, vera delineatio.
Lucas Ianß
Wagenaer.

Cum Priuilegio ad decennium.

NOORDT

M A R E   S E P T E N T

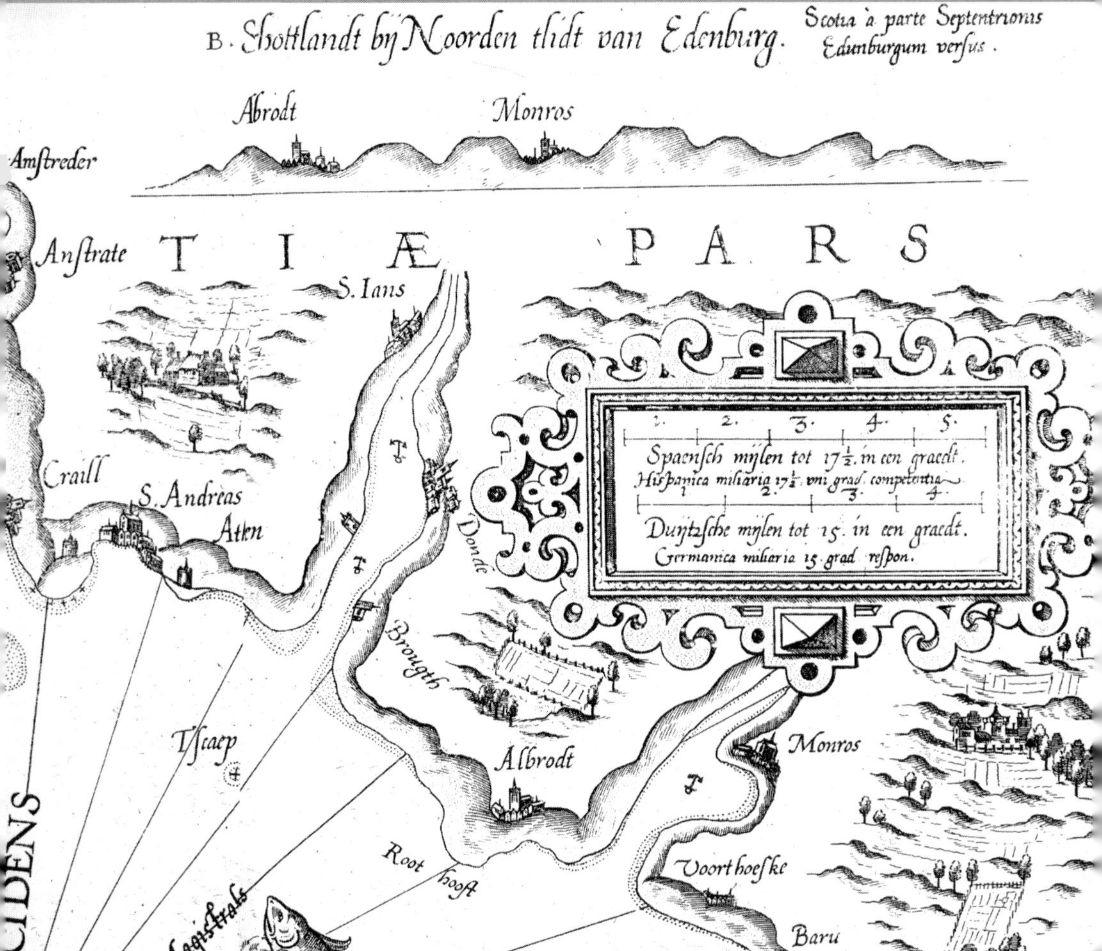

Abrodt   Monros

Amstreder

Anstrate   T I Æ   P A R S

S. Ians

Craill   S. Andreas
          Atkn

Donde

Tscaep   Brougth

Albrodt   Monros

Root hooft   Voorthoeske

OCCIDENS   Baru

Noordt West Magistrals   Aberdein

                                      Steenbay
                                      De
                                      Torrey

SEPTENTRIO

Noordt Oost

ZEE

Graets

I O N A L E

Spaensch mijlen tot 17½ in een graedt.
Hispanica miliaria 17½ vni grad. competentia.

Duytsche mijlen tot 15. in een graedt.
Germanica miliaria 15 grad. respon.

12

Ioannes à Doet.
Fecit.

the expense of a rival. In such a hostile environment armed trading was prevalent at sea.

This predatory aspect of mercantilism increasingly came to the fore as the eighteenth century progressed and explains the support of the mercantile community for the series of dynastic and revolutionary wars that are a hallmark of the era. Between the introduction of the first of the Navigation Acts (1646) and their dissolution by Huskisson (1823), the English and Scottish marines were embroiled in ten major wars. Hostilities at sea dominated trade for over one-third of the period, to which may be added a number of years when international tensions severely affected sailing patterns and frequency. At one time or another, the vessels and seamen loyal to the British crown were pitted against the privateers and naval forces of every other major Atlantic maritime power – with the exception of Portugal, Britain's oldest ally.

During this era, national security was increasingly viewed in terms of the fighting strength of the navy and the armed merchant marine relative to its rivals. A large navy was not, in itself, a guarantee of survival; much depended on the political will to unleash such a force to retain the nation's share of overseas trade. As Pitt the Elder declared, 'When trade is at stake it is your last defence: you must defend it or perish.'[7] It was not, however, until the Seven Years War (1756–63) that he came to fully realise the advantages of supporting a European continental war as an instrument in extending Britain's strategic global ambitions. By merging 'continental' and 'blue water' policies, he prophetically declared, 'We will win Canada on the banks of the Elbe'.[8] Superior naval power proved its worth as the crushing defeats inflicted on the French fleets at Quiberon Bay and Cape Lagos paved the way for the military successes in the West Indies and Canada – culminating in the capture of Quebec.

The overseas empire seized by Britain from her war-depleted rivals after 1760 vindicated Pitt the Elder and his aggressive brand of mercantilism in the eyes of most contemporary commentators. Johnson went so far as to acclaim him as 'the greatest statesman by whom Commerce was united with, and made to flourish by, War'.[9] Typical of this root-and-branch conversion to the benefits of aggression was the open letter of gratitude

7   J. Ben Jones, *The Hanoverians: A Century of Growth, 1714–1815* (Leicester, 1972), p. 15.
8   *Ibid.*, p. 86. Blue-water policy stressed naval power and colonial and commercial considerations, while continental policy stressed military strength and the balance of power on mainland Europe.
9   *Ibid.*

sent to the dying King George II in July 1760 by the Convention of the Scottish Royal Burghs. [10]

With an empire secured, the mercantilist system grew more complex as Britain sought to monopolise and control the produce of her overseas possessions. This was achieved by channelling their conveyance to the European markets through designated British home ports. By 1784, over a hundred commodities had join the original 1696 list of produce and goods subject to regulation at the ports of Britain and her colonies. [11] The promotion of the fisheries – 'the nursery of seamen' for the navy in the eventuality of war – fitted readily with the prevailing mercantilist outlook and so received state funding via the bounty system.

The American War of Independence (effectively 1776–83) breached this system, built, as it was, upon a body of piecemeal legislation accumulated over the previous hundred years. In doing so it exposed the contradictions and fallacies of such a restrictive and inhibiting attitude to trade and international relations. This study, therefore, concludes with the aftermath of this war and the first sweeping rationalisation of the mercantilist system (1786–1790) ordered by Pitt the Younger.

While the Navigation Acts survived the review intact – indeed, if anything strengthened – the partial dismantling of the high-tariff customs regime signalled a retreat from the high mercantilist stance. This shift in government attitude laid the foundations for a more flexible order in international trading relations after the French Revolutionary and Napoleonic Wars.

THE SCOTTISH EXPERIENCE OF MERCANTILISM AND WAR

The Scottish marine, in terms of number of vessels committed to the great overseas trades, was a relatively insignificant player in the great international mercantilist arena. However, the development of Scotland's shipping industry and institutions offers valuable insights into the formation and working of British mercantilism.

Prior to Act of Union of 1707, Scotland was an independent trading

---

10   H. and J. Pillan and Wilson (eds.), *Extracts from the Records of the Convention of Royal Burghs, 1759–79* (Edinburgh, 1918), p. vi.

11   Huskisson's *Reciprocity of Duties Act* (1823) started the dismantling of the Navigation Acts, which were not wholly abolished until 1849.

nation with its own maritime institutions. In seeking to develop their own variety of mercantilism the arguments of the 'bullionist' and 'ballance of trade' schools of political economy were influential, albeit belatedly, in the deliberations of the Scottish Privy Council and its Committee on Trade.

Scottish overseas trading aspirations were, however, severely curtailed by the powerful alliance of English shippers and the London-based Merchant Adventurer Companies. The former primarily sought to deny Scottish access to the carrying trade of the English plantations, while the latter were to the fore in protecting their monopolies by denying the creation of Scottish equivalents. The ambiguous status of Scotland under the Stuarts – regally joined but commercially and fiscally separate from England – frustrated virtually every attempt at catering for Scottish aspirations within the existing English Navigation Acts.

The succession of William and Mary to the English throne in 1688 radically changed this relationship and unleashed pent-up national aspirations and Jacobitism in the North. The ensuing acrimonious defence of Scottish maritime sovereignty against the outrages perpetrated by English commanders in Scottish waters, and the tensions created by Jacobite attacks, present a unique example of the interplay of aggressive mercantilism and the war dynamic in national affairs.

In the critical decade that followed, the precarious co-existence of the Scottish marine and the enforcers of the English Navigation Acts rapidly deteriorated to the point of open conflict. By the mid-1690s the advocates of the 'ballance of trade' school in Edinburgh circles were able to harness the rising tide of national indignation to join the international contest for wealth as a matter of national survival. In the view of one supporter of the newly formed 'Company of Scotland':

> It's beyond all Controversie that it is in the Interest of all
> Nations to increase Trade; the Increase of which begetteth
> Wealth, and Riches, which in time of Warr doth more
> contribute to the preservation of a Nation then the multitude
> and valour of its Men.[12]

The Company's failure to establish a trading emporium overseas on the Darien isthmus – together with the great loss of men, ships and capital –

---

12   Anon., *A letter from a Gentleman in the Country to His Friend at Edinburgh: Wherein it is clearly Proved, That the Scottish African and Indian Company is Exactly Calculated for the Interest of Scotland* (Edinburgh, 1696), p. 3.

effectively ended Scotland's attempt at forging her own mercantile empire and system.[13]

After the Union, the fortunes of the Scottish marine were closely tied to those of the emerging British Empire. Government interest in the maritime affairs of 'North Britain' was sustained by the recurring Jacobite emergencies and the orchestrated accusations of widespread sharp practice at the Scottish ports made by the influential English mercantile lobby. The result was a series of customs inspections, surveys and reports on the state of the Scottish marine and ports that is second to none in detail and scope.

The impact of conflict is particularly relevant to the Scottish maritime experience during the mercantilist era as the isolated location of many Scottish ports and sea areas in wartime actively encouraged enemy raiders to penetrate deep into Scottish home waters. During the American War of Independence the more outlying coastal communities came under direct attack to the detriment of their seaborne trade. This study strives, therefore, to integrate 'naval' with 'maritime' history at both the national and regional levels. In doing so it relates and analyses the interplay of mercantilism and war during the period 1650–1790.[14]

To this end the impact of major events, domestic and international, on Scottish maritime affairs has been placed in the context of changes to the prevailing system. The proliferation of hostilities across one and a half centuries presents, however, too unwieldy a subject to be encompassed in a single seamless chronological sweep. This is particularly the case at the regional level of enquiry where the diverse experiences of Scotland's maritime communities add a further major variable. The 'war and peace' aspect of this study has, therefore, been divided into three periods: 1651–1755, 1756–75 and 1776–90. These divisions encompass three distinct phases in Scotland's participation in the evolving mercantilist trading system. Each period has at least one major war during which conflict was the principal catalyst for change.

---

13   As Armitage has succinctly concluded; 'In sum, the Darien Scheme venture was an alternative to dependency and corruption within Britain, and to poverty and universal monarchy in Europe'. D. Armitage, 'The Scottish vision of empire:intellectual origins of the Darien Scheme', in J. Robertson (ed.), *A Union for Empire: Political Thought on the British Union of 1707* (1995), pp. 97–118.

14   The 'lack of coherence' between the differing schools and interest groups has been identified as the primary reason why maritime studies invariably fails to deliver to their full potential, namely as a microcosm of national history. N.A.M. Rodger, 'Britain', in J.B. Hattendorf (ed.), *The State of Naval and Maritime History* (Newport, 1994), pp. 45–58.

Even after the Union with England, the greatest maritime power in Europe, the Scottish fleet remains a clearly discernible entity within the British marine for the remainder of the eighteenth century. Furthermore, prior to 1790, the numbers of Scottish vessels and masters in the customs categories – foreign, coastal and fisheries – are such as to be sufficiently manageable to allow individual elements of the marine to be identified and their wartime experiences collated. This treatment is usually only possible for vessels and commanders of the Royal Navy, the East India Company and Greenland whalers. Through this analysis the pivotal role of a very small number of Scottish masters and their vessels in wartime, notably in the earlier periods, becomes apparent.

CHAPTER I
THE ADVENT OF
THE MERCANTILIST ERA

England, with Scotland in tow, was set on a collision course with her European rivals in trade after 1650.[1] The Navigation Act of that year targeted the Spanish for expulsion from the English colonial trade while the second Act (1651) extended the exclusion of rival vessels to the domestic carrying trade of England and the fisheries. This highly aggressive move was aimed squarely at the Dutch with the intention of provoking the first of the three Dutch Wars.[2]

Scotland's membership of the English camp was effected without her consent. Indeed, the Navigation Act of 1651 was drafted as Monck's military subjugation of Scotland was being consolidated and hence anticipated the subsequent Union of Scotland and England. The inclusion of the Scots under the terms of the Act was implicit, as vessels 'that belong only to the people of this commonwealth and the plantations' had a right of entry to the English plantation trades.[3] Scotland was finally declared a full member of the Cromwellian Commonwealth by the Council in State of 12 April 1654 – too late to participate in the first assault on the Dutch marine.[4]

---

1   The earlier Act of 1646 was a prototype and lacked the necessary rigour or means of enforcement.

2   Analysis of the pressure groups is available in: J.E. Farnell, 'The Navigation Act of 1651, the First Dutch War, and the London Merchant Community', *Economic History Review* (1964), VXVI, pp. 439–452.

3   *Acts and Ordinances of the Interregnum,* I, p. 913, as quoted by E. Lipson, *The Economic History of England* (London, 1948), III, p. 123. A general view of the problems facing Scotland at this time is available in: G. Donaldson, *Scotland: James V – James VII* (Edinburgh, 1965). A more detailed analysis is available in T.M. Devine, 'The Cromwellian Union and the Scottish Burghs: The Case of Aberdeen and Glasgow, 1652–60', in J. Butt and J.T. Ward (eds.), *Scottish Themes* (Edinburgh, 1976), pp. 1–16.

4   Chapter 4 reviews the impact of the invasion on shipping activity in and out of the Scottish ports. Prior to 1654 wartime restrictions had been placed on Scottish communication with the colonies.

OLIVER CROMWELL (SCOTTISH NATIONAL PORTRAIT GALLERY)

TUCKER'S REPORT OF 1656

The Scottish marine was hardly in a condition to respond to the opportunities created by the war at sea or to exploit the access to English trade gained by her membership of the Commonwealth. Monck's invasion had laid waste many of the seaports of the east coast of Scotland, and a particularly severe winter that year, during which a great storm wrecked many vessels, compounded the losses already suffered by acts of war.[5] In the aftermath Cromwell's agent in Scotland, Thomas Tucker, undertook his *Report upon the settlement of Revenues of Excise Customs in Scotland A.D. 1656*. Part of that report is his much quoted 'doomsday' survey of the surviving stock of Scottish hulls that offers, when consolidated, a baseline for future comparisons.[6]

Table 1.1. Estimates of Scottish shipping by Customs precinct, 1656

| Precinct | Number | | Tonnage | |
	Lowest	Highest	Lowest	Highest
1 Aberdeen	14	14	540	540
2 Ayr	10	11	203	208
3 Bo'ness	5	5	480	480
4 Dundee	22	22	874	874
5 Inverness	8	8	118	118
6 Kirkcaldy	50	50	1,741	1,741
7 Leith	12	13	800	1,300
8 Glasgow	18	20	1,020	1,045
Total	139	143	5,776	6,306

Source: T. Tucker, *Report upon the settlement of Revenues of Excise Customs in Scotland A.D. 1656*

5   J.D. Marwick (ed.), 'Report by Thomas Tucker upon the settlement of Revenues of Excise Customs in Scotland A.D. 1656', *Miscellany of the Scottish Burgh Records Society* (Edinburgh, 1881), pp. 1–48. The reappraisal displayed in Table 1.1 includes the following adjustments to the original data: a. the dry capacity burthen entries for Montrose (in lasts) and Orkney (in chaldrons) have been converted to a tons deadweight measure using R.E. Zupro, 'The weights and measures of Scotland before the Union', *Scottish Historical Review* (1977), LVI, pp. 119–145; b. the unspecified tonnages of listed coasters at Leith and Culross have each been awarded the average for their description and locality, i.e. 40 tons and 100 tons respectively. Appendix A offers a fuller interpretation of tonnage measurements prior to 1790.
6   *State Papers Domestic*, 1658–1659, pp. 7–10. Dutch masters and hulls regained a foothold in England's carrying trade as neutrals during the war with Spain.

This comprehensive survey of thirty ports found approximately 140 vessels, the majority located on the east coast. Their combined tonnage did not exceed 6,400 tons, with the majority of vessels under 60 tons burthen. By contemporary English and European standards this marine was truly insignificant in all aspects and indicative of the retarded state of the Scottish economy.

SCOTLAND'S EXCLUSION AFTER 1660

The diminutive size of the Scottish marine did not, however, protect it from being selected for exclusion by the London merchants and shipmasters. Within a year of Tucker's report they were petitioning the Lord Protector and the Parliament of 1658 for a redefinition of the terms of the 1651 Act. The eventual outcome of this highly emotive campaign was a new Navigation Act, passed in September 1660 by the first Parliament of the Restoration.[7] This Act decreed that the master and three-quarters of the crew had to be of English nationality. The explicit statement that only 'his Majesty's subjects of England, Ireland and his plantations are to be accounted English and no others' recategorised the Scots as a 'foreign' nation, along with the Dutch.

This exclusion of the Scots was not an oversight. Article XVI of the Act tacitly acknowledged the plight this legislation would cause the Scottish economy by making concessions on the direct importation of Scottish grain, salt and cured fish. The specified conditions were that this trade had to be carried in a Scottish-built hull commanded by a Scottish captain and a crew three-quarters of whom were to be 'his Majesty's subjects'. As it was common knowledge that the Scottish marine was then almost entirely foreign-built, such prohibitions and conditions were blatantly discriminatory: 'by which means our [Scottish] shipping is in a manner debard from traiding to England, becaus by their Act of Navigation our ships can import nothing but what is the produce of this Kingdom'.[8]

By December 1661 the Scots merchant community in London had been mobilised to petition 'in swa farr as it is prejudiciall to the Scotts

---

7   *Act of Parliament of England*, 12 Chas. II, Cap 18 (1660), confirmed by 13 Chas. II, Stat. I, Cap 14.

8   *Register of the Privy Council of Scotland [RPC]*, series iii, VII, p. 653.

shipps' – but to no avail.[9] Their mission was certain to fail as the Scottish Parliament had already retaliated with its own *Act for the Encouragement of Shipping and Navigation* some months earlier. This piece of legislation vainly sought to emulate the English model by ordering that all goods imported 'from the original places, whence they are in use first' for domestic consumption or re-export were to be carried by Scottish vessels via a Scottish port. The far-sighted exceptions were companies wishing to trade out of Scotland with Asia, Africa, America, Muscovy and Italy.

This stance was taken as a hostile act by the English Merchant Adventurer Companies who were then actively seeking royal charters from Charles to enshrine their monopolies in those areas of the world. Furthermore, the Scottish Act defined a 'Scottish' ship as one navigated by a crew of whom three-quarters, as well as the master and owners, were of Scottish domicile. There was no requirement that the hull be British-built.[10] These conditions had to be verified by certificate under pain of confiscation of the vessel. The only tangible effect of this Act was, however, to encourage a few Dutch and English masters to seek naturalisation as Scottish burgesses.

Further extensions to the English Navigation Acts, in 1662, 1663 (the Staple Act) and 1664, completed the Scots exclusion from the domestic and plantation trades. The first decreed that all coastal trading must also be in hulls built in the King's dominions (the Scottish coastal fleet was then mostly foreign-built). This brought a renewed outcry for 'relief' from Scottish 'merchants, mariners and coal and salt owners … debarred from all trade and commerce with England'.[11] The second Act established the means of enforcement of the English Acts abroad. It authorised colonial governors to appoint deputies, known as the 'clerk to the naval office' (later shortened to the 'naval officer') to police all aspects of colonial seaborne trade within their jurisdiction.[12] The last Act imposed the strict requirement that all European goods and manufacture destined for the colonies must pass through an English or Welsh port in an 'English' hull as prescribed by the Statutes. This was the final blow to Scottish trading aspirations that

9   *Extracts from the Burgh Records of Edinburgh, 1655–8,* M. Wood (ed.) (Edinburgh, 1940), p. 272, petition, 2 December 1661.

10   *Act of Parliament of Scotland,* VII, p. 257. Smout rightly draws attention to the significance of the omission of the origin of the hull requirement, which underlined Scotland's dependence on purchasing foreign-built vessels at this time: *Scottish Trade,* p. 48.

11   *Extracts from the Burgh Records of Edinburgh,* p. 311, petition, 14 November 1662,.

12   The date of appointment of naval officers differed between colonies; e.g, Jamaica c. 1676, Massachusetts 1682 and Virginia 1692.

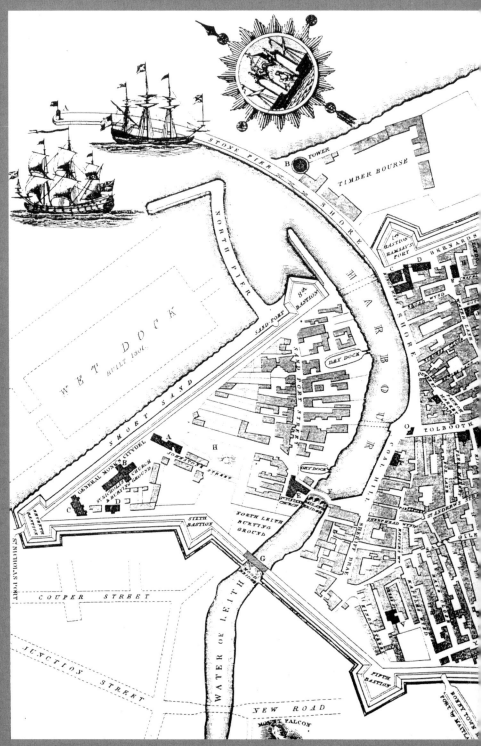

LEITH'S FORTIFICATIONS DATING FROM 1565

BALTIC STREET

SECOND
BASTION

LADY'S WALK

CONSTITUTION ROAD

CHARLOTTE STREET

CHARLOTTE LANE

EASTERN FORTIFICATION
FROM CAPT. COLLINS ANNO 1681.

ROAD TO SEAFIELD

GOAT-FOLD LANE

LINKS
LANE

St MARY'S CHURCH

COMBS ALLEY

BURYING GROUND

KIRK GATE OR ST ANTHONY'S PORT

St ANTHONY STREET

St ANTHONY STREET

THIRD
BASTION

FOURTH
BASTION

LEITH WALK

EASTERN ROAD

LEITH LINKS

MOUNT PELHAM

MOUNT SOMERSET

SCALE OF   FEET
100   0   100   200   300   400   500

were already reeling from the introduction of the *Book of Rates* that increased English customs import duties on most Scottish goods.

This deadlock between two trading nations tied by a common allegiance to the Stuart monarchy prompted urgent diplomatic efforts to claim exemption for the Scots from alien status. The matter was first referred to a small *ad hoc* committee (July 1664) headed by Lord Lauderdale, then the Lord Treasurer.[13] There it was argued that the favourable balance of trade that England enjoyed with Scotland could allow 'the admission of the Scotch' to the home market, without prejudicing English trading interests or customs. This opinion was duly presented to the Council for Trade who proposed lowering the domestic market duties on a reciprocal basis. The Council, however, remained adamant that any such relaxation of trading restrictions should not concede access to the English plantations or encroach on the trade preserves of the Royal Chartered Companies.

The whole sovereignty issue was finally referred to a Royal Commission, set up in 1668, 'for settling the freedom of trade between the two countries'. Predictably, the Scottish Commissioners cited the Union of the Crowns (1603) as entitling the Scots to participate in the domestic carrying trade of England. As to access to the colonies, they proposed a compromise whereby all colonial commodities imported by Scottish vessels, but not destined for consumption in Scotland, would pass through English ports.

THE EXCLUSION OF IRELAND, 1664

This proposal came too late to substantially change the hardening attitude within the vested interest groups of English manufacturers and merchants. Only the year before, the English parliament had voted to renege on the inclusion of Irish shipping as 'English' under the original terms of the 1660 Act. In 1664, a new Statute forbade the exporting of anything other than 'horses and victuals' to the colonies by Irish traders and, by inference, from receiving imported commodities directly from the colonies. This rigid interpretation of the English Navigation Acts was subsequently confirmed by a further Act in 1671 and remained in force until 1705 when a concession was made on the direct exporting of linen from Ireland.

---

13   The Scottish commissioners' initial brief (6 May) also included settling trade with France – as one of the 'thrie nations' – which had recently imposed a levy of 50 sous per ton on all 'stranger vessels' entering her ports; *Ibid.,* p. 347.

In between times Irish-Scottish trade suffered a further blow when an Act of Scottish Parliament (1703) re-established the prohibition on the importing of Irish meal and livestock. As this protective measure served the interest of the landowners on the west coast of Scotland, it was destined to remain on the statute books for the next fifty years. Such selective discrimination in trade was not wholly one-way. The Scottish linen industry faced periodic bans on exporting to Ireland (1667 and 1704–5) and incurred an import duty until 1716–7.

On balance, however, the west-coast Scottish shippers would appear to have openly benefited from the general exclusion of Irish shippers from the British colonial trades and were able to exploit their geographic location to secure a sizeable share of the re-export market in colonial commodities to Ireland.[14] Such market opportunities were, however, largely unforeseen in 1668 when the Royal Commission on Anglo-Scottish trade affairs pronounced.

THE SECOND DUTCH WAR

The resumption of war (1664) against the Dutch and their allies temporarily allayed the internal squabbling over trading access, as the glittering prospect of plundering Europe's greatest fleet struck up a common *esprit de corps* between the erstwhile rival marines. The outcome was a truly dramatic windfall of mainly Dutch prizes taken by a few determined Scottish privateering masters. This elite group of war-hardened mariners are worthy of individual note as they later served as the captains of guard ships and masters of foreign-going armed traders in subsequent wars.

Less tangible, though more significant in the long run, was the legacy of judicial reforms stemming from this and the following third Dutch War. These were crucial to the Scottish marine's future participation in the new international system of passes at sea which produced major dividends during the following years of peace.

---

14   A review of trade policy is available in D. Woodward, 'Anglo–Scottish Trade and English commercial policy during the 1660s', *Scottish Historical Review* (1977), 56, no.162, pp. 153–176. The Irish–Scots trade relationship has been examined by L.E. Cochran, *Scottish Trade with Ireland in the Eighteenth Century* (Edinburgh, 1985), p. 9.

Table 1.2. Known Scottish letter-of-marque vessels and privateers during the Second Dutch War, 1666–7

Vessel	Port	Captain(s)
Adventure	Burntisland	Andrew Reioch [or Reiode]
Adventure	Leith	John Mortoun
Agnes	Leith	Hendry Donaldson
Ann	Anstruther	Anstruthers
Anna	Prestonpans	John Kerr
Anthony	Leith	William Wood
Barbara	Leith	James Bennet
Batchelor	Bo'ness	William Mather & James Waterstown
Batchelor	Kirkcaldy	William Bosewell
Bell	Leith	John Keir
Benjamin	Montrose	Ephraim Ruchinson
Boniventur	?	Robert Orrock
Bonaccord	Aberdeen	John Seaton & Francis Anderson
Bruce	Pittenweem	John Achcson [or Aitchison]
Catherine	Leith	Andrew Hall
Charles	Kinghorn	James Wood
Chambers	Glasgow	?
Chieftain	Anstruther	Wm Anstruther & John Alexander
Chieftain Rothes	Leith	Rbt Chenie & Rbt Marshall & Alex Stewart
C[h]ristian	B'ness	Alexander Allan
Dauphin	Inverness	William Geddes
Dove	Kirkcaldy	David Groat
Fisher	Bo'ness	James Gib
Fortun	Glasgow	George Dishington
Fortune	Burntisland	James Seatoun & Robert Angus
Fortune	Leith	Thos Dishington, Jas Dawnie & Geo Cheyne
George (friggato)	Glasgow	Robert Allan [or McAllan]
Gift of God	?	John Robertson
Good Fortun	East	William Ged
Greentree	Montrose	George Wilkinson [or Walker]
Hopewell	St Andrews	Wm Mortoun & John Black & John Mastertown
Hound	?	William Buchan
Hunter	Kirkcaldy	David Hunter
Isobel	Kirkcaldy	Matthew Anderson & James Brown
James	Leith	Patrick Logan
Jean	Greenock	John Hunter
Jean	Leith	Thomas Binning (Younger)
Jennet	?	Ronald Murray

Vessel	Port	Captain(s)
John	Leith	John Gillies
Katherine	Leith	John Hendry
Lamb	Ayr	John Blair
Lamb	Leith	John Brown(e)
Lesley	Leith	James Alexander & James Binning
Lion	Glasgow	George Breddon(e)
Marcell	Kirkcaldy	John Sympson
Margaret	Peterhead	James Seatoun
Margaret	Kirkcaldy	William Martin
Margaret	Leith	James Martin
Margaret	Linlithgow	David Wilson
Margaret	Queensferry	Alexander Stewart
Mary	Kirkcaldy	Peter Gedd
Mayflower	Ayr	John Kennedy
Morton (cutter)	Wemyss	Peter Winchester & David Blyth
Nonsuch	?	Andrew Smeaton
Prince Rupert	?	Davis Coustoun [or Cowstoun]
Providence	Dundee	John Masteroun & David Forest & Thos Gray
Providence	Glasgow	John Scot
Rainbow	Glasgow	George Chambers [or Chalmers]
Revenge	Leith	Thomas Binning
Rothes	Leith	William Hamilton
Speedwell	Burntisland	Michael Seton
Swallow	Burntisland	John Allan
Thistle	Leith	Gideon Murray & John Black
Thomas	Dundee	Thomas Bower & Thomas Lion
Union	Inverness	Thomas Lion
Wemyss	Burntisland	John Wemyss

Source: GCA, Maxwell of Pollock MSS T-PM 107/7/20/4; RPC; Stair's Institutions; London Gazette.

THE SCOTTISH PRIVATEERS

At first the new-found patriotic fervour in the North for the prosecution of the King's war at sea against the Dutch was inhibited by the idiosyncrasies of the Scottish Admiral – then the heritable office of the Duke of Richmond and Lennox. His lengthy absence from Scotland and initial lack of interest resulted in only three privateering commissions being issued by the spring of 1666.[15] This bureaucratic *impasse* was resolved, without loss of face, when the Scottish Privy Council undertook the necessary administration in his name. In this way, some twenty-five commissions were issued during the three months of April, June and July. By then, the early successes of two captains – Gideon Murray on the *Thistle* and William Hamilton on the *Rothes* (both commissioned 5 April 1666) – had fuelled a short but intense public mania for privateering:

> The people of Leith and Edinburgh are very hearty and zealous
> for the service of his Majesty in this war with the Dutch and
> the French and a general rendezvous is appointed in this city for
> the putting into a positive way as may be most appropriate for
> the publick good.[16]

During the course of this war over sixty Scottish vessels, a sizeable proportion of the Scottish marine, sailed with a letter of marque commission.[17] It is, however, highly likely that the majority of these vessels were opportunist armed traders rather than dedicated privateers. Indeed, the relatively higher costs incurred to fit out a small vessel as a cruising privateer prohibited most owners from speculating in such ventures.

For those who did, most of the outlay went on victualling and equipping the large crew required for fighting at close quarters. Cannons on Scottish privateers at that time were generally of very small calibre and ineffective at range. Prizes were, therefore, secured by closing and boarding rather than by stand-off bombardment. The *George* 'frigatto' of Glasgow (60 tons) provides a good example of the stores and armaments of a privateer of the period. She departed with provisions for six months for her crew of sixty men, who were heavily armed for boarding: thirty-two muskets, twelve half-pikes, eighteen pole-axes, and thirty swords. By way of contrast she carried only three barrels of gunpowder for her five cannons on this extended cruise.[18]

On the west coast the highly speculative venture of sending out a privateer attracted a select group of local merchant burgesses and landed gentry. The promoters of the *George* numbered sixteen, led by Provost

---

15   *RPC*, II, pp. 152–175. This hereditary office has been reviewed by A.R.G. McMillan, 'Admiralty Patronage in Scotland, 1702–1705', *Juridical Review* (1938), pp. 81–6.

16   *London Gazette*, Edinburgh Report, 7 July 1666

17   See; table: 1.2.

18   J. Pagan, *Sketches of the History of Glasgow* (Glasgow, 1847), p. 77.

William Anderson of Dowhill, John Walkinshaw and Sir George Maxwell of Newark.[19] On the east coast, the nobility would appear to have taken the lead. For example, the *Bruce* 'frigatto' of Pittenweem (size unknown) was owned by: Charles, Earl of Haddington, Sir William Bruce of Kinross, Sir James Stanfield of Newmilns, Sir Robert Baird of Saughton Hall, Mr John Dempster of Pitliver and Mr Thomas Stewart of Blair.[20]

During the early stages of this war the expectation of a quick and exceptional return on their investment was fully justified. The rate of capture by Scottish privateers, cruising as far a field as the Spanish and Norwegian coasts, quickly reached a peak in August 1666:

> Nor are our privateers wanting to make the Hollanders sensible
> of the war, having brought in here nine prizes in eight days to
> or about Leith and many more expected daily besides six or
> eight more we are informed are taken about Brasse Sound in
> Jutland.[21]

In the seventeen months of hostilities (April 1666 to August 1667) successive reports in the *London Gazette* recounted to its mainly southern readership, as a matter of national pride, the exploits of a dedicated core of around twenty Scottish privateers. These reports listed at least 108 Dutch, French and Danish prizes brought into the east coast ports of Scotland that, apparently, vied for the business.[22] This tally was approximately a fifth of that taken by their English counterparts for that war (552 vessels) and so was a remarkable achievement for such a small number of masters.[23]

The impact of such an influx of prize hulls into the Scottish marine over the following decades can hardly be overstated. Though only a quarter of the prize reports in the *London Gazette* incidentally mention the tonnage

---

19 Maxwell occasionally deputised for Lennox in Admiralty matters at this time.

20 NAS, Bruce of Kinross MSS, GD 29/46/8 and 29/48. The Court of Session handed down judgement on two of her prizes brought into Cromarty Roads in 19 February 1673. Sir William Bruce was obliged to attend the London Admiralty concerning the matter of compensation as late as 21 June 1684. He may well also have held shares in the privateer *Wemyss* of Burntisland, as the same missive collection includes a Cromarty Vice-Admiralty decree condemning her prize: GD 29/43.

21 *London Gazette*, Leith Report, 21 August 1666.

22 *Ibid.*, successive reports, 1666–7.

23 Professor Davis calculated that over the three Dutch wars the number of prizes captured by English vessels totalled c.2,000 – 2,700, at a loss of 500 to its own marine; R. Davis, *The Rise of the English Shipping Industry* (London, 1962), p. 51.

of the captured vessel taken into a Scottish port, their combined tonnage amounted to c.6,150 tons. This figure virtually matches the entire tonnage of the Scottish marine surveyed by Tucker ten years earlier. The value and size of the prizes and their cargoes were equally impressive. Heading the list were: a Dutch East Indiamen (900 tons) carrying silks; an Archangel trader (400 tons) with potash, 'turkey leather' and furs of great value; and the ex-HMS *Convertin[e]* (58 guns).[24] These were in addition to; four hulls over 400 tons, six over 300 tons, five over 200 tons and ten over 100 tons burthen – and their cargoes.[25]

But the easy pickings were rapidly coming to an end. By the spring of 1667 the Scottish privateers started to encounter a more resolute enemy. In one incident the most active flotilla – comprising the *Bruce* (John Acheson), the *Rothes* (William Hamilton) and the *Lamb* (John Brown[e]) – was brought to action by a Dutch man-of-war from which they only just managed to extricate themselves. Indeed, the *Lamb* was so badly holed along the water line in the engagement that Browne was forced to transfer his crew to a prize.[26] Furthermore, on their return to Leith, Hamilton's hard-won prize sank in the mouth of the harbour.[27] This was not an isolated incident, Gideon Murray on the *Thistle* was forced to disengage having received a similar mauling from two large Dutchmen.[28] One unnamed Scottish privateer (22 guns) was less fortunate and was sunk, having refused to surrender to a man-of-war. Likewise, two prizes taken by 'Scots companies' cruising off Galicia were retaken by a warship (40 guns).[29]

The Dutch offensive also carried the war back to the east coast of Scotland. On 30 April 1667 a Dutch naval expedition in excess of thirty men-of-war appeared off Leith intent on wreaking havoc and retribution on the ports of the Forth. In the midst of the panic that ensued onshore, Leith looked to its meagre and neglected defences. As fate would have it,

---

24   The cargoes noted were a fair cross-section of the European north–south trade and included Iberian wine, nuts, treacle and citrus fruits. Not all was sold on the Scottish market. The customs records for Newcastle during the customs year 1665–6 included Scottish imports of 76 tons of French wine and 545 cwt. of brown sugar taken from Dutch prizes; Woodward, 'Anglo–Scottish Trade', p.156.

25   *Ibid.*, supplemented by M. Wood (ed.), *Extracts from the Records of the Burgh of Edinburgh* (London 1950) as quoted by S. Mowat, *The Port of Leith* (Edinburgh, 1994), p. 214.

26   *London Gazette*, Leith report, 13 April 1667.

27   Wood, *Extracts of the Burgh of Edinburgh*, p. 32.

28   *London Gazette*, Leith report, 9 April 1667.

29   *Ibid.*, two reports, 19 May 1667.

the sunken wreck of Hamilton's prize probably did as much to keep out the fireship sent in by the Dutch as the chain boom strung across the harbour mouth. The three warships of the Stuart navy, then in the upper Forth, prudently kept away until such time as a southerly wind took the Dutch fleet across to the opposing Fife shore where they attempted to bombard Burntisland. This scheme was also foiled as a company of local privateering captains managed to unship their heaviest cannon in time to mount a defensive shore battery. After a feeble exchange of shot the Dutch abandoned the entire project and stood out to sea sailing north, belatedly chased by the naval squadron under the command of Sir Jeremy Sands.[30]

The Dutch never again returned in force and by June of that year the balance had fully swung back in favour of the Scots privateers: 'of late scarcely a day has come passed in which there has been two or three prizes sent in, so much that the harbour [at Montrose] is so thronged that they are forced to send several of them to other places'.[31] It was, however, a short-lived revival as hostilities were concluded in August.

The Scottish merchant marine suffered only negligible losses as very few Dutch privateers ventured into Scottish waters.[32] This situation was the direct result of the Dutch official ban on manning privateers while their navy remained short of skilled seaman. This edict was repeated every summer from 1665 onwards and only relaxed in the winter months. For those Dutch privateers that did sail, the few prize opportunities presented by the diminutive Scottish marine probably discouraged forays so far north and into such hazardous waters in winter.[33] Luck would also seem to have favoured the Scots. Their one major loss of the Second Dutch War – the *Glasgow* (300 tons) – was subsequently recaptured from the prize crew by her own sailors in a daring episode and brought back safely to the Clyde.[34]

---

30   Mowat uses the *Extracts of the Burgh of Edinburgh* in her coverage of the military preparations and civil panic caused by this visitation; *Port of Leith*, pp. 214–5.

31   *London Gazette,* Montrose report, 26 June 1667.

32   The only loss during the first Dutch war was the capture of *Makrell* of Leith, Claude Brown master. She was taken by a Spanish privateer near Bayonne in 1653 and later valued at 8,000 pieces of eight; Wood, *Extracts of the Burgh of Edinburgh, 1665–8*, p.7, entry April 1653.

33   The few that did cruise in Scottish waters had such terror-inducng names as the *Mother and Virgins* and the *Provoked Cheese Maker* (names used by a number of hulls); J.R. Bruijn, 'Dutch Privateering during the Second and Third Dutch Wars', *Course et Piraterie,* papers to the 15th Conference of the Commission Internationale d'Histoire Maritime (San Francisco, 1975), II, p. 415.

34   *London Gazette,* Glasgow report, 5 February 1667.

THE THIRD DUTCH WAR

By the end of the Second Dutch War, however, the political and the judicial climate had changed dramatically. Charles II had become deeply concerned at the diplomatic repercussions of the rough handling of neutrals in the North Sea by Scottish privateers. During the heady days of 1666–7, the condemnation of a neutral vessel and cargo as prize was virtually assured at the notorious Vice-Admiralty Court at Cromarty. As Lord Stair later recalled, the rules of evidence accepted in this outpost of Scottish justice were farcical:

> It was alleged that the confession of the ship's company, taken by the Admiral Depute at Cromartie, was extorted by holding swords and pistols to the breasts or that famine was so extorted at sea when they were taken, it was found sufficient to enervat their testimonies.[35]

Such a wanton disregard for legal process was symptomatic of the general disrepute into which the office of the Lord High Admiral of Scotland had been allowed to lapse under Lennox. His only serious interest was to encourage inflated valuations of the prizes brought in so as to enhance his tenth share as Admiral.

At the outbreak of the Third Dutch War in March 1672 (with France now an ally of Britain) Charles made his displeasure known to the Scottish Privy Council. As a consequence Dutch vessels seized in Scottish ports at the time of the declaration of war were ordered to Leith, from where they were released with a safe conduct pass.[36] Obstructions were also placed in the way of the Scottish privateering masters putting to sea. This was achieved by refusing to issue new privateering commissions and granting only a single voyage extension to the holders of old commissions until his Majesty's pleasure was known. In the interim, securing such an endorsement involved the captain attending on the Lord Chancellor.

In response, two of the most active privateering masters – Bennet and Browne – got up a petition to the Scottish Privy Council (July 1672). This denounced the deliberate policy of keeping them from the sea; 'seeing that the petitioners are put to vast charges and expense to outreicking of their

35 Sir James Dalrymple of Stair, *Institutions of the Law of Scotland* (Edinburgh, 1681), p. 218.
36 As required by Article 32 of the Treaty of Breda (1668).

several frigates and furnishing the same with soldiers, mariners and provisions'.[37] Their other grave concern was the number of recent judgements handed down by the new judicial process that found against the Scottish privateer. Consequently reinstating the captured vessel to its rightful owners – with costs. Furthermore, all outstanding and future prize matters were now to be referred solely to the Judge Admiral of Scotland sitting in the Court of Session at Edinburgh, a lengthy and rigorous process. Despite such obstructions, it is plainly evident, from the large number of prize cases relating to this short conflict, that privateering activity was aggressively resumed by Scottish masters.[38]

CHANGES IN SCOTTISH PRIZE LAW

The timely death of Lennox (April 1673) presented Charles II with the ideal opportunity to bring Scottish maritime affairs within his more immediate control.[39] To this end he appointed his brother James – then Duke of York and Albany and Lord High Admiral of England – to the vacant office of Lord High Admiral of Scotland.[40] While James consolidated his new position, Charles directly instructed the Scottish Privy Council (in June) to enforce strict observance of the six main English prize rules. These were publicly displayed at Edinburgh 'Mercat Crose' and the 'Custome House' at Leith and filled the legal vacuum in Scottish prize law until peace was proclaimed in February 1674.[41]

With the end of hostilities the Judge Admirals, deputised by York to sit at Edinburgh, continued in their task of establishing the new legal

---

37 *RPC*, III, p. 555.

38 Ninety-one prize cases, heard between 4 May 1672 and 10 January 1673, were noted by Judge Robert Hodson Cay, 'List of Prize Question Tried in the High Court of Admiralty in Scotland '(1806), PRO, *Treasury In-letter*, T.1. 973 (3131); as quoted in T. Baty, 'The Judge Admiral of Scotland', *Juridical Review* (1954), pp. 146–7. Mowat's recent review of the Registers of Decreets (NAS AC7) has found an even higher number: 109 prizes taken by Scottish privateers in 1672.

39 Only the month before the death of Lennox, the principal contractor for masts in the Baltic for the English navy had written to London concerning two Gothenburg mast ships taken by Scots privateers' ... against all right and reason condemned'; R.G. Albion, 'Forests and Sea Power', *Harvard Economic Studies* (Cambridge, Massachusetts, 1926), No.29, p. 223.

40 *Ibid.*, pp. 30 and 42. James was the last Lord High Admiral of Scotland to receive this office by letters patent.

41 *RPC*, IV, pp. 69–71.

precedents in Scottish prize law that would redress the legal excesses of the last two Dutch Wars. This was, understandably, a protracted process, and the last ruling was not handed down until June 1680: 'There have been many questions as to the rights and Interests of Allies and Newters, very fully and accurately debated ... for the clearing of the important points that occur in these controversies and for vindicating of the publick justice of the Kingdom.'[42]

The following year the precedent-making cases were collated and published by Lord Stair, the President of the Court of Session, as part of his seminal *Institutions of the Law of Scotland*.[43] This new corpus of legal pronouncements finally brought Scottish prize law into line with English and Continental codes of practice established by the Treaty of Breda (1668) and the Anglo-Dutch Maritime Treaty (1674). These treaties ended this series of wars and created a new British-Dutch understanding which lasted until the outbreak of the American War of Independence (1776).

THE 'BULLIONIST' AND 'BALLANCE OF TRADE' SCHOOLS

As Scottish jurists moved slowly towards the international consensus as to what constituted the 'Law of Nations' at sea, so the same spirit of reasoned enquiry inspired moves to unlock the prosperity of the nation. The formulation of Scotland's national trade policies had, since the Union of the Crowns (1603), been primarily the concern of the Scottish Privy Council. In 1663, however, the Convention of Royal Burghs took the initiative and embraced the 'bullionist' approach by promoting an embargo on the export of specie to pay for imports, the only exceptions being payment for essential purchases of Norwegian timber and, in famine years, grain from the Baltic. This embargo had, however, the undesirable effect of hindering the Scottish traders' entry into the rapidly expanding north–south European trades.[44]

The Order in Council of 1670, on the other hand, tacitly acknowl-

---

42   Stair, *Institutions*, p. 213.

43   E.J. Graham, 'The Scottish Marine in the Dutch Wars', *Scottish Historical Review* (1982), LXI, no. 171, pp. 72–3.

44   The most acclaimed 'bullionist' tract, *A discourse of the Common Weal[th] of this Realm of England*, was first published in Edinburgh in 1549 (and reprinted in 1581).

edged the influence of the more sophisticated arguments of Thomas Munn and 'the ballance of trade' school. This edict attempted to redress Scotland's adverse balance of payments by freeing the small herring industry from all export duties while reintroducing the embargo (previously imposed in 1667) on the import of Irish cattle and victuals. The latter was brutally enforced in July 1672 with the violent capture of an Irish 'bark' carrying meal off Arran in the Firth of Clyde that left dead and wounded amongst the Irish crew.[45] After 1674, however, such tactics were moderated and redirected against the property of the offenders, with the seizure of cargoes and burning of any Irish boats found in the west-coast ports.[46]

The benefits of these initiatives were short-lived. The fishing industry initially responded with a significant increase in barrels for export before royal edicts, claiming to conserve the inshore fish stocks of the firths, limited the scale of expansion. Charles's intervention was almost certainly revenue-driven as he was then actively investigating the prospects of selling patents for the fisheries to large companies.[47] This initiative also failed as the local expertise simply did not exist, in Scotland or elsewhere in the British Isles, to match the Dutch in their techniques of offshore catching and onboard curing of herring.

Similarly, the enforcement of the embargo on Irish imports, by the sequestration of their small open boats, only raised a temporary barrier to Irish imports before they resumed as a contraband trade – with the collusion of local officials – through Galloway and Argyll.[48] At worst this embargo simply denied the Irish the means to purchase Scottish exports, an elementary lesson in the benefits of reciprocity in trade that was not understood until Queen Anne's time.

---

45   *RPC*, III, p. 592.

46   For example, orders were sent in 1674 to Robert Kennoway, Lord Cochrane and the Collector for the Clyde respectively, *Ibid.*, II, pp. 552 and 592; see also order to seize Irish meal boat at Ayr from which the food was to be given to the poor and boat to be sold by roup, *Ibid.*, IV, pp. 132 and 148.

47   Smout, *Scottish Trade*, p. 222.

48   For example, warrants were issued after the lapse of the temporary licence of 1675 against merchants caught still importing Irish victuals. Amongst them was Provost Graham of Dumfries who was arrested, along with the tidewater at Portpatrick and other accomplices, on charges of importing *c.*100 Irish cattle and oxen. In the Firth of Clyde area over twenty warrants were issued for colluding with Irish smugglers. The outcome was that the tidewaiter at Ayr went into hiding in Ireland, four soldiers at Dumbarton Castle were cashiered and a number of burgesses of Glasgow and Renfrew fined; *RPC,* IV, pp. 453, 582–3 and V, pp. 55, 99, 101–2.

THE BARBARY CORSAIRS

After the peace, the favourable trading conditions created by Charles II's policy of neutrality in a still warring Europe actively encouraged Scottish shippers to venture further afield again.[49] During the 1670s the southern European trades offered the best prospect for high value-added trading as Scottish barrelled fish was readily exchanged for salt, spirits, wine, nuts and citrus fruits. Profits in this trade could be very high. Indeed, the irrepressible Glasgow entrepreneur Walter Gibson made enough on his venture out to St. Martin on the Ile de Ré (off La Rochelle), with 300 lasts of Clyde herrings out and brandy back, to purchase his chartered Dutchman – *St. Agate* (450 tons) – and two other smaller vessels.[50] In 1672 another group of Glasgow entrepreneurs, led by Provost John Bell, pushed further south to Cadiz with the *Providence* which returned safely with a rich cargo of Spanish sherry sack, the first accredited direct import of this luxury commodity through a west-coast port.[51]

Such returns, however, reflected the high risk of capture by Barbary coast corsairs in the southern approaches to the British Isles and the Bay of Biscay during that decade.[52] The absence of an effective French naval presence in the latter sea area had allowed the Barbary galleys (often manned by renegade Christians) to penetrate as far north as the waters around southern Ireland and the Scilly Isles from their bases on the North African coast.

The first report of a Scottish loss to this particular outbreak of piracy was that of the *Golden Salmond* of Glasgow. Owned by a consortium headed by the enterprising William Anderson of Dowhill, she was taken *en route* to Cadiz by a 'salleeman' man-of-war in March 1671.[53] Despite the safe return of the *Providence* the following year, losses continued to mount as the decade progressed. In 1675 the *Mary* of Inverkeithing was overwhelmed by 'Turks' and her crew were carried into slavery.[54] In the following summer the crew of the *William & Jean* of Glasgow had the good fortune to retake

---

49   This neutrality stance is evident in the Scottish Privy Council's decree that a French vessel fitting out at Leith as a privateer was only free to leave if it remained a merchantman; *RPC,* IV, p. 309.

50   J. McUre, *The History of Glasgow* (Glasgow, 1736, reprinted 1830), p. 169.

51   *Ibid.,* p. 170. Bell took the dual precautions of equipping her with both a 'Turks' (Mediterrenean) Pass and forty-eight guns.

52   Earlier reports of Scottish vessels taken by Barbary corsairs date from the 1640s.

53   *RPC,* II, p. 574.

54   *RPC,* IV, p. 489.

their vessel from the Algerine prize crew put onboard after their capture *en route* to Cadiz. But their hopes of a safe passage home were short-lived, as a boarding party from a passing Portuguese frigate exploited the presence of the disarmed crew of 'Turks' to carry her into Lisbon as prize.[55] In September of that year the *Isabel* of Montrose was carried into Tangiers while attempting the return passage from La Rochelle.[56] Sometime before July 1678 the *Anna* of Pittenween was taken on the same route and her crew imprisoned, despite sailing in the company of three English vessels.[57]

These incidents, while involving small numbers of vessels and men by English standards, represented a significant reduction of the diminutive stock of Scottish sea-going hulls and a serious drain on the pool of experienced long-haul mariners.

The fate of the unfortunate crews taken captive demonstrated how inferior Scottish maritime prowess and institutions were at this time. Scotland, as an independent nation state, did not have the naval force to emulate Admiral Blake's bombardment of Algiers and Tunis (1654) or the diplomatic leverage to secure the release of her nationals from the horrors of captivity. Nor did Scots have the customs organisation to levy an equivalent to the English 'Algerine Duty' on vessels entering their ports to fund ransoming *en masse*.[58]

The ransoming of Scottish crews was therefore left to the charity of their kinsmen at home. This was a very costly and uncertain process that often took years.[59] The method of collection involved direct appeals to the principal city corporations, while agents authorised by the Scottish Privy Council toured the maritime parishes touching the Christian conscience of their congregations on Sundays.[60]

---

55   *Ibid.*, V, p. 59.
56   *Ibid.*, V, p. 281.
57   *Ibid.*, VI, p. 288.
58   In 1641 an Act of the English Parliament set aside a percentage of all customs duty to redeem captives. Such ransoming *en masse* was organised by intermediaries, usually the Order of Redemptionist Fathers. In the first 'redemption' (1646) Elizabeth Mancor of Dundee was ransomed for £200 and Alice Hayes of Edinburgh for £1,100 sterling; S. Clissold, 'The Ransom Business', *History Today*, XXVI, No.12, p. 787.
59   The ransom for Walter Noble, one of the crew of the *Golden Salmond*, was set at 400 pieces of eight; *RPC*, IV, p. 113. He was eventually released and served as master on a succession of Clyde vessels including the *Mayflower* of Glasgow, crossing to the 'Caribees' in March 1685; NAS E72 19/1/8/9.
60   Eight wives of crewmen lodged a petition protesting against the collectors' delay in amassing the ransom for two men; *RPC*, VI, pp. 364 and 573.

A The Mary Rose.
B The Hambororough Frigatt a Merchant
C The Roe Ketch
D a Scotch Merchant bound for Cadiz
E a Pinck which came with us from
   Tangier bound for Salee
F The Half Moon an Algier Man of Warr
   who Charging first, had 40 Gunns
   and 400 men
G Orange Tree being the Vice Admirall
   36 Gunns 250 Men
H Seaven Starrs 30 Gunns 300 Men
I White Horse 39 Gunns 240 Men
K The Hart 28 Gunns 260 Men
L Golden Lyon the Turks Admirall, he
   had 34 Gunns 300 Men
M The Rose Coase following the Prise.
N The Prise
O a French Merchant

A 'SCOTCH' MERCHANTMAN (D) ASSISTS IN REPELLING ALGERINE
MEN-OF-WAR. ENGRAVING BY HOLLAR, 1670

THE NEW INTERNATIONAL ORDER AT SEA

Such an unsatisfactory state of affairs was not allowed to continue, especially when it impinged on the grander schemes of the monarch. In December 1676, James assumed the exclusive right to issue foreign-going passes to Scottish masters, thereby taking full control of Scotland's overseas trade. During the Barbary corsair emergency of the following year, he went so far as to temporarily place the issuing of 'Mediterranean passes' to Scottish traders in the hands of the English Admiralty.[61] This move may have been designed to bring them under the protection of English agreements with the Barbary States. It is more likely that his need was to curb the number of diplomatic incidents at this particular time.[62]

As part of the general accord that followed on from the Treaty of Nijmegen (July 1678) that formally concluded the Dutch Wars, delicate negotiations were undertaken between the major European trading nations and the Barbary States. The outcome was a comprehensive international pass system. This was the first practical dividend of the new consensus on the Law of Nations at sea and signalled an end to the worst excesses of the early mercantilist system in European and western Mediterranean waters.[63] At the inauguration of the system the issuing of these indispensable foreign-going passes to Scottish masters was placed under the direction of a new Scottish civil office – the 'General Surveyor'.[64] To facilitate trade Scotland was divided into three administrative districts – the Lowlands, the North, and the Isles – served by issuing offices at Edinburgh, Aberdeen and Lerwick respectively. The new system required separate passes for each leg of a voyage, which were valid for a year and a day. After that time the messengers-at-arms were empowered by 'Letters of Horning' to secure old passes so that 'they do not abuse for covering of foreigne trade or otherwayes therby'.[65]

---

61 *Ibid.*, V, p. 52.
62 The English Admiralty only issued passes to 'British-built' vessels, and so foreign-built Scottish vessels were denied. England had then gone on the offensive against the Tripoli corsairs. Naval boats, under the command of Clowdisley Shovell, burned craft found in Tripoli harbour (1676) and cruised the Barbary coast (1677–86).
63 The signatories were Spain, Holland, Sweden, Denmark and the corsair states (Algiers, Tunis and Tripoli). In addition Spanish and Dutch passes carried by neutrals were also deemed valid against French privateers.
64 *RPC*, V, p.217. The first of whom was Hugh Dalrymple, son of Lord Stair.
65 *Ibid.*, pp. 135–6, 217 and 442. An example of a Mediterranean pass via Campvere was that issued for the *Margaret* of Aberdeen, Captain Thomas Gordon (1692); *State Papers* (Scotland) Warrant Books, VXV, No.334.

THE REHABILITATION OF THE
OFFICE OF LORD HIGH ADMIRAL

Such treaties and advances in international maritime co-operation, however, only served to highlight the general disregard into which the authority of the Lord High Admiral of Scotland had fallen. In the more isolated waters of the Outer and Western Isles, sporadic warfare flared between rival foreign marines in blatant contempt of Scottish sovereignty.[66] General lawlessness and acts of piracy were regularly perpetrated by and against the local communities, with judicial retribution rarely seen to be exacted on the transgressors.[67] It was, therefore, a matter of urgency that the Duke of York, as Lord High Admiral of Scotland, restore the tarnished credibility of this office.

In 1680 the Scottish Privy Council, no doubt at his behest, reaffirmed the independent and supreme authority of the Lord High Admiral, 'it being certain that the Admirall has not only a civill jurisdiction but a supream jurisdiction ane *imperium marum* for judgeing and punishing all thefts, roberies and other crymes committed at sea or within the seamark'.[68] The following year his new marine judicial system was enshrined in a statute of the Scottish Parliament that effectively stripped the Vice-Admiralties of their power to hear and condemn prizes. Such matters were now deemed to be the sole prerogative of the Judge-Admiral sitting at the Court of Admiralty at Edinburgh, as the Statute 'Prohibit[ed] and Discharge[d] all other Judges to meddle with the decision of the said causes in the first instance, except the Great Admiral or his Deputes allenarly'.[69]

In the international arena the Lord High Admiral of Scotland was seen to hold firm on the issue of Scottish sovereignty. The *cause célèbre* was the case of John Niven, master of the *Fortune* of London, who had absconded with his French-owned cargo while *en route* from La Rochelle to Ostend.

---

66   Prior to the Act of Union, engagements between Spanish, Dutch and French squadrons repeatedly occurred in the waters of the Outer Isles. In one incident (1640) four Dutch naval escorts of the incoming East Indies fleet were overwhelmed in Shetland waters by ten Spanish privateering frigates fitted out at Dunkirk for this mission.
67   Major expeditions against pirates' nests were mounted by the Convention of the Royal Burghs in the Firth of Clyde (1590 and 1643) and the Western Isles (1610). The occasional execution of pirates captured in Orkney waters continued until at least 1725; NAS, Morton MSS, GD 150, box 136.
68   *RPC*, VI, pp. 535–6.
69   It became a Scottish Statute in 1681, as quoted by Baty, 'Judge Admiral', from the 'Memorial for the Judge Admiral of Scotland, 1802', PRO T.1/901 *Treasury In Letter.*

When he resurfaced in Burntisland he was imprisoned in the local tollbooth on a holding charge of 'crimes against the personage of the Lord High Admiral of Scotland' while the question of jurisdiction was decided. The French laid claim to ultimate jurisdiction in what was, as they saw it, an act of piracy. Failing that, they pressed for a 'paine of death' penalty through the Scottish courts. York rejected both demands and had Nevin prosecuted for sedition and breach of contract in the Scottish Court of Admiralty – having first pardoned him of slander.[70]

THE SHIFT WESTWARD

The establishment of the Law of Nations in Scottish and western European waters did not, however, extend to all zones of the Mediterranean. In the southern and eastern areas elements of the Barbary corsairs and the Sultan's navy regularly broke agreements. The experience of the Scottish *Turkie* frigate serves as an example. She was taken on her return passage from Leghorn, in 1681, by six Turkish men-of-war sailing under the French flag. It was a bloody engagement during which the captain and several of the crew were killed and the survivors carried off to enslavement in Algiers.[71]

Given such a volatile state of affairs in that sea region, it was understandable that John Dunlop, a Scottish merchant in London, pressed his younger brother William to secure personal insurance against ransom before sailing for Venice via Cadiz.[72] In his letter John quoted William 'six guineas per £100 [as] the usual rate on a passage for the Straits [of Gibraltar]'. This was at a time when a new armistice had recently been agreed between the British Crown and the Ambassador of the 'Emperor of Morocco' that greatly reduced the threat from the Barbary coast corsairs in Biscayan and Iberian waters. Ominously, he did not attempt to quote a rate for insurance on the highly dangerous second leg to Venice.[73] As it was, William duly sailed in September 1682 for Cadiz on the *Londoner* (22 guns)

---

70   For the progress of this long-running case, see *RPC*, VI, pp. 439, 440, 452, 520, 535 and 536.

71   *Ibid.*, IV, p. 582 and VI, p. 190.

72   Letter to father in Glasgow, 9 September 1682. William had just completed his training in 'ciphering, writing and book holding' in Rotterdam; GCA, Dunlop of Garnkirk MSS, 120 D12/11.

73   *Ibid.*, D 12/29.

in the company of two other armed English merchantmen (36 & 16 guns) – 'so they need not fear no Salee man'.[74]

Such real dangers were, of course, only one of a number of factors that actively encouraged young Scottish merchant adventurers to look to the Americas rather than the Mediterranean or the Levant when seeking their fortunes. The subsequent actions of William Dunlop typify this westward shift in outlook as he abandoned his planned trip to Venice and took passage westward on an English West Indiaman. His first port of call was New York, a place where 'he has not heard of any hurricanes there, nor is the hazard of pirates great'. From there, armed with letters of introduction and credit and using the Scottish network abroad, he made his way from West New Jersey to Curacao and Jamaica where he met an untimely death at Port Royal in November 1683.[75]

The fact that all Dunlop's passages were made on English vessels and his letters home delivered via England points to the general effectiveness of the English Navigation Acts at this time. His unrestricted progress, on the other hand, demonstrates the accommodation secured by the Anglo-Scottish Commission of 1668 that allowed Scottish merchants to settle and trade within the English colonies. This august body did not, however, concede any concessions on the crucial issue of the exclusion of Scottish vessels and ports from the direct carrying trade to and from the colonies and plantations.

THE EARLY ATLANTIC TRADERS

The Clyde masters had established a direct regular trade with the Caribbean isles prior to the Restoration and the Navigation Act of 1660. As Cromwell's agent Tucker reported in 1656, 'here hath likewise beene some who have adventured as farre as the Barbadoes; but the losse they have sustayned by reason of theyr going out and comeing home late every yeare, have made them discontinue goeing thither any more'.[76] The

---

74 *Ibid.*, D 12/15 and 16.

75 *Ibid.*, D 12/36, 41 and 6/25. William's prime connection in London was James Hamilton who gave him £131 sterling and introduced him to the 63-year-old Scots Quaker, Gavin Laurie. Laurie was recommended for his 'great trading experience' and drew up a list of goods suitable for New York or the Leeward Isles market. He also gave William a letter of introduction to his son, the Governor of West New Jersey.

76 As quoted by Marwick, *Miscellany*, p. 26. No doubt, the appointment of the Scots peer, the Earl of Carlisle, as governor of this island (1650) had much to do with its attractiveness as a destination.

surviving evidence supporting his observation is fragmentary but sufficient to indicate that he was referring to the Royal Burgh estuary ports of the Firth of Clyde that served the merchants of Glasgow at this time – Ayr, Irvine and Dumbarton.[77]

Ayr would appear to have taken the lead with the departure of the *Rebecca* of Dublin from Ayr for Barbados, Monserrat and the neighbouring isles in 1642.[78] Two years later, the bark *Blessing* of Ayr was sent out 'towards Barbadois for the importing of tobacao'. This was a wholly local venture commanded by the Ayr merchant Andrew Rowane who subsequently made his way to St.Kitts. This enterprise was cut short by his death, and in 1646 the *Bonadventur* of Irvine was sent out from Ayr to retrieve his stock from the island. The outgoing cargoes probably included some reluctant passengers, as a general confession was heard in the town the following (plague-ridden) year that sought forgiveness for 'their ungodlie and unlawful gaine by alluring and cariing of children to the West Indies'.[79] Other ventures followed. Three years later, the *James* of Ayr returned home with 'a stock of tobacco newly come fra the Isle of Barbadus worth £1533. 6/8d' belonging another deceased Ayr burgess, William Kelso. During the Commonwealth the *Gift [of God]* of Ayr was reported arriving safely at Barbados.[80]

With the Restoration and the strengthening of the English Navigation Acts (1660–3) this trade continued under various guises, primarily by sailing under English colours. As part of the deception, the Ayr burgess owners of the *Unicorn* arranged a sale of convenience to their English master John Hodgson so that he could pass her off as 'English-owned' in

---

77 Principally the surviving port books, burgh records and reports to the Convention of Royal Burghs. Tucker was made a burgess of Ayr and would have been familiar with its trading ventures. There are earlier isolated references to transatlantic passages, namely the *Grace of God* returning to Dundee from Newfoundland (1600); the *Janet* of Leith to the West Indies (1611); and the *Golden Lion* of Dundee to the Chesapeake (1626).

78 NAS, RD 1/544/6. I am grateful to D. Dobson for calling this source to my attention.

79 For the voyage of *Bonadventur*: A. Dunlop, *The Royal Burgh of Ayr* (Edinburgh, 1953), p. 198. The confession was noted in the Records of the Sailors' Society of Ayr (now lost); see D.A. Lyon, *Ayr in the Olden Times* (Ayr, 1928), p. 24. I am grateful to Tom Barclay for his assistance with these data and what follows on Hodgson, his vessels and associates.

80 Dunlop, *Ayr*, p. 198, and Minutes of the Council of Barbados, 1 August 1655 as quoted by D. Dobson, *The Mariners of the Clyde and Western Scotland* (St. Andrews, 1994), p. 17.

his subsequent voyages to St.Kitts (1663–6).[81] The capture of St. Kitts, Monserrat and Antigua at the start of the Second Dutch War, however, temporarily halted this trade until the *status quo* was eventually reinstated with the peace settlement.

Thereafter, the subterfuge was resumed with the replacement of the *Unicorn* that Hodgson purchased on a visit to Merseyside in 1668. Renamed the *Unity*, this small 'English-built' vessel (28 tons) made three passages from Ayr to the West Indies before she was captured returning from Monserrat in early 1674.[82] The *Unity's* cargo manifests (sugar, ginger, indigo and tobacco) of her two previously completed voyages throw light on the wider regional interests served by the Ayr network – fronted as it was by Englishmen. Along with local Ayr merchants, the part-owners of the cargo included a Glasgow merchant and two Belfast 'passengers'. The latter had secured an accommodation with the Collector of Customs and Town Council of Ayr to land their goods.[83]

By then Ayr's connections with Monserrat and Barbados were sufficiently well-established to discard the 'English master' facade. It may be that the appointment of the Duke of York as the High Lord of Admiral of Scotland (1673) – with his known benevolence towards Scottish trading aspirations – encouraged such boldness. That year, Hodgson took the *Unity* out to the Monserrat for the last time.[84] She probably sailed in company with the Ayr privateer *Lamb,* under charter to Belfast merchants, heading for Barbados.[85] Thereafter it was local masters. In 1678 David Ferguson took out the *Swan* (40 tons) and James Chalmers (Hodgson's Scottish brother-in-

81 Hodgson was well connected, from Kendal (Westmorland), and married into an Ayr shipmaster family. He may well have been a master with Cromwell's supply fleet to the local garrison. The bond he signed with the owners of the *Unicorn* stated: '... that the sale of said vessel is only granted to me per forma as a confident person; and I bind and oblige myself to redeliver the said rendition to the said owners and their partners at such times as I shall be required.'; CL Ayr Burgh Records, Bond December 1661.

82 She was taken weeks after the end of hostilities and so Hodgson was sent by her owners to Holland to negotiate her return or seek compensation; *Ibid.,* Accompt of expenses, January 1675.

83 The Irishman Laurence Orum was 'forgiven his transgression' of selling his tobacco and indigo to the town treasurer, on payment of £20 Scots; while his compatriot, John Donallie, had to pay £3 Scot for a licence to sell his tobacco to any freeman of the Burgh; *Ibid.,* Port Books Nov. 1672–73 and Council Minutes 21 September 1672. The key figure in such accommodations was the Collector – Yaxley Robson – ex-commander of the Cromwellian garrison, business associate of the Earl of Eglinton and future Provost of Ayr (1682).

84 The voyage of the *Unity*: E. 72/3/3.

85 CL Ayr Burgh Records, Dean of Guild Court Book, B6/24/3.

law) the newly acquired *James* (100 tons) to Monserrat. Chalmers made one more visit before his death (1681).[86]

Much of the sugar carried back was declared 'free of [Scottish] customs' on arrival as it was destined for the 'Glasgow Sugarie' for refining, prior to re-export. By the time of the last voyage of the *James*, the other 'creeks' on the North Ayrshire coast had joined in and risked their best vessel on ventures to such Scots-friendly islands as Nevis, Barbados and Monserrat.[87] Their success, however, only served to increase the glut of tobacco and sugar on the home market at this time.

By way of contrast, conclusive evidence that vessels belonging to the upper Clyde made transatlantic passages prior to Tucker's observation (1656) – and, indeed, for twenty-five years afterwards – remains elusive. While the surviving records of Dumbarton (the only 'free' Royal Burgh seaport on the upper Clyde at that time) list the departure of three vessels (1627–8) to support Sir William Alexander's settlement in Nova Scotia, none was cited as belonging to Dumbarton or a neighbouring anchorage.[88] Likewise, the often quoted reference to the *Antelope* 'of Glasgow' arriving in the upper Clyde in 1646 with 20,000 lb. of tobacco 'fra Martanik' is sufficiently ambiguous as to be referring to a re-export delivery from France.[89] What is known for certain is that Dumbarton was particularly vigilant and aggressive in policing the upper Clyde southern bank anchorages of Crawfordsdyke and Newark Bay. Vessels found in these bays were boarded and searched. Those found trading in breach of the royal burgh's exclusive 'right to communicate' in foreign trade were summarily arrested and their cargoes confiscated. It would seem, therefore, that the vessels of the unfree burghs were not, as yet, in a position to be directly involved in the transatlantic trading. Indeed, it was not until after the building of the first quay at the

---

86   The voyage of the *Swan*: NAS, E. 72/3 /4; the *James* (replacement for the *Unity*): NAS, E. 72/ 3/7,11 and 12 (the mate took command of her for the passage to Monserrat in 1683).

87   Notably in April 1684 when Saltcoats directly sent out the *William & James*, James Kyler. The *Jean* of Largs also departed from Port Glasgow under the command of Ninian Gibson; *Ibid.*, E. 72/96/6 and 72/19/9.

88   The *St.Lawrence* was described as 'of Lubeck'. The others were the *Eagle* and the *Morning Star*, both cited without a home port. The latter name was common to the vessels from the Baltic ports at this time but has yet to appear in any record of an ocean-going Scottish vessel.

89   As quoted by F. Robert and I.M.M. McPhail (eds.), *Dumbarton Common Good Accounts, 1614–1660* (Dumbarton, 1972), p. 266. The re-export interpretation is based on the facts that: the *Antelope* also had onboard 'daills' [planking] which, in all other contemporary entries, are of European origin. On the other hand the tobacco was described as belonging to 'frenchmen planters'.

virgin site of Newark Bay – sanctioned for foreign trade under Glasgow's status as a Royal Burgh – that the first unequivocal reports of 'New Port' Glasgow's involvement emerge. This was the departure of the one-time letter of marque vessel – the *Rainbow* of [Port] Glasgow – for the plantations in February 1671, just before hostilities with the Dutch resumed.[90]

Ten years passed before it can be said that a regular transatlantic trade had been finally established. In 1681, at least five locally owned vessels were reported clearing for the plantations: the *Alexander* and the *Friendship* for Virginia, the *William & Jane* for New York, the *John* for New England and the *Benjamin* to the West Indies (twice). They were followed by the *Catherine* and the *Walter*, the latter running the Atlantic for two successive years (1682–3), having been diverted from her usual run to Cadiz. All were described as 'of Glasgow'.[91]

The Ayr–Glasgow connection remained quite pronounced at this time, as evident from the three tons of wine carried to Virginia onboard the *Alexander* of Glasgow for the Ayr merchant, David Ferguson. In 1682, James Crauford (the younger) – a fellow burgess of Ayr – was chosen by the Scottish Carolina Company as the supercargo on board the small *James* of Irvine that sailed that October (from Port Glasgow or Irvine) under the command of the veteran George Dreddan.[92] Amongst the small select band sailing with him was the adventurous Glasgow merchant William Anderson.[93] Their exploratory mission was twofold: to find a site for a Covenanters' colony that was sufficiently removed from the main English plantations; and to test the local market for Scottish goods. Two years later, this ill-fated precursor of the Darien Scheme got underway. The first settlers were transported on the larger *James* of Ayr (David Ferguson commanding) to found Stuartstown in South Carolina under the leadership of Lord Cardross.[94]

90   The voyage of the *Rainbow*: RPC, II, p. 299. At the same time the *Glasgow Merchant* also left but the home and departure port(s) is not known; RPC, III, pp. 259 and 678.
91   The voyage of the *Benjamin*: NAS Port Book, E. 72/19/1 and 2; the *Catherine*: E72/19/1,5 and 9: and the *Walter*: E. 72/19/5,6 and 8.
92   Dreddan had previously crossed the Atlantic to the plantations as the master of the *Glasgow* (port unknown) in 1670: RPC III, p. 299. He may also be George 'Breddon' – master of the letter-of-marque *Lion* of Glasgow (1666): Table: 1.2.
93   They carried an array of Scottish manufactured textiles and domestic goods, the property of William Cochrane and Sir George Campbell (amongst others), to test the local market.
94   L.G. Fryer, 'The Covenanters' lost Colony in South Carolina', *Scottish Archives* (1996), 2, pp. 98–106. The *James* of Ayr does not reappear in the port books of Ayr or her neighbours and may have been lost with the venture. The last vessel to reach the settlement was the *Carolina Merchant* (170 tons) which departed from Gourock in 1685.

AYR, c.1690. REMNANTS OF THE CITADEL AND BARRACKS ON THE RIGHT. ALSO
ST JOHN'S CHURCH. PARTIALLY DECKED BOATS WITH LEE-BOARDS LIE GROUNDED
AT THE QUAYSIDE. (FROM SLEZER'S *THEATRUM SCOTIAE*)

In 1686 disaster struck when two determined Spanish attacks launched from St.Augustine wiped out this settlement. This ended the dream of founding a colony to which Scottish vessels carrying 'Scotch goods' could directly trade for mainland plantation tobacco.[95]

TRANSPORTATION AND THE
RISE OF THE TOBACCO TRADE

Elsewhere on the eastern seaboard of America the writ of the English Navigation Acts held force – though with varying degrees of rigour. It followed that the vessels that carried settlers from Leith, Montrose, Aberdeen and Kirkwall to the 'Scots Lots' in the post-Restoration 'proprietory' colonies – West and East New Jersey – were invariably English charters.[96] The latter colony, under the tolerant governorship of the Aberdonian quaker Robert Barclay, attracted the largest numbers after 1680.[97] Likewise, entering the New England ports with 'Scotch goods' was left to American and English charters.[98]

There remained, however, a loophole enabling Scots traders to enter directly from a Scottish port with a paying cargo without breaching the English Acts. This was by transporting felons, political prisoners or bonded servants. In January 1663 Lord Lauderdale, then Secretary of State for Scotland and confidante of Charles II, set the precedent by granting to John Browne, the Scottish merchant and master mariner, a licence to trade with four vessels to the Americas.[99] This was probably in response to a request made the previous year by the Edinburgh magistrates to be allowed to transport undesirables directly to the colonies. What is clear is that from 1666 onwards a number of Leith vessels were licensed to transport felons

95   Fryer, having examined the Bute Archives relating to this venture, states that national and individual commercial interests were the prime motives driving this scheme.

96   See printed advert for the *Henry & Francis* of Newcastle, June 1685: NAS RH18/1/93. She left Leith two months late with emigrants and a variety of locally manufactured goods: *Ibid.*, E72/15/32.

97   For example, the *Thomas & Benjamin* of London, Thomas Pearson, landed 130 men, women and children collected from Leith, Montrose and Aberdeen, at Sandy Hook in 1684.

98   For example, the *Swallow* of Salem which entered Boston from Port Glasgow with 'Scotch goods' in 1682; as quoted by D. Dobson, *Ships from Scotland to America, 1628–1828* (Baltimore, 1998) p. 117.

99   BL, MSS 35126, licence 16 January 1662/3.

NEW YORK, c.1670

and indentured servants to Virginia or Barbados.[100]

While the Royal Commission of 1668 on Anglo-Scottish affairs deliberated, Scottish aspirations to settle a colony through which a direct trade in plantation commodities could be undertaken found a champion in the Duke of York – then the High Lord Admiral of England. Using his personal influence and authority, he proposed a Scottish plantation and entrepôt at New York as a channel for Scottish enterprise. His motives were far from selfless as he held the royal patent for this newly acquired English colony (the ex-Dutch New Amsterdam). Under his scheme Scottish entrepreneurs, 'in Vessels from Scotland', were encouraged 'to pass from Scotland to New York with such persons of the Scots Nation as shall desire to plant there, and to trade between the said places as they shall have occasion. Or remain at New York upon the account of the fisheries'.[101]

In May 1669 an Order of Council duly authorised York to license the

---

100   The first to Virginia with convicts would appear to have been the *Phoenix* of Leith – Wood, *Extracts of the Burgh of Edinburgh*, entry 25 April 1666 – and the *Job* of Leith returning in March 1667: Mowat, *Leith*, p. 220. Later that year the *Elizabeth* of Leith and the *Good Intent* of ? departed with consignments of criminals for Virginia and Barbados: *RPC*, II, p. 358. The most regular was the *Ewe and Lamb*, 1666–72, while the largest was the prize and ex-warship *Convertine*. The latter was chosen to remove the remaining Covenanters held in Greyfriars churchyard to Virginia (1668): Mowat, *Leith*, pp. 216–7.

first Scottish vessels under this scheme. These were two Leith hulls – the *James* (150 tons) and the *Hope* (350 tons). To ensure that the original aim of promoting a Scottish settlement was achieved, the Council imposed the condition that at least four hundred Scottish subjects were conveyed on their first voyage. This onerous requirement was probably the reason why the owners of the smaller *James* appears not to have taken up their licence. The owners of the *Hope*, on the other hand, persisted and petitioned the Scottish Privy Council to instruct all Sheriffs and Justices of the Peace to deliver to them 'strong and idle beggars, vagabonds, Egyptians [gypsies], comon and notorious whores, theeves and other dissolute and louse persons banished or stigmatised for gross crymes'.[102]

While this human cargo was being assembled, a new Order in Council (June) extended the access to the English colonial market with the addition of the clause – 'or any other of His Majesty's plantations in America'. This new privilege was granted under certain conditions first mooted by the Scottish representatives to the Royal Commission, namely, that they give security to the English customs and only carry goods that were the produce of England, Scotland or Ireland, and that they returned directly to an English port to report and pay duty on any colonial goods imported.

This new clause justified switching the destination of the *Hope* from New York to Virginia in order to attract more steerage volunteers and to secure a more lucrative return cargo of tobacco for the promoters. Even so, finding the requisite numbers of passengers proved laborious for the recruiting agents; John Kennoway wrote to his brother: 'I heir that Sir Wm [William Bruce of Balcaskie, later Kinross] is to send some vessellis to Virginie. It is reported heire that thair is severall unsuffi[cient] persons taken to send thairin.'[103] The prohibitive expense of incarcerating and transporting felons to Edinburgh or Leith seems to have dissuaded outlying magistrates from adding to the numbers onboard. The *Hope* and her human cargo never cleared Scottish waters as she was wrecked with few survivors on Cairnbulg Sands in Fraserburgh Bay in late December 1669.[104]

---

101 As quoted by Mowat, *Leith*, pp. 216–8.
102 Act of the Privy Council (Colonial), I, no. 848, as quoted by P. Gouldesburgh, 'An Attempted Scottish Voyage to New York in 1669', *Scottish Historical Review*, 40 (1961), p. 56.
103 NAS, Bruce of Kinross MSS GD 29 1962/23. The other owners, at one time or another, were William Binning, James Currie (both later Provosts of Edinburgh), James Standsfield (later of Newmilns) and Robert Baird of Saughtonhall.
104 She may have been heading for the Moray Firth or Cromarty to collect more prisoners, as one collecting agent was ' a merchant of Tain': *Ibid.*, p. 62.

Despite this initial disaster an annual autumn sailing from Leith with felons for the plantations continued until 1672. After that date the frequency of passages increased to accommodate a glut of criminal and political prisoners sentenced to transportation. In 1673 the English Quaker and merchant of Leith, 'Moreis Trent', was authorised to transport 'a great multitudes of vagabonds, idle and sturdie beggars and louse and masterles men, and women who have no visible way of liviliehood'.[105] Their departure on the *Hercules* was delayed by a warrant to search the vessel for 'frie' persons illegally carried on board.[106] The clearing out of undesirables to America continued with the *St Jo[h]n* of Leith transporting a party of 'Egyptians [gypsies]' moved from Dunbar to Edinburgh tollbooth for embarkation.[107]

Around this time the liberal interpretation of the June amendment to the Order in Council was successfully challenged, no doubt arising from Scottish abuse of the privilege. The curtailment of Scottish sailings to Virginia brought a rapid retort from the colonists in 1675. They complained that the reintroduction of the commodity trading ban on Scottish vessels threatened to cut their supply of cheap labour as '[Scots]men will not bring [bonded and unfree] servants when they bring no other commodities'.[108]

The ongoing political and religious troubles of Scotland continued to produce a flow of felons for transportation to Virginia and Maryland. The Glasgow merchants, in their determination to penetrate the tobacco trade, seized the opportunity created by the lucrative contracts awarded by the Secret Council (1678–9) to convey to the plantations, as slaves, those remaining Covenanters who had refused the 'Bond'.[109]

The contract for the first year had gone to English vessels brought up to sail directly from Leith. The second-year contract to convey between three and four hundred prisoners from Leith was, however, won by William Paterson of Glasgow. His chartered vessel – the *Crown* of London – was wrecked on the coast of Orkney and the 258 prisoners crammed under secured hatches left to drown while the captain and his crew saved themselves. News of their inhuman conditions in passage and their pitiless fate raised a general public

---

105 *RPC*, IV, p. 83. Trent probably settled after the disbanding of the Cromwellian garrison at Leith.

106 *Ibid.*, p.103. The *Hercules* left Leith for Virginia in September under Captain Edward Say.

107 *Ibid.*, pp. 490 and 144.

108 *State Papers American and West Indies, 1675–1676*, p. 304 as quoted by Lipson, p. 127.

109 *RPC*, XI, pp. 78 and 257. To sign the bond was to renounce the Solemn League and Covenant and accept the State's supremacy in religious matters.

JAMES VII & II

outcry.[110] The departures from Leith continued undeterred until December 1685 when the last consignment of prisoners embarked for the plantations on board the *John & Nicholas* (180 tons/12 guns).[111]

The solution to the perils of going north about *en route* to the Americas was to ship directly out of the Clyde. In May 1684 James Montgomerie of Glasgow contracted with the Edinburgh city fathers to rid them of all 'dissolut women' held in the House of Correction – between the ages of twenty and thirty – to the Carolinas for a fee of 30/- per head.[112] Around

110   J. Grant, *Old and New Edinburgh* (London, undated), III, p. 189.
111   Mowat, *Leith*, p. 218.
112   They were conveyed to Port Glasgow by ten soldiers of the town guard: Wood, *Extracts Burgh of Edinburgh (1681–89)*, pp. 162–3.

the same time Walter Gibson's consortium formally contracted with the government agent for transportation, Robert Malloch, to handle regular consignments of prisoners and undesirable elements 'in shackles' from Greenock and Port Glasgow to Virginia and the Carolinas.[113] His principal vessel was the *Pelican* of Glasgow commanded by his brother James Gibson and aided by two others vessels – the *John* and the *Friendship* of Glasgow – when numbers required.[114] Consignments of prisoners were subsequently shipped from the Clyde until the mid-1690s, after which the increasing availability of negro slave labour in the eastern seaboard plantations undermined the commercial viability of transportation.

The Clyde shippers' switch from the West Indies to New England in search of tobacco had not gone unnoticed. As early as 1680 Edward Randolph – the Surveyor General of Customs for the American Plantations – reported that 'many ships full laden with tobacco' gave bond to the Naval Officers' Office at Boston that they were bound for unpatrolled Newfoundland. He was, however, certain that they intended to sail straight for 'Scotland, Canada and other foreign places'.[115] Such was the lure that even the normally dedicated *James* of Ayr forsook her regular destination in the West Indies for a solitary passage to Virginia in July 1681. There are indications, however, that she still took the usual precaution of carrying a few bonded servants to legitimise her entry into this English colony.[116] In the same month the *Hope* 'of Edinburgh' cleared out of Leith for New England, keeping alive the Forth's interest in the Americas.[117] Others would appear to have found a Scottish port to be a safe conduit for the illegal transportation of tobacco, as with the arrival of the *Providence* of Coleraine

---

113 *RPC*, VII, p. 653. The *Pelican* took 180 prisoners in one shipment. A *résumé* of Walter Gibson's trading exploits prior to his bankruptcy and imprisonment is available in W.F. MacArthur, *History of Port Glasgow* (Glasgow, 1932), pp. 32–3.

114 NAS, Port Book E. 72/19/1/2. The *Pelican*'s first consignment of twenty-two prisoners departed from Greenock in July 1684: D. Weir, *History of the Town of Greenock* (Glasgow, 1829) p. 67.

115 R.G. Lounsdury, *The British Fishery at Newfoundland, 1634–1763* (Newhaven, 1734, reprint London, 1969), p. 44.

116 The *James* of Ayr was declared free to leave for America by the Lords of the Committee of Council, having been searched by soldiers of the Major General for a fugitive and stolen goods in 1678. Such official permission to sail directly for America would imply that she was carrying servants; *RPC*, V, p. 528. Ayr Burgh records of this period make occasional reference to banishment to the Americas and authorise the 'Master Mariner' of the port to contract their shipment out of the port: J. Crighton, *Contributions to Scottish Maritime History* (Ayr, undated), p. 16.

117 NAS, Port Book, E. 72/3/4.

at Ayr with Virginian tobacco, having touched at Londonderry on her voyage back from the plantations.[118]

By the end of the decade the turmoil of the Glorious Revolution provided the ideal cover for Walter Gibson (Provost of Glasgow by 1688–9) and his circle of merchants and masters to drop all but token pretence when running commodity cargo directly from the Clyde to America and tobacco back. In the few years it took William and Mary to secure the British throne from the threat of a Jacobite invasion, the damaging effect of their incursions had become all too blatant. In 1692 Randolph (by now a Scotophobe) vented his frustration, at the inability of the English navy to deter their activities, to William Blathwayt, the Secretary-at-War:

> I find yet in these 3 years last there has been above 5 ships
> trading legally in all those rivers and nigh 30 sayle of Scotch,
> Irish and New England men. I humbly inclose to your honours A
> forg'd certificate (No. 4) produced to Major King by William Hall
> of Boston allowed of by Mr Layfield he clear'd his ship having
> 110 hds [hogsheads] aboard ye 7th April 1689 and went to
> Scotland since which time to ye 25th May 1692 above 1644 hds
> has been shipt off by interlopers ... above 20 Scotch, Irish and
> New England vessels within these [last] 8 months have sayld out
> of ye Cape with their loading of tobacco for Scotland and
> Holland and ye man of warr had not discover'd one of them.[119]

Prior to 1696, duping the Naval Officers at the American port of entry and exit was a relatively simple and practised affair. Scottish and chartered English vessels concealed their outward passage from a Scottish port by registering and clearing from an English port *en route* – usually Whitehaven. This device is evident in the instruction from the Glasgow owners of the *Antilop* to her captain, Cabel Chapin – 'y[e]t caire may be taken about cleiring in England' – on his voyage from the Clyde to the Chesapeake in 1693.[120] The return passage was not usually a matter of concern as they

118   *Ibid.*, E 72/3/16.
119   C.M. MacInnes, *The Early English Tobacco Trade* (London, 1926), p. 179.
120   GCA, Shawfield MSS 1/42–43, letter 21 October 1693. Those who did not take this precaution did so to their cost, as with the detention of John Watson's unregistered ship in the West Indies when found with Maryland tobacco onboard – after conveying her cargo of bonded servants to Pennsylvania: NAS, Court of Session Processes 29/1752.

sailed directly back to the Clyde, avoiding English Customs altogether. The only real danger was interception by English warships and privateers in Scottish waters.

Despite these hazards and the upheavals that followed the Protestant Succession, the trade to the Americas was firmly established by the mid-decade. In 1695 (the year before the introduction of the stringent 'Plantation Register' system) the Crown Agent for Customs in Scotland reported that twenty-four vessels were trading to the American colonies in defiance of the Navigation Acts.[121] This figure is not far off the number of vessels trading to the Chesapeake during the main decade of the legal 'tobacco era' (1760s) in Scottish history.

After the comprehensive Plantation Register system was implemented (1696), other routes were found to evade the colonial customs service in the Chesapeake and so maintain the illegal direct trade to Scotland. One such involved carting hogsheads of tobacco overland to ports in Pennsylvania and Massachusetts for shipment to the Clyde via Newfoundland. The unresolved status of Newfoundland – as an extension of His Majesty's realm of England but 'not a true plantation' – gave the Clyde shippers and their Whitehaven allies in the tobacco trade an exit point from the Americas away from direct customs surveillance.[122]

THE DELIBERATIONS OF
THE COUNCIL OF TRADE

The Duke of York, despite his reputation for oppressive handling of Scotland's internal affairs, can be credited with displaying commendable knowledge and vigour in his ongoing attempts to resuscitate the Scottish economy. This was at a time when Charles II had nothing but contempt for the trading aspirations of his Scottish subjects.

In January 1681, York found the vehicle for his schemes when he assumed the chairmanship of the Scottish Council of Trade.[123] The status

---

121 MacArthur, *Port Glasgow*, p. 34.

122 D. S. Macmillan, 'The "New Men" in Action: Scottish Mercantile and Shipping Operations in the North American Colonies, 1760–1825', *Canadian Business History* (Toronto, 1972), pp. 50–51. He holds the opinion that supposed Scottish involvement in the Newfoundland fisheries was a cover for illegal trading.

123 This, previously ineffective, committee was first convened by the Scottish Privy Council in the same year as the Scottish Navigation Act (1661).

of this Council was further enhanced by his reconciliation with the Whigs and his appointment as a Royal Commissioner (holder of the King's warrant) to Scotland in July of that year. Thus empowered, his first act was to summon leading merchants 'to advise anent the causes of the decay of trade and what they would propose for the remeid ther of".[124] Their recommendations formed the basis of a new national strategy that would replace the piecemeal legislation of the previous two decades.

The outcome of their deliberations was a series of memoranda which fully embraced the 'ballance of trade' solution to 'the disease' of a haemorrhage of bullion out of the domestic economy. The crux of their deliberations was embodied in the critical appraisal of the state of trade presented by the Provost of Linlithgow. Indeed, his highly pragmatic conclusions provided the blueprint for government intervention in Scotland's seaborne trade for decades to come. He emphasised the pressing need to resolve the recurring monetary crises and recover the nation's prosperity by the elimination of the persistent trade deficit that had accumulated over the past decade with England, France and Holland.

The most formidable barrier to achieving this aim was, in his opinion, the alarming deterioration in the volume of Scottish exports to England. This had been brought about by the doubling of duty incurred by Scotland's 'alien' status in the English *Book of Rates* (1664), compounded by the subsequent prohibitions on Scottish imports on wool and woollen manufactures, fish and grain (except in famine years). All of which came on top of existing discriminatory tariffs on coal and salt. The Provost went on to predict that any further tightening of the English Navigation Acts and raising of duties would ruin both the English market for Scottish linen and the overland trade in cattle. He concluded that, as England had displaced Holland as the principal market for Scottish produce, goods and commodities, the only logical course of action was to seek 'ane union of traid ... seing ane union betwixt the kingdoms cannot be hoped for'.[125] Such a customs union, he conceded, would not include free access for Scottish shippers to the colonial trades.

His recommendations for redressing the balance of trade with Scotland's European trading partners was relatively simple in comparison. The Dutch trade (mostly in household goods and utensils) was not, he considered, a cause for concern as it 'was great now in decay' and the

---

124 *RPC*, VII, p. 652. He stated that the 'old way' had been that the Dutch 'carried and bought ... .taking [the] risk'of the seaborne trade of Scotland.
125 *Ibid.*, p. 653.

balance of trade was currently in Scotland's favour. The drain of bullion to France, Scotland's oldest commercial ally, was a serious concern and primarily due to the salt trade in which the French had an absolute advantage in both price and quality. The solution proposed by the Provost was to place an outright ban on its import so that all domestic consumption would henceforth be of locally produced salt. Furthermore, he believed that the export trade to France could be readily boosted by offering £2,000 sterling to the French customs farmers in exchange for a waiver on the recently introduced import levy of fifty sous per ton of cargo. He looked forward to an increase in the neglected trade with Spain which he believed was 'our own fault [as] we have no more advantage [in trade]'. He blamed the debased home coinage as a major obstacle to the 'South' trade. The solution he proposed was that the internationally respected Spanish gold pieces of eight and silver ducatoons should be actively acquired as a substitute for the unwelcome Scottish coinage when trading abroad.

He also identified the purchase and hire of foreign hulls as worthy of special consideration by the Council. Until then the acquisition of Norwegian and Dutch-built hulls had been deemed unavoidable if Scotland's shipping stock was to be maintained. The elimination of this drain on the nation's coinage was, therefore, a prime target for direct intervention. A ban on the purchase of foreign vessels would also have the highly desirable effect, he assumed, of nurturing the virtually non-existent home shipbuilding industry. The growth of which was the key to fulfilling the 'British-built' condition of entry under the terms of the existing English Navigation Acts.

Such deliberations were influenced by a current surplus of tonnage 'latly built and bought' by Scottish owners. The Provost believed that since the last review of the Scottish marine at end of the Second Dutch War (estimated at 215 vessels) the number of Scottish wholly or partly owned 'ships, busses, barks and great boats' had doubled. The Council therefore issued a decree in February 1681 that placed an outright ban on the purchase or co-ownership of foreign hulls, under pain of confiscation.[126] This decree was not, however, put into effect until 1 May 1682. This was to allow vessels already ordered to be delivered and for existing 'co-

---

126 *Ibid.*, p. 671. The rigour of its enforcement is evident in the number of petitions received by the Privy Council for permission to purchase foreign hulls during the years of the embargo. An example is that of the shippers of Montrose who had lost six or seven vessels in the space of twelve months. Their plea was granted in 1685 on condition it was not taken as a precedent by others: *Ibid.*, XII, p. 140.

ownerships' with Dutch or other foreign partners to be liquidated. At the same time all import duties on shipbuilding materials were removed to encourage the home industry.

But there was an inherent problem to this simplistic solution. The previous influx of captured Dutch hulls into the Scottish marine had proved to be a mixed blessing. As the Council noted, some of the prizes were 'so great in bulk as not proper for our trade'. This was an indirect indictment of the retarded state of development of the Scottish east-coast ports.[127] On the other hand those prizes under 200 tons, the majority, had been easily absorbed into the expanding Scottish marine but were largely responsible for stifling the indigenous shipbuilding industry.

The English shipbuilding industry, by contrast, had not been adversely affected by the vast influx of prizes taken by her privateers. England's numerous deep-water ports readily deployed the large Dutch bulk carriers in their rapid post-war expansion in the European trades. This had been achieved without any significant detriment to her shipbuilding industry which had long since specialised in the building of armed traders for the Atlantic and beyond.[128]

The question posed by the Provost of Linlithgow was: which of these two diverging design concepts in hulls and rig should the Council actively promote?[129] The Dutch-formula hulls maximised carrying capacity for specific trades while minimising operating costs, as typified by the ubiquitous 'fluyt' boat. This design formula – a large and full tumble-home (curvature of the hull from the waterline to the deck) hull with a narrow deck from which an easily managed sail plan was hoisted – produced a very high tonnage-to-crew ratio. This gave the economies of scale that allowed the Dutch to dominate the peacetime north-south carrying trade of Europe.[130] The alternative concept – which the Provost of Linlithgow referred to as the 'Swedes' formula – was the 'frigatto' (frigate) design of hull, best typified by the 'brig'. This design was based on a different concept centred on a wide flushed deck hull, with much less tumble-home, that served as a stable gun platform 'so as to provide in war and trade'.[131] The Swedes had promoted the 'frigot way' for some time by offering

127   *Ibid.*, XVIII, p. 679.
128   English traders to the Americas, Africa, the Mediterranean and the East were invariably armed because of the risk of piracy, privateers and the prospect of returning to a war in European waters.
129   *RPC*, VI, pp. 657–8.
130   R. Davis, *The Rise of the Atlantic Economy* (London, 1973), p. 181.
131   *RPC*, VII, p. 654.

remission of half the duties payable on the launching of hulls.[132]

The English shipbuilders had already embraced the frigate design as their buyers expected armed trading in peacetime and valued the option of up-gunning the vessel as a 'running ship' or privateer in wartime. That these vessels required a larger crew than their Dutch counterparts was rapidly becoming a secondary issue. For, as the few Scottish 'frigatto' privateers had demonstrated, survival was rapidly taking precedence over profitability in the new order.[133]

It was clear that Scotland's dual aspirations – of owning a marine that could win a share in the highly competitive European peacetime carrying trades, while securing a foothold in the hostile trading environment of the Atlantic – could not be fully met by one design. In the certain knowledge that any future Scottish assault on the trade of others would be opposed, the Council of Trade elected to recommend the frigate design. In practical terms, however, this decision had little direct impact as the Council had already decided to remove import duties on all shipbuilding materials, leaving the matter of the hull design in the hands of the purchasing shipowners.

THE ROYAL BURGHS'
MONOPOLY OF FOREIGN TRADE

Running parallel to the lengthy deliberations on a national trading policy, and equally important to the unleashing of Scotland's overseas trading potential, was the breaking of the Scottish Royal Burghs' monopoly to 'communicate in foreign trade'. This legal anachronism, a legacy from the medieval period, had been confirmed as late as 1633 by an Act of the Scottish Parliament. This privilege was conceded in recognition of the Royal Burghs' assumption of the burden of collecting the cess (local tax) on behalf of the Scottish Exchequer. Since then their hold on trade had been increasingly challenged by the rise of the 'new' ports. The outcome was a series of legal disputes between the 'free' and 'unfree' burghs over access to overseas trade during the period 1669–1710.

The first such challenge arose in 1669 when the Duke of Hamilton declared his intention to raise the status of his town of Bo'ness to that of a free port by its elevation to a Burgh of Regality.[134] While the implications

---

132   *Ibid.*, pp. 652–3.
133   Dutch losses are discussed in Bruijn, *Course et Piraterie*, p. 415.
134   Records of the Convention of the Royal Burghs of Scotland as quoted by T. Pagan, *The Convention of the Royal Burghs* (1920), pp. 133–4. As the Lord Superior, most of the township were his feuars (ground renters).

of this precedent were being considered, a test case was brought against the unfree Burgh of Falkirk by the Royal Burgh of Linlithgow, supported by Stirling. The eventual outcome was a compromise embodied in a new Act of the Scottish Parliament (1672). Under its terms the 'right to communicate in trade' was conceded to the new unfree Burghs of Regality or Barony in return for their undertaking to relieve the members of the Convention of Royal Burghs of an agreed proportion of the cess tax.[135]

The collective response of the unfree burghs was, with the notable exceptions of Glasgow and Arbroath, to ignore this offer to legitimise their trading activities. The principal reason was that they stood to lose the cost advantage they currently offered as a haven from the cess tax for their resident merchants and shipmasters. Since the customs house was invariably located at the head port (the neighbouring Royal Burgh), trading through the unfree port, also gave the shipper ample opportunity to evade customs duties. Indeed, the loss of trade experienced by the free port to their unfree neighbours was such as to prompt several of them to petition to have their Royal Burgh status nullified.[136]

The Convention of Royal Burghs sought to retrieve the situation by securing the 'total rescission' of the 1672 Act, thereby re-establishing its members' monopoly of overseas trade.[137] At their annual meeting in 1681 the Convention resolved to exploit their tax leverage with the Treasury to expedite matters. It was not, however, until June 1690 and a change of monarch that their privileges were reinstated by an Act of the Scottish Parliament.[138] This Act went beyond the previous *status quo* as it not only confirmed their monopoly, but also prohibited burgesses from holding partnerships with 'unfreemen', and from loading or unloading or hiring vessels or crews at unfree ports.[139]

This draconian legal move brought a somewhat belated response from the main offender – Greenock. At the July Convention of 1691, Sir John Shaw (the younger) appeared as the representative of his burgh and

---

135   Between the Restoration and the Union, fifty-one Burghs of Barony and Regality were created.

136   A more detailed report ion this clash of interest is available in J. Marwick, *The River Clyde and the Clyde Burghs* (Glasgow, 1909), pp. 121–156.

137   The fine of £200 Scots imposed by the Lords of the Treasury on Sir John Shaw of Greenock and associates for importing leather (1681) was ordered to be given to the relief of a prisoner held captive by the Turks; *Ibid.*, p. 121.

138   *Ibid.*, p. 127.

139   *Ibid.* p. 129–30. In the lower Firth of Clyde action was taken against vessels belonging to Saltcoats and Newton-on Ayr.

conceded the principle of relieving the cess tax. He refused, however, to be drawn on how much his burgh would agree to contribute, which was perceived for what it was – a stalling manoeuvre 'mor ingenuous and poynted than the rest, yet in regaird he wold not liquidar his offer'.[140]

THE REGISTER OF 1692

The next move in the Convention's offensive was already in hand. Its prime objective was to demonstrate to Parliament the degree to which fraudulent trading via the unfree burghs had contributed to their decline. This was achieved by a survey – the *Register containeing of the State and Condition of every [Royal] Burghs within the Kingdome of Scotland* – that was presented to Convention held the following year at Dundee (July 1692).[141]

It was commissioned in 1690, and fifteen instructions were issued to those entrusted with completing the local report so as to ensure a standardised and comprehensive survey. The seventh instruction is of particular interest as it required them to 'take exact accompt of what ships, barks, boats and ferry boats they have belonging to them, the names of the saides ships, ther burden, and value of each of them, and how imployed and by whom.'[142]

The validity of the Register of 1692 as a reliable source of shipping data has since been questioned on two grounds. Firstly, it was conceived as part of a political agenda and, secondly, it was compiled from reports undertaken by local notaries who had a vested interest in portraying a morbid scene of decay in the trade and shipping at their ports. In defence of the integrity of the survey and its findings it can be argued that the checks and balances that the architects of the Register included from the outset were as even-handed and objective as can be reasonably expected from this era.

Indeed, the Register's compilers were fully aware of the need to pre-empt the inevitable allegations of bias and collusion that would be levelled at them by the powerful patrons of the unfree ports. To this end, two groups of 'visitors', raised from the membership of the Convention, were commissioned to tour the Royal Burghs to ensure the correctness of the local report. To avoid charges of partisan reporting or collusion, the

---

140   *Ibid.*, p. 130.
141   *Ibid.*, pp. 53-157.
142   *Ibid.*, p. 53.

visitors were chosen from the opposing coast to the one they were inspecting. It followed that the Royal Burghs on the Clyde and south-west coast were visited by James Fletcher, Provost of Dundee, in company with Alexander Walker, Baillie of Aberdeen, while those on the Forth and east coast were visited by John Muir and James Smalet, the Provosts of Ayr and Dumbarton respectively.[143] Furthermore, those responsible for the primary compilation of the shipping stock at the major ports usually had a high degree of competence in maritime matters as they were either master mariners or merchants. In the case of Leith, the largest and busiest Scottish port, the shipping list was compiled by Walter Learmouth, 'shor master'.[144]

From a modern viewpoint, the fact that a few of the maritime Royal Burghs were not visited and hence omitted (Wick, Dornoch, Kirkwall, Brevie and Galloway) also requires consideration. Their absence, however, is a minor concern as it is fairly certain that they owned no vessels of consequence, other than a few open boats, at that time.

Much more to the point is the grave reservation that, as with Tucker's report (1656), the Register of 1692 was taken in the depth of a trade cycle aggravated by war and hence gives an unrepresentative view of the Scottish ports and their shipping stock for the era.[145] While this was undoubtedly the case, it can be readily argued that warfare at sea was virtually endemic to the period. Therefore, war-affected trade cycles and adverse sailing conditions were, to all intents and purposes, common and hence representative of the early mercantilist period.

The inescapable fact remains that, given the dearth of statistical information on Scottish shipping since Tucker's report, the vessels listed at each port in the Register of 1692 offer a second unique pre-Union insight into the progress of the Scottish marine.

Transforming the shipping data in the Register of 1692 into a national survey of all Scottish ports of consequence requires, however, an allowance for the unreported shipping of the unfree ports. At the time of its compilation (1690) the majority of these unfree ports – Campbeltown, Saltcoats, Alloa, Prestonpans, Port Seton and Peterhead – were still undeveloped anchorages and as yet to be raised to the status of Burgh of Barony or Regality and so can be largely discounted. This leaves the fleets of Greenock and Bo'ness to be deduced for inclusion with those of the reporting Royal Burghs.

143   Ibid., p. 38.
144   Ibid., p. 56.
145   T.C. Smout, 'The Overseas Trade of Ayrshire', Transaction of the Ayrshire Archaeological and Natural History Society, 6, pp. 56–7.

The Greenock vessels engaged in overseas ventures were, fortunately, well documented in the complaints made to the Convention by the neighbouring Royal Burghs of Dumbarton and Glasgow, which referred to four vessels – *John, Neptune, George* and *Hendrie.*[146] Further details of these offending vessels are available from the Glasgow reporter's admission that his merchants were still heavily involved as 'co-partneries' outside the Royal Burgh, in direct violation of the Convention's previous ban. This was evident in the case of the *John*:

> the half whereof was laitle bought by two merchants in Glasgow
> at ane roup, but they hearing of the lait act of the royall burrows
> dischairgeing ther haveing any partnership with unfreemen in
> shipping they stopt to be any farder concerned therin.[147]

This ship, at 130 tons, was almost certainly Greenock's largest vessel at this time. It is, therefore, reasonable to conclude that the total tonnage of the four reported monopoly breaking vessels of Greenock could not exceed 520 tons. By way of comparison the Register of 1692 listed the recently developed deepwater harbour of 'Newport' Glasgow – 'the second trading royall burgh of the kingdome' to Leith – as supporting four vessels of one hundred tons and over and a further five hulls of over fifty tons. It is highly unlikely that Greenock's foreign-going fleet matched or exceeded that of its neighbour.

There still remains the unspecified number of partially decked and open boats based at Greenock. Tucker's earlier report mentioned that these smaller craft served as coastal carriers trading mainly to Ireland or the Isles 'with small smiddy coals' or were engaged in herring fishing within the Firth of Clyde. The solution would seem to lie in a comparison with the report from the haven of Renfrew, a few miles upriver, which had the largest fleet of fishing boats recorded in the Register of 1692. They numbered twenty-four open boats of three or five tons, served by two larger salt boats of twelve and fifteen tons respectively, all of which amounts to no more than 150 tons.[148] It would seem reasonable to assume that Greenock's flotilla of small boats did not greatly exceed that of Renfrew at this time. If this 'inshore' element is added to Greenock's foreign-going fleet, the composite estimate is around 670 tons – roughly half the total declared for Port Glasgow.

---

146 J.L. Dow, *Greenock* (Greenock, 1975), p. 62.
147 Marwick *Miscellany*, p. 75.
148 *Ibid.*, p. 119.

The estimate for the Bo'ness fleet is somewhat more difficult. Tucker remarked that the Bo'ness anchorage once rivalled Leith for the title of premier port of Scotland but failed to report any indigenous vessels there or along the immediate coast.[149] It may well be that only Dutch and Leith shippers visited the undeveloped anchorages at Bo'ness and Grangepans at that time: fleeting visits to land goods for the west-coast markets, without paying duty. Circumstantial evidence lends support to this view as only three out of the forty-odd Forth privateers, commissioned during the Second Dutch War (1664–7), declared Bo'ness as their home port.

By 1690, however, it was fairly evident from the number of complaints being raised by her neighbouring Royal Burgh of Linlithgow that a shipping fraternity was firmly established at this new Burgh of Regality of Bo'ness. The Linlithgow reporter to the *Register* referred to the rising prosperity of the unfree burgh and the 'great prejudice' it had on the surrounding towns and villages, 'who wrong ther trade by venting aboundance of staple comodities to the countrey'. As with Greenock, the promoters behind the rising numbers of foreign-going vessels at Bo'ness can be traced back to those very Royal Burghs making the complaints to the Convention. The evasive response made by the freeman merchants of Linlithgow to the enquiring magistrates, 'that they being surprized could not satisfie them therin at the tyme, but desired that they have four moneths tyme to consider on it, that if there were any unfreemen concerned with them', speaks volumes.[150] In contrast, the Glasgow reporter openly acknowledged his merchants' involvement in illegal partnerships in three vessels on the upper Forth – one of 200 tons (the largest in the *Register of 1692*) and two of 150 tons each.[151] These hulls were of a size that could only work regularly out of Bo'ness on that particular stretch of the Forth. As external co-partnery was usually the hallmark of a major venture, it is likely that these vessels were the largest of the Bo'ness fleet at this time.

As to smaller coastal and fishing craft, the later eighteenth-century Customs annual shipping returns for Bo'ness record only a few small craft belonging to the port of Bo'ness (when separated from its creeks). The southern shore of the precinct had then little direct involvement in the inshore fisheries or the coal trade of the Forth. The impression given by this profile is that of a home fleet composed of a few large sea-going vessels and small craft, not too dissimilar to that of the port of Kirkcaldy,

149   *Ibid.*, p. 19.
150   *Ibid.*
151   *Ibid.*, p. 75.

her nearest rival in the Forth at this time.

Without any compensatory element for the omitted fleets of Greenock and Bo'ness, the Register of 1692 (when adjusted for the few inconsistencies in reporting) listed *c.*232 vessels (totalling *c.*8,400 tons).[152] With the removal of all fishing boats (three to five tons), this figure drops to *c.*127 vessels (*c.*7,160 tons) described as 'ships' or 'boats' capable of an offshore passage.[153] When the ports of Greenock and Bo'ness are included (by generously crediting each with fleets the size of their comparable rivals Port Glasgow and Kirkcaldy respectively), the final tally for Scotland rises to just over 10,000 tons – half the estimate for the era in peacetime.[154] Within this stock, the number of Scottish vessels capable of foreign-going voyage at this time was around 150, of which at least a third were open or partially decked 'barks' and 'doggars'.[155]

The requirement to assess the condition of their vessels was generally ignored by the reporters to the Register and is a great impediment to the overall assessment of the Scottish fleets as they entered a prolonged period of warfare.[156] Only the Kirkcaldy return (a close third behind 'New Port' Glasgow) specifically mentioned the age of its fourteen trading vessels (1,215 tons).[157] Of this fleet, eight vessels (nearly half the tonnage of the port) date from the Dutch Wars – the oldest being thirty years – and were a motley collection of 'fluyt boats', 'pinks' and 'doggars'. Most of the remaining seagoing stock predates the Council of Trade's embargo, ten years earlier, on acquiring foreign-built vessels.[158] This decision would

---

152 The total was achieved a. by taking the higher number where vessel numbers or tonnage quoted are between two figures (e.g. 7 or 8 barks); b. by awarding five tons to every fishing boat mentioned (based on Rothesay report); c. by awarding forty tons (the average) for every trading 'bark' or 'boat' listed without a specified tonnage (e.g. the Irvine report).

153 The general usage of the terms 'ship' and 'boat' is to distinguish those hulls with a deck. Tucker did not report 'boats' under five tons.

154 Smout holds the opinion that between 1660 and 1707 the Scottish fleet (excluding boats engaged solely in fishing or coastal trade) was *c.*20,000 tons in normal peacetime trading conditions: *Scottish Trade*, p. 54. This would imply that the disasters of the late 1680s had halved the fleet.

155 Hulls below forty tons were often open or partially decked at this time.

156 It must be borne in mind that at this time it was common, especially with the smaller communities of the east coast, to refer to a vessel by the owner/ master's name (e.g., 'George Tod's ship') rather than by the vessel's name and port.

157 Marwick, *Miscellany*, pp. 83–4.

158 The newest vessel was declared as ten years old, which makes it possible that she was bought as a new hull before the embargo was implemented on 1 May 1682. See Glossary for description of types of vessel.

appear to have created an ageing fleet that was ill-prepared to meet the combined attrition of war and natural disasters at sea. If the state of the Kirkcaldy fleet was typical of the east-coast stock of vessels, then hull and rigging fatigue must have been a contributory factor to the high numbers reported lost at sea in the years immediately prior to 1692.[159]

While the numbers lost in the intervening period amount to an insignificant tally compared to other trading nations, they constituted a major setback for individual ports. In the twelve months prior to the survey, Leith lost three of her larger vessels to enemy privateers.[160] This left the premier port of Scotland with an assortment of only twenty-nine vessels.[161] The loss of the *Swan* of Ayr, wrecked in the West Indies that year, was the final entry in a catalogue of misfortunes at sea: 'within these twenty or thertie years, fourty saill of ships wherin the toun were concerned [were] lost'.[162] With her fleet virtually annihilated, trade through this once prosperous Ayrshire port stagnated. The closure of the French markets and the general slump in foreign trade after 1688 led to the dereliction of hulls at other lesser ports. Dumfries bemoaned the fate of her small fleet: 'lyen up these three or four years for want of trade and soe are ruinous'.[163]

The general impression created by the Register of 1692, intentional or otherwise, was that there had been a dramatic reversal in the fortunes of the Scottish marine since the short-lived revival of the previous decade. The Scottish marine now barely matched one ton for every hundred of English shipping.[164] It must have seemed to the reporters to the Register of 1692, as they looked towards the new century, that the situation could hardly get worse.

---

159   An example is the report from Dundee that lists a loss of ten vessels and cargoes valued at c.70,000 merks: Marwick, *Miscellany*, p. 63.

160   All three were attempting to run wine back from France. Of note was the *Charles* of Leith, Edward Burd master, carried into Dunkirk: Wood, *Extracts of the Burgh of Edinburgh*, 6 November 1689.

161   Marwick, *Miscellany*, pp. 56–7.

162   *Ibid.*, p. 78.

163   *Ibid.*, p. 92.

164   English statistics are taken from Davis, *English Shipping*, p. 25.

CHAPTER 2
THE DEFENCE OF
MARITIME SOVEREIGNTY
1688–1707

During the reign of last two Stuarts, the offices of High Lord Admiral of England and Scotland had been made wholly subordinate to the central policies of the monarch. As a consequence, the commanders of the Stuart navy were expected to defend the United Kingdom without undue concern for the separate maritime jurisdictions of the two nations.

The accession of the House of Orange to the British throne in 1688 abruptly ended this understanding and reopened the question of maritime sovereignty. In this climate of rising national consciousness and assertiveness, the new distinctions – between Scottish Jacobite and Williamite and national trading interests – were of little concern for many English naval and privateering commanders. Without an absolute monarch dictating a common code of conduct, it was inevitable that their highly partisan behaviour in Scottish waters would lead to confrontation and, ultimately, schism between the two nations.

THE END OF
ABSOLUTE RULE

The Scottish establishment's instinctive reaction to the end of absolute rule was to reassert the national institutions and aspirations. South of the Border, the alliance of manufacturing and mercantile interests was just as quick to exploit William's desperate need to raise the revenue necessary to fund his extensive European military campaigns. As a result the move towards protectionism in both domestic and overseas trades along strictly national lines was greatly accelerated, and the gradual *ad hoc* rehabilitation of the Scots into the English mercantilist system was discarded and replaced by intolerance. Indeed, it was during the 1690s that the elaborate fiscal regime based on high import duties was created along with rigorous new instruments of subordination to the *modus operandi* of the English mercantilist system.

THE SECURITY CRISIS
IN THE 'WESTERN SEAS', 1688-90

The new incoming English establishment viewed Scotland as, first and foremost, a security problem. The Protestant Succession had created a Jacobite threat on the northern flank of Britain that elevated Scotland to the position of a strategic frontline state. This position dragged her into a much wider European conflict.

The geography of the principal Jacobite areas – essentially those inhabited by the Catholic Gaels in Ireland and Scotland – was highly favourable to naval incursions by their French allies. Indeed, a link-up of the Irish and Scottish Jacobites to secure Scotland for the deposed James II would require military landings and supply from the sea. For this to happen the French navy (or her privateer squadrons) would have to gain control of the 'western seas' for a limited period. The spring of 1689 seemed destined to witness this development.

By March the deposed James II was holding court in Dublin, courtesy of Tyrconnel's army and a contingent of Louis' navy. With the exception of a few stubborn Protestant strongholds in Ulster, Ireland was secure for James, and a union with his supporters on the west coast of Scotland seemed within his grasp.

To contain the situation the Scottish Estates imposed, in early April, an embargo on all sailings from the west coast.[1] On the east coast a major seaborne intervention by the French was expected at any time, so much so that Leith was thrown into disarray by the appearance of a large fleet in the Forth – which turned out to be a Dutch military convoy.[2]

During the summer months of May, June and July this invasion scare was extended to the whole of Britain. The southern coast of England

---

1   E.V.M. Balfour-Melville (ed.), *Accounts of the proceedings of the Estates in Scotland (1689–90)*, Scottish History Society (Edinburgh, 1954), I, p. 41. A few days later, this embargo was extended to all vessels sailing for France without finding caution; *Ibid.*, p. 49.

2   *Ibid.*, p. 41.

braced itself for a grand naval battle for control of the Channel that would be the prelude to a French invasion. As it transpired, the French navy was content to continue to play the Irish card and did not seriously consider the grander scheme of a direct invasion across the English Channel until 1692.[3]

THE 'SCOTCH FRIGATES'

After asserting its independence, the Scottish Parliament – summoned by William to legitimise his claim to the Scottish Crown – had to provide a defence force to meet the expected Jacobite seaborne invasion. In the absence of a 'Scots Navy', authority was immediately given (March 1689) to three commissioners – Sir James Montgomery of Skelmorlie, John Anderson of Dowhill and James Boswell of Kirkcaldy – to oversee the fitting out of two armed cruisers to meet the threat in the west. These were the *Pelican* of Glasgow (200 tons/18 guns) and the *Jannet* of Glasgow (tonnage unknown/12 guns). Both were ex-merchantmen of the 'frigate' design and were manned by 200 prime sailors recruited from the ports of the Clyde, Forth and Ulster. Their respective commanders were William Hamilton and Alex Browne (then at Irvine), sailing under quasi-naval commissions to 'sink all ships belonging to the late King James ... from the point of Cornwall to the Isle of Skye'.[4] These two guard vessels represented the extent of naval power that an independent Scotland could muster at the commencement of a century of endemic maritime warfare.

Their fitting out attests to both a sense of urgency and the absence of an indigenous armaments industry. The war-hardened Commissioner Boswell and his two commanders (all masters of Forth privateers during the Dutch wars) were empowered to appropriate whatever cannon they could find from the laid-up Clyde fleet. Munitions were acquired in a similar manner. Delivered onboard were the 'balls and granadoes' seized from the house of an Edinburgh Jacobite along with four hundredweight of gunpowder impounded from a Londonderry master who had put in at Greenock having failed to run the blockade. To augment the fighting

---

3   J.R.R. Ehrman, *The Navy in the War of William III* (Cambridge, 1953), p. 382. A general review is available in D. Aldridge, 'Jacobites and the Scottish Seas, 1689–1719', *Scotland and the Sea* (Edinburgh, 1992), pp. 76–94.

4   *Acts of the Scottish Parliament*, IX, p.17 and *RPC*, XIII, p. 412. These vessels were owned by Provost Walter Gibson and Robert Campbell (late Dean of the Guild of Glasgow) respectively who later petitioned for compensation: NAS, Leven and Melville MSS, GD 26 9/260.

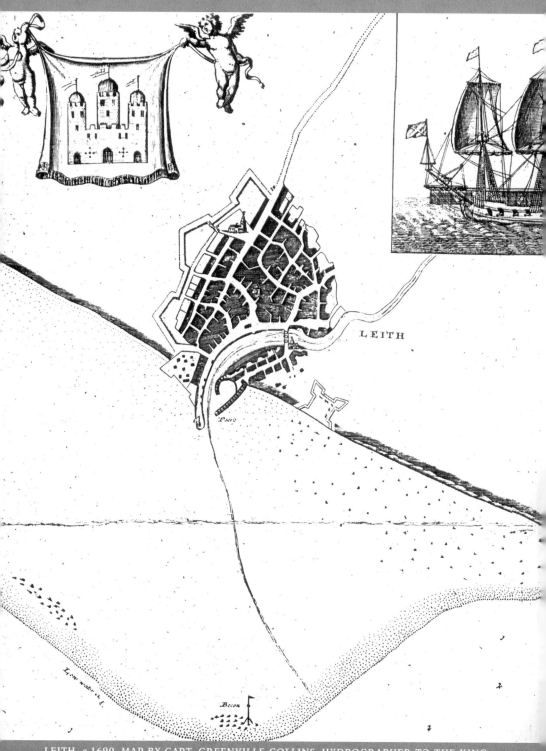

LEITH, c.1690. MAP BY CAPT. GREENVILLE COLLINS, HYDROGRAPHER TO THE KING.
MUCH OF THE INLAND FORTIFICATIONS HAD BEEN DEMOLISHED SINCE 1660
(NATIONAL ARCHIVES OF SCOTLAND)

Prospect of LEITH from the East

N. Yeates fecit

TO THE
Right Honourable
Sr. IAMES FLEMING
Lord PROVOST of ye City
of EDENBURGH,
And ye rest of ye Honble Councill
of the sd Burgh.
This Mapp is humbly Dedicated by
Capt. Greenvile Collins
HYDROGRAPHER to the
KING.

Low water Mark

strength of the crews, a company of soldiers, equipped with small arms and shot from Dumbarton Castle, were embarked to serve as marines.[5]

Events, however, overtook the preparation of the two armed cruisers. An indecisive naval action in Bantry Bay (1 May), during which Admiral Herbert's fleet narrowly escaped defeat, left the French naval presence in Irish waters largely unscathed. The fall of the besieged Protestant strongholds of Enniskillen and Londonderry in Ulster appeared imminent as their seaborne supplies were cut off. To meet this immediate crisis a further three privateers were hastily commissioned by Lord Hamilton, as President of the Scottish Parliament. Two were Ulster blockade-runners, based in the Clyde, who had been supplying their besieged kinsmen while evacuating women and children.

It is symptomatic of the general confusion of the time that these captains were elevated to the rank of quasi-naval officers by rather odd commissions that can only be properly described as 'letters of reprisal'.[6] Their legal position was, however, regularised by official letters of marque under the royal warrant by late May.[7] Their writ was to search all 'highland birlins' for arms that might find their way to Claverhouse's Jacobites on the mainland of Scotland.

By then the 'Scotch frigates' had put to sea with orders to co-operate with the small English naval squadron cruising off the coast of Northern Ireland under Commodore Rooke on HMS *Dartmouth* (265 tons/32 guns).[8] At first Hamilton on the larger *Pelican* met up with the English warships blockading a large party of armed Macleans marshalling on the Isle of Gigha.

Thereafter, he appears to have detached himself from Rooke's

---

5   *RPC*, XIII, successive entries pp. 413–450 and *Accounts of the Estates* I, p.47.
6   These letters were granted in lieu of personal loss at the hands of Jacobites to Captains William Burnsyde of the doggar *Vine* of Londonderry (40 tons) and Andrew Douglas of the *Ph[o]enix* of Coleraine (50 tons). A third privateer, an unnamed vessel of Irish/ Scottish ownership under the Irvine skipper John Woodsyde, joined them in the same month: *RPC*, XIII, pp. 386–388. A fuller discussion of the legality of the two types of commission in the Scottish context is available in E.J. Graham, 'Privateering – the Scottish Experience' (unpublished M.A. dissertation, University of Exeter, 1979), pp. 2–4.
7   *RPC*, XIII, pp. 395–7, 29/30 May 1689. The Ulsterman Burnsyde also held a commission from the Post Master General to act as courier to the commander of William's forces in Ireland.
8   Rooke's squadron – *Dartmouth, Bonadventure* and *Swallow* – was ordered to cruise the North Channel after escorting the transports conveying Major General Kirke's relief force. His instructions were to prevent 'any insult from the French and Scottish [presumably Jacobite] privateers'.

squadron and joined up with Brown on the *Jannet*. Crossing to the Irish coast, they set about destroying ferryboats found in the Jacobite-held ports. A few were spared to transport Protestant refugees to safety on the Mull of Kintyre.[9] Their efforts, combined with those of a few determined Ulster masters sailing out from the Clyde and Whitehaven, undoubtedly saved the Protestant cause in Ireland while William assembled his forces.[10]

During those critical months the fate of Ulster hung in the balance. In June a boom was raised across the River Foyle, severing the supply route by sea to Londonderry.[11] That summer only a few Glasgow merchants found the nerve to venture an armed vessel to the other Ulster ports with supplies.[12] The majority of the Clyde fleet chose to stay in port for fear of capture by the three French men-of-war known to be at Carrickfergus. This French squadron was preparing to ferry a large Jacobite force (1,200 men) across the North Channel to Skye or Mull from where they could link up with Claverhouse in the Highlands.

In the same month as the Londonderry siege tightened, the two Scottish frigates cruising in the North Channel fell in with the French squadron escorting seven 'fly boats' transporting the first contingent of 400 soldiers to Mull and Inverlochy. Apparently Hamilton and Browne mistook them for Rooke's frigates and closed to within hailing distance. At such a range there was no possible escape. The ensuing contest, between vastly ill-matched adversaries (two of the French frigates carried 35 guns), resulted in the sinking of the *Jannet* and the capture of the *Pelican* with great loss of life. Of the 120 crew of the *Pelican*, only thirty survived the seven-hour engagement to be taken prisoner and eventually ransomed.[13] The loss of these guard ships left the Clyde and the west coast defenceless

---

9   *Accounts of the Estates,* I, p. 111.

10   The *Phoenix* had the distinction, in company with the *Mountjoy,* of breaking the boom across the River Foyle in late July with 800 bolls of Scottish meal for the starving garrison, *Ibid.,* pp. 396 and 406.

11   The *Elizabeth* of Coleraine, Captain William Boyd, arrived at Saltcoats on the Firth of Clyde with the last evacuees, returning with forty volunteers to Londonderry.

12   Two vessels which did make a passage were the *Mayflower* of Irvine (tonnage and armaments unknown) and the *Prosperitie* of Glasgow (45 tons/ 4 guns) captained respectively by Hugh Brown and William Adair: *Ibid.,* pp. 451 and 555.

13   British Library, contemporary news sheet (London, 1689) which was, at the time of research, unlisted and bound with the *London Gazette* for that year. The *Pelican* was used by the Jacobites to land a group of officers on Mull before she was audaciously recaptured in Dublin Bay by the yacht *HMS Monmouth,* Sir Clowdisley Shovell commanding: *London Gazette,* 19 April 1690. She was not, however, returned to her Scottish owners and was probably sunk as a breakwater off Sheerness.

at a time when naval events in the English Channel were to open the way north for the French privateering squadrons.[14]

ENGLISH WARSHIPS AND
PRIVATEERS IN SCOTTISH WATERS

On the same day (10 July 1690) that William triumphed at the Battle of the Boyne in Ireland, the Anglo–Dutch fleets were defeated by the combined French Mediterranean and Brest fleets off Beachy Head. The English Channel was now open for the French army to attempt an invasion of the south coast to reinstall James II in London. To meet this emergency Sir Clowdesley Shovell's squadron was recalled from the Irish Sea, leaving the North Channel momentarily uncontested. To fill this gap William found it expedient to sanction a few English naval vessels to cruise Scottish inshore waters to deny the Scottish Jacobites further seaborne reinforcements from Ireland.

In the vanguard was HMS *Dartmouth*, released from the Irish station to cruise the west coast of Scotland. Her new captain, Captain Pottinger, was the forerunner of a new generation of naval officers who clearly took their orders from the English Admiralty while in Scottish waters. Their high-handed behaviour over the next decade presented a series of challenges to the competence of the Scottish Admiralty and, by implication, to the integrity of the independent sovereignty of Scotland.

A month prior to the arrival of HMS *Dartmouth* relations between the two Admiralties had been strained by an incident in the English Channel. It was a relatively minor affair, but one which serves to highlight the English establishment's lack of concern for Scottish interests at sea and their deep suspicion of the loyalty of Scots found voyaging abroad. The incident involved the detention of the *Barbara* of Irvine while conveying Sir Robert Barclay and family to the spa at Bath. This party were roughly handled, as suspected Jacobites, by the commander of the English frigate that recaptured their vessel from a French privateer sailing under a letter

---

14   It was not until the following spring that English vessels reappeared, with dramatic effect, with one 30 gun frigate sinking six out of the ten privateers encountered. Thereafter, three small frigates cruised the western isles to cut off communications with the Scottish mainland and Ireland. The next replacement Scottish guard ship for the West Coast was commissioned in April 1690 – 'charges ... to the Treasury' – was a lightly armed vessel expected to 'command all the small vessels upon the coast'; *Accounts of the Estates*, II, pp. 130–3.

issued by James in exile. The Scottish Privy Council took up their case with the English Admiralty but received little satisfaction.[15]

With national sensibilities already aroused, Pottinger's actions were to be deeply provocative in two distinct ways. Firstly, he exploited his position as the only effective naval force in the Clyde to requisition two vessels to make up a flotilla. One was a newly completed frigate-design hull – the *Lark* – which he placed under the command of the Ulsterman Andrew Douglas. The second – the sloop *Lamb* of Glasgow (100 tons/ 20 guns) – he placed under the command of the Clyde transatlantic master, Ninian Gibson.[16] Pottinger also demanded, and got, six months' credit from the Glasgow baillies for supplies, as well as the services of four Clyde pilots, fifty seamen and the recently ransomed lieutenant of the *Pelican*. Turning his crew ashore to intimidate the local inhabitants seems to have expedited matters in his favour.[17] Although there is no evidence that he pressed Scottish sailors into his service, his high-handed conduct verged on total disregard for the authority of the Scottish Admiralty. It was his later activities in Scottish waters that brought him into open conflict with the Scottish establishment sitting in Edinburgh.

In the few months he was on station, prior to his death, Pottinger succeeded in breaking the fragile and as yet untried new understanding as to the conduct of English warships in Scottish waters.[18] In addition to raiding Skye – where he burnt the house of Donald Macdonald – without prior approval, he took it upon himself to enforce the English Navigation Acts on all vessels he encountered in Scottish waters trading to the colonies. Stormbound and war-damaged Irish and English vessels in from the Atlantic seeking shelter in the Clyde, without having first declared in an

---

15   A. McJannet, *The Royal Burgh of Irvine* (Edinburgh 1938), pp. 251–2. A similar fate also befell the *Concord* of Glasgow: *RPC*, XVI, p. 75.

16   *RPC*, XV, p.180, XIII pp. 434 and 450. The Scottish Privy Council belatedly added their seal of approval to the *Lamb*'s quasi-naval role by granting her a letter of marque (4 May 1691), 'to take, seize upon, and apprehend and in the case of resistance to fyre, sink or destroy the shipps and goods of the French, Irish or Scottish highlands in rebellion': *Ibid.*, XVI, p.277. The *Lamb* may have been the unnamed Glasgow vessel commissioned by the Estates the previous April.

17   *Ibid.*, XIII, p. 504. Aberdeen provided twenty of the seamen under the direction of a committee set up by the Privy Council.

18   HMS *Dartmouth* was lost off Mull that October along with most of her crew including her captain. Her wreck has since been the subject of a major investigation: C.J.M. Bell, 'The *Dartmouth*, a British frigate wrecked off Mull, 1690', *International Journal of Nautical Archaeology and Underwater Exploration*, VII (1978), pp. 29–58.

English entrepôt, were seized along with illicitly trading Scottish merchantmen.[19]

What could have been overlooked as over-zealous diligence was fully exposed as blatant self-interest when Pottinger arranged for his prizes to be escorted to an English port by the *Lamb* – in complete disregard of the jurisdiction of the Scottish Admiralty Prize Court. The Privy Council of Scotland declared that it was 'ane unheard off practique to secure Scottish merchant vessels without any just pretence'.[20] Their immediate response was to intercept and impound them, pronouncing that 'prizes must be tried in the jurisdiction of the Admiral of where the prize lies – Scotland'. An urgent diplomatic note indicating their displeasure was also relayed to the London Admiralty, with the request that Pottinger should be disciplined:

> acquaint him it is their opinion that no ships in Scotts harbours
> can be summarily seized by ane order of England. Scotland
> being ane independent nation, but if England have any
> pretences to ships in Scotts harbours, the same shall be fairly
> and legally tried.[21]

In their subsequent correspondence with the Lord High Admiral of England (the redoubtable Earl of Nottingham) such complaints against English commanders become a regular event. In April 1691 they denounced Captain Roope on HMS *Sheerness* who, without consulting the Scottish Admiralty, attempted to seize a neutral – the *Emanuell* of Flensburg – in Leith Roads on a charge of carrying contraband.[22] This simmering dispute between the Admiralties erupted again in June of that year. The reason this time was the piratical behaviour of Captain Ivory (or Evory) of the English frigate *Pembroke* who attacked the *John* of Greenock as she entered the Clyde from Bilbao, before going on to terrorise the whole firth. Ivory, they claimed:

> did summarily seize the said ship by way of fact and force,
> shooting great guns at the said ship and putting out their

---

19   George Lockhart lead the Glasgow merchants who petitioned for the return of their vessels 'loadned with Tobacco' that Pottinger had seized. The Privy Council responded firmly: ' the ships are Scots bottoms and belong to Scotsmen and … justice shall be done': *RPC*, XV, pp. 384 and 444.

20   *Ibid.*

21   *Ibid.*, p. 590.

22   J. Grant, *The Old Scots Navy* (London, 1914), p. 101.

majesties flag; and having turned out the waiters put in by the custom office … did also violently seize and possess himself of three gabards or lighters that were sailing up the water … refusing to show any warrant or commission for such a procedure, but, on the contrary threatening to throw the surveyor of New Port Glasgow overboard.[23]

'Communicating with the enemy' was the other pretext used by the masters of English warships on the Scottish station to seize a Scottish vessel as prize. In 1690 the yacht HMS *Monmouth* took the *Mary* of Glasgow prize for carrying letters from James II to Lord Melville.[24] This was at a time when virtually the entire English establishment was openly in communication with James.

One of the difficulties in handling the situation had been the lack of an effective administrative head at the Scottish Admiralty. William, prior to his departure on military campaigns, had deemed the office of the High Lord Admiral of Scotland vacant. In the interim, the Lords Commissioner of the Scottish Privy Council acted when necessary until the Duke of Hamilton received the gift of the office in 1692.[25]

In 1693, however, their combined authority was powerless to check an English privateer cruising the Firth of Forth, stopping and searching, with impunity, passing traders for possible contraband.[26] More sinister was the behaviour of a privateer – the *Elizabeth* of Argyll (70 tons/16 guns/80 men) – the property of the Duke of Argyll. Acting under an English letter of marque, its predatory master, Hugh Campbell, boarded and detained Scottish vessels entering the Clyde, sending those with cargoes suspected of breaching the English Navigation Acts south for condemnation.[27] Such behaviour prompted the Lords Commissioner for the Treasury (that September) to commission the Glasgow merchant William Cross to fit out

---

23   *RPC*, XV, pp. 329–30.

24   *Ibid.*, XV, p. 147.

25   William Dundas, advocate, had been gifted the office of Judge Admiral in December 1690. The Duke of Hamilton was the Lord High Admiral from March 1692 until his death in April 1694. Thereafter the Scottish Privy Council was effectively in control of such affairs until January 1697.

26   After 1691 the records of the Privy Council are held as unedited manuscript: NAS, PC, 1/49, 24, 8 May 1693.

27   NAS, PC 1/48, 530, 10 June and 27 December 1692. Her English letter of marque was the only one granted to a Scottish vessel out of a total issue of 490, which would suggest that this practice was stopped thereafter: PRO HCA 26/1–3.

a twenty-gun vessel to cruise the Clyde and the North Channel 'for the security of trade' as well as seizing the enemies of the crown.[28]

THE CROWN'S RESPONSE
TO THE SOVEREIGNTY ISSUE

Such was the gravity of the situation that a direct appeal was made, in William's absence, to the Queen. The test case concerned the actions of another English privateer – the *Countess* of London – whose master ransacked a Flensburg vessel while in the Forth. This was the second English vessel that month to board a neutral without warrant. When ordered to restore his plunder, he sailed away and had to be chased by HMS *Sweepstake* commanded by the redoubtable Andrew Douglas. Douglas was, by then, a commissioned naval officer in what was, to all intents and purposes, an English navy. Having caught up with the privateer, he extracted an agreement from its master to submit himself to judicial proceedings on berthing in the Thames, thus placing him under English Admiralty jurisdiction.[29] As a result, the Admiralty in London was forced to pronounce on the competence of the Scottish Admiralty to hear cases relating to incidents that had occurred within Scottish waters.

The Queen's reply to her Scottish Privy Councillors that August was both placatory and assertive:

> til now that the business was determined in the Court of our
> [English] Admiralty we could make no return to yours, but now,
> by admitting your plea to return the ship to be judged there in
> our Admiralty of Scotland, you may be well satisfied of our
> care and concern we take of the rights, immunities and honour
> of our ancient Kingdom as well as of its wealth and trade.[30]

The 'immunities and honour' the Queen referred to were the other outstanding grievances of the Scottish maritime community, namely, the pressganging of her sailors by passing English warships and the rough handling frequently meted out to Scottish ships driven in distress into the Channel ports.

---

28   NAS, E 90/9.
29   NAS, PC 1/49, 106–9, 29 June 1693.
30   *Ibid.*, 1/49, 117, 19 August. 1693.

As to the first issue, the succession of William and Mary had rendered void the old levy system of providing Scottish seamen for the Stuart navy. This, however, was used as justification by English naval commanders to resort to the pressgang to make up their complements. The worst years were 1690–2 when the London press took to preying on Scottish vessels entering the Thames.[31]

The second issue – the rough handling of Scottish crews in English ports – can best be illustrated by the case of the *James* of Glasgow. This vessel, having survived attacks from enemy privateers during a winter passage to the Canaries, was stranded in Porthleven, Cornwall, where the inhabitants looted her cargo and rig and stripped her crew 'naked'.[32] As with the previous *Barbara* of Irvine incident, Scottish protestations proved quite futile.

In general the Queen's letter was a satisfactory, if not decisive, reply to a specific set of Scottish grievances. It did not, however, resolve the conflicting and, at times, ambiguous views held by the two nations on the fundamental issue of the inviolability of Scottish maritime sovereignty. To defuse this situation a commission was sent north to 'interrogate witnesses' and to put the questions, 'whether or not Scotland be a free nation independent of the kingdom of England and whether or not the Admiralty of Scotland be a supreme court independent of England'.[33] Had this commission resolved these fundamental questions at this opportune moment, then the violent collision of national interests over the ill-fated Darien Scheme might have been averted.

At the time of the receipt of the Queen's letter, however, the friction between the two nations appeared to be easing with the removal of the immediate security threat to the Protestant Succession. Ireland had been reconquered and 'pacified', for the time being, by the Treaty of Limerick. In the Highlands, the death of Claverhouse at Killiecrankie left the Scottish Jacobites without an effective military leader. Only the handful of rebels defiantly holding out on the strategically positioned Bass Rock in the Forth symbolised the armed struggle for the Jacobite cause in the lowlands.

---

31   *RPC* records a number of petitions for the release of Scottish crews pressed at London around this time, e.g., petition by David Wood, master of the *Bonadventure* of Montrose, to have his crew released in February 1690: *RPC*, XV, p.78.

32   GCA, Shawfield MSS 1/82, a sworn declaration by crew taken by Glasgow magistrates, 28 May 1694. The *Christian* of Anstruther, Captain Smith, had a similar experience when brought into Teignmouth: University of Edinburgh Library, Laing Manuscript, II, 490/1, as quoted by Smout, *Scottish Trade*, p. 67.

33   NAS, PC 1/49, 117, 26 September.1693.

FRENCH PRIVATEERS IN SCOTTISH WATERS: JEAN BART (TOP LEFT) AND
RENÉ DUGUAY-TROUIN (TOP RIGHT). BOTTOM: DUGUAY-TROUIN, ON THE *BELLONE*,
CAPTURES A DUTCH 38-GUN FRIGATE OFF ORKNEY IN 1702.
SEE ALSO FORBIN (PAGE 152).

THE ONSLAUGHT OF FRENCH PRIVATEERS

At sea, the French naval advantage gained at Beachy Head was short-lived. The heavy losses suffered by Tourville's grand fleet at the Battle of Barfleur, together with the crippling losses sustained at La Hogue, amounted to a national disaster for the French which ended any prospect of a French-led invasion across the English Channel. By mid-1693 the remnants of their navy were demoralised and blockaded in their home ports. Thereafter, the offensive role passed to French privateers.

In the vanguard were the St. Malo and Dunkirk squadrons led by the legendary exponents of the *guerre-de-course* – Bart, Forbin and Duguay-Trouin. Under their daring leadership the war at sea entered a new phase that again placed Scotland in the forefront of the struggle. The small French privateer 'capers' (ex-fishing craft) that had first pestered the North East and Orkney in the summer of 1690 were, henceforth, joined by the hunting packs led by French ex-naval units on hire to these privateering 'admirals'.[34] The first of these large flotillas raided Orkney waters in June 1693 and would have been entirely successful in its designs had not the timely arrival of HMS *Centurion* and *Kingfisher* scattered them – taking nine of their number.[35]

As the fighting strength of these French squadrons rapidly increased, they became willing and able to attack such naval escorts in order to capture whole convoys.[36] Their cruising pattern was to sweep the North Sea, from Norwegian as well as French bases, to intercept the returning Baltic and White Sea convoys. The response of the allied navies was to gather off the Belgian coast to entrap the privateers heading home with their prizes. To frustrate this counter-move the French privateers often went north-about Scotland at the end of the foray. This gave them the further opportunity to raid the Dutch Spitzbergen whalers and the herring fleets that marshalled in Orkney and snap up any incoming Atlantic traders before returning home via the western approaches.

Scottish renegades provided many of the pilots and masters of the enemy privateers that worked closer inshore during this period. In one incident, in 1694, a shore party, of five seamen under a lieutenant from a

34   Eight privateers had infested Orkney waters that summer. One of them narrowly missed laying hands on the strong box containing the year's Crown rents and several months customs revenue, having forced the vessel carrying the bullion to Leith to run ashore: *RPC*, XV, p. 338.

35   *London Gazette*, 12 August 1693.

36   Between 1688 and 1697 St Malo privateers alone captured 3,384 merchantmen and 162 escorting men-of-war: D. Macintyre, *The Privateers* (London, 1975), p. 83.

French privateer lying off Stranraer, were caught and all found to be renegades.[37] Indeed, by 1697 the Scottish Privy Council felt it necessary to issue a proclamation outlawing any such association with the enemy.

THE FORTH GUARD SHIPS, 1690—6

It was anticipated that the east coast would bear the brunt of these assaults. As early as 1690 the Scottish Privy Council had commissioned guard ships to protect the Forth. In keeping with the scale of the problem, as then perceived, the three vessels initially selected were larger ex-merchantmen – the *Red Lyon* (200 tons/14 guns), the *James* of Queensferry (190 tons/6 guns) and the *Providence* of Kirkcaldy (160 tons/12 guns).[38] To cut off the supplies run by the French privateers to the rebels on the Bass Rock, the *Lamb* of Glasgow (100 tons/20 guns) was brought round from the Clyde to cruise in company of the *Providence*.[39] As enemy activity surged in the winter of 1693, the *Lyon* (200 tons/20 guns/48 men) joined the two Bass Rock blockade ships based at Dunbar.[40]

What seemed a formidable force was, in fact, only a deterrent against the smaller enemy privateers. When the supplying of the Bass rebels was taken up by the more powerful French ex-naval frigates – *Railleuse* (42 guns) and *Sauvage* (20 guns) under the command of Scottish renegade Robert Dunbar – the guard ships prudently stayed in port. Nor did they cruise outside the Forth, thereby allowing Dunbar the option to go north-about after his visit to the Forth in June 1693, attacking houses on Orkney as well as shipping on his way.[41]

The inadequacies of deploying armed merchantmen against such formidable forces were plainly evident. The Duke of Hamilton addressed the Scottish Parliament on the matter that very year, as did the King's letter to the Committee of Trade. Both dwelt on the pressing need to find a solution to the privateering menace as the naval intelligence for the following sailing season produced an even bleaker forecast:

---

37   NAS, PC 1/50, 21, 11 October 1694.
38   *RPC*, XV, p. 75, commander John Boswall.
39   *Ibid.*, pp. 311–13. These blockade vessels carried companies of soldiers.
40   *Ibid.*, p. 358. She was probably the doggar, commanded of Edward Burd (the younger), hired to cruise around the Bass with forty soldiers in January of that year: NAS E.90/8
41   Dunbar had been the master of the Forth customs boat in 1688. His knowledge of the Forth was, therefore, considerable. For his raid on Orkney, see J. S. Bromley, 'Jacobite Privateers in the Nine Years War', *Statesmen, Scholars and Merchants* (Oxford 1972), p. 25.

A list of the officers and land soldiers aboard of the Providence
Captain John Boswell command & taken in & Mustered be
Baillie Robert Haas in Dunbar the eight day of Aprile
Patrick and ye ... four years

Lieutenant   John Dupant   Thomas Davison drumer

Serjants   James Dickson   William Mass
             James Gibson   John Mill

Corporals   ... Stot   John Whyt
             Patrick Wilson   Ferguss Marborne

                                            William Grahame
             Soutinalls   Andrew Davidson
             William Fa...   John Mar Gilbert
             ... Robertson   James Stot
             John Doan   John Campbell
             James Gary   David Borthwick
             John Lindsay   Gilbert Richie
             James Gordon   James Prymor
             James Wright   Thomas Barbea
             Andrew Lall   Geo. Buchannan
             George Mardonald
             Peter Wilson   John Glouny
             Andrew Witherinton   Robert Wood
             Mathew Whyt   James Pyper
             William Bobberty   John Dumphy
             ... Smith elder   Alex Chatham
             Alex Smith yer   John Baity
             Alex Mertton   John Floyde
             Robert Hardy   George Robison
             George Roes   Wm Macfarlane
             Dury Cumming   John Murray
             John Nicoll
             William Barty
             John Brooke   aboard of the Providence this & Captain
Boswell command the first John of Aprile 1694:
Mustered aboard conform to the above written vote of officers
& soldiers fiftie two be us

                                    Robert Haas
                          John Dupont Lt

> We have received information from prisoners that the French do
> not intend to set out their grand fleet this year, but would have
> many cruisers abroad, of greater force than formerly, that will
> sail two together and far exceed the strength of the guard ships.[42]

The only viable solution was the deployment of comparable naval raters in
Scottish waters. The only naval vessel then on regular station in the North
was HMS *Dolphin*. She cruised the Western Isles bombarding castles, when
not 'fishing for plate from an old wreck in the North Sea'.[43]

The prospect of concentrations of English warships gathering in the
firths of Clyde and Forth, at a time when the behaviour of their privateers
was a bone of contention between their lordships in London and
Edinburgh, was politically unacceptable. But the alternative – the
acquisition of a Scottish navy – was too heavy a burden for such a weak
economy.

THE CREATION OF THE 'SCOTS NAVY'

The limitations of the Scottish public purse necessitated a compromise.
Estimates undertaken in April and May 1695 put the cost of a navy of three
or four frigates at between £24,000 and £36,000 pounds sterling.[44] The
request to their sovereign for the procurement of men-of-war to protect
their coasts was, therefore, a qualified one:

> It may please your Majesty to order two English fifth or sixth
> rate frigates ... for our security and if his majesty will lend us
> the ships we will furnish and pay the men, for there is a
> necessity that the ships be subject to our orders, lest otherwise
> they trouble our merchant ships.

Added to this plea was a request to check the predatory behaviour of
English privateers in the North: 'and we hope his Majesty will give orders
that no commissions shall be given by the Admiralty of England to trouble
ships within our waters, specially ships belonging to our merchants'.[45] The

---

42   *Calendar of State Papers, domestic series,* p. 424 (Dublin Castle report, 13 April 1695).
43   *Ibid.,* p. 415.
44   *Ibid.,* p. 428.
45   NAS, PC 1/58, 650–1, 20 March 1693.

ambiguity of this last phrase may well have been intentional so as to embrace the delicate matter of Scottish privateers obtaining English letters to prey on their own merchantmen – as the *Elizabeth* of Argyll had done that year.

This request was granted and three naval hulls of a rating sufficient to deter the new generation of French privateer were fitted out at London in 1696.[46] The commissioning of Scottish skippers was more than diplomatic expediency as the lack of Admiralty coastal charts for the North meant that local knowledge was essential if the inshore raiders were to be checked.

Table 2.1. The vessels and masters of the Scots Navy of 1703

Royal William	5th rater/367 tons admiralty/32 guns/145 men – Captain Edward Burd (previously captain of the guard ship *Lyon*)[47]
Royal Mary	6th rater/284 tons admiralty/24 guns/115 men – Captain Bosswell (previously Special Commissioner and captain of the guard ship *Providence*)
Dumbarton Castle	6th rater/ tonnage unknown/24 guns/115 men – Captain George Lyon (previously captain of the West Indiaman *Walter* of Glasgow)

Source: NAS, PC 1/53, 1–18, successive entries June to July 1703; tonnage details: Clowes, *The Royal Navy*.

Control of their own defences did not, however, signal the end of seizures of Scottish merchantmen in home waters. Aware that the Scottish Admiralty was tolerant of breaches of English Navigation Acts and passively condoned the wine trade with the enemy, the more avaricious commanders of English warships in northern waters followed Pottinger's example and sent their Scottish prizes south. This combination of personal gain and higher allegiance was particularly evident in the actions of the Right Honourable Archibald, Lord Hamilton, commander of HMS *Litchfield*. He took the *Ann* of Kirkcaldy with a cargo of French wine off the Shetlands (1696) and sent her direct to Great Yarmouth.[48] A similar fate

---

46　Their upkeep was essentially that outlined by the original proposal made by the Scottish Parliament.

47　Members of the Burd family feature regularly in the history of Leith for this period.

48　The confessions of her crewmen stated that she was 'hired to go to St. Sebastian but … sailed directly to Bordeaux': PRO HCA, 32/33,6. She was described as a Dutch-built doggar (40 tons) at least twenty years old.

THE BASS ROCK, c. 1690 (FROM SLEZER *THEATRUM SCOTIAE*)

also befell the *Kath[e]rine* of Dysart when she was taken prize (1697) by *HMS Woolwich.*[49]

Confrontation between the English and Scottish naval services flared even within the confines of the upper Forth. HMS *Nonsuch* fired on the *Royal William* for not dipping her flag in deference to the English navy: 'the [Scottish] Admiralty here can hardly believe it, yet Burd says that some of them shot sharp at him, as he came down the river'.[50] This act, perhaps more than any other since Pottinger's excesses in the Clyde, served to indicate the extent of English naval captains' contempt for Scotland's maritime pretensions. Fortunately, the cessation of hostilities with the Treaty of Ryswick deferred further escalation of this type of behaviour, as the Scottish navy was immediately de-commissioned and laid up at Burntisland.

THE DARIEN SCHEME

The conflict of national interests now focused on the ill-fated Darien Scheme. This grandiose and morale-boosting plan to catapult the independent nation of Scotland into the same league as her neighbour was born out of national frustrations that had built up during the early war years.

The Committee of Trade met in 1693 to finalise their recommendations for the promotion of Scottish merchant adventurer companies, just as English outrages against the Scottish maritime interest were becoming all too excessive. By June 1694, the Scottish Parliament had passed the fateful *Act for Encouraging of Forraign Trade.* This mimicked the established English model by offering 'letters patent' to any company that sought to trade with the world beyond European waters. As before, Africa was the preferred area owing to the weak position of the English Royal African Company and the allurements of the slave trade.

The timing of the launch of Scotland's bid for trading parity was fateful. The death of Queen Mary, late in 1694, removed a moderating hand in Anglo–Scottish affairs. Furthermore, events in England conspired to defer, for a short time, any immediate backlash to the Scottish formation of a merchant adventurer company. Firstly, there was the change in the English administration as the incoming young whig *junta* paid little attention – in their ardour to prosecute the King's European war – to the depth of

49   NAS, PC 1/51, 94, 20 January 1697.
50   As quoted by Grant, *Old Scots Navy*, p. 209.

COAT OF ARMS OF THE COMPANY OF SCOTLAND TRADING
TO AFRICA AND THE INDIES (BANK OF SCOTLAND)

resentment in the North. Secondly, William's absence abroad leading his military campaign extended the period of indecision in London.

When William finally returned from his victory at Namur, in 1695, he encountered the wrath of the English merchant interest, orchestrated by the East Indies and Africa companies.[51] By then the creation of the 'Company of Scotland trading to Africa and the Indies' – empowered for thirty-one years to make treaties and plant colonies – was well advanced. It is little wonder that the English lobby immediately pressed for, and secured, a new Navigation Act (1696). This definitive Act finally closed the remaining access loopholes of the 1664 Act and confirmed the territorial exclusiveness of the English chartered companies' monopolies. Under their threat of further sanctions the London subscription list to the Scottish Company was closed and withdrawn.

51   The insecurity was heightened by the fact that the East India Company's charter was due for renewal.

The severity of this backlash surprised many Scots at the time, as evident in the reaction of Sir James Ogilvy, Secretary of State for Scotland: 'I am sorry our Indian Act occasions so much trouble; for I think it will do little hurt to England seeing that we want [for] a fleet'.[52] His comment underlined the fact that the Scottish marine was then quite incapable of attempting a serious assault on the preserve of others – as things stood.[53] Indeed, of the shipping stock recorded in the Register of 1692, only fifteen vessels were deemed to be of ocean-going size.[54] Of these, none was remotely comparable with the large East Indiamen of the English companies, many of which were seconded to the Royal Navy during the war years.

The commission given to the Company's agents – Alexander Stevenson of Edinburgh and James Gibson of Glasgow – was, therefore, to enquire abroad as to the purchase of 'five or six ships of about of 600 tons each ... fit for voyages to the East Indies'. Their subsequent purchase of three very large and two smaller hulls from Dutch and Hamburg yards fell somewhat short of this order but still represented a virtual doubling of Scotland's foreign-going tonnage.[55] Their acquisition and preparation over the next two years was followed closely by London. Indeed, their equipping with heavy armaments was carefully noted by Sir Paul Rycaut, then residing in Hamburg, who reported his observations to the appropriate English ministers – Sir William Trumbull (Secretary of State) and William Blaythwayt (the Secretary-at-War).[56]

As their fitting-out neared completion, there was a real apprehension that a pre-emptive strike by the armed East Indiamen of the English chartered companies was in the offing. As a precaution the Scottish Admiralty ordered Burd on the *Royal William* to convey the commissioning crew for the *Caledonia* (600 tons) to Hamburg and to escort her back, along with the *Instauration* (350 tons), a decision that speaks volumes as to the tacit

---

52   *Carstares State Papers and Letters* (1774), 10 December 1695, as quoted by Grant, *Old Scots Navy*, p. 270.
53   The introduction provides analysis of the shipping listed in the *Register* of 1692.
54   W.C. Dickinson and G.S. Pryde, *A New History of Scotland* (Edinburgh, 1962), II, p. 74.
55   While an exact contemporary list of the new company vessels, as opposed to those hired, has not survived, they can be identified from the substantial documentation of this venture. See: G.P. Insh, *Papers relating to the ships and voyages of the Company of Scotland Trading to Africa and the Indies* (Edinburgh 1924). Also by the same author, *The Darien Scheme* (London, 1947).
56   Insh, *Papers relating to the ships*, pp. 6– 48. Successive reports, 10 August 1696 to 12 November 1697. The company agents were also empowered to negotiate for a free port status with the Hanse towns without William's authorisation.

involvement, if not benevolent attitude, of the Scottish establishment.[57]

Table 2.2. The vessels of the Darien Scheme and their fate

Vessels		Master	Fate
First fleet	*St Andrew*	Andrew Pennicuik (Commodore)	abandoned at Fort Royal
	Unicorn	Robert Pinkerton	abandoned at New York
	Caledonia	Robert Drummond	returned to Scotland and sold
	Endeavour	Mallock	abandoned at New York
	Dolphin	?	castaway at Cartagena
Relief ships	*Dispatch*	Andrew Gibson	wrecked outgoing on Western Isles
	Hopeful Binning	Alexander Stark	hired Bo'ness vessel returned with evacuees
	Olive Branch	William Jameson	destroyed by fire at Darien
Second fleet	*Rising Sun*	James Gibson	wrecked on Charleston bar in hurricane
	Hope	James Millar	castaway on rocks at Colorados, Cuba
	Hope	Richard Dalling	hired Bo'ness vessel sold at Cartagena
	Duke of Hamilton	Walter Duncan	hired vessel wrecked on Charleston bar
	Speedy Return	?	returned to Scotland

Source: G.P. Insh, *Papers relating to the ships and voyages of the Company of Scotland*

The series of calamities that followed the first fleet's departure for the Isthmus of Panama from Rothesay Bay (July 1698) and the second fleet's sailing from Greenock (September 1699) have been fully recounted by others.[58] Suffice it to say that William's desperate need to the maintain the fragile Peace of Ryswick with Spain provided him with 'invincible' reasons for abandoning the colonists and their 'raging madmen' at home – as he described the supporters of the scheme.[59] His displeasure manifested itself in his proclamation to all English colonies in the Americas to deny succour

---

57 *Ibid.*, p. 57. 'Instructions from the Company to Captain Tennant on the *Caledonia*, 20 August 1697'.

58 The location of the settlement at 'New Caledonia' was ill-conceived as the climate was unhealthy and it was within reach of Spanish forces. Earlier proposals to colonise a part of Spanish Florida might have reduced such risks considerably.

59 The comment was made to Heinsus: G. Clerk, *The Later Stuarts, 1660–1714* (Oxford, 1955) p. 285.

to any of the survivors from the abandoned colony. This condemned hundreds on board the fleeing company vessels to die of malnutrition-induced illnesses. This followed hard on the first full accounts to reach home of the horrors already suffered from tenacious Spanish attacks and the ravages of disease. The overall effect was to embitter Scottish public opinion and engender a sense of English treachery that took decades to dissipate.

The loss was more than just the sacrifice of the best Scotland had to offer in seamen, vessels and capital. It was a catastrophe that shook the collective confidence of Scottish society. Of the thirteen company vessels that crossed the Atlantic in the two forlorn expeditions, only three returned to the Clyde – the *Caledonia, Hopeful Binning* and *Speedy Return.*[60]

The Company of Scotland simply did not have the resources or the political allies to recover from such a setback. With one exception – the voyage of the *African Merchant* to West Africa (returning in July 1700) – all their subsequent attempts to recoup losses proved equally disastrous. In that year the Company marshalled its remaining capital and few hulls for two small-scale, high-risk ventures into the eastern trading preserve of the English chartered companies. Sailing under the Articles of Agreement (validated by the Company's letters patent), one venture deployed the ship *Speedwell* (250 tons), John Campbell, on a direct voyage from Port Glasgow to China in early 1701.[61] The other project involved the dispatch of two authorised company vessels from the Clyde to Africa – the ship *Speedy Return*, under Robert Drummond (late of the *Caledonia*), in company with the brig *Content*, Alexander Stewart.[62]

Both ventures, despite the triumph of their safe navigation to their declared destinations, came to an ignominious end in foreign ports. The *Speedwell*, having been twice driven back by typhoons from the final approaches to Macao, was brought into a haven in the Straits of Malacca so that her badly damaged hull could be careened. As fate would have it, having survived the worst of the China Seas, she was wrecked on a prominent rock in the harbour while being refloated. The super-cargo blamed 'our ignorant, selfe-willed and obstinat commander' for deliberately

---

60   The *Caledonia*, at 600 tons, was the largest of the company vessels and was sold to William Arbuckle of Glasgow on her return to the Clyde. Arbuckle subsequently (sometime around 1710) sold her to Francis Collins of London who renamed her the *Reviver* in her new role as a government contract naval stores ship.

61   Insh, *Papers relating to the ships*, pp. 231–7. Sailing Instructions, 12 December 1700.

62   *Ibid.*, pp. 245–248.

sending ashore the more competent chief mate during the operation.[63] Thousands of miles across the Indian Ocean, the *Speedy Return* and *Content* were also lost due to their captains' negligence: boarded by pirates in the notorious harbour of the Isle of St. Mary (off Madagascar) while their masters were being entertained ashore.[64]

Such intrusions into the preserve of the great English Merchant Adventurer Companies did not, of course, go unnoticed. In the year of their departure the English 'Lord Commissioners for Trade and the Plantations' belatedly sought the opinion of the Attorney and Solicitor Generals in London as to 'how far Scotchmen were aliens' in their role as shipmasters in the plantation trades. The reply was probably not what they expected: 'We are of the opinion that a Scotchman is to be accounted, as an Englishman, within the [Navigation] act, every Scotchman being a natural born subject'.[65] Such learned opinion was, however, studiously overlooked by those in authority in England in the years that followed.

THE RENEWED PRIVATEERING ONSLAUGHT

This unresolved state of affairs was inherited by Anne on her succession to the British throne in March 1702. Her policy was to continue to support the autonomy of Scotland's maritime institutions and acquiesce in her trading aspirations.

By May of that year, war was resumed with France and her new ally Spain.[66] It was, therefore, an irony of fate that had the Scottish venture against the Spanish possession of Darien been launched then, it would have been well received, if not applauded, by Anne and her English subjects. As it was, the remnants of the Scottish marine left in home waters would, again, require protection from the French privateer squadrons.

These came quickly and were initially unopposed. Duguay–Trouin's squadron rounded Orkney unchallenged in the autumn of that year. The Dutch whaling fleet was his target and he would have been entirely successful had not a severe storm scattered his pack. The outcome was that

---

63   *Ibid.*, pp. 241, correspondence from the supercargo Robert Innes.
64   *Ibid.*, pp. XII–XV.
65   G. Chalmers, *Opinions of Eminent Lawyers* (London, 1814), I, pp. 361–3.
66   Queen Anne immediately moved to check the recurring pressgang problem by publicly reaffirming her late father's order 'that our subjects of Scotland should not be impress[ed] from onboard Scots ships by the English for the sea service': *Edinburgh Gazette*, 18 June 1702.

NOLIN'S MAP OF NORTH SEA SHIPPING LANES (PARIS, 1702), SHOWING THE
NORTHERN ROUTE TAKEN BY ENGLISH AND DUTCH EAST INDIAMEN

only three prizes were taken – two of which were subsequently wrecked on the Scottish coast.[67] Undeterred, French privateers were back in the same area the following spring and caught the entire Dutch herring fleet and naval escorts in Bressay Sound (Lerwick). A battle ensued in which the Dutch Admiral's frigate – the *Wolfswinkel* – was blown up and almost the entire fleet of herring busses captured and burned (c.150 vessels). Only a few were spared to carry the stranded crews back to Holland.[68] This was a severe setback to the Dutch exploitation of the Scottish fisheries. Their harvesting of this great source of wealth had, until then, gone on relatively undisturbed since the end of the Dutch Wars.

The Scottish mainland coast was defenceless against such attacks. The *Royal William* lay in a dilapidated state at Burntisland while the two smaller 'Scots navy' cruisers – *Royal Mary* and *Dumbarton Castle* – were unavailable for duty. Although they had been recommissioned by March 1703, their captains – Thomas Gordon and Matthew Campbell – had leased them for private armed ventures to the West Indies and Italy respectively.[69] The revenue from such a cost-cutting exercise to the Scottish purse was more than negated by the additional wear and tear to these elderly hulls, already strained by years of patrolling the Scottish seas. On their return they had to be sent south to be refitted at Chatham, at the expense of the Crown, and were not back on their Scottish stations until July 1703. The *Royal William* required a full survey before the decision was taken to refit her in 1704. By September 1705 she was back on station as the flagship of the energetic and promoted Commodore Gordon.[70]

The condition of the *Royal Mary*'s hull remained a matter of grave concern to those who sailed on her. Henry Clerk, an officer serving onboard, mentioned her very poor state in a bitter letter to his family (August 1706). He reported that during a fifteen-hour chase of a French privateer found in Aberdeen Bay she had sprung a bad leak and barely

---

67   Macintyre, *Privateers*, p. 101.

68   J.R. Nicholson, *Lerwick Harbour* (Lerwick 1987), p. 4. This estimate of Dutch losses is the most conservative, as the *Statistical Account of Scotland* report of the parish of Lerwick puts a much higher figure (c.500).

69   *State Papers Domestic (Scotland)*, Warrant Books, xix, 6 Nov. 1703. Gordon on the *Royal Mary* captured the *Catherine* of Rotterdam (120 tons) *en route* from Tenerife with wine and brought her into Burntisland: NAS HCAS AC9/88, Gordon v Russell.

70   Gordon took the credit for the capture of the Spanish privateer *Holy Trinity* of Ostend: NAS HCAS AC7/107 Register of Decreets, XII, entries, 22 June and 17 August 1705. The capture of the Scottish vessel *St. Andrew* by a Middelburg privateer the following year was seen as an act of reprisal for Gordon's zeal in taking a German vessel at this time.

made it back to Leith with her prize. Indeed, after her arrival her pumps had to be continuously manned for seven days to stop her sinking.[71]

His correspondence also gives insights into the operations and internal politics of the Scots Navy at this critical time in the nation's history. The pursuit of the Frenchman took the *Royal Mary* 120 miles directly out into the North Sea. This was in direct defiance of Commodore Gordon's prime order to keep the 'thin shelled' *Royal Mary* within thirty miles of the shore. Ostensibly, his reason was to avoid the risk of her falling in with a French privateering squadron known to be off the Norwegian coast.[72] Clerk, however, believed that Gordon – ever mindful of prize money and glory – had an ulterior motive. By ordering his new captain – James Hamilton junior of Orbiston – to stand offshore at that specific distance, Gordon, on the *Royal William*, had a clear run along the more probable inshore course for interception. Indeed, Clerk reckoned that Gordon took considerable exception to his captain's success.

The poor maintenance of these warships was, fortunately, hardly tested. The French privateering wolf packs abandoned the North Sea that year for the rich new hunting grounds around the Iberian peninsula and the southern approaches. Indeed, it was not until 1707 that Forbin's squadron reverted to the old cruising pattern of rounding Scotland after cutting up the incoming Moscovy Company convoy off Norway. With this exception, this temporary lull in hostilities in northern waters, and the clearance of the smaller inshore raiders by the guard ships, allowed the Scottish marine to revive while English and Dutch shipping losses mounted in the south.[73]

---

71   The intruder was the *Angelica* of Havre de Grace (60 tons/60 men/10 guns): NAS HCAS AC8/67, 9/185. For detailed billing of repairs carried out at Leith: *Ibid.*, AC 8/78 James Robertson (carpenter) v Hamilton.

72   NAS, Clerk of Penicuik MSS, GD 18, 4136. I am grateful to Michael Dun for calling my attention to this letter.

73   NAS, McPherson of Cluny MSS, GD 80/ 568: letter from William Niven regarding the Dunkirk squadrons off the Scottish coast and the capture of two Aberdeen vessels. On the west coast the *Dumbarton Castle*, Captain Matthew Campbell, had a success that year, taking the St. Malo privateer *St Peter & St. Paul*, Captain Jean Petit, and her prize the *Happy Entrance* of Dublin: NAS HCAS AC8/61 and AC 9/210 Campbell v Petit 1706. The year before Campbell had taken the French privateer *Aime Mary*: *Ibid.*, AC7/ 107, 24 July 1705. Convoying is illustrated by the case heard before the High Court of Admiralty of Scotland, in 1705, in which the owners of the *Antonia* of Leith sued their master, James Cuthbertson, for the cost of the vessel (£4000 Scots). She was taken by a French privateer owing to his delay in sailing and hence missing the convoy to London: NAS HCAS AC9/128 Pringle v Cuthbertson.

CALAIS.

NOUS ſouſſignez *Jacques du non* —
Commandant le Vaiſſeau le *L'Hirondelle* — de Calais,
& *Jean ffishe et* — Maître du Vaiſſeau
le *heleyne delile* — ſommes convenus de ce
qui ſuit. C'eſt à ſçavoir que moy *Jacques duno* —
reconnois avoir Rançonné ledit Vaiſſeau le *heleyne delile*
appartenant à *Gorge Wanderame* —
Bourgeois de *aſmoute en écoſe* — du port de *40 liſte* Tonneaux ;
le 15.ᵉ *auvil* du preſent mois de *d'auvil* — mil ſept cens *1710*
allant de *ymoute* — à *Nauf Castel* ſous pavillon de *danoir* —
& Paſſeport de *Puglitaine* — chargé de *ſix caste de poiſſont*
En barils — pour le compte de *Gorge Wanderame* —
Bourgeois de *aydermoute* —
lequel Vaiſſeau je ſuis convenu de Rançonner moyennant la ſomme
de *cent quatre Vingt livres* — *pour laquelle j'ay remis ledit Vaiſſeau en liberté pour aller au Port*
de *Neufcastel* — où il ſera tenu de ſe rendre dans le tems &
eſpace *de quinze Jours* — après l'expiration duquel tems le
preſent Traité ne pourra le garentir d'être arrêté par un autre Armateur ;
Pour ſûreté de laquelle Rançon j'ay reçu en ôtage *Jean ffishe* —
Capitaine — ſur ledit Vaiſſeau : Priant tous Amis &
Alliëz de laiſſer ſûrement & librement paſſer ledit Vaiſſeau le *heleyne*
delile — pour aller audit Port de *Neufcastel* —
ſans ſouffrir qu'il luy ſoit fait pendant ledit tems & ſur ladite route
aucun trouble ou empêchement, *pendans quinze Jours date*

Et moy *Jean ffishe sud Capitaine* — tant en mon nom, que celuy
deſdits, *Gorges Wanderame* — Propriétaires dudit Vaiſſeau & des Marchandiſes, me ſuis ſo100000000000 —
de ladite Rançon de *lad. ſomme ly deſſus éscrite* —
pour ſûreté de laquelle j'ay donné ledit *Capitaine* — en
ôtage, promettant de ne point contrevénir aux conditions du preſent
Traité, dont chacun de nous a requis un double que nous avons ſigné
avec cedit *Capitaine* — reçû pour ôtage. Fait à Bord du Vaiſſeau
le *L'Hirondelle* — le *traize auvil* —
de l'année mil ſept cens *dix*

Nº *354*

THE IMPENDING SCHISM

It was, however, during these years that Anglo–Scottish relations entered their darkest days as tit-for-tat legislation escalated the maritime sovereignty dispute to a constitutional crisis of sinister dimensions. The cycle of confrontation commenced with an Act of the Scottish Parliament that legalised the import of Madeiran and French wines and liquors. This provocative move was meant to redress the Scots trading disadvantage and challenge the legitimacy of seizures by English warships in Scottish waters. This legislation broke with the Tory grand strategy of an economic blockade to defeat Spain and France, then holding sway in the Queen's Council.

Escalating the level of confrontation was the Scottish Act (1703) that forbade any future monarch to declare war on behalf of Scotland without first gaining the consent of the Scottish Parliament. In that year, the gauntlet was finally thrown down over the supremely sensitive matter of the Hanoverian succession with the Scottish 'Act of Security'. This Act prepared the way for the dissolution of the Union of the Crowns unless

> There be such conditions of government settled and enacted as
> may secure the honour and sovereignty of this Crown and
> kingdom, the freedom, frequency, and power of parliament, the
> religion, freedom, and the trade of the nation, from English or
> any other foreign influence.[74]

The eventuality of armed external interference in Scottish domestic affairs was covered by a clause that empowered the Scottish Parliament to muster every able-bodied man to form a national militia. The royal assent to this Act was, understandably, withheld by the Queen. At the same time the English Parliament set about drafting a retaliatory and proscriptive measure against the Scottish community and interest in London.

Under such volatile political conditions, the contest at sea resumed in earnest with the *Annandale* outrage. The Company of Scotland fitted out this armed merchantman (220 tons/20 guns/48 men) for a further voyage to the East Indies, ostensibly to retrieve the valuable cargo of the wrecked *Speedwell*. She sailed with letters of marque issued under the company

---

74 A general view of Anglo–Scottish antagonism is available in D. Defoe, *The History of the Union of Great Britain* (Edinburgh, 1709), pp. 141–5.

patent and was commanded by an English master – John Ap-Rice – later denounced by his Scottish employers as 'a rogue'.[75] In January 1704, she was detained at the Downs on her outward passage and condemned as legal prize for intending to breach the monopoly of the English East India Company.

This private action, undertaken by agents of the English Company, succeeded in deterring other would-be speculators from taking up with the Scottish Company. The previous month, James, Earl of Morton, had signed Articles of Agreement with the Scottish company to send out his vessel – *Morton* (100 tons/ 14 guns) – to the East Indies. Lying in the Thames, she was within immediate reach of the agent of the English Companies, so he prudently cancelled her departure. A similar scheme to fit out the galley *Hannah* on behalf of the Company by the London merchant Ainsworth was also dropped, even though she lay out of harm's way at Burntisland.[76]

THE TRIAL OF CAPTAIN GREEN

In December 1704, the myth of a possible peaceful co-existence of English and Scottish trading companies in the colonial world finally exploded when the Lord High Admiral of England openly sanctioned the seizure of all Scottish vessels found trading in breach of the English monopolies.[77] The opportunity to retaliate offered itself that same winter when the small English East Indiaman – *Worcester* (130 tons/16 guns/32 men) – put into Burntisland under stress of weather. She was, in fact, a private trader with the second-rank English 'Two Million Company' on her home run to London, having rounded Scotland to avoid capture in the English Channel. Indeed, had she been a large 'regular' of the East India Company, it is doubtful whether the agents of the Company of Scotland would have secured her in compensation for the *Annandale*, without an immediate fight or retaliation later.

---

75 *State Papers Domestic* (Scotland), XIX, 3 January 1704. A second letter of marque was issued (20 February 1704) against the French and Spanish to the galley *Alexander* of Queensferry, John Stewart. No information has come to hand to determine whither it was used or not.

76 The Morton agreement was signed in December 1703; for reproduction, see Insh *Darien Scheme*, pp.251–2. Ainsworth had the *Hannah* arrested for debts owed to him by the Scottish Company while awaiting his orders, NAS HCAS AC 9/183, Heggan v Ainsworth and Miller; and AC10/25 (1706).

77 *Historical Manuscripts Commission, House of Lords Report*, new series, VI (1704–6), pp. 233–8, as quoted by Whatley, 'The Union of 1707', p. 156.

LEITH SANDS c.1690, WHERE CAPTAIN GREEN AND TWO OF HIS OFFICERS
WERE HANGED (FROM SLEZER'S *THEATRUM SCOTIAE*)

As it was, the seizure of the *Worcester* completed the stalemate that
now made it impossible for the company vessels of one nation to survive
in the territorial waters of the other unmolested.

The dispute took on national proportions when her captain Thomas
Green and a number of his seamen were charged with piracy and the
murder of the crew of the overdue Scottish Company vessel – *Speedy
Return*. The actions of Captain Hews on HMS *Winchester*, then visiting the
Forth, aggravated the prisoners' situation further when he took to searching
Scottish vessels, 'firing at them if they refused to comply with his
demands'.[78] The trial and conviction of Captain Green and a few of his
officers on hearsay evidence was a sop to the baying Edinburgh mob and
a travesty of Scottish justice, not least because it was known in Admiralty
circles that two crewmen of the *Speedy Return* had recently landed at
Portsmouth and testified to the true fate of their vessel – taken by
Madagascan pirates.[79]

The public execution of Green and two of his fellow officers on Leith
Sands took place within days of the planned passing of the English 'Aliens
Act'. This piece of retaliatory legislation would have effectively severed
Anglo–Scottish trading links by expelling the Scottish merchant
community in London. The *Worcester* tragedy did, however, have the effect
of displaying the enormity of Scottish disaffection towards their
overbearing neighbour and shocked both establishments into seeking a
way round the *impasse*. To this end the Queen ordered her commissioners

---

78 NAS, PC 1/53, p. 370, 12 March 1705.
79 NAS HCAS AC9/126 and 150, Fiscal -v- Green. Clerk of Penicuik gives a graphic
and contemporary report on this case: NAS, MSS GD 18/6072, *Account of the trial of Capt.
Thomas Green and crew for piracy.*

from the two nations to reconvene in London in 1705 to formulate a full political and economic union as a matter of urgency.[80]

THE FINAL SOLUTION —
THE INCORPORATING UNION

The first article of the proposed Treaty of Union – the surrender of national sovereignty to create 'one kingdom' – was fully debated the following year by the Scottish Parliament. Towards the end of their deliberations the Scottish Commissioner, William Seton of Pitmedden, gave a highly succinct account as to why his signature was on the draft treaty. His pragmatic observation was that Scotland's future co-existence as an independent trading nation with England could never be peacefully resolved as 'two Kingdoms subject to one Sovereign, having different Interests, the nearer these are one to another, the greater the Jealousie and Emulation will be betwixt them.' Nor, after the experiences of the past decade, could the allegiance to a common monarch ever again be taken as a guarantee of fair play or even-handedness, as:

> Every monarch, having two or more Kingdoms, will be obliged to prefer the Counsel and Interest of the Stronger to that of the weaker, and the greater Disparity of Power and Riches there is betwixt these Kingdoms, the greater Influence, the more powerful Nation will have on the Sovereign.

In his view the 'remedy' for Scotland's dire economic state and hopes for prosperity through foreign trade required at least 'the Assistance of England'. He left his audience in no doubt that *Realpolitik* dictated that, with the onslaught of virulent mercantilism in Europe, 'no money or Things of value can be purchased in the Course of Commerce but where there's force to protect it'. The harsh reality was that an independent Scotland was 'behind all other Nations of Europe ... being Poor and without Force to protect its Commerce ... till it partake of the Trade and

---

80   A comprehensive review of publications on the Act of Union is available in C.A. Whatley, 'Economic causes and consequences of the Union of 1707: a survey', *Scottish Historical Review* (1989), LXVIII, pp. 150–181. More recently the same author has reviewed learned opinion in *Bought and Sold for English Gold? Explaining the Union of 1707* (East Linton, 2001).

Protection of some powerful Neighbour Nation'.[81] From the English point of view any attempt by Scotland to ally in this way with a rival naval power – Holland or France – was simply unthinkable.[82]

To the man on the street the message was the same. As the pro-Unionist Rev. Dr. John Arbuthnot sermonised from Ecclesiastes X at the Mercat Cross of Edinburgh, in December 1706, 'Better is he that labourth and aboundeth in all things, than he that boasted himself and wanteth bread'. For him the prospect of prosperity and stability under the Union was infinitely preferable to national bankruptcy and social strife as an independent nation.[83] Given the wholly adverse circumstances that Scotland was bound to face in the future, it is difficult to perceive what feasible alternative there was to an 'incorporating union' with England – for the Scottish maritime community at least.[84]

The resulting Act of Union of 1707 was a competent piece of diplomacy from point of view of the maritime interest. Each grievance was taken into account and neutralised: Article IV finally conceded Scottish access to the colonial markets of England; Article V redefined the shipping of both marines as of 'British' sovereignty under the protection of a British navy; Article XV allocated a generous amount (£219,094 pounds sterling) as the 'equivalent' to compensate for the higher taxation that Scotland would bear after the Union. Much of this funding was used to compensate the shareholders of the Company of Scotland for the termination of their company.[85] This was a simple but effective solution that left the English monopolies intact while refinancing the Scottish merchant community to engage in the other trading opportunities the Union would accord them.

The significant concession that the Scots gave in return was the surrender of their sovereignty. In maritime matters Article XIX stripped the Scottish Admiralty of effective power while leaving the edifice in place as a concession to national sensitivities: 'yet the Court of Admiralty

81   Abbreviated version of *A speech in Parliament On the First Article of the Treaty of Union 1706,* as quoted in Appendix I ; Whatley, *op. cit.*

82   Daniel Defoe, *The advantages of Scotland by an incorporate union with England, compared with those of a coalition with the Dutch or league with France.*

83   H. See and A.A. Cormack, 'Commercial Relations between France and Scotland in 1707', *Scottish Historical Review* (1926), 23, p. 279.

84   In *Bought and Sold for English Gold?* Whatley offers 'a new synthesis' that concludes there was nothing inevitable about the Act of Union.

85   *Act of Parliament,* 5 Anne, Cap.11 (1706). It is thought that one quarter of the Nation's available capital had been sunk in the Company of Scotland.

established in Scotland should be continued, subject to future regulations and alterations by the parliaments of Great Britain'. The office of Lord High Admiral of Scotland, however, set an additional problem for the Commissioners as the Duke of Richmond and Lennox successfully championed his claim to have the office recognised as his heritable title.[86] This was conceded as a proprietary right and the commissioners were obliged to buy out the office in a separate arrangement.

The passing of the Act of Union terminated Scotland's attempts as an independent sovereign state to achieve a breakthrough in the plantation and colonial trades without 'the Assistance of England'. The Darien Scheme and the events surrounding her efforts to defend her own coastline with guard ships proved that the nation was wholly incapable of providing the necessary 'force' to promote and protect her maritime interests. On virtually every count Scotland had been found deficient. She had neither the necessary stock of shipping and masters, nor the political allies, by which to force an entry into and sustain a presence in the preserve of others.

Even in home waters, her attempts to control the import of basic foodstuffs with the ban on Irish victuals had to be suspended from 1695 onwards as a succession of crop failures headed the list of misfortunes that befell the Scottish economy during the 'hungry nineties'.

---

86   The basis of his claim dates back to the ratification of the separate jurisdiction of the Scottish Admiral in 1609 and 1681.

CHAPTER 3

THE IMPOSITION OF ENGLISH MERCANTILISM

The harmonisation of the Scottish Customs and Excise regimes with their English counterparts was crucial to securing the Act of Union. Queen Anne's instruction (5 June 1706) to her Commissioners negotiating the terms of the Union was explicit on this matter that: 'there be the same Customs and Excise and all other taxes and the same prohibitions, restrictions and regulations of trade throughout the United Kingdom of Britain'.[1] Implementing this directive in the midst of war proved, however, to be a highly fraught business which had profound implications for both the course and development of the Scottish marine.

Indeed, it would not be overstating the case to assert that the introduction of this new fiscal regime was the most immediate, tangible and dramatic change to daily life felt by the inhabitants of 'North Britain'.

THE OLD CUSTOMS SERVICE

Prior to 1707, excise was largely deployed as a local tax, normally levied for a limited period on brewing ale in the area to fund a specific project – such as a harbour improvement. Customs, on the other hand, was a national collection delegated to private, profit-driven 'tax farmers' whose licence might include one or more precincts. This arrangement had hardly altered since the Customs and Excise Commission, headed by Tucker, had set up the first national system some fifty years earlier.

The shortcomings of tax farming[2] can be illustrated by the contract

---

1   As quoted by G. Smith, *Something to Declare* (London, 1980), p. 34. The Scottish Board of Customs Commissioners was established by PRO Patent Roll, 6 Anne, P6, No.16 (1707).
2   *RPC*, XI, p. 31. The English tax farmers had been systematically phased out after 1671. In 1696 the English Customs Service was subsequently upgraded to a professional body under the central direction of the Commissioners of a Board of Customs – answerable to the Treasury: Hoon, *The English Customs System*, p. 7.

concluded between the Crown Conservator (under the gift of the Great Seal) and the partnership of Mylne of Barton and Charles Murray This agreement (covering 1681–84) granted them the right to farm Leith, the principal customs precinct, on payment of an annual rent of £23,000. The amount of revenue actually raised was essentially a private concern as a clause in their contract stipulated that, for an additional £3000 per annum, they could have the customs books of the port 'burn[t] to ashes' at the expiry of their tenure. This practice partly explains the piecemeal survival of the early customs registers and the lack of credible national trade statistics prior to the Union.[3]

It was also an ill-disciplined service. The collectors deputised by the farmers resorted to accommodation rather than enforcement to ensure an adequate flow of revenue for their paymasters. This meant accepting understated or fraudulent cargo declarations from belligerent shippers. Indeed, a report to the Scottish Parliament in 1698 declared that it was common practice for the local tidewaiters to dispense with the onboard survey. This cross-examination of the master's 'report book' (cargo manifest) against what was found by 'rummaging' in the hold and cabins prior to berthing was, and remains, the basic deterrent against wrongful declaration or the broaching of cargo.[4] The replacement of tax farmers in the major firths by salaried crown officers lagged at least a decade behind England. The 'foreign customs' of Leith was still in private hands in 1702, and during the next five years little headway was made at the other precincts to change over to a professional crown service. Such was the inertia that the Treasury was obliged, for a number of years after 1707, to renew the farmers' licences for the remote customs precinct of Shetland.[5]

Furthermore, the customs coverage was incomplete as whole stretches of the more inaccessible north-western coastline were left unsupervised. Even within the major firths, customs supervision at the previously unfree ports was insufficient to discourage large-scale evasion. Prior to the establishment of new customs headports at Alloa and Bo'ness, it had been found necessary to station soldiers on Inch Garvie Island in the middle of the Firth of Forth. This was to discourage the passage of vessels seeking to

3   The convenient fire at the ledger office at Leith in 1683 probably saved them this additional fee. The surviving Scottish port books for this period are held by the NAS, Exchequer [E.]series.
4   Smout, *Scottish Trade*, pp. 32–42.
5   The Leith Customs tack syndicate, 1697–1702, was headed Sir Archibald Mure. Details of the Shetland tack are available in H.C. Smith, *Shetland Life and Trade, 1550–1914* (Edinburgh, 1984), p. 213.

avoid customs at Leith by landing their cargoes on the upper shores.[6]

Such a piecemeal arrangement was entirely at odds with the incoming system that was firmly based on the 1696 reorganisation of the English Customs Service. This new professional regime was founded on the modern concepts of uniformed and impartial enforcement at the quayside, full coverage of the coastline, and rigorous accountability to a central authority.

SMUGGLING AND SHARP PRACTICE

The disciplining of a nation already addicted to tax avoidance was a thankless and daunting task. The distractions of intermittent warfare since the Glorious Revolution encouraged both direct smuggling along the coastline and illicit and sharp practices at the quaysides of the Scottish ports. The first great spur to this activity had been the quadrupling of English import tariffs (with only a few essential raw materials exempt) between 1690 and 1704. As Scottish tariffs had not followed suit, those commodities that attracted a high duty in England (notably tobacco and spirits) were often landed at a low-duty Scottish port – to be slipped on to the English and Irish domestic markets at a later date.

This disparity actively promoted collusion between Scottish and northern English merchants. By 1701 the problem had mushroomed to the point where Charles Godolphin – the ablest of the English Commissioners of Customs – was given special leave from his London duties to inspect the north-west ports of England.[7]

To the outrage of London and Bristol merchants lobbying at Westminster, such practices gave the Scottish traders and their accomplices a cost advantage in both home and foreign markets. The scale and breadth of this fraud was, they claimed, self-evident from the meagre contribution that Scottish Customs made to the Exchequer. As they pointed out, in the years immediately prior to the Union, the Scottish contribution averaged c.£30,000 (just over two per cent of the British Customs collection).[8] This situation was acknowledged in a retrospective report submitted in 1710 to

6   Mowat, *Leith*, p. 205.
7   E. Carson, *The Ancient and Rightful Customs* (London, 1972), p.118 and Hoon, *English Customs*, p. 3
8   J.M. Price, 'Glasgow, the Tobacco Trade and the Scottish Customs, 1707–1730', *Scottish Historical Review*, LXIII (1984), p. 7. Professor Price believes this report was compiled by Thomas Fullarton, an English Customs officer raised to the position of Scottish Commissioner in 1709.

the new Lord Treasurer, Robert Harley, by the Earl of Wemyss. Entitled *A Brief Account of the Customs of North Britain*, it stated that, before the Union, half of the gross receipts from Scotland from those

> principal Branches of Importation from whence the Customs did arise were first 1,600 Tuns of Wine & Brandy, and 2,000 hhds of Tobacco, the Wine and Brandy was Imported from France, and Holland, some of the Tobacco from England, but most of it was stolen in from the plantations.[9]

The second great spur came with the pronouncement in January 1707 that the Union of Scotland and England would become effective as from 1 May. This sparked a rush to land colonial commodities at the Scottish ports while the tariff differential still existed. During the intervening four months it was estimated that tobacco imports into Scottish ports surged to 2.13 million pounds – double the annual rate. The super-profit was made after the Union when these cargoes, as the legal stock of North Britain, were free to move onto the English domestic market without incurring further duty.

The Atlantic-facing Solway and Clyde ports particularly benefited from this short-lived bonanza. Vessels running directly in from the colonies had virtually unrestricted access, while their close proximity to England and Ireland was highly advantageous when the Union came into force. The propagandist for the Union, Daniel Defoe, informed the readers of his *Review* that he was 'told by a merchant in Dumfries, that there have been 4,000 hogsheads brought from England into that Town only'.[10] This figure had, undoubtedly, a large element of journalistic licence, as such a store would amount to around two million pounds of tobacco – equivalent to the entire annual Scottish trade in this commodity at that time.[11] While the actual amounts that passed through Dumfries in those months will probably never be known, the impression remains that this speculative boom created a remarkable upsurge in shipping activity.

After the speculator's moment had come and gone, the imposition of high import tariffs on almost all luxury goods guaranteed the accelerating growth of 'the trade' – as direct smuggling was known. The Isle of Man, the fiscal rights of which were the prerogative of its owner, the Duke of

9   *Ibid.*, p. 6.
10 *Ibid.*
11 Calculated on the basis that the tobacco in the average hogshead was then *c.*500 lb.

Atholl, quickly established itself as the epicentre of 'the trade' on the west coast. In direct response, the newly installed Scottish Commissioners allocated their first revenue sloop to the Galloway coast, at a cost of £160 to build and £10 to provision with small arms.[12]

RESTRUCTURING THE
SCOTTISH CUSTOMS SERVICE

The separate Scottish Boards of Customs and Excise were first authorised to sit at Edinburgh in June 1707. Introducing the highly unpopular excise regime was a costly but relatively simple matter of drafting in professional English 'gaugers' to staff all levels.[13] By comparison, the major restructuring of the existing Scottish Customs Service along English lines was one of the greatest adminstrative undertakings of the immediate post-Union period.

The authority to do so was conferred from London in the months following the Union. In July, the Lord Treasurer of Scotland received the Treasury warrant to 'compound and regulate all matters and abuses relating to the seizure of goods, wares and merchandise, imported and exported, into and out of, Scotland'.[14] Whitehall, however, retained the main instruments of enforcement of the (now British) Navigation Acts, namely, the registration and regulation of Scottish shipping in the colonial trade. These were placed under the supervision of the Board of Trade and Plantations sitting at London.

Similarly, the various Inspectors General responsible for collating trade statistics – the new *political arithmetick* of policy makers – also sat in London. The Scottish Board of Customs at Edinburgh was, therefore, required to forward each precinct's quarterly report on the enumerated commodities imported/exported (by quantity and *official* value) directly to London. This remained the situation until the creation of a Scottish Board of Trade in 1723 when quarterly and annual extracts were generated from Edinburgh-held registers for use in London.[15]

---

12   G. Smith, *King's Cutters* (London, 1983) p. 34. An analysis of the smuggling on the west coast is available in L.M. Cullen, 'Smuggling in the North Channel in the eighteenth century', *Scottish Economic and Social History* (1987), 7, pp. 9–26.
13   J.F. Mitchell, 'Englishmen in the Scottish Excise Department, 1707–1823', *Scottish Genealogist*, XIII, pp. 16–28.
14   BL Harleian MSS 2263, Warrant dated 22 July 1708 and signed by Godolphin, then Lord Treasurer of England.
15   This office had been enlarged to cover Scotland by Treasury decree: PRO Treasury Papers, 1, No.94. The majority of eighteenth-century Customs annual reports are held in the PRO Customs 17 series.

Port Glasgow

Christmas Qua[r]. 1707 Establishment £ 190.17

Officers	Salaries	Reasons why	Short paid
David Graham Collector	25 — —		
Christo: Hilton Comptrol[er]	17.10		
James Howson Land Surv[eyo]r	15 — —		
Hugh Cranford Searcher	10 — —		
John Bewick Computer	12.10		
W[m] Curwen Landwaiter	8.15 —		
Tho: Kennedy Ditto — — —	8.15 —		
Geo: Scot Tyde Surveyor	11.5 —		
Rob[t] Cunningham Watch Keep[er]	5 — —		
James Morison Cooper — —	1.10 —		
Edw[d] Blenkarn Tydesm[a]n	3.15 —		
John Jackson Ditto —	3.15 —		
Norman Goodlet Ditto —	3.15 —		
Rob[t] Campbell Ditto —	3.15 —		
Ninian M[c]Aulay Ditto —	3.15 —		
John Moire Ditto —	3.15 —		
Tho: Grey Ditto —	3.15 —		
Walt[r] Caripbel Ditto —	3.15 —		
Tho: Summervill Boatm[a]n	3.2.6		
Benj[a] Boakin Ditto	3.2.6	He never appeard	3.2.6
Dan[l] M[c]Alla Weigh[er] & Marker	3.15 —		
Richard Newsham Weigh[er] & Mark[er]	3.15 —		
John Moor Gen[l] Surveyor	30 — —		20 — —
Charles Ady Riding Officer	12.10		
Philemon Caddun Ditto —	12.10		
Total £	**214 — —**	**Total £**	**03.2.6**

In those politically charged months following the Union the base of this bureaucratic pyramid in Scotland had to be built virtually from scratch and at great speed. Political expediency dictated the key appointments to the extent that the integrity of the new organisation was suspect for decades to come. The mould was set by the incoming patent-holding Commissioners and their senior advisors, the majority of whom were Godolphin's nominees from the south. They were, with one notable exception, political appointees little versed in customs procedures.[16] The same held true of the first wave of managerial appointments at Edinburgh and the main headports, many of which were filled with equally inexperienced – as often as not disreputable – Englishmen. As the Board had an aversion to re-employing staff from the old customs regime in any position of authority, the few Scots who were appointed to promoted posts had little or no previous experience.

Such was the appalling lack of expertise available to the Board in the weeks preceding the Treasury warrant that the newly appointed Clerk to Board had to be set to hand-copying two books brought from London. These handwritten transcripts of learned opinion on case precedent and procedure served as the basic guides by which the incoming Commissioners sought to emulate the English model after July.[17]

From such an inauspicious start, the service in Scotland struggled in the years that followed to establish its credentials with London and restore its credibility with its detractors. The administrative model provided the means for addressing the first problem. At the most senior level in Edinburgh the interpretation of current practice and government legislation became the prime concern of the 'Solicitor'. Transmitting the Board's dictat to the Collectors at the headport was the duty of the 'Secretary'. Managing and auditing the accounts of the collection and generating the trade statistics required by the Board of Trade in London was the work of the 'Receiver General', 'Comptroller General' and 'Examiner'. Each had a clerk, as did the Collectors at the premier precincts.[18] This hierarchy was mirrored at the major headports, though the number of promoted posts depended on the scale of activity through the precinct.

---

16   Only Lionel Norman of Berwick, a late replacement for the West Country politician and Harley supporter, John Henley, had served as a Collector.
17   The largest (c.90 pages) was *Reports and Presentations of the Commissioners att London and the Opinions of Her Majesty's Sollicitor and Attorney General*. Robert Savage was paid £6 for this labour, 27 May 1707, NAS, E508 1/2/6–10.
18   Successive entries.

To kick-start the system a number of the more able officers were dispatched on special duties, such as to observe and instruct local officers in regulating the duties on salt intended for the fisheries. Initiative was rewarded, as with the *ex gratia* payment made to the landwaiter and searcher at Inverness for his 'extraordinary diligence and expense in visiting the remotest parts of the West and North Highlands'.[19]

At the quayside little of worth was inherited from the outgoing tax-farmers. At most the cramped 'King's cellar' was the only major asset to be passed on. Generally missing were the substantial weighing beams and accurate weights and measures essential for the uniform collection by the elaborate post-1707 high-tariff system. At Leith, two premises had to be rented to serve as the 'customshouse' and 'customs warehouse' and an iron chest procured for the safe keeping of the collection.[20]

Even with such expenditure in the first year of the new order, the quantity of enumerated goods still managing to circumvent the 'tidewaiters' at the 'legal quay' was a major concern. It was, therefore, found necessary to appoint 'landwaiters' to inspect the carters leaving the port or entering the major cities. By May 1708 landwaiters were installed at the six gateways in the city walls that still enclosed Edinburgh and one at the end of Leith Walk.[21] Over the next two years the other main precincts made similar appointments along with riding officers to tour the coastline.

Removing the deep and widely held suspicion of the professional integrity of the Service was a seemingly intractable problem. Hindering the process was the recruitment of unsuitable personnel from the outset. Unlike their superiors, many of the low-ranking customs officers, supernumeraries and boatmen had been previously employed by the outgoing tax farmer. As such their receptiveness to English training in enforcement and general loyalty was suspect. They were often reported as being insufficiently detached from the local shipping fraternity they were meant to be policing. Left to their own devices, especially at the more remote precincts, they often reverted to their old accommodations with the local masters. Many observers laid the blame for the prevailing culture of mistrust, within and between the ranks, at the Board's doorstep. It was their undisguised preference for English collectors of dubious record and commitment – rather than elevate indigenous staff of merit to positions of authority – that perpetuated low morale and lack of grassroots professionalism. As Defoe commented:

---

19   NAS E508 salaries series.
20   The old customs house at Leith had previously been burned down.
21   NAS E508 salaries series.

In the [Scottish] Customs the clamours against the Englishmen being employed has laid hold of, but the conduct of the commissioners here likewise answered the pretence, no sooner had the officers sent by the commissioners in England ... done the work they came about, viz. in directing and instructing the officers in Scotland, but the greatest part [went] back again.[22]

The English tobacco lobby seized on this image of a Scottish Customs Service incurably riddled with incompetent and corrupt officers and infested by closet Jacobites. This became the central plank of their campaigns to undermine the trading access terms of the Act of Union.[23] They, of course, conveniently ignored the fundamental role of the government's high-tariff policy in creating and nurturing the smuggling menace at every port in Britain – not just Scotland.

They focused instead on the two widespread abuses reported at the Scottish quayside: collusion between merchants and corrupt officials when weighing goods for duty purposes; and the fraudulent claiming of 'draw back' of import duty on goods. The latter involved claiming the refund on duty paid on imported goods damaged in transit or destined for re-export but, in fact, resurrected or relanded illegally on the domestic market. On both counts the competence, vigilance and integrity of the local customs officers was the decisive factor in containing the problem.[24]

THE 1710 CUSTOMS ESTABLISHMENT

There was, undoubtedly, substance to these allegations. The solution was a series of purges, commencing in 1710. Godolphin's new establishment of that year removed a significant number of the personnel of 1707 and dispensed entirely with supernumeraries. The problem of adequate coverage was also addressed at the same time with the creation of new, permanently staffed customs houses at Alloa and Anstruther Easter in the Forth and Greenock on the Clyde.

22   Defoe, *History of the Union*, p. 18.
23   Price, 'Glasgow, the Tobacco Trade', pp. 1–36.
24   The scale, range and economic impact of smuggling during this era is examined in R.C. Nash, 'The English and Scottish Tobacco Trades in the Seventeenth and Eighteenth Centuries: Legal and Illegal Trade', *Economic History Review*, second Series (1982), XXXV, pp. 354–372. Also T.C. Barker, 'Smuggling in the eighteenth century: the evidence of the Scottish tobacco trade', *Virginia Magazine of History and Biography* (1954), LXII, pp. 357–99.

During the restructuring the upper Clyde ports received the largest allocation of staff, in recognition of their emerging dominance in the post-Union boom in salt, coal, herring, sugar and tobacco. The Collector of the new super precinct of Port Glasgow – which then included the ports of Greenock and Dumbarton, Glasgow and the Isles of Bute and Cumbraes and most of Argyllshire – received the largest budget (£995). His deputised Collector at the Broomielaw quayside, eighteen miles upriver in the heart of Glasgow, was allocated £100 to maintain a Comptroller, one landwaiter, three landcarriagemen and two boatmen. The number of officers serving in this substantial establishment, with its other outposts at Greenock and Dumbarton, doubled between 1707 and 1712 to over sixty. This was justified by the need to supervise the increasingly complex re-export trade in colonial commodities. The bulk of colonial commodities landed at the legal quays at Greenock and Port Glasgow were, after inspection, dispatched directly to the European market by sea. An increasing proportion, however, was sent upriver in gabbarts to the Broomielaw. From there, what was not destined for domestic consumption was carted overland to Bo'ness and Alloa on the Forth for re-export to the Low Countries.[25]

Even with Godolphin's ninety new permanent appointments, Scotland still remained one of the weakest links in the Customs Service of mainland Britain. Godolphin's successor and rival – Lord Harley – having railed against the expense of such manning levels, was forced to authorise further increases to their number on taking office. Even so, criticism of the Scottish Service continued to mount during the war years as the scourge of smuggling through the Scottish ports made its impact elsewhere. In 1711, the English Board of Commissioners found it necessary to send a circular to their customs officers to be ever vigilant against false declarations made on French wine and brandy routed through Scottish ports and then sent coastwise as 'produce of Portugal'.[26]

Not that the Scottish Board was complacent. In 1716 they wrote to their Collectors, chastising them for the fact that 'the duties of the tobacco [collected] since the Union ... fall vastly short of what the consumption of Scotland ought to pay'.[27] It has since been calculated that during the period

---

25   Price, 'Glasgow, the Tobacco Trade', footnote p.10.

26   The letterbooks of Scotland's largest wine importer of the period – Oliphant & Co., of Ayr – indicate that the importing of preferred claret under the guise of 'Portuguese' was commonplace in the eighteenth century; J. Fergusson, 'A wine merchant's letter book', in Pares, R. and Taylor, A.J.P. (eds.), *Essays Presented to Sir Lewis Namier,* reprinted in *Ayrshire Collections,* (Ayrshire Archaeological and Natural History Society), IV, pp. 216–224.

27   This referred to loss of duty on domestically consumed tobacco owing to the market being glutted by illegally landed supplies.

1715–17 the amount of tobacco smuggled was around sixty-two per cent of that legally imported.[28] Such was the growth of the tobacco re-export trade and its shadow economy that an additional post of 'Inspector General of Tobacco in Scotland' was created by the Treasury (1718) and awarded to David Graham, the Collector at Port Glasgow. His appointment did little to stem the influx of directly smuggled goods as he was soon the centre of a great scandal that led to his dismissal from the Service.

THE KING'S BOATS

The explosion of smuggling cannot, of course, be laid solely at the door of corrupt or inept local officers. This phenomenon had been greatly exacerbated by a major error of judgement made by their Lordships at the Treasury acting on Godolphin's 1710 review. This was their decision to dispense with the five customs sloops then stationed at Leith, Montrose, Aberdeen, Inverness and Dumfries.[29] These seagoing vessels had been found by the local officers to be suitable for visiting local creeks or offshore cruising and staying on station in bad weather. Their superiors were of a different opinion. They maintained that their upkeep was expensive in (£1,400 per annum) and, without further consultation, declared them unsuitable for 'the deep coasts, islands, firths and tides of Scotland'. They were sold out of service and replaced by fourteen open-oared 'King's Boats' which were stationed around the coast from Dunbar to Dumfries, including Stornoway, Lerwick and New Port Glasgow.[30]

These King's boats came in two sizes – 'small' and 'bigge'. The former rarely left the immediate vicinity of the harbour roadstead while the latter were able to put to sea and raise a small sail in the right conditions. Neither possessed the seaworthiness to remain on station in adverse weather to deter the illegal trans-shipment of goods from merchantmen entering the lower firths. The much harassed Collector of Dundee explained to his superiors, in June 1725, that he was unable to challenge passing vessels because his 'bigge' boat had been 'beat to pieces by a storm'. This left him

28   Nash, 'The English and Scottish Tobacco Trades', p.364. A more comprehensive view of the Scottish tobacco trade is T.M. Devine, *The Tobacco Lords* (Edinburgh, 1975).
29   At the setting up of the service at the timeof the Union – two local vessels had been hired and one purchased to patrol the Forth, the west and the northern coasts. The latter was taken by an enemy privateer in the Moray Firth.
30   Smith, *King's Cutters,* p.34

with the 'small' boat that was 'insufficient for the business' as it 'cannot stand on station'. Furthermore, the boat crews were only supplied with side arms. These were a wholly ineffective defence against the swivel cannons of the well-armed smuggling 'bucker'. As a direct consequence, the first phase of the war against the smuggler was fought, unsuccessfully, onshore at the place of landing.

In 1716 this basic mistake was grudgingly conceded by the Treasury, and a small lightly armed cruising yacht – *Royal George* (80 tons), Captain Lane Whitehall – was allocated to the busy Firth of Forth to intercept incoming smugglers at sea.[31]

THE DEMORALISATION OF THE SERVICE

At the root of the smuggling problem was the widespread resentment of the greater level of interference under Hanoverian rule and bitter reaction to the fiscal *diktat* of London. The latter introduced the modern concept of relatively high and universal taxation.

Set against this anti-establishment background, the Collectors' correspondence from the outlying stations to their superiors in Edinburgh paints a bleak picture of a highly frustrated and intimidated Service. On the one hand their attempts at enforcing order, without the support of a militia, were denigrated by their superiors. On the other, their best efforts were systematically thwarted by organised gangs prepared to resort to violence. The apparent ease with which these smuggling 'companies' could conduct their business without interruption was largely due to the wall of silence maintained by the local inhabitants. While most were too frightened to speak, many where openly supportive of the smugglers to the point of turning out as a mob to obstruct the enforcement of the law. It is rare to find an account in the Customs correspondence of the period where a smuggler was successfully brought to trial after a serious incident. In almost every instance the accused fled the scene of the crime with the help of a mob, usually fronted by jeering women, or escaped from custody with the connivance of the jailer.

---

31   The Scottish Customs Board had previously petitioned the Treasury to have a small frigate of 24–30 guns stationed in the Firth of Forth (1712): PRO Treasury 1/146/13. Whitehall was inept as he allowed the crew of an arrested Elie smuggler to stay aboard their vessel overnight whereupon they broke open the sealed hatches and sold fifty casks of brandy over the side: NAS HCAS AC 9/723.

Undoubtedly, the greatest threat to the morale of a serving Customs officer – other than deadly assault against his person – was an allegation of corruption. These were often maliciously levelled against effective officers by the business associates of the smuggling fraternity.[32] Their slanderous charges ranged from collusion with local smugglers, laid against the Collectors of Inverness and Aberdeen, to that made against the tide surveyor at Aberdeen that he openly used the King's boat for his own smuggling runs.[33]

This, at times lethal, blend of intimidation and collusion pervaded the Scottish coastal communities and was a cause of grave concern for the policymakers in London and the 'beleagued native oligarchy' in Edinburgh.[34] Following the death of Queen Anne (1 August 1714), the question of the loyalty of individual Customs officers to the Hanoverian Succession heightened the level of collective neurosis and atmosphere of 'impermanence' within the Service.

The Jacobite Rebellion of 1715 turned this obsession into something approaching an inquisition that broke the careers of a number of local Customs officers. In such a climate of suspicion, an accusation of harbouring Jacobite sympathies often led to dismissal – whereas overt loyalty was publicly rewarded. In the latter category, one Scottish officer received an *ex gratia* payment of £50 for having been 'barbarously assaulted and maimed for expressing his affection for the Government of the times, on the occasion of the King's coronation'.[35]

Such events were extensively quoted by the English tobacco merchants' parliamentary lobbyists in their anti-Scots campaign. This reached a climax with a petition to the Treasury during the winter session of 1721–2. Robert Walpole, as the newly appointed First Lord of the Treasury, skilfully deflected their demands to exclude tobacco from the terms of the Union or to scrap the Union itself. His tactic was to allay their basic grievances with placatory measures so as not to lose their support for his impending keynote budget.[36]

---

32   Extracts from the Scottish Customs letterbooks pertaining to smuggling as compiled by F. Wilkins: *Strathclyde's Smuggling Story* (1992); *Dumfries and Galloway's Smuggling Story* (1993); *The Smuggling Story of the Two Firths* [Forth and Tay] (1993); and *The Smuggling Story of the Northern Shore* (1995).

33   Smith, *King's Cutters,* p. 34.

34   D. Szechi, 'The Hanoverians and Scotland', in M. Greengrass (ed.), *Conquest and Coalescence* (London, 1991), p. 123.

35   Smith, *Something to Declare,* p.55.

36   This budget completed the fiscal restructuring, started back in 1696, by dismantling the remaining tariffs on exports (with the exception of wool).

THE CUSTOMS INSPECTIONS, 1722–3

In April 1722, the Treasury was seen to act on allegations of widespread evasion of duty at the Scottish ports. Four acting 'surveyor generals' were created and the positions filled, as usual, by political appointees under the leadership of a Scottish Customs Commissioner – the Englishman Humphrey Brent. Without professional serving officers on this investigating team, it rapidly descended into to a paper exercise. Brent concentrated most of his efforts on examining the Edinburgh-held Scottish Customs registers, the bulk of which had been compiled under the direction of the first Scottish Comptroller-General (John Crookshank) who had recently been dismissed for incompetence (1719).[37]

In the summer of 1723 – as new regulations regarding the tobacco trade were being issued by the Treasury – a more business-like team of three senior and experienced English Customs officers was dispatched north, led by Robert Paul, the 'assistant-comptroller-general', who visited the major Scottish ports – starting with Port Glasgow. After their tour, eight reports were submitted between June and October of the following year.

One of their recommendations – the need to restore seagoing revenue cruisers in all the major firths – was acted upon almost immediately. The Treasury set aside its reservations on spending and sanctioned the acquisition of seven new sloops from English yards, having first ordered that the old *Royal George* be sold out of the Service. The first of these – *Princess Caroline* – was stationed at Montrose some time around 1725. The other new vessels deployed were also named, in keeping with the political correctness of the day, after the Hanoverian royal family – *Prince(s) William* and *Frederick* and the *Princess(es) Amelia, Anne, Louisa* and *Mary*.[38]

The other phyrric victory scored by the English merchants' parliamentary campaign was the political fob of disbanding the Scottish Customs Board in favour of a British Board sitting in London. By the following year (1726) this 'unified' Board was operational, having

37 Price, 'Glasgow, the Tobacco Trade', p. 20.
38 Smith, *King's Cutters*, pp. 34–5. The use of royal names for new vessels entering the Scottish Customs service was upheld while a Hanoverian monarch remained on the British throne, the exception being the *Cumbra[y]es* wherry stationed at Millport on the Firth of Clyde which, presumably, predated the new order or, being a wherry, was not considered appropriate for a royal name. These Customs cruisers were frequently assigned to military service in times of war or crisis or to aid the Scottish Excise Service (which did not have its own cruisers until 1763).

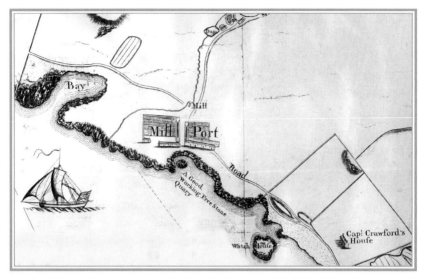

MILLPORT, GREAT CUMBRAE, BASE FOR THE CLYDE CUSTOMS CRUISER.
THE HOUSE OF THE CAPTAIN OF THE REVENUE CRUISER IS TO THE RIGHT
(BUTE FAMILY ARCHIVES)

amalgamated the seven commissioners sitting at London with the five who had previously sat independently at Edinburgh. These Scottish Commissioners were then deputised to return to Edinburgh. They returned with new powers to issue 'plantation certificates', which had, until, been then the sole prerogative of the London-based Board of Trade and Plantations.

THE FAILURE TO ESTABLISH
A BONDED WAREHOUSE SYSTEM

Matters, however, did not greatly improve with the reorganisation, as the smuggling gangs and perpetrators of fraudulent practices at the quayside adapted in turn. In the late 1720s, the zealous Collector of Customs at Liverpool felt compelled to write to his superiors: 'I have lately discovered and detected a most notorious fraud … scarce to be equalled in North Britain … and I am told some of our merchants carry on the same fraudulent trade in Glasgow.'[39] The particular abuse he had uncovered was

---

39 In 1729, he listed all the vessels leaving his port that he suspected were intent on relanding their tobacco in Ireland or Scotland. Both the Irish and Scottish Customs Services declined to act on his information: J. Paxton and J. Wroughton, *Smuggling* (London, 1971), p. 24.

a new variation on the 'draw-back' swindle: bundles of unwanted low-duty tobacco stalks were wrapped in leaf and re-exported as solid 'parcels' of spun leaf on which the higher duty was reclaimed.[40]

This continuing stream of allegations of malpractice in the North instigated a new campaign by the English tobacco merchants in the early 1730s. Their aim was now to remove the Scottish ports from the list of those permitted to receive enumerated goods.[41] Their lobbying resulted in the setting up of a Committee of Investigation (1732) which again confirmed the existence of widespread and large-scale abuse. This evidence was used, in turn, by Robert Walpole to justify the element in his Excise Scheme of 1733 that sought to impose a bonded warehouse system on the re-export tobacco trade. This measure, which would have stopped the draw-back frauds at a stroke, had been actively considered back in 1713. Unfortunately, the hysteria generated throughout the country by the main tax proposal – a higher malt duty – forced a withdrawal of the bill, killing off the warehouse scheme in the process.

Although there was no rioting in the North on the scale of the previous malt tax riot (1725), it did refuel anti-government sentiment in Scotland as a whole. The smuggling fraternities were quick to harness this rising groundswell of hostility and resurgence of Jacobite sentiment to isolate the local agents of government within the coastal communities.[42] In 1733 reports of violence and intimidation streamed from the Collectors at the head ports. The correspondence of the Collector at Inverness, writing in May of that year, serves to illustrate the degree of organised hostility he was facing daily:

> Yesterday morning some ill-disposed villains … carried away
> the Customs boat across the ferry, and with saws and axes have
> cut her in two by the middle, left the one half on the beach,
> and disposed of the other to the waves. The execution of this is
> owing no doubt to the common people, but the contrivance to
> greater heads, and that it has been premeditated appears by the
> tools they had provided themselves with to perform it. 'Tis hard
> to tell where this will end. The warehouse has been twice
> broken open, the boat destroyed, the expresses from the

40   Later on stalks were ground down to make a new product – 'Scotch snuff'.
41   Enumerated goods were those listed under the terms of the Navigation Acts and liable for 'draw-back' of import duty if re-exported.
42   As Szechi rightly concludes, 'patriotic anti-Unionism in Scotland had nowhere else to go but Jacobitism after 1707': Szechi, 'The Hanoverians and Scotland', p. 126.

outports stopped and the letters taken away, a person under
suspicion of being an informer dragged across the Firth and his
ears cut out, and hints every day given to myself to take care of
my life, in short no part of the face of the earth is peopled by
such abandoned villains as this country.[43]

The inability of the local Customs officers to deal with this level of civil
disobedience led to the promise of yet another inquiry into the competence
of the Scottish Customs Service.[44]

London's remote control of the Scottish Customs Service did little to
help. The facade of a unified Customs Board was maintained until the
departure of Walpole from office in 1742, after which a separate Scottish
Customs Board was quietly reconstituted at Edinburgh. By then the respon-
sibilities of the service had grown in line with the seemingly ever-increasing
list of goods on which duty was payable, including locally produced salt.

THE CURB TO SCOTTISH TRADING ASPIRATIONS

This restructuring of national fiscal policy to create a protectionist barrier had
profound consequences for the post-1707 Scottish economy, dogged as it was
by recurring financial crises and a lengthy depression. The imposition of a
high-tariff regime destroyed the hopes of the Scottish Royal Burghs to revive
their traditional trade with France after the war. In the interim few legitimate
alternatives to smuggling had occurred to support Scottish trading aspirations.
As the contemporary commentator 'Bass' John Spruell pointed out, Scotland
had entered the new century lacking any manufacturing base of consequence
from which to promote exchange to the plantations and colonies.

It would not be exaggerating to claim that the recovery of Scotland's
overseas trade in the 1730s owed as much to illicit trading and sharp practice
as to the erratic rise in the volume of legal trade. Indeed, by 1750, the black
economy nurtured by Walpole's budgets was so firmly rooted at every Scottish
port that its corrupting influence touched every level of Scottish society.[45]

---

43 NAS CE 62/1/1, Collector of Inverness to Board, 18 May 1733.
44 A graphic account of the 'reign of terror' at Montrose is available in D. Fraser, *The
Smugglers* (Montrose, 1971).
45 The network of west-coast 'friends' and customers of the smuggling baron George
Moore numbered in excess of 300 individuals: F. Wilkins, *George Moore and Friends: Letters
from a Manx merchant, 1750–1760* (1994), appendix II, pp. 287–292.

Not every Scottish Customs Commissioner, however, condemned the smuggler as a canker in society. Adam Smith, in his later role as a political economist, chose to denounce that great folly of successive governments – the mercantilist system – as the real culprit. In doing so, he collectively absolved the smuggler as an entrepreneur who 'would have been in every respect an excellent citizen had not the laws of his country made that a crime that nature never meant to be so'.[46]

---

46 As quoted in Smith, *Something to Declare*, p. 93. Adam Smith's family were profes-sional Customs officers who held senior positions within the new establishments at Alloa and Kirkcaldy.

CHAPTER 4
THE IMPACT
OF THE UNION

The ownership of vessels served as a prime non-monetary indicator of regional and national prosperity throughout the eighteenth century as hulls were readily bought and sold in direct response to changes in business confidence. Changes in the numbers, tonnage and distribution of vessels offered the administrators of the day tangible evidence of the impact of new legislation, trade cycles and war. This fairly sensitive barometer went some way to compensate for the acknowledged limitations of contemporary methods of measuring, in *official* values, the bilateral foreign-going trade during an era noted for endemic smuggling.

Measuring the immediate impact of the Union by listing the vessels owned by the Scottish ports was one of a number of onerous tasks given to Robert Paul's team of Customs officers as part of their inspection of the Scottish Customs Service (1724–5).[1]

PAUL'S REVIEW OF THE YEARS 1707–12

Paul fulfilled his mission by examining the 'Accompts sent from North Britain' held by the 'Register-General of Trading Ships' at London.[2] This prime source, which has since disappeared, was probably as valid and complete as any available for the period. Under the terms of the Act of Union, all Scottish vessels were required to register as part of the British marine – under pain of confiscation.[3] The survey's declared objective was,

1   Appendix B discusses the credibility of this survey.
2   The Register General position had been created in 1701 and upgraded to a full office – answerable to Godolphin – in 1707. Paul's handwritten survey is dated 24 March 1725 (1724 O.S.): BL, Harleian MSS 6269. The dual dating system (e.g. 1724/25) was used by Customs until 1752 to cover the difference between the Scottish New Year (1 January) and the Church of England New Year (Lady Day – 25 March).
3   The increase in tonnage owned since the Royal Burgh's 1692 Register may be partly owing to the introduction the '1694 formula' for measuring the tonnage of a vessel in the North: see Appendix A.

therefore, to compile an alphabeticall list of all ships and vessells with their respective Tonnage that appear by the generall register kept at London to have traded in any Ports of North Britain from Christmas 1707 to Christmas 1712 distinguishing such of them as have been registered pursuant to the Act of Union by the letter 'R'.

Fortunately, the author clarified the rather ambiguous last statement in his title. In a postscript he defined those vessels 'Marked in this list with the letter 'R' as appearing to be registered at the time of the Union', i.e., registered by the end of December 1707. This choice of starting date was to allow a period of grace (granted by the Royal Proclamation of 28 July) in which returning long-haul Scottish vessels could register as British.[4] The unique survey was addressed to Robert Harley, the Lord Chancellor, which indicates that these data were of considerable importance to the establishment of the day.[5]

THE SCOTTISH FLEETS, 1707–12

The 'R' vessels (registered by December 1707) provided the inspectors with their benchmark against which the growth of the Scottish fleet was measured over the next five years. The Review listed 215 vessels (14,485 tons), which gives an average of 67 registered tons per vessel for the Scottish marine. The range of tonnage of vessels was between 6 and 600 tons, which is impressive but somewhat misleading as only three vessels exceeded 200 tons – the *James* of Montrose (350 tons) and the *Lyon* and the *Viceroy* (both 600 tons) of Leith.[6] Of the outstanding vessel stock just over half was less than 50 tons and eighty per cent was less than 100 tons. By group frequency the smaller hulls in the 11 to 70 tons class stand out as the dominant element in the 1707 Scottish marine. In terms of the geographic distribution, the Firth of Forth ports dominated with just over two-thirds of the total tonnage, a percentage that rises to over three-quarters when

---

4   Published in the *London Gazette*, 11 August 1707. An example of the penalties incurred by losing the status of 'free British bottom' was the case of the *Anne* of St Andrews that was declared 'unfree' by the Scottish Commissioners of Customs (1723). This error cost the master his bounty payment on grain to Norway: NAS HCAS, AC 9/815, Seton v Binning.

5   This need to quantify the economic benefits of the political Union resurfaces later in the century.

6   These vessels were possibly trading from London: Smout, *Scottish Trade*, p. 52.

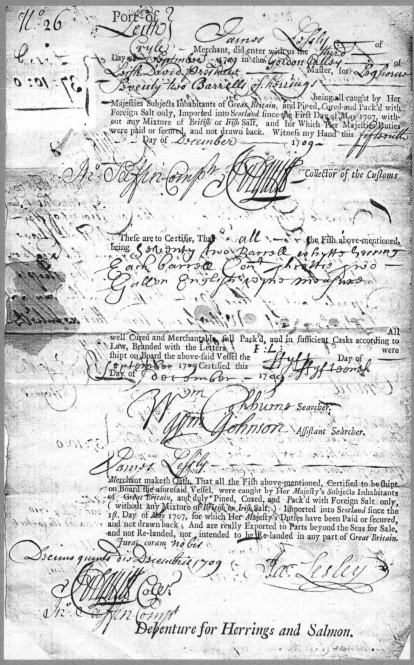

CUSTOMS DEBENTURE, DECEMBER 1709, FOR BARRELLED HERRING
BOUND FOR LEGHORN ON THE *GORDON* (GALLEY), CAPTAIN DAVID
PERSHAW (PRESHAW) (NATIONAL ARCHIVES OF SCOTLAND)

joined with that of the North-East ports.[7] The Firth of Clyde, then only just emerging as a major shipping area and still heavily reliant on English charters, supported less than a tenth of Scotland's tonnage.

When the comparison is made between the 'R' hull stock of 1707 and that accumulated over the next five years (up to December 1712), the full impact of the Union becomes apparent. The tonnage of the Scottish ports had increased three and a half times (50,232 tons), while vessel numbers had risen even faster, increasing fivefold (1,123 hulls).

These figures do not, however, represent the fleet as it existed in December 1712 as the sale of hulls abroad and losses at sea would have reduced their numbers over the intervening five years. Cross-referencing with the available shipping intelligence reports in the contemporary newspapers suggests that this rate of attrition might be in the region of ten to fifteen per cent.[8] Even if this adjustment were to be made, the Scottish marine of 1712 was of a size and number that could readily sustain a presence in all of the maritime activities – 'foreign', 'coastal' and 'fisheries'. Here at last, it would seem, was the critical mass of shipping that had hitherto eluded the efforts of the Scottish Council of Trade since the 1680s.

The composition of the registered fleets had also undergone significant change since 1707. A much greater proportion was now in the smaller tonnage classes. By 1712 the lower tonnage classes (less than 50 tons) made up just under three-quarters of the total tonnage. If this view is extended to vessels under one hundred tons, then the vast majority of the marine is encompassed. The greatest increase (an additional 178 vessels) was in the smallest category of open boats (5–10 tons) engaged in ferrying, inshore fishing and conveying coal and salt in the firths. This is in contrast to a gain of only five vessels for the larger (190+ tons) oceangoing class of vessel.[9]

---

7   This increase may have been partly owing to more owners of small hulls deciding to register their vessels in anticipation of a 'foreign-going' passage – to Ireland and Norway – than to newacquisitions.

8   This impression is derived from the number of vessels mentioned in contemporary newspapers as are: the *Edinburgh Gazette* (1699–1708); *Edinburgh Courant* (1705–9); *Edinburgh Flying Post* (1709–11); *Scots Courant* (1710–16); and *Scots Post Boy* (1711–12). The four out of five of the vessels, along with their port of origin, listed in the shipping intelligence reports (from a sample of *c.*200 entries over the period 1707–1712) have a namesake in the 1725 Review. It is not possible to match one source with the other with absolute certainty as the 1725 Review gives the vessel's name, port and tonnage but not the master – while the newspapers usually give name and port but rarely the master and tonnage.

9   Customs used the term 'boat' to mean an undecked vessel. Those under five tons – not capable of open sea voyages in normal circumstances – were not included in the port books or Customs shipping registers.

CHANGES IN TRADING PATTERNS

This change in the composition of the fleets reflected the shift in trading patterns at this time. As the surviving port books of Dundee and contemporary commentaries indicate, the wartime dislocation and upheaval in Scottish foreign-going trade before and after 1707 had been more than counterbalanced by a general expansion of the coastal trade in coal, salt and meal.[10] These commodities enjoyed tax exemptions or bounties for a limited period under the articles of the Act of Union.[11]

It is, therefore, predictable that when the vessels of the Review are matched with their trading destinations, as listed in the *Scots Courant* for the last full year of the survey (1711), the smaller hulls (up to 50 tons) were deployed mainly as coastal traders.[12] This class of hull ran the whole of the east coast, venturing as far as Lerwick and London. On the west coast the most cited destinations outside the Clyde were the northern English ports, Ireland and the Isle of Man.

Vessels of the 50 to 80 tons class regularly undertook lengthy offshore passages and were sent as far afield as Portugal, Spain, the Canaries and the Baltic – often on a triangular or round-about trading route. Above 80 tons was the small number of transatlantic traders from the west coast, the smallest being the galley *Anne* of Glasgow (85 tons) that set out from Port Glasgow for Barbados in November 1711, having first delivered tobacco and coal to Dublin.[13]

There were only a handful of hulls above one hundred tons, which underlines contemporary comments that the first sustained upsurge in the Atlantic trades from the west-coast ports was serviced by a mixture of

10   This conclusion is consistent with that expressed by Whatley, *Bought and Sold for English Gold?*: notes by Smout on his research into Trinity House of Leith Fraternity records; the Danish Sound Tolls; Aberdeen Shore dues; and S.J. Monaghan 'The Dundee Shipping lists as a Record of the Impact of the Union upon the Dundee Shipping Industry, 1705–10', unpublished MA dissertation, University of Dundee, 1988. I have to thank Iain Flett for access to the original registers held by Dundee District Archive and Record Centre.

11   After 1707 King William's bounty on the export of 'corn' was extended to Scotland: 5/- per quarter of wheat, 3/6d on rye and 2/6 on malt. At the same time imports were prohibited until wheat reached 48/- per quarter, rye 32/- and malt 24/-.

12   The *Scots Courant* for that year reported c.185 shipping movements. Most reports name the vessel, home port, captain, cargo and destination. They very occasionally mention tonnage, crew size or armaments.

13   PRO HCA 26/15, letters 17 October 1711, voyage reported by the *Scots Courant,* 24 November 1711.

chartered English and Irish vessels and only a few select acquisitions to the Clyde fleet. Even so, by December 1712 the Clyde ports' share of the nation's total tonnage had doubled to twenty per cent.

THE WESTWARD SHIFT

This westward shift in the distribution of the Scottish marine following the Union is plainly evident in the new ranking order of individual ports by 1712.[14] While the main Forth precincts of Leith and Bo'ness retained the top two positions by accumulated tonnage – by a very large margin – the Clyde precincts were closing the gap. Port Glasgow now supported the fourth largest tonnage (previously ranked seventh) closely behind Kirkcaldy (previously third) and just ahead of Aberdeen (previously fifth). The Irvine precinct, which included Saltcoats, had risen to eighth position (previously seventeenth). The recently built harbour at Greenock (1710), while supporting only half the tonnage of Port Glasgow, already held twelfth place ahead of Inverness. Conspicuous by their failure to consolidate their pre-Union position in the tobacco-carrying trade were the Solway ports with only twenty-seven small vessels (415 tons).

THE LESSER PORTS

A unique feature of the Review is that it catalogued the vessels by their home anchorage rather than under the collective identity of the head port – as was the practice with all later official shipping returns. By doing so the Review credits ninety Scottish ports and creeks – from Annan to Eyemouth – with supporting a registered vessel before December 1712. Their contribution should not be under-estimated as these lesser ports and creeks supported half the number of registered hulls (one third by tonnage). A few, notably those engaged in the coal trade, were ports in their own right and supported a substantial number of vessels.[15]

The proliferation of creeks was greatest along the Forth, notably the coal and ferry ports on the opposing shores of the upper Forth that came under the Customs precinct of Bo'ness. This precinct encompassed the havens and anchorages of Grangepans, Limekilns, Rosyth, Torrie,

14   See Table 4.1.
15   See Table 4.2

Table 4.1. A comparison of the registered Scottish fleets, 1707 and 1712

Port	1707			By 1712		
	Number	Tonnage	Rank by tons	Number	Tonnage	Rank by tons
1 Aberdeen	22	94	[7]	88	3408	[5]
2 Ayr	1	60		10	372	
3 Alloa	18	502	[10]	60	1976	
4 Anstruther	19	1192	[5]	58	2173	[9]
5 Bo'ness	26	2451	[2]	104	6913	[2]
6 Caithness/Thurso	0	0		10	298	
7 Campbeltown	0	0		30	395	
8 Dumfries	0	0		7	132	
9 Dunbar	1	30		23	640	
10 Dundee	25	1315	[4]	57	2922	[6]
11 Fort Willian	0	0		0	0	
12 Inverness	7	415		26	1136	
13 Isle Martin/Ullapool	0	0		0	0	
14 Irvine	1	20		90	2325	[8]
15 Kirkcaldy	18	1690	[3]	69	3867	[3]
16 Kirkcudbright	0	0		2	25	
17 Leith	39	3354	[1]	106	8202	[1]
18 Montrose	6	584	[9]	72	2669	[7]
19 Oban	0	0		1	10	
20 Kirkwall	0	0		13	265	
21 Perth	0	0		3	140	
22 Port Glasgow	15	959	[6]	73	3716	[4]
23 Glasgow	1	30		4	86	
24 Greenock	6	285		63	1582	
25 Prestonpans	6	725	[8]	26	2082	[10]
26 Rothesay	0	0		13	199	
27 Stornoway	0	0		0	0	
28 Stranraer	1	60		12	207	
29 Portpatrick	0	0		15	154	
30 Tobermory	0	0		0	0	
31 Wigton	0	0		3	104	
32 Zetland	0	0		3	118	
	212	14613		1041	46116	

Source: BL *Harleian* MS 6269.
Note: Not all vessels are included in this list as the compiler omitted to include the
tonnage of five hulls. Likewise, a further sixty-odd hulls have not been included as, while
they were listed with their tonnage, there is no home port mentioned. This computes to a
shortfall of c.7.5% between the total tonnage and that apportioned by precinct in the
table.

Blackness, Culross, Inverkeithing and North, South, and East Queensferry. Their contribution to the overall Customs precinct tally (*c.*6,224 tons) was half by number and one-third by tonnage over the five-year period since 1707. When their contribution is removed, the first clear view of the home fleet of the head port of Bo'ness becomes available (*c.*3,800 tons).[16] This major port had already eclipsed the declining Kirkcaldy (*c.*2,778 tons) and was on a par with the emerging Port Glasgow (*c.*3,461 tons).

A similar situation applies to the head port of Irvine on the lower Clyde where half the declared tonnage of the precinct belonged to the neighbouring creek – the newly completed (1700) coal port of Saltcoats.[17] More typically, the contribution of the creeks in supplying the smaller craft to the precinct's fleet can distort the average tonnage figure for the head port by as much as thirty per cent.[18] Bo'ness was, again, the most impressive example as it had the highest average tonnage of any head port in Scotland. The statistics for the few head ports that do not follow this general pattern (Caithness, Campbeltown, Dunbar and Stranraer) are distorted by the presence of a solitary large hull at one of their creeks.

These larger hulls were characteristically three or four times greater than the average tonnage registered for their home port.[19] They carried the aspirations of their community in foreign-going ventures with surplus local produce – as often as not barrelled fish.[20] It would appear that many of the lesser east-coast ports supported one or two hulls that were too large to operate a regular trade from their home port, requiring a spring tide to enter and leave fully loaded.[21] Their conspicuous absence from the local shipping intelligence, especially during the war years, points to their heavy involvement in 'round-about' overseas trading from home or from a major port in their area.

---

16 Bo'ness became the head port of the precinct in preference to Blackness during the reorganisation of the 1710 Establishment.

17 Saltcoats never attained or requested its own precinct though a salt officer was eventually appointed to the port in the mid-1750s.

18 See Table 4.3.

19 See Table 4.4.

20 In the case of Caithness it was the *Three Brothers* of Tain (150 tons); at Campbeltown it was an un-named 'frigot' (50 tons) of 'New' Tarbert; at Dunbar it was the *Sophie and Margaret* of Eyemouth (60 tons); while at Stranraer precinct it was the *Margaret* of Ballantrae (30 tons).

21 The commentator for Kirkcaldy to the *Statistical Account* (1791) lamented the previous dispersal of his port's home fleet to serve the great ports: 'Some of the largest of them are employed in the trade to the Mediterranean, the West Indies and America, and of these some have been occasionally absent from this place for three or four years'.

ARMED TRADER, THE GALLEY *SANDWICH* AND PINNACLE BOAT, AT LOCHRYAN,
1734, AS DRAWN BY ITS MASTER, CAPTAIN JAMES ROGERS OF LEITH
(NATIONAL ARCHIVES OF SCOTLAND)

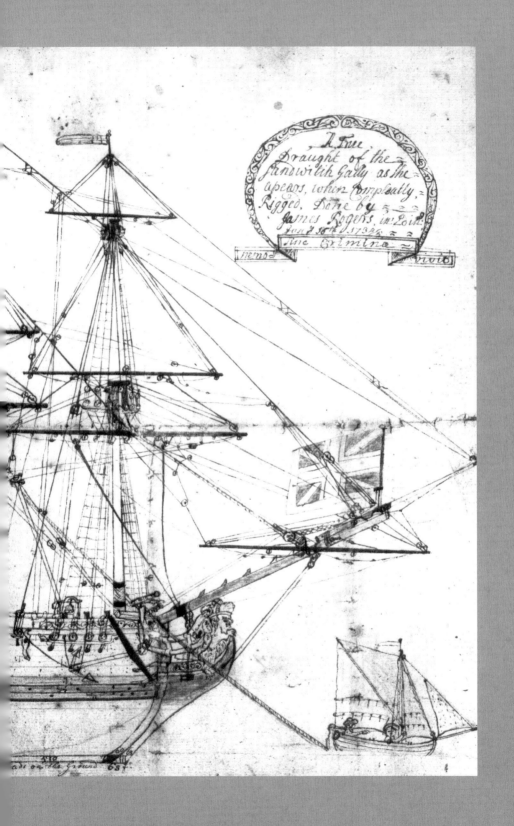

A True Draught of the Sandwith Gally as she apears, when Compleatly Rigged, Done by James Rogers, in Lon. Jan'y 10th 1732/3

Sine Crimine

Table 4.2. Distribution of vessels between head ports and their creeks, 1712

Precinct	Head port		Creeks		Precinct Total	
	Number	Tonnage	Number	Tonnage	Number	Tonnage
1 Aberdeen	39	2155	49	1253	88	3408
2 Ayr	10	372	1	6	11	378
3 Alloa	55	1846	5	130	60	1976
4 Anstruther	14	581	44	1592	58	2173
5 Bo'ness	37	3844	50	2380	87	6224
6 Caithness/Thurso	3	44	7	254	10	298
7 Campbeltown	19	238	11	157	30	395
8 Dumfries	6	124	1	8	7	132
9 Dunbar	19	515	4	125	23	640
10 Dundee	57	2922	0	0	57	2922
11 Fort William	0	0	0	0	0	0
12 Inverness	16	693	10	443	26	1136
13 Isle Martin/Ullapool	0	0	0	0	0	0
14 Irvine	42	1186	48	1136	90	2325
15 Kirkcaldy	31	2778	55	1778	86	4556
16 Kirkcudbright	2	25	0	0	2	25
17 Leith	103	7982	3	220	106	8202
18 Montrose	41	2040	31	629	72	2669
19 Oban	1	10	0	0	1	10
20 Kirkwall	8	160 main isle	5	105 other isles	13	265
21 Perth	2	100	1	40	3	140
22 Port Glasgow	60	3461	10	255	73	3716
23 Glasgow	4	86	0	0	4	86
24 Greenock	41	1334	22	248	63	1582
25 Prestonpans	20	1955	6	127	26	2082
26 Rothesay	2	20	11	179	13	199
27 Stornoway	0	0	0	0	0	0
28 Stranraer	10	171	1	30	11	201
29 Portpatrick	15	154	0	0	15	154
30 Tobermory	0	0	0	0	0	0
31 Wigton	3	104	0	0	3	104
32 Zetland	3	118	0	0	3	118
Total	663	35018	378	11199	1041	46116

Source: BL Harleian MS 6269.

Table 4.3. The average tonnage at head ports and their creeks, 1712

Precinct	Head port Average	Creeks Average	Precinct Average
1 Aberdeen	55	26	39
2 Ayr	37	6	34
3 Alloa	34	26	33
4 Anstruther	42	36	37
5 Bo'ness	104	48	60
6 Caithness/Thurso	15	36	30
7 Campbeltown	13	14	13
8 Dumfries	21	8	19
9 Dunbar	27	31	28
10 Dundee	51	0	51
11 Fort William	0	0	0
12 Inverness	43	44	44
13 Isle Martin/Ullapool	0	0	0
14 Irvine	28	24	26
15 Kirkcaldy	90	33	52
16 Kirkcudbright	13	0	13
17 Leith	77	73	77
18 Montrose	50	20	37
19 Oban	10	0	10
20 Kirkwall	20	21	20
21 Perth	50	40	47
22 Port Glasgow	58	26	51
23 Glasgow	22	0	22
24 Greenock	33	11	25
25 Prestonpans	98	21	80
26 Rothesay	10	16	15
27 Stornoway	0	0	0
28 Stranraer	17	30	18
29 Portpatrick	10	0	10
30 Tobermory	0	0	0
31 Wigton	35	35	35
32 Zetland	39	0	39
Averages	53	30	44

Source: BL Harleian MS 6269.

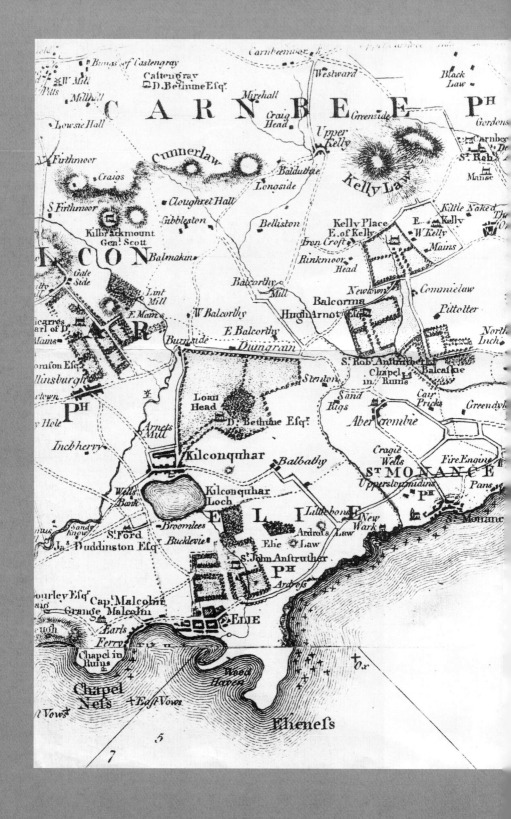

LEFT. ELIE, USED BY CUSTOMS CRUISERS FOR CAREENING
THEIR HULLS. FROM AINSLIE'S MAP (1775) OF FIFE,
KINROSS AND THE FIRTHS OF FORTH AND TAY

ABOVE. A SINGLE-MASTED SLOOP, BACKBONE OF THE
POST-UNION SCOTTISH FLEET

Table 4.4. Extract of larger Scottish hulls, 1707–12

Head port	Vessel	Tonnage	Average tonnage of precinct
Aberdeen	*Johannah*	130	39
	Christian	120	
	Arthur	120	
Alloa	*Robert*	300	33
Anstruther (Elie)	*Mary*	200	37.5
Bo'ness	*Christian*	300	66.5
	Isabel	280	
(Queensferry)	*James*	180	
(Burntisland)	*Elizabeth*	120	
Caithness (Tain)	*Three Brothers*	150	30
Dumfries	*Kirkconnel*	60	19
Inverness	*Three Brothers*	120	31.5
Irvine	*Endeavour*	100	26
	Leopard	90	
Kirkcaldy	*Mary* (galley)	220	56
	Isabel	200	
	Lamb	165	
	Mary (frigate)	160	
Leith	*Lyon*	600	77
	Viceroy	600	
	Adventure	300	
Montrose	*James*	350	37
Port Glasgow	*Hopewell*	200	61
	American Merchant	160	
	Elizabeth	160	
Greenock	*Resolution*	150	25
Prestonpans	*Marion*	250	80
	Margaret	250	

Source: BL *Harleian* MS 6269.

THE ATLANTIC TRADERS IN 1711

The tonnage data on individual vessels in the Review serve as a key when collating the information available on passages for other contemporary sources. By matching the stock of vessels with the information available from the run of shipping intelligence reports in the *Scots Courant* for 1711, letter of marque commissions and Admiralty court disputes, a snapshot of trading activity in the Atlantic in a wartime year can be created.[22]

In that year (noted only for a few minor security scares in Scottish waters) fourteen passages were reported outgoing to America and nine to the West Indies. However, only eight of the vessels involved in the America trade were Scottish-owned. This number matches that reckoned by Defoe to have been fitted out in Scotland for the English plantations in the first year after the Union.[23] Of the six tobacco ships reported entering the Firth of Clyde, only two were returning to their home port – the remaining four were chartered from Whitehaven and Workington.[24]

By way of contrast the east coast sent out four – all locally owned vessels – to Virginia that year.[25] These reports also recorded the kernel of the new trade in rice, oil and resin from the Carolinas, with three Clyde vessels arriving home with these commodities that summer.[26] Completing the tally were two Boston-owned vessels that made the crossing to Scotland, probably only to conform with the Navigation Acts before sailing on to their southern European market.[27]

Of the three armed West Indiamen sent out from the Clyde, the most interesting is the *Betty* of Bo'ness [ex-*Elizabeth*] (100 tons) as she serves as an example of the transfer of vessels from the east to the west coast at that time. This well-armed vessel was brought round from the Forth by her captain – John Finlayson – and was described as 'of Port Glasgow'

---

22   PRO HCA 26/13. Fifteen Scottish vessels took out letters of marque during the 1707–13 period (eleven vessels were from the east-coast ports and the remaining four from Port Glasgow). None exceeded 200 tons: the smallest at 35 tons was the Clyde-to-Belfast armed packet *Dolphin* of Port Glasgow. Even so they represent the cream of the Scottish armed traders running the Atlantic and the north–south trade of Europe.

23   Defoe, *History of the Union*, p. 415, quoted by Smout, *Scottish Trade*, p.177.

24   *Hope* (70 tons) and *American Merchant* (160 tons), both of Port Glasgow: *Scots Courant*, 26 February and 21 April 1711.

25   *Friendship* (130 tons) of Leith; *Concord* (150 tons) of Queensferry; *Johanna* (130 tons) and *Antelop* (details unknown) of Aberdeen: *Ibid.*, 16 August, 13 April and 26 May 1711.

26   *Margaret* (details unknown); the galley *Expedition* of Port Glasgow(100 tons/6 guns); and *Endeavour* of Irvine (100 tons); *Ibid.*, 1 August, 23 June and 4 December 1711.

27   *Dolphin* and galley *Speedwell* of Boston reported at Inverness: *Ibid.*, 26 May 1711.

thereafter. In March she sailed from the Clyde in convoy under the protection of HMS *Queensborough* as far as Dublin. Her cargo was barrelled herring and baled goods for the West Indies. By November of that year she was safely back at her new home port, having made a seven-week passage from Antigua with sugar and cotton.[28]

The other two Port Glasgow vessels also returned safely with West Indian sugar for refining at the three Glasgow sugar houses.[29] At this time any additional demand for unrefined sugar was met by imported stock shipped up from Bristol.[30]

THE 'NORTH—SOUTH' TRADERS

As the years covered by the Review (1707–12) were war years, sailing south into the war zones of the 'Straits' and the Western Mediterranean was a high-risk venture. The galley *Dee* of Aberdeen (150 tons), which set out for Livorno in late 1710, was well prepared for damage to the extent of carrying three sets of sails and spare cordage.[31] On the west coast the galley *Glasgow* (190 tons) carried a crew of fifty and a list of supplies indicative of a vessel determined to defend herself on her voyage to Lisbon via Sligo.[32] On the safer offshore passage to Madeira most of the Scottish traders reported in the shipping intelligence were under 70 tons and only lightly armed.

Armed trading offered the chance to engage in prize taking when the opportunity offered. A case in question was the letter-of-marque galley *Gordon* of Leith (80 tons) owned by very business-orientated Captain

28 PRO HCA 26/15, letters 21 February 1711, outward bound; *Scots Courant*, 15 March 1711. Reported at Glasgow from Antigua with sugar after seven-week passage; *Ibid.*, 5 and 12 November 1711. In her two voyages from Greenock – one to Sweden, the other to Antigua – she made a cumulative loss of £5,092. The vessel was eventually arrested and rouped (1714) in lieu of debts outstanding against the master. Thirty-six 'firelocks' were part of the inventory: NAS HCAS AC 8/139, 168 and 9/511.

29 The galley *Resolution* of Glasgow (150 tons) and *Elizabeth* of Glasgow (160 tons). Their respective voyages were to Jamaica and Barbados: *Scots Courant,* 30 May and 12 September 1711.

30 Delivery of sugar to the 'westerie sugar house' from Bristol by the *Speedwell* of Liverpool: *Edinburgh Courant*, 9 May 1710. *Two Brothers* of Greenock, Captain James Boyd, in from Bristol with sugar and cider: *Scots Courant*, 2 April 1711.

31 PRO HCA 26/15, letters 23 September 1711; outward report: *Scots Courant*, 15 December 1710.

32 PRO HCA 26/15, letters 16 September 1710; reported as carrying fifty men on her initial passage to Lisbon: *Scots Courant,* 3 November 1711.

Thomas Gordon R.N. She voyaged as far afield as Archangel, Bergen, Riga and Cadiz during the war years under the command of David Pershaw. Very much in the mould of his owner, he grasped the opportunity to board and seize two French-owned vessels – *Enfro* and *Mademoiselle* 'of Stockholm' – posing as neutrals. They were major prizes as the former was 'of so great a burthen that she cannot come into [Leith] harbour until the springs'.[33]

The largest number of Scottish vessels identified in the Review were engaged in trading to the Low Countries, the Baltic and Scandinavia. Most sailed unarmed and without letters of marque as the Anglo–Dutch North Sea convoy system offered adequate protection after 1710. During 1711 the Danish Sound Toll Records listed sixty-seven passages by Scottish masters outwards (west-going) and sixty-nine passages inwards (east-going) through the Baltic. This was double the number of the previous year. Their eastward destinations were primarily Danzig (38), Königsberg (7) and Sweden (19).[34] The sailing season of 1711 was, of course, one of the better years, as there followed a marked deterioration in security in the Baltic area followed by outbreaks of plague in the Eastlands.

THE REVIEW AS A BENCHMARK

The Review provides the third benchmark against which the progress of the Scottish marine – at national, regional and local levels – can be measured. The next comparison does not, unfortunately, become available until 1759 (another war year) when annual national shipping statistics – collated from the Scottish head ports returns – were reinstated. In that year the Scottish marine numbered 909 vessels totalling 47,751 tons.[35] This tally is inferior – in both number and tonnage – to the accumulated Scottish marine of the immediate post-Union as listed in the Review. It would, therefore, appear that during the intervening decades of economic stagnation (1712–23), depression (1725–34) and gradual recovery (1735–58), the fleets of Scotland consolidated and adapted to the new trading environment rather than undergoing further expansion.

33   PRO HCA 26/13, letters 11 May 1708 (various spellings of
Pershaw/Preshau/Pereshaw). Petition: NAS HCAS AC 10/73 and prize case AC 9/305,
Pershaw v Stanley. Inward report: *Scots Courant*, 23 February 1711.
34   I am grateful to Professor Hans-Christian Johansen of Odense Universitet, Denmark
for access to the Danish Tolls database for the years 1661–1795. A fuller analysis is
provided in the following three chapters.
35   Glasgow University Library, MSS GEN 1075.

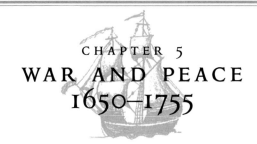

CHAPTER 5
WAR AND PEACE
1650–1755

Domestic upheavals and international wars were prime catalysts in the development of the Scottish marine and its supporting industries. From the mercantilist point of view, war was the other, more drastic, means by which the seaborne trade of foreign rivals could be reduced and their colonies seized. As it has been aptly remarked of this age, it was 'not one in which the successful businessman was at all wedded to peace'.[1]

Even in peacetime, the process of enforcing the exclusion of others, by arrest and forfeiture, was enshrined in the first Navigation Acts. Thereafter, the elaborate body of protectionist legislation – a myriad of tariffs, regulations, exemptions and bounty payments – aggressively promoted the nation's shipping, trade and fisheries to the detriment of rivals.

CROMWELL'S INVASION

Scotland's bloody baptism into this new order came with the imposition of the Cromwellian Commonwealth. Prior to 1651 the fragmentary Customs records for Leith for the maritime year (Martinmas to Martinmas) 1638–9 offers a pre-invasion benchmark against which the subsequent disruptions to shipping activity can be measured.[2]

It was a crucial year in Scottish history as the nation was in foment over Charles I's imposition of his canons and liturgy, culminating in the mass signing of the National Covenant in Greyfriars churchyard (February 1638). As this crisis spiralled towards civil war, elements of the Stuart Navy

---

1   E.J. Hobsbawm, *The Age of Revolution* (London, 1973), p. 87.
2   The following data and Table 5.1 were extracted from tables collectively entitled *Ships into Leith, 1624–1738* compiled by S. Mowat from the primary sources held at the Edinburgh City Archives (shore dues) and the National Archives of Scotland (Customs).

arrived in the Forth during the summer with orders to stop and search vessels for arms and dissidents.

Against this background of impending insurrection the shore dues (paid by all vessels) recorded by the farmers of Leith Customs, listed the inward passage of c.350 vessels during the maritime year (commencing 11 November) 1638. The vast majority were Scottish vessels sailing under Scottish masters (c.320 entries) of which one third (c.100 entries) belonged to Leith and the main havens of the Forth – Bo'ness, Prestonpans, Kinghorn, Kirkcaldy, Burntisland, Dysart, Anstruther and Pittenweem. Most of the remaining two-thirds was an assortment of small coasters from the havens of the east coast as far north as Elgin, all of which serves to illustrate the full extent to which Leith was the epicentre of trade on the eastern seaboard of Scotland. In all, just under a third of all recorded passages in that maritime year (c.132 entries) were 'foreign-going', a small contingent of which (c.30 entries) were foreign vessels – mainly from Denmark and the Baltic ports.

Some twenty years later, the 'primegilt' (paid by all Scottish-owned vessels incoming from a foreign-going passage) list for Leith for the first maritime year after the Restoration (1660–1) recorded only thirty-seven foreign-going passages – a drop of two-thirds. The Restoration compilers of the Calendar of State papers laid the blame for this severe contraction of overseas trade squarely on the Cromwellian Union (1652–60). During the Interregnum, if they are to be believed, 'almost all the ships and vessels of His Majesty's subjects of Scotland were during the last usurpation: taken, burnt or destroyed'.[3] They were, however, selectively mute on the highly adverse effect of the new English Navigation Act of 1660 that recategorised Scottish traders as 'aliens'.

Even so, and allowing for an element of retrospective propaganda in their claim, Cromwell's invasion and subjugation of Scotland were, undoubtedly, a traumatic event for many of the Scottish ports, in varying degrees. After Cromwell's victory at Dunbar (September 1650) and his unopposed entry into Leith, the parliamentary warships that had been blockading the Forth moved northwards to support Monck as he advanced up the east coast and attended at the sacking of the port of Dundee. Local commentators claimed that the thoroughness of this looting was such as to deny the local shippers the means to regain their seaborne trade for years to come. This does not appear to be an exaggeration. The English sea captain Richard Franck felt compelled to write, after his visit in 1656, 'Give

---

3   *Calendar of State Papers*, Charles II, CXXXIII, p. 141.

me leave to call it deplorable Dundee, and not to be exprest without a deluge of tears'.[4] The Fife ports were also subjected to much abuse after their occupation in July 1651. Anstruther was described as 'very spoyled' by the seizing of vessels and the burden of maintaining the soldiers quartered in the town.[5]

For others the occupation was but the final blow. Kirkcaldy, until then the second port of Scotland, reported losing ninety-four vessels during this turbulent period (1644–60) in the nation's history. Ayr, the most adventurous of the Clyde ports, had to bear the cost of quartering an uninvited military garrison in excess of a thousand soldiers, on top of heavy losses sustained in high-risk ventures to the West Indies. Back in 1638, Ayr had reported twenty 'guid ships' that were reduced to six by 1645. When Tucker surveyed the port, four years after Monck's entry into the town, its decline was such that there were only three locally owned vessels – two open boats of three and four tons and a bark of one hundred tons – to be found.[6]

Not all ports seem to have suffered to the same degree as Ayr, Dundee and those of Fife. The *Shore Work Accounts* of Aberdeen and the *Register of Ship Entries* for Dumbarton (ranked third and fourth by commerce and wealth respectively) provide statistical evidence that is at odds with the dire picture painted by the commentators. Both these Royal burghs would appear to have maintained the core of their maritime trades during the imposition of the Cromwellian Union – after which they staged a qualified recovery.[7] If the Dumbarton *Register* can be taken as an indicator of prosperity of the upper Clyde fleets – Dumbarton was then the entrepôt for Glasgow – it would appear that they flourished during the Interregnum.[8] The fact that they were not selected as the garrison ports may explain the contrast in their experience to that of their neighbours along the coast.

The physical legacy of the Commonwealth, from the maritime view, was the fortification of selected ports. Following Cromwell's military

4   R. Franck, *Northern Memoirs* (1658), reprinted in Hume Brown, *Early Travellers*, pp. 208–9.
5   S. Stevenson, *Anstruther* (Edinburgh, 1989), p. 10.
6   Set against this tally only one English supply ship appears to have been lost to Scottish forces.
7   Devine, 'The Cromwellian Union', pp. 1–16. Monck's entry into Aberdeen was followed by looting, though not on the scale experienced by Dundee.
8   This is the also the opinion of Marwick (*The River Clyde*, p. 94) who noted that Dumbarton had the collective confidence, in 1655, to build its first common quay.

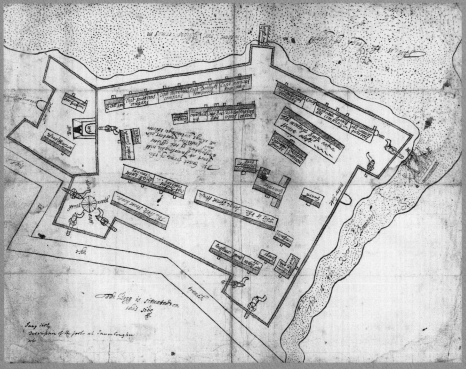

INVERLOCHY STAR FORTRESS (LATER FORT WILLIAM)

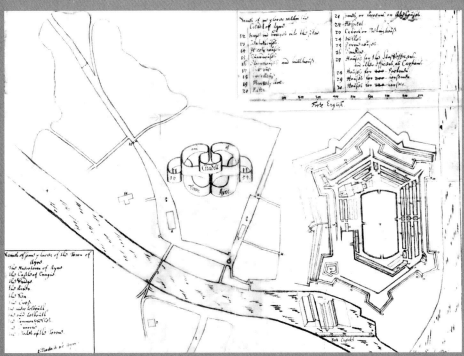

AYR CITADEL (BOTH ILLUSTRATIONS PROVOST AND FELLOWS
OF WORCESTER COLLEGE, OXFORD)

success at Dunbar, seaborne supply and communications consolidated his hold over Scotland. The surrender of Leith gave him effective control of the Forth and Edinburgh, the retention of which required the immediate fortification of the port and town. As this military base was being secured, the subjugation of the rest Scotland proceeded by a similar process at selected ports to the north and west.

Time was of the essence for the occupying forces. To raise the citadel and quay at Inverness, stonework was stripped from an old chapel. At Inverlochy, at the western end of the Great Glen, the fortress was thrown up with whatever local materials were to hand. In addition to these labours, a forty-ton vessel was built and dragged on rollers across the six miles of land from Inverness to Loch Ness where it was launched and armed with cannon to deter armed parties of Highland raiders crossing the Great Glen by boat.[9]

On the west coast 'divers barkes came into Ayr with provisions for the troops, [escorted by] four frigates and several vessels for their assistance' that summer.[10] Their primary objective was to secure a base in the Clyde area as the main seaborne supply line from Liverpool and Whitehaven for Monck's drive into the South-West of Scotland. As at Inverness, his troops flung up a large star fortress to control the town and harbour. The citadel – enclosing twelve acres – was, reputedly, built of masonry stripped from Ardrossan Castle and shipped down the coast by the transports.[11] Further north the harbour at Stornoway was also fortified, though on a much smaller scale.

THE EXCLUSION OF THE DUTCH FROM THE FISHERIES

The Anglo–Dutch conflicts fought out in Scottish waters prolonged the misery of the east-coast ports engaged in the fisheries. The eviction of the Dutch, along with the Danes, from the 'gold mine' of the fishing grounds around Scotland was a central tenet of the now dominant English *Mare*

9   A.G. Pollitt, *Historic Inverness* (Inverness, 1981), p. 110 and A.D. Cameron, 'The Hub of the Highlands', *Inverness Field Club* (Inverness, 1975), p. 237.
10   They were unopposed as the Royalist frigate HMS *Peter,* dispatched by Charles to hold the region, had been 'cast in at Troone' sands from which the Earl of Eglinton retrieved her guns (1650): NAS, Lothian MSS GD 40 V/24–5.
11   Dunlop, *Ayr,* p. 199. When shown the building costs, Cromwell is reported to have enquired if its walls were made of gold.

Clausum school of maritime sovereignty. At their zenith (1640) the Dutch had an estimated 500 herring busses in Shetland waters which fished for up to four months, closely supported by their 'jager' supply and hospital ships.[12] This harvesting of such enormous wealth from the waters of the new Commonwealth was anathema to the English mercantilist doctrine of exclusivity and its closely related interest in limiting the reservoir of able seamen available to the Dutch navy.

Commonwealth warships were consequently dispatched to Shetland to contest the Dutch presence in the 'grand fishing' at the outbreak the First Dutch War (1652). Only bad weather stopped Admiral Blake's fleet of eighty warships engaging with the Dutch defending force, led by van Tromp, off Burravoe (Isle of Yell). In the subsequent pursuit down the east coast Blake captured 150 Dutch busses off Buchan Ness (Aberdeenshire), the first in a series of major blows struck against the Dutch presence in the northern fisheries. To deter their return or possible acts of retaliation, Cromwell ordered the building of a new fortification at Lerwick to command Bressay Sound. Thereafter, Commonwealth warships were stationed in northern Scottish waters and by the end of hostilities (1654) four frigates – *Primrose, Duchess, Unicorn* and *Sun* – were enforcing the exclusion zone, when not serving as escorts.[13]

The Scottish ports did not, however, appear to have taken the opportunity to participate in any significant numbers in the northern herring fisheries during this enforced absence of the Dutch or join the escorted annual cod fleet to Iceland.

In the first year of peace (1655) Cromwell's ruling Council of State moved to recruit the Scots to the mercantilist cause by 'giv[ing] all due enc[o]uragement to the trade and commerce of that nation [Scotland] and to advance manufactures and fisheries there'. The Council's benevolent measures had, however, little impact on the war-ravaged east-coast fishing ports. As the burgesses of the debt-ridden Anstruther reported the following year:

> We hadd within this few yeares of shippes nineteen now we
> have only (three of them small and worth little) four, we hadd

---

12   E. Balneaves, *Windswept Isles* (London, 1977), p. 154. The great debate between Britain and the Netherlands over the issue of 'open' and 'closed' seas is a theme examined by C.R. Boxer, *The Dutch Seaborne Empire* (London, 1965).

13   Mowat, *Leith*, pp. 191–3, gives a summary of naval movements around the Forth and the North-East in 1654.

of barks five now we have but one, of late we hadd boates
going to ye Orknay fishand and busching fifteen … Since …
we was a burgh we had sundtrie vessels sumtymes a guid many
that went to the Isles fishing, this yier we have not one.[14]

The few foreign-going passages from the east-coast ports did, however,
benefit from the protection of the annual frigate-escorted convoy between
Leith, Elsinore and the Norwegian coast. Those sailing south from Leith
were escorted as far as Newcastle where the next convoy marshalled for
London and hence onwards to the English Channel and the French ports.[15]

THE COUNCIL FOR
THE ROYAL FISHING

On his restoration Charles II continued this policy of displacing the Dutch
in the grand fisheries, though his motives were driven more by a sense of
profit than political doctrine. His personal interest in the promotion of
'fishery companies' ran to the extent of chairing a meeting at Worcester
House, attended by Lauderdale and Prince Rupert, when outfitting of
herring busses and boats and fishing techniques were discussed in the
greatest detail.[16] The outcome was the creation of a 'Council of the Royal
Fishing of Great Britain and Ireland' whose primary aim was to sell royal
patents to interested parties.

The strategic importance of the Shetlands to such royal designs on the
grand fisheries was fully recognised. The royal master mason, John Mylne,
was dispatched to build the pentagonal Fort Charlotte on top of the earlier
Cromwellian fortification at Bressay Sound. This, paradoxically, at a time
when Charles II was ordering the demolition of the citadels at Ayr and
Leith. On completion this new fortress was rarely garrisoned, though its
very existence was sufficient to forestall a planned invasion of the islands
by the Dutch Admiral Van Gent during the Second Dutch War (July 1667).
On that occasion he was content to wait, unopposed, in the Sound to escort
home the Dutch East Indies fleet. At the end of the third and final conflict
(1674), however, the Dutch returned in force to bombard the empty fort,

14   Stevenson, *Anstruther,* p. 132.
15   Mowat, *Leith,* pp. 191–3.
16   GCA, Maxwell of Pollock MSS, T-PM 107/7/20/4.

setting half of Lerwick ablaze in the process.[17]

This unchallenged incident signalled the virtual abandonment of the defence of Shetland and any consistent attempt at imposing an exclusion zone in the 'grand fisheries' in those waters. It followed that, for well over a century thereafter, the only defence this extensive sea region received was from the passing armed escorts of the annual northern convoys – the Iceland cod fleet, Greenland whalers, Archangel traders, and the Muscovy and the Hudson Bay Companies. What meagre naval resources were occasionally allocated to patrol northern waters tended to congregate further south at the marshalling area of Scapa Flow in Orkney. As a result enemy raiders were, for over a century, allowed well-nigh complete freedom of action in Shetland waters and the option of an unopposed north-about passage between the Atlantic and the North Sea as part of their cruising strategy.

Royal interest in developing the relatively unexploited inshore fisheries of the west coast of Scotland followed a similar pattern. The monarch's open preference for royal patent-buying companies, as opposed to indigenous enterprise, manifested itself in his obstructive edict that banned the local communities from fishing in the Firth of Clyde and adjacent lochs until 25 July of each year, 'upon pretext that the same does spoile the scooles of herring and damnifie the fishing'. As the monarch's interest in fishery companies waned, this restriction was relaxed. After 1676 it became lawful for local fishermen to 'wet their nets' a month earlier, so extending the inshore fishing season from 15 June to 25 December.[18]

THE CHANGES
TO OVERSEAS TRADING

The windfall of prizes from the Second Dutch War and improved security in European waters at the end of hostilities encouraged a resumption of Scottish foreign-going voyages in reasonable numbers. The most adventurous undertaking recorded in the surviving Customs books for

17   Gifford of Busta (writing in 1733) states that the original garrison numbered 300 men under the command of a native, Colonel William Sinclair, with twenty or thirty cannon. The annual upkeep was put at £28,000 sterling. The garrison was withdrawn towards the end of the Third Dutch War: Balneaves, *Windswept Isles*, p. 158.
18   *RPC*, V, p. 183. Charles' schemes were partly obstructed by the revived Scottish Parliament's attempt at resurrecting the east coast Scottish burghs' interest in the Orkney fisheries by bestowing 'above strangers' (preferential) status on them (1660).

Leith for the year 1667 was the departure of a flotilla of three Forth vessels – *David* of Burntisland, *Unicorn* of Queensferry and *James* of Pittenween – for Tangiers.[19] This armed venture was an impressive piece of opportunism, undertaken in the wake of Blake's punitive expedition to the Barbary Coast that resulted in the capture and retention of Tangiers harbour for the British Crown.

By then the peace with Holland had revived the more mundane but regular trade with the Low Countries. The choice of entrepôt had, however, altered considerably since 1638, as Rotterdam and Amsterdam now clearly surpassing the old staple ports of Campvere and Middelburg. Furthermore, the drift in Scotland's foreign-going trade away from France and more towards England (and her colonies) – as later described by Provost of Linlithgow's to the Council of Trade in 1681 – had already set in.

Table 5.1. The place of embarkation of 'foreign-going' passages arriving at Leith, 1638–67

| Year | 1638 | 1660 | 1661 | 1662 | 1663 | 1667 |
Source	S	P	P	P	P	C
Norway	39	*6*	*9*	*19*	*15*	6
Baltic	20	*6*	7	5	7	11
Germany	0	*1*	0	*1*	0	6
Low Countries	28	*6*	8	7	6	27
England	13	8	*10*	6	7	21
France	35	*10*	*12*	25	*10*	5
Spain	4	0	*4*	0	*1*	0
America	0	0	0	0	0	2
Total	139	*37*	*50*	*63*	*46*	78

Source: NAS E71–2, Leith shore dues (S), primegold (P) and Customs records (C) (Scottish vessels only in italics), compiled from S. Mowat, *Ships into Leith, 1624–1690.*

The advance of Scotland's seaborne trade after the conclusion of the Third (and last) Dutch war (1674) was hampered by domestic events. Firstly, a royal edict placed an embargo on the departure of all foreign-going vessels from Scottish ports during the months March–June 1678. This draconian measure was taken to ensure compliance with the national levy of five hundred Scottish sailors for the Stuart Navy. While coastal traders were technically exempt from the embargo, the general uncertainty and loss of

---

19   Extracted from Mowat, *Ships into Leith, 1624–1690,* database of Leith Customs Records.

such a significant number of seamen adversely affected all levels of shipping activity.[20] The second was the security crisis surrounding Argyll's Rebellion.

ARGYLL'S 'REBELLION IN THE WEST'

The commissioners entrusted by Charles II to contain the Scottish nation, racked by religious and civil strife, intuitively placed security above prosperity. In 1682 their chairman, the autocratic Duke of York, returned from his brief sojourn in London and set about imposing stern and arbitrary measures aimed at tightening control over the movement of dissenters and rebels. His decree of 1684 required all masters of vessels entering and leaving Scottish ports to present a list of passengers to his officials for vetting, an onerous task that impeded commerce.

This threat from disaffected nationals aboard was dramatically underlined the following year by Argyll's 'Rebellion in the West' (April–June 1685) in support of the Duke of Monmouth. Argyll had previously fled from London to Holland where he purchased, and later secretly armed in Norway, two 'frigots' which he renamed – *Anne* (22 guns/190 tons) and *Sophia* (20 guns/243 tons).[21] These vessels conveyed him back to Cowal, Argyllshire, following his appointment as 'Commander of the Invasion of Scotland'. His primary mission was to create a diversion that would draw government forces north just before Monmouth made his bid for the throne in the south. His two frigates were essential to the plan and would have been the dominant force in Scottish waters had their arrival gone unopposed.

Their final approach was, however, shadowed by three warships of the Stuart navy – HMS *Kingfisher, Mermaid* and *Drake*. This flotilla had been dispatched from England under a resolute commander, Captain Hamilton,

---

20   *RPC*, X, pp. 304 and 374. It is tempting to suppose that the levy per port reflects the level of merchant shipping at each, but this does not seem wholly compatible with known shipping data. It would seem more likely that the levy also reflected a historic contribution, the number of fishermen in the area and an element of relief for those burghs accepting a higher level of cess tax.

21   *RPC*, IX, p. 173. Argyll's agents had recruited an assorted crew including fifteen Dutchmen with the promise of a voyage to Surinam. After their capture, both vessels (with the approval of the Scottish Privy Council) were sequestrated and renamed: the *Ann* became HMS *Dumbarton* (sixth rater) and served on the Virginia station, while the *Sophia* became HMS *Sophia* (fire ship): W.L. Cowes, *The Royal Navy* (New York, 1960).

ARGYLL'S WARSHIP *SOPHIA*, BY VAN DE VELDE, SKETCHED SHORTLY
AFTER CAPTURE (NATIONAL MARITIME MUSEUM, LONDON)

who quickly cornered his quarry at Inveraray. The capture of Argyll's warships effectively put an end to his grand scheme to invade lowland Scotland. As a consequence the planned major rebel landing at Largs was aborted and was replaced by two smaller token landings at Greenock. These landing parties – led by Lord Cochran and Major Fullarton – re-embarked for Cowal after a few skirmishes with the local militia and before Hamilton's flotilla arrived to entrap them. Thereafter, the rebellion collapsed and its supporters were driven down the length of the Mull of Kintyre, escape from which was sealed by the English warships.

In many ways the maritime aspects of the rebellion set a precedent for future incursions by English naval commanders into Scottish waters. In executing the orders of the English Lord High Admiral, they paid little heed to the disruption they caused to the seaborne trade of the monarch's loyal Scottish subjects. Indeed, by July the area of disruption was greatly extended to 'scour' the Irish and western seas for arms and fugitives. HMS *Drake* was detailed to patrol the Firth of Clyde and North Channel for the rest of the summer while HMS *Mermaid* was detached to cruise the west coast as far as Orkney. During this manhunt the herring fleet at Campbeltown was confined to port and all traders sailing the west coast were stopped and searched.[22]

There was no compensatory windfall for the Clyde shippers as the mopping-up operation was entirely an English affair. Captured rebel prisoners were conveyed on royal yachts to London for trial and execution, and a London-bound English merchantman was chartered to carry south the box containing the quartered body and severed head of the maltster Rumbold for public display.[23] The lack of involvement of Clyde shipping can be surmised from the fact that only one petition, of a petty nature, was made to the Privy Council relating to maritime matters arising from the rebellion.[24]

22   Weir, *Greenock*, pp. 67–9. HMS *Drake* was probably the unnamed frigate that anchored off Largs to receive Lieutenant Lawder escorted by a troop of dragoons that summer: *RPC*, XI, pp. 90, 148 and 304.
23   *RPC*, XI, pp. 132 and 483.
24   That lodged by Laurence Wallace, the Collector at Portpatrick, asking permission to seize a boat used to convey rebels and to restore one known to have been stolen by them: *Ibid.*, p. 165.

THE BENEFITS OF CONFLICT

The next great political upheavals – those arising from the Glorious Revolution – did, in some ways, serve Scottish maritime affairs well. To check Claverhouse's descent from the Highlands required the rapid deployment of men and supplies. During this emergency a large number of the 'great' and 'small' boats of ferry ports of the Forth were kept busy transferring General Mackay's troops across to Fife. Equipping the garrisons in the forts on either side of the Great Glen also employed a smaller number of the large decked vessels of Leith, Pittenweem and Queensferry. They were kept busy conveying a wide range of essentials from cannon and shot to coal.[25]

In the Clyde, troop movements and the need to maintain a seaborne supply to the garrison at Inverlochy (Fort William after 1690) were a boon to local boatmen, merchants and the growing victualling industry. The latter contracts brought the areas south of Ardnamurchan Point within the orbit of the Clyde ports. Likewise, feeding William's military forces in Ulster built up such a momentum that, after 1690, there were times of glut in the storehouses at the main Ulster ports. More lasting was the establishment of a twice-weekly dispatch boat from Portpatrick across to Donaghadee (first mooted in 1678) at the expense of the Post Master General for Scotland.[26]

The distractions of war allowed the Clyde shippers to resume their illegal trading to America in earnest, despite the occasional efforts made by English naval commanders in Scottish waters to enforce the English Navigation Acts. Likewise, after 1690, the number of Irish and English merchantmen using the North Channel to clear in or out of the Atlantic, or heading north-about to avoid the English Channel, also rose rapidly. As a result the outermost anchorages of the Firth of Clyde became well-frequented marshalling areas and storm havens, so much so that, by the end of the War of Spanish Succession (1713), the Privy Council found it necessary to authorise fifteen pilots to operate out of Loch Ryan.[27]

Moreover, the restocking of the livestock slaughtered by the opposing armies and the mass migration of over 20,000 lowland Scots families to the

---

25   NAS, E 28/ 447 series contains lists of claims made by local masters to the General Commissioners of Supply – James Oswald and John Dunlop.

26   This service replaced the old *ad hoc* use of the *Mayflower* sailing out of Irvine: *RPC*, V, p. 286 and X, p. 165.

27   *Ibid.*, X, p. 458. Temporary pilots had previously been hired to guide William's military transports from this haven across the North Channel in early 1690.

Ulster provinces during the 'hungry nineties' greatly increased maritime activity in the Firth of Clyde and Galloway peninsula. This activity was sustained, thereafter, by kinship links and the rise of the great export trade in Ayrshire coal to Ireland.[28]

William's European land campaigns also created a demand for military transports which placed a premium on suitable vessels. William Walkinshaw and Thomas Peters of Port Glasgow contracted their respective vessels – *Unity* (150 tons) and *James* (110 tons) – to carry soldiers to the Flanders campaign at a rate of twelve shillings sterling per month.[29] On the east coast Leith became established as a naval repair and victualling station for the reconstituted Scots Navy and English and Dutch convoy escorts.[30]

SCOTTISH LOSSES TO CONFLICT

Scottish shipping losses to war and disaster during the fifty years prior to the Darien Scheme have been put at upwards of a hundred vessels.[31] Set against this tally, the gains made by the Clyde shippers from the troubles of the 1690s appear to be poor compensation. But this simple comparison does not fully impart the dynamic effect of conflict on setting the stage for future opportunities in trade. To appreciate this it is necessary to compare Scottish losses and levels of wartime disruption with those experienced by her primary rivals – the competing English and Dutch marines.

In the case of the former, the commentator Coke calculated that during the Dutch Wars (1652–4, 1664–7 and 1672–4) the prizes taken by the English marine outnumbered their losses four-to-one. On the other hand Cromwell's ongoing war with Spain (1655–60) incurred very heavy losses to the English marine (estimates range between 1,000 and 1,800 vessels), with few Spanish prizes to compensate.[32] The balance of maritime

---

28   Outward voyages to Ulster from the North Ayrshire and upper Clyde ports leaped from 106 (1688–9) to 355 (1689–90): Smout, 'Overseas Trade of Ayrshire', p.63. In 1696–7 Ulster destinations dominated the passages to and from Port Glasgow (295 of 347 inward and 138 of 196 outwards): NAS, TD 64, Customs searcher's report boo, Port Glasgow, 1696–7.

29   McArthur, *Port Glasgow*, p. 38.

30   There had been much rivalry with Burntisland and South Queensferry for this work: Mowat, *Leith*, pp. 226–7.

31   R. Renwick (ed.), *Extracts from the Records of the Burgh of Glasgow* (Glasgow, 1912), III, pp. xxi and 393.

32   R. Coke, *Discourse of Trade* (1670), p. 27 as quoted by R. Davis, *English Shipping Industry*, footnote to p. 316.

power by the end of that cycle of warfare was, therefore, still in England's favour and so did little to promote the use of Scottish vessels.

This was to change dramatically after 1688. William's and Anne's wars against the French (1689–1713) were harrowing times for the English marine. During the War of the League of Augsburg (1689–97) the English Admiralty estimated that the final number of captured English merchant vessels was around 4,000. The vast majority, Pepys believed, were taken in the last four years of the conflict when the French abandoned fleet actions and unleashed their privateering flotillas. The attrition of the English marine continued unabated during the War of Spanish Succession (1702–13). By 1707 it was estimated that a further 1,146 English vessels had been taken.[33] Equally damaging was the fear of capture in southern home waters as English merchants complained that 'having of late years been such great sufferers by the ill-timing of convoys and want of cruisers … they dare no longer engage the remainder of their estates to carry on their several trades'.[34] Their Dutch counterparts fared little better against the French and sustained very heavy losses until the introduction of the Anglo–Dutch convoy system (1710).

THE TRADING OPPORTUNITIES CREATED BY WAR

This high level of disruption to the operations of rival marines in established markets would appear to have provided an increase in trading opportunities for the Scots – despite the occasional loss of a vessel in the process. The Scots were able to exploit their distance from the principal theatres of war and clear access to the Atlantic to penetrate long-haul markets where survival took precedence over carrying capacity. The southern European trades, once dominated by the Dutch running the English Channel, were the main targets for Scotland's small 'Swedes'-formula armed traders.

The lure of high-value cargoes from these areas was enhanced by: the establishment of an English naval presence at Lisbon (after the 1703 Anglo–Portuguese Accord); the capture of Gibraltar and Minorca (1705

---

33   *Ibid.*, p. 317.
34   *Ibid.* The incidence of cases raised in the Scottish High Court of Admiralty against partners who had failed to honour ransom notes indicates that a number of Scottish vessels were captured. In one example, William Fairfoull, apothecary of Arbroath, was abandoned in a French prison for six months, having been 'persuaded' to go as the hostage: NAS HCAS, AC8/98, Fairfoull v Spink.

THE COMTE DE FORBIN

ADMIRAL THOMAS GORDON, WHEN AN ADMIRAL IN THE RUSSIAN NAVY
(PRIVATE COLLECTION)

and 1708 respectively); and the recruitment of the Tripoli corsairs to the British war effort. In combination, these reduced the risk of capture in southern waters and so revitalised the direct trade from Scotland to the Iberian and Mediterranean markets.

Although the number of Scottish voyages to these areas was initially small, their contribution to the domestic market was significant. Notable was the departure in 1708 of the *Neptune* from the Forth and the *Concord* of Glasgow to Livorno (Italy) for oil, coffee and chianti. Their departure marked the return of Scottish traders, after a lengthy absence, to these once highly dangerous waters.[35] Merchants at the more outlying Scottish ports were also encouraged by the new security situation to send out a venture. One such was the attempted voyage of the *Three Brothers* of Tain from Portmahomack (Dornoch Firth) to Lisbon with barrelled fish. The lack of local expertise in trading so far south is evident in the fact that the Inverness owners contracted an English captain and a French supercargo to ensure success.[36]

After 1707 the Clyde transatlantic shippers were quick to benefit from their newly legalised access to America as a source of cheap vessels and shipbuilding materials. They were also in prime position to exploit the new commodities – naval stores, provisions and rice – that had recently been added (1705) to the list of enumerated goods under the English Navigation Acts. To the fore, however, was the promising long-term market opportunity in the re-export trade in American tobacco. This too can partly be attributed to the War of Spanish Succession, for as British privateers cut off the French supply from her West Indian colonies, so French cruisers made good the loss with captured English Virginian tobacco. After the end of hostilities the French consumer's taste for this lighter leaf remained entrenched. This new market opportunity was seized upon by the merchant classes of Scotland who now had a legitimate right of access and a geographic advantage to exploit.

The dispatch of the sons of lairds to the colonies as British officers

---

35   The *Neptune* was captured off the Barbary Coast in April 1708, but reappears trading in November 1714. It must be presumed that she was recaptured or released or (more likely) replaced by a namesake: GCA, Shawfield MSS, 2/397, 332, 373 and 365.
36   Inverness Burgh Records, MSS CTI/IB 36/1: Contract between James Dunbar and William Fraser and factors to Captain Plowden owner. It was a troubled venture: William Tolmie of Fortrose appears to have bought out Plowden before the *Three Brothers* sailed. At sea she experienced heavy weather and had to put back into Greenock with a bad leak. There the vessel was arrested for outstanding debts against Plowden, prompting a number of the crew to desert: NAS, HCAS, AC 10/69, Petition by Thomas Tolmie.

during the war greatly strengthened trading links, no more so than in St Kitts where Colonel William Macdowall and Major James Milliken concluded their tour of duty by marrying the widow and daughter of the greatest plantation owner in the island. Returning to Scotland as rich men in the late 1720s, they set up a direct trade in West Indian sugar to Port Glasgow that effectively cut out the Bristol middlemen. In doing so, they laid the foundation for the great West Indian trading house of Alexander Houston & Co.[37]

THE DEFENCE OF SCOTTISH
WATERS AND THE CONVOY SYSTEM

Complementing this increase in trading opportunities abroad was a substantial improvement of security within home waters during the last years of the War of Spanish Succession. After the Union, the strategic planning of the seaward defence of North Britain rested with the Lords of the Admiralty sitting in London. Their acquisition of Scottish maritime sovereignty cleared the way for a major reorganisation of naval coastal defences. Two vessels of the 'old' Scots Navy – *Royal William* and *Royal Mary* – were absorbed into the British Navy and diplomatically renamed HMS *Glasgow* and HMS *Edinburgh* respectively. The third, the smaller sixth-rater Clyde escort HMS *Dumbarton Castle,* kept her name but served only a very short term under the new establishment before she was captured off Waterford after a spirited defence of her convoy in April 1708.[38] Of the Scottish commanders, only the great opportunist, Captain Thomas Gordon, was commissioned into the British Navy and given command of HMS *Leopard* (50 guns), then attached to Byng's squadron.[39]

The Earl of Nottingham's strategy, as Lord High Admiral of Great Britain, to bring the war to an end was to cut off the vital supplies to

37   G. Eyre-Todd, *History of Glasgow* (Glasgow, 1934), III, p. 150.
38   She was taken by a Brest privateer twice her size – an ex-Royal Navy fourth-rater *Jersey* (42 guns / 456 men) – which serves to illustrate the extensive use of hired naval craft by French privateers raiding the Irish Sea and St. George's Channel at this time. In this context a contemporary's description of the Old Scots Navy as 'all very small and of little importance' seems valid: Clowes, *Royal Navy*, p. 251.
39   Gordon's career – his rise from master of the *Margaret* of Aberdeen to Rear Admiral of the Russian Navy, including his collusion with Scottish Jacobites – occupies substantial sections of Grant, *Old Scots Navy*. Of the other captains, James Hamilton died in the West Indies in December 1709 while the gallant Matthew Campbell was held prisoner at St. Malo, and later Dinan, until his exchange in the same year: *Ibid.*, pp. 356–7.

France hitherto delivered in vast quantities from the holds of prizes brought in by her privateers. To this end an elaborate convoy system was developed to cover all the major sea-lanes of the British Isles.

In 1708, while these plans were still being finalised, the French attempted a belated major military landing in the Forth, in the hope of diverting men and resources from the victorious Marlborough on the French border. The expedition involved ten thousand soldiers conveyed, along with James in person, by a squadron of five ships-of-the-line and three privateering frigates under the overall command of Forbin, the one-time privateering commodore. The scheme, which had the potential to alter the course of European history, was thwarted as much by Forbin's bad navigation and lack of resolve as by the size of Byng's squadron sent north to intercept him. The only person to cover himself in glory was Thomas Gordon, who had the great good fortune to engage and capture, off Montrose, the straggling French frigate *Salisbury*.[40]

That same year (1708) the Cruiser & Convoy Act was passed. Forty-three cruisers were withdrawn from the fleet to act as convoy escorts. Twelve were allocated to protect North Britain – nine on the east coast and three on the west coast. Scapa Flow, Aberdeen Bay and the Firths of Clyde, Forth and Cromarty became designated marshalling areas.[41] By agreement, units of the Dutch Navy were invited to operate in Scottish waters as escorts for the whaling fleets and the North Sea convoys. This was the basic blueprint for the defence of British trade until 1775. It must be said in passing that the deployment of such naval resources would have been quite beyond the means of an independent Scotland close to bankruptcy after the failure of the Darien Scheme.

The Cruiser & Convoy Act was not, however, immediately implemented, and in the interim the Convention of Royal Burghs continued to petition, unsuccessfully, for naval guard ships for the Forth, Clyde and Orkney. The full convoy system was finally inaugurated in October 1710 and proved effective, although ponderous, in holding the privateering threat in check during the last years of the war. The northern coastal convoy system involved shepherding some forty vessels at a time between the marshalling areas. Escorts arriving and departing from these

40 *Ibid.*, p. 200. The *Salisbury* was a British warship previously taken by the French and so its recapture ensured Gordon's promotion. Details of the invasion attempt are available in J.S. Gibson, *Playing the Scottish Card: the Franco–Jacobite Invasion of 1708* (Edinburgh, 1988).

41 The contemporary newspapers report shipping movements from these areas from this time onwards.

anchorages usually did so with the knowledge and approval of the provost of the head port. From there, seasonal convoys set out to destinations as far afield as Archangel, the Baltic and the Atlantic (west of Kinsale).[42]

A measure of their success is the final tally of the English marine losses for the War of Spanish Succession. These have been estimated as low as 2,000 vessels by the time hostilities were suspended in late 1712. Such losses were more than compensated for by the 2,200 prizes taken by mainly English privateers.[43] All the indications are that Scottish losses and gains to warfare during this period were very low in comparison and certainly did not exceed double figures.[44]

The principal convoy escorts on the northern stations were all naval sixth-raters. While HMS *Flamborough, Glasgow* and *Strumbolo* plied the sea-lanes between Newcastle and Leith, HMS *Seaforth's Prize, Queensborough* and *Aldborough* did their duty from the Clyde to Kinsale.[45] The weak link in the chain was the coast between Leith and Orkney that was patrolled by the solitary HMS *Mermaid* – when not acting as escort to the Holland convoy out of the Forth.

JACOBITE-COMMANDED PRIVATEERS
IN SCOTTISH WATERS

The northern convoy system was never really tested as the disgrace of Forbin and the absence of the gravely ill Duguay-Trouin terminated the operations of the larger French privateer flotillas in the North Sea after 1708.[46] The next generation of enemy privateers, which first appeared in substantial numbers during the spring of 1711, consisted of much smaller vessels and posed no real threat to the naval escorts.

They were, however, capable of widespread disruption to local shipping activity in between the passing of convoys, especially along the

---

42   Smout holds the opinion that Scots rarely accepted or solicited convoy from English ships: *Scottish Trade*, p. 67. This may have been the situation prior to 1710, given the previous history of rough handling and pressing seamen, but attitudes on both sides would appear to have changed substantially after 1710. The shipping reports from the lowland newspapers, quoted hereafter, testify to the success of the convoy system.

43   Davis, *English Shipping*, p. 317.

44   This estimate is based primarily on contemporary newspaper reports quoted in this chapter.

45   P. Crowhurst, *The Defence of British Trade* (London, 1977), pp. 349–351. HMS *Flamborough* replaced the escort HMS *Greyhound* which was wrecked on the east coast.

46   Forbin was banished to internal exile after his failure to land James in the Forth in 1708.

unguarded stretches of the North-East coast. Their tactic was to hover in pairs off the Fife, Aberdeenshire and Orkney ports, bringing local fishing and coastal traffic to a halt for weeks at a time.[47] Even in the well-patrolled firths small enemy privateers – as often as not commanded by zealous Scottish Jacobites based in Calais – were capable of penetrating the naval screen to spread panic in the coastal communities. Those that infested the Forth were particularly audacious, taking vessels in sight of Leith. Two even took the time to dispatch a shore party to the Isle of May to plunder the lighthouse.[48]

In the long term, however, the escorts and guard ships won the war of attrition as they invariably captured those raiders that lingered too long in Scottish waters. In the space of a few weeks HMS *Mermaid* took the Calais privateer *Pontchartrain* off Buchan Ness (along with her most recent prize *Virginia Merchant* of Aberdeen) and later caught up with her consort, *Favourit Carrel*.[49] The honour of capturing the most daring and persistent privateer, *Agrippa*, which had 'taken many prizes on the coast for several years', fell to HMS *Flamborough*.[50]

The first appearance on the west coast of a determined enemy cruiser was in June 1711. The reports on this particular incursion offer interesting insights into the nature of marine warfare at this time, as well as illustrating the vulnerability of the outlying coastal communities to enemy raiders. The intruder – the St. Malo privateer *Desmarell* (4 guns/70 men) – was commanded by a Scots renegade by the name of Smith. He first entered the Clyde from the North Channel in pursuit of a homeward-bound Rotterdam vessel heading north-about Scotland from Lisbon. The Dutchman sought safety in Loch Ryan where her crew fled ashore to join up with the male population of the town of Stranraer to repel the invader. This combined force (around one hundred men) was, however, unable to stop the long boat from the privateer putting aboard a prize crew and making off with the merchantman.

47   *Scots Courant*, 20, 21, 27 March; 2, 9, 13, 24 April; 4, 7, 11, 16, 23 May; 2, 8 June, 3, 8, 24 September; 6 October and 5 November 1711.

48   *Ibid.*, 14 May 1711. A year later a small Calais privateer carried off the sheep from the Isle of May after landing two Aberdonians they had been holding for ransom: Clark, *Aberdeen*, pp. 112–3.

49   NAS, HCAS, AC 8/128 and 131, Applications by Captain Collier to have them declared prize.

50   The *Agrippa* was cornered off the Bass Rock; NAS, HCAS, AC8/129, application by Captain Howard to have her declared prize. HMS *Strumbolo* was also at the scene of the capture, having just taken a smaller privateer in the same area.

The following month Smith was back in the same sea loch, this time chasing the galley *Expedition* of Port Glasgow on her outward passage to Belfast and the West Indies. On this occasion his prize crew succeeded only in running their new charge onto the Skar rocks at high tide. Unable to get her off, Smith threatened to burn her to the waterline unless her master agreed to a ransom of £300. A week later, however, the security of the Galloway peninsula and the Firth of Clyde was restored when the *Desmarell* was captured by an armed packet – *Dolphin* of Glasgow (35 tons/10 guns/60 men) – on her run to Belfast with dispatches.[51] The fact that Smith was caught careening the *Desmarell* on Sanda Island, off Campbeltown, points to how far he had assumed that the North Channel was unpatrolled at that particular time.

The public indignation these renegade captains inspired, on both sides of the Border, was evident from the treason trials and public executions to which they were subjected. The 'pirate' Alexander Dalziel, the notorious Scottish commander of the privateer *Agrippa*, serves as an example. After his capture in the Forth he was not brought before the Scottish High Court of Admiralty on a charge of piracy but sent in chains to the Old Bailey for trial under the highly contentious Treason Act of 1708.[52] He was subsequently publicly executed (1713) in London, even though hostilities had effectively ceased the previous year and most prisoners-of-war had been exchanged.[53]

The scares of 1711 at the outlying ports were the exception rather than the rule. Under the protection of the convoy system Scottish merchantmen engaging in coastal and overseas trading out of the major ports flourished. During those first years of Anglo–Dutch naval collaboration, at least five Clyde vessels availed themselves of escort protection to trade to Archangel, then Russia's sole entrepôt prior to the opening of St. Petersburg in 1714.[54]

---

51   *Scots Courant*, 2 June, 13 and 17 August 1711. That Smith was cleaning his hull would indicate that he had been cruising for some considerable time and did not expect to encounter a naval unit in these waters. NAS, HCAS, AC8/130, application by Captain Russell to have her declared prize. Smith may have been the Aberdonian Jacobite, Alexander Smith, who was prosecuted in December 1693 by the Lord Advocate for hiring out a French privateer.

52   This Act, passed after the failed 1708 invasion, required only one witness to convict a Jacobite and caused uproar in Scotland as it was seen as usurping Scots Law (which had required two witnesses) as guaranteed by the Act of Union.

53   *Scots Post Boy*, 26 June 1712.

54   Convoy reports: *Scots Courant*, 10 March 1711 and 9 June 1712. The vessels were the *Janie*, the galley *Expedient* and *Vigilant* of Port Glasgow and the *James* and *Hope* of Greenock. The *Janie* was subsequently wrecked though her cargo was salvaged by the *James. Ibid.*, 24 April 1711.

THE REBELLION OF 1715

After the Treaty of Utrecht (1713) the peace with France held firm for nearly two decades and so political conditions were generally favourable for Scottish overseas traders. This accord was the product of diplomatic moves undertaken on the death of Queen Anne to end Britain's isolation in Europe and to secure international recognition of the Hanoverian Succession. The moment for reconciliation came when Philip V of Spain challenged the legitimacy of the Regent Orléans' administration after the death of Louis XIV (September 1715). Through this mutual need for recognition, the governments of France and Britain made their peace. In the process James in exile lost his principal backer at a time when the benefits of the Union had eroded support for his cause in lowland Scotland.

In such a changing political climate the 1715 Rebellion in the North was undertaken without French naval support or any hope of a seaborne military invasion. Furthermore, Byng's squadron in the English Channel ensured that the local Jacobites did not receive arms or supplies covertly out of the French ports in contravention of the new Barrier Treaty. Mar's rising in the North-East for the Old Pretender was, therefore, destined to be a localised land campaign whose only hope of success was a decisive and quick victory.

Following the inconclusive Battle of Sheriffmuir, fought on the same day as the surrender of the English Jacobite host at Preston, the cause was lost. Government forces led by the Duke of Argyll recovered the Fife ports in December, allowing Dutch reinforcements to be landed in time to join his march north. When James was finally landed at Peterhead from a French fishing boat (2 January 1716), his adherents had already scattered. He spared them further retribution by reboarding, with Mar, the *Forerunner* at Montrose for France a month later.[55]

The short duration of this disastrous episode hardly allowed time for any major naval operations to get underway in Scottish waters or for the disruption to seaborne trade to spread beyond the North-East coast. In the months following James's departure, a few belated seizures were made off this coast by the newly dispatched cruisers HMS *Deal Castle* and *Royal Ann*, galley.[56] Of much greater consequence to Scottish maritime affairs was the

---

55 Aldridge, 'Jacobitism', p. 87.
56 They were petty affairs involving the arrest of three small local vessels for allegedly carrying the goods of the known rebel, Henry Crawford of Crail: NAS, HCAS AC 9/559 and 565 Willis v Short. HMS *Deal Castle* had recently served as an escort with *Sheerness* and *Penzance* on the Leith – London route.

central government's decision to strip the ordnance from the fortifications raised at a number of the east-coast ports during the emergency. This was in order to deny any future Jacobite uprisings a fortified harbour from which to defy the Royal Navy.

As part of the 'Triple Alliance' (concluded in 1717 by Britain, France and the Austrian Empire) the Regent Orléans was obliged to banish James, first to the papal city of Avignon, and finally to Italy. The Regent also found it expedient to finally implement the full terms of the Treaty of Utrecht and the Barrier Treaty (signed 1713). These required France to demolish the near-impregnable defences and sluices of Dunkirk and the neighbouring Fort Mardyck. The Dunkirk privateering fraternity, which had proved such a potent force during the *guerre de course* era, was thereby scattered south to St. Malo and Morlaix and north to the warring ports of the Baltic.

MILITARISM IN NORTHERN EUROPE

During the period 1717–31 the spirit of Anglo–French accord was largely maintained, despite the schemes of the residual Jacobite element at the French court. The mutual need was to preserve the Alliance against the threats brewing in both northern and southern European waters. In the Baltic the clash of the vaulting ambitions of the militaristic 'hero kings' – Charles XII of Sweden and Czar Peter of Russia – sparked the Great Northern War (1700–21) which involved most of the states in the Baltic region and their continental allies. In the Mediterranean the collision of Austrian and Spanish ambitions over Sicily threatened to ensnare British interests in that sea area.

The impact of these conflicts on Scottish overseas trade to the contested regions was both immediate and direct. Less apparent, however, was their influence in diverting Scottish entrepreneurial energies away from the traditional European north–south trades and towards the transatlantic colonial trades.

The crisis years were 1715–20 when Sweden moved against British interests in the Baltic. This was in retaliation for Britain's part in the recruitment of Holland into, what was now the 'Quadruple Alliance'. As a mark of his contempt for the House of Hanover, Charles XII granted refuge to prominent Jacobites from the failed 'Fifteen Rebellion, notably in the Courland area of the Baltic. He then raised the general state of tension at sea by passing the Ordnance of Privateer (1715). This set in place the option of unleashing Swedish privateers on British vessels found trading in the Baltic, without formally declaring war. Moreover, after his invasion of Norway (1718), his Navy had access to North Sea bases from which to raid the east coast of Britain.

As it happened, most of his naval forces were committed to the Eastern Baltic. This left only a few ill-equipped privateers to prosecute the war in the west. A small number of the Gothenburg-based privateers were manned by motivated ex-Dunkirkers and Scottish Jacobites – such as John Norcross. They managed to take only a few passing Scottish vessels before the death of Charles XII halted all offensive action.[57]

In Mediterranean waters, Britain's relations with Spain reached a state of open hostility after Byng's total destruction of the Spanish fleet off Cape Passaro (July 1718). This act of war brought instant retaliation from the Spanish Prime Minister Alberoni who ordered the seizure of all British merchantmen found in Spanish ports. Furthermore, to take the war to Britain, a grand scheme was hatched with a faction within the Swedish court. This proposed a Spanish-led invasion of England in tandem with a Swedish descent on the eastern seaboard of Scotland from the Norwegian coast. To carry out this plan Ormonde's Irish Jacobites, waiting in northern Spain, were to be escorted by elements of the Spanish navy. At the same time, three Swedish men-of-war were to be covertly slipped into a French port to convey the Old Pretender.[58]

This master plan failed to materialise. Charles XII was by then militarily over-committed in the Eastlands and lacked the naval power to deliver an invasion force from Norway. The Swedish warships assigned to convey James from France were consequently stopped from sailing. In the south the 'Second Spanish Armada' – five men-of-war and twenty-two transport – was dispersed by violent storms off Cape Finisterre and never reached Ormonde's Jacobites waiting at Corunna.[59]

---

57 Details of Scottish renegades at Gothenburg are available in A. F. Steuart, 'Sweden and the Jacobites, 1719–20', *Scottish Historical Review*, XXIII, pp.111–127. One Scottish vessel taken in Gothenburg was under the command of David Pershaw, one-time privateer captain employed by Thomas Gordon. He exploited the moves towards peace to sell his cargo of herring, before it was condemned, to the Swedish government: NAS, HCAS AC 9/926 Maisters v Gordon.

58 The arrival of the latter was under pretence of calling in while sailing south to found a Swedish colony on the pirate haven of St Mary's Isle (Madagascar): Aldridge, 'Jacobitism', pp. 87–8.

59 *Cambridge Modern History*, VI, pp. 104–106.

Although the grand invasion scheme had collapsed, a small Spanish flotilla of two frigates departed from Paajes with Don Pedro de Castor's regiment of three hundred men on board. Avoiding the British naval detachment of five frigates lying in wait for them off the Scilly Isles, they reached Hebridean waters. There they rendezvous'd with a small Jacobite party led by the Earl Marischal. This group of exiles had earlier been clandestinely landed direct from France and immediately squabbled with the Spanish commanders over who held the superior commission. The captains of the two Spanish frigates quit Scottish waters after landing their charges on the shores of Loch Duich. Their abrupt and unscheduled departure provided the pursuing British warships – HMS *Worcester, Enterprise* and *Flamborough* – with the prefect cover to slip close inshore. Flying the Spanish flag, they caught the cheering Spanish encampment at Eilean Donan Castle wholly unprepared for the murderous bombardment that followed.

Of the original landing party, 274 Spanish soldiers were eventually rounded up by Major General Wightman in Glen Shiel and marched to London, from there they were immediately repatriated to Spain under a Swiss guard, thereby ending what had become more of a diplomatic embarrassment than a threat to the British Government.[60] Soon afterwards the Swedes also withdrew their direct support of the Jacobite cause. This decision was hastened by the appearance off Stockholm of Sir John Norris's squadron, in company with a Dutch fleet. The newly installed King of Sweden had little choice but to make his peace with Britain.

French-inspired invasion scares, however, continued to interrupt the activities of Scottish traders abroad. In 1719, the ever-vigilant British Ambassador to the French court – the Earl of Stair – sent a stream of alarmist reports gathered by his spy network. They warned of military preparations for yet another projected Jacobite landing. As a precaution a British naval squadron was discreetly fitted out so as not to jeopardise Anglo–French relations.[61] The result of this continuing turmoil was that Scottish traders found in the English Channel were stopped and searched by both British and French men-of-war. Likewise, wary French officials resorted to obstructive and lengthy administrative procedures to discourage their presence in French ports.

---

60   *Edinburgh Evening Chronicle*, 23 June 1719.
61   The second Earl of Stair, son of the Lord Advocate, was recalled the following year. An interesting example of French diplomatic caution at this time was the arrest of the renegade Norcross on his arrival at a French port in 1717 with an Inverness-owned vessel as prize. His Swedish privateer and crew were allowed to sail home to Gothenburg but he was handed over to the English authorities: Wilkins, *Northern Shores*, p. 26.

Table 5.2. Passages made by Scottish masters through the Danish Sound, 1685–1724

Source: Extracted from the *Danish Sound Tolls* database compiled by H.C. Johansen (Odense Universitet, Denmark)

Peacetime trading conditions in the Mediterranean were finally stabilised when Spain accepted the terms of the Alliance and acknowledged the Hanoverian Succession (1720). As Spain was the last major financial backer of the Old Pretender, her withdrawal of support meant that Jacobitism became a dormant force in British and European politics for the next two decades.

THE OVERALL IMPACT OF WAR, 1685–1724

The effect of these wars and security scares on the general level of Scottish maritime activity in the Baltic trades is evident from the Danish Sound Toll Records. This continuous series of data recorded all passages 'outwards' (going west) and all passages 'inwards' (going east) through the Sound by the domicile of the master.[62] The sharpest decline in passages made by Scottish masters was during the war years of the 1690s, with only eight voyaging to the Baltic in 1694. After the conclusion of the War of the League of Augsburg (1697), there was a rapid recovery that lasted until the outbreak of the War of Spanish Succession (1702–1713).

With the resumption of the French *guerre de course* in the North Sea, the number of passages made by Scottish masters was again adversely affected. By 1710, however, the success of Anglo–Dutch naval collaboration encouraged an upsurge in their number. The next substantial dip in passage numbers was during the 1715–19 security crisis in the Baltic commencing with the Swedish Ordnance of Privateer. When open hostilities finally broke out at sea, during the short-lived War of the Quadruple Alliance (1718–20), it was largely contained within the Baltic. It became a naval affair involving a few punitive Anglo–Dutch naval actions against the Swedes.[63]

During the 1690s, when all factors seemed to conspire against the Scottish interest at home and abroad, as few as eight per cent of all

---

62   The occasional small mismatch in any given year is probably due to a few vessels being caught ice-bound late in the season or captured/sold/wrecked/detained for repair in the Baltic. The limitations of this source of shipping data are well known: primarily that they do not specify the name of the vessel, its tonnage or home port. As the domicile of the Scottish master was usually that of the home port of vessel during this early period, the data – listed in Table 5.2 – can be held to display the levels of Scottish shipping activity to the Baltic during the years of war and peace.

63   A paltry ninety-eight British vessels took out a letter of marque against the Swedes. The only Scottish vessel was the Dunbar whaler – *Happy Janet* (200 tons): PRO, HCA 26, commission 9 July 1719.

Table 5.3. Passages made in and out of the Baltic by English and Scottish masters, 1685–1724
Source: Danish Sound Tolls[64]

passages made by British masters were undertaken by Scottish-domiciled masters. The recovery of their normal share of the peacetime carrying trade (*c*.27%) followed the cessation of hostilities in 1698.

By way of contrast, during the early years of the War of Spanish Succession – when the English marine suffered their heaviest losses – the Scottish masters increased their share of British-originating passages from thirty-eight per cent (in the first year of the war) to sixty-four per cent by 1709. By 1710, however, the improvement in the security situation, with the introduction of the Anglo–Dutch convoy system, brought a strong recovery in English and Dutch shipping activity in the North Sea. As a consequence the Scottish share of the conveyance of British trade halved to a more typical twenty-nine per cent.

Overall, the ups-and-downs in the number of passages made by Scottish masters followed those of their English and Dutch rivals. As might be expected, the number of passages leapt during the years of peace and contracted in wartime in a direct response to the threat of capture. During the 1715–20 crisis in the Baltic the combined number of passages made by British and Dutch masters slumped to well under half the annual peacetime number as they reacted to the Swedish threat.

With the conclusion of the Great Northern War the number of voyages made by the Anglo–Dutch masters in the Baltic trade gradually recovered, reaching pre-war levels in 1722.[65] Numbers advanced rapidly thereafter, more than doubling by 1725. In competitive peacetime conditions the Scottish masters accounted for between twenty and thirty per cent of all passages made by British-domiciled masters, who were, in turn, beginning to erode the Dutch dominance of the Baltic trade from 1712 onwards.

'ROUND-ABOUT' TRADING IN EUROPEAN WATERS

The other highly significant change, evident from the Danish Sound Toll Records, was the advent of regular 'triangular' and 'round-about' trading in European waters by Scottish masters after the Union. Prior to 1707, Scottish vessels trading to the Baltic – the vast majority from the Forth and

---

64   The maximum number of Scottish vessels involved can be calculated by dividing by two the number of Scottish passages. As quite a number of masters made three or more voyages per year, this figure in peacetime must be considered high.

65   See Table 5.4.

the North-East ports – had been effectively excluded from working out of the English ports by the levy of double duty as 'foreign vessels'. Their normal sailing pattern was, therefore, to run directly from Scotland to the Baltic and back, with an occasional foray to a Continental staple port.

After 1707, Scottish traders – as full members of the British mercantilist system – began to switch their attention to serving the English market and those of her allies, principally Portugal. Such unrestricted access presented Scottish owners and masters with their first real opportunity to emulate the Dutch as contracted carriers to other nationals. It also allowed the Scots to 'trade-up' a series of cargoes on their own account around Europe, thereby breaking free from the historic limitations of bilateral trading in Scottish commodities of low value to the European market.

This trend first gathered, at times faltering, momentum with the improvement in security after 1710. The conclusion of the War of Spanish Succession (effectively 1712) produced a short-lived surge in the number of secondary destinations before the deterioration in relations with Sweden again deterred Scottish traders from entering the Baltic. The end of the Great Northern War (1720) did not, however, signal a quick return to normal trading levels. The spread of pestilence during the next two years – through Portugal and France into the Eastlands – greatly hindered the free movement of vessels. A number of Scottish masters unilaterally cancelled their intended passages to the stricken areas, much to the displeasure of the charter party.[66] By January 1722, the Swedish authorities were demanding passports and certificates of health from all British ships trading in their area. Similarly, all vessels arriving in Scottish waters from the affected regions were required to air their cargo as part of their forty-day quarantine.[67]

Around the same time Scottish masters heading south-about – through the English Channel – to French or Portuguese ports faced the additional hazard of capture from three Algerine corsairs. These raiders had exploited the distractions of the Great Northern War to venture beyond the Bay of Biscay in search of prey. This was a major breach of security that caused general havoc in the southern approaches to the English Channel for nearly

66   *Edinburgh Evening Chronicle*, 17 February 1721. An example of litigation arising from cancellation of a voyage due to fears of plague was that raised by the Edinburgh merchant Thomas Mitchell against James Blair, master of the 40-ton *Margaret* of South Queensferry. Blair should have delivered coal to Bordeaux and taken on a cargo of wine from Mitchell's factor, Robert Gordon: NAS HCAS, AC 9/840.
67   *Edinburgh Evening Chronicle*, 19 January 1722.

Table 5.4. Point of departure of Scottish masters eastwards through the Danish Sound, 1685–1724

Year	Denmark	Sweden	Norway	Scotland	England	Holland	France	Portugal	other
1685		1	3	43			1	2	
1686			3	45			1	1	
1687			1	48			5		
1688				60	1		4		1
1689				36					
1690				18		1			
1691				37					
1692				39	1				
1693				15		3			
1694				8					
1695				13					
1696				22					
1697				19					
1698				58		1	1		
1699		1		55		1	3	2	
1700				71		1	1		1
1701			1	49	1		3		
1702				45	1				
1703				41					
1704				43					
1705				46					
1706				44					
1707		2	1	60					
1708			1	35		1			
1709				29		1			
1710			1	32	2	1			
1711			4	62	1				
1712			10	64		1			
1713		1	7	65	5	1	11	2	
1714		3	4	61	14	2	1	1	
1715		3		59	3		3		
1716		1		40	4		2		
1717	1			45	1	1	1	1	
1718			1	39	2			1	
1719			4	64	8				
1720	1	3	11	57	4	1		6	
1721		3	2	88	3		1	1	
1722				83	2				
1723		1		58	8		1	2	2
1724		3	1	61	9	1	1		3

Source: *Danish Sound Tolls.* War years are in bold.

two years: so much so that the situation was not fully retrieved until direct naval action was taken against their North African bases.[68] It was not until the mid-1720's that the hectic domestic conditions and turbulent European affairs of the preceding three decades finally gave way to a more settled period in seaborne trade.

The new scale of the involvement of Scottish vessels in round-about trading on the European north–south routes can be gathered from the legal disputes that arose between owners and masters. In 1725 Alexander Simpson – the tenant of Balbethie and one-sixth owner of the *Alexander* of Pittenween – sued his master for his share of the profits on no less than thirty passages made by this vessel to Danzig, Hamburg, Norway, France and Lisbon.[69] Around the same time, James Murray of Edinburgh pursued his captain for neglect of his charge – *James* of Leith. During her sixteen-month round-about trading venture she had sailed from; Leith to Lisbon, the Scilly Isles, Cadiz, back to the Scilly Isles, Alicante, Ostend, Bimmell and, finally, back to Leith.[70]

In all such instances the ability to record the earnings generated by these intermediate overseas passages wholly eluded the 'political arithmetick' of the Customs Service of the day. As a consequence this dynamic multilateral trading activity received no attention from statistical compilers then and little, indeed, since. To this omission must be added the unrecorded and vast coastal trade to England and Wales, and smuggling. The inescapable conclusion is that the detailed documentation of bilateral foreign-going trades – such as in tobacco – hold an over-inflated position in Scotland's absurd 'ballance of trade' figures for the eighteenth century. These trade statistics by *official values* are, at best, an indicator of the legally declared bilateral overseas trade of the nation.

THE COLONIAL TRADES

Leading the fitful recovery during the 1720s – which slowly lifted both England and Scotland out of the economic doldrums – was the upturn in trading in colonial commodities. The major opportunities fell to the west-

---

68   First attacks reported *Ibid.*, 23 July 1719. The Algerine privateer *White Horse*, Solomon Ryce, took (and later released) four Scottish vessels returning from Bordeaux – *Mary* of Eyemouth, *James & Rachel*, galley *Edinburgh* and *May* of Leith: NAS, HCAS, AC 9/985.

69   *Ibid.*, AC 9/882 Simpson v Donaldson.

70   *Ibid.*, AC 9/882 and 9/6397.

coast shippers to exploit their north-westerly location in the expanding Atlantic economy and the Irish market.

After the conclusion of hostilities with France, the seemingly ever-expanding European market for tobacco created a short-lived boom that attracted numerous ventures to the Chesapeake from the Atlantic-facing ports of Britain: so much so that by 1721 the area was experiencing a glut of shipping. The local commentator Robert Carter reported 'a swarm of ships in all our rivers' and counted some forty vessels in both the Rappahannock and York Rivers. As the supply of available tobacco was insufficient to provide all with cargoes, the freight charges tumbled from a wartime peak of £13 to £8 per ton that year.[71]

In the long term such narrowing profit margins would benefit the lower running cost Scottish traders, by allowing them to squeeze out many of their English rivals. In the short term, however, the chartered English hull remained a necessary outlay in the Clyde's rise in an uncertain market.

THE UPPER CLYDE PORTS, 1721-2

The extent of chartering during this formative period – in the absence of almost all Customs registers and port books – can best be gathered from contemporary newspapers and civil actions brought before the Scottish Admiralty Courts.

With the former source, the isolated and rare short run of 'shipping intelligence' published in the *Edinburgh Evening Courant* – January 1721 until October 1722 – gives a fairly clear view of the composition of the foreign-going fleets working the upper Clyde ports.[72] This was at a time when the Clyde ports were on the threshold of challenging the domination of the English ports in the carrying trade of key colonial commodities: a challenge that galvanised the English tobacco lobby into launching its first vitriolic parliamentary campaign against Scottish traders and their sharp practices.

During that twenty-one-month period, the *Courant*'s Greenock correspondent logged some fifty reports of foreign-going voyages to and from the upper Clyde ports. Of the thirty-nine arrivals, seventeen vessels conveyed tobacco (sixteen from Virginia and one from Maryland). The continuing reliance on the chartered hull is evident in that only seven

---

71 A.P. Middleton, *The Tobacco Coast* (Maryland, 1989), p. 323.
72 The reports indicate that the Atlantic-going passages from the Clyde, though firmly established, had hardly increased in number or frequency of voyages since the post-Union year of 1711.

GLASGOW, C.1720 (FROM SLEZER'S *THEATRUM SCOTIAE*)

carriers were Clyde-owned. The outstanding ten belonged to Whitehaven (8), Londonderry (1) and Maryland (1).

The direct importing of sugar from the West Indies, on the other hand, was marginally more in the hands of the Port Glasgow shippers, with six out of the nine incoming cargoes carried in Clyde-owned vessels. A few of these (possibly only two) were returning from the final leg of the triangular slave trade. The safe arrival of the *Hanover* of Port Glasgow (60 tons) from St. Kitts, with less than twenty tons of sugar on board, marked the end of a bungled, bloody and loss-making slaving voyage. Her sister ship – *Loyalty* of Port Glasgow – had earlier aborted her planned voyage from Guinea to Virginia after being boarded, ransacked and four of the crew kidnapped for ransom by local pirates.[73] The cumulative effect of such heavy losses – compounded by a blatant lack of expertise and mounting antagonism from the Royal Africa Company – killed off any further involvement of Clyde vessels in slaving in preference to the tobacco trade.

The Greenock agent's reports of outward foreign-going passages, for reasons that are not immediately apparent, numbered only eleven.[74] Of significance was the clearance of the *Christian* of Fort William for Virginia underlining the ability of the more remote and undeveloped ports to support a major venture now and then. Also reported was the advertising for cargo and passengers, weeks in advance of its departure, for the brig *Jean & Mary* of Boston on her regular homeward passages from Greenock. Finally there was the passage by the galley *Houston* of Glasgow to Holland and Archangel with tobacco. The choice of the last destination was to avoid clashing with the Russia Company of London which was then vigorously defending its monopoly at the more accessible port of St. Petersburg. The Greenock agent also noted the direct importing of Scandinavian iron and deals to the Firth of Clyde (first documented in the 1690s) in vessels returning home from Northern Europe.

SHIP AND CARGO MANAGEMENT

It was during the 1720–40 period that the 'supercargo' gave way to the 'resident factor' mode of trading abroad. On regular short-haul trades the

73   The losses incurred on the *Hanover* were the subject of a lengthy legal action: NAS, HCAS, AC 9/1042, Horseburgh v Bogle. Those of the *Loyalty* of Glasgow are noted in *Ibid.*, AC 9/718, Daniel v Graham.
74   Possibly because the first outward port of call was within the British Isles, e.g. the *Loyalty* called at Liverpool before sailing for the Guinea Coast.

master, as sole or part owner of the vessel, had complete authority over his charge and cargo and often traded on his own account as well as those of his partners. When contracted by a third party, however, or venturing to new markets, the time-honoured way was for a supercargo – experienced in dealing with matters pertaining to the disposal and acquisition of cargoes at foreign ports – to take over the business role. This left the safe navigation and handling of the vessel to the captain.

Under the old system, the business competence and integrity of the supercargo often decided the ultimate profitability of the voyage. He decided the next port-of-call and duration of stay. In the case of the unwarranted six-month detention of the *Squirrell* in the worm-infested waters of St. Kitts (1722–3), the owners charged the supercargo – rather than the master – with gross mismanagement of the vessel's safety.[75]

As to the profitable purchase and disposal of the cargo, the voyage of the *Christian* of Leith (70 tons) to Newfoundland (1726–7) with a small cargo of thirty-two barrels of biscuits is a well-documented example of the shortcomings of this trading system. The journal of the novice supercargo – Edward Burd junior – records a master and crew attempting their first northern transatlantic passage and his own ineptitude in dealing with wily Newfoundland fishermen.[76] Their subsequent passage to Barcelona to trade their dried Newfoundland cod for Spanish brandy was managed little better.[77]

This venture was instigated by Claud Johnson – the most senior and energetic Scottish merchant in London – in the depths of a depression. His choice of destination is all the more interesting as both locally and Icelandic-caught white fish was then readily available and regularly exported directly from Scotland to Catholic Southern Europe.[78] It may well be that the age-old problem of finding an adequate profit from the

75   NAS, HCAS, AC 9/1022, Clark v Inglis.
76   His father had previously been the commander of one of the Bass blockade vessels and old Scots Navy.
77   NAS, RH9/14/102. An analysis of the business aspects of this voyage is available in T. McAloon, 'A Minor Merchant in General Trade: the case of Edward Burd 1728–39', *Scottish Themes*, pp. 17–27 and R.K. Hannay, 'Gibraltar 1727', *Scottish Historical Review* (1918), XVI, pp. 325–334.
78   Inverness Burgh Records, CTI/ INV/ M 11/1–8 contains extensive correspondence on local fisheries and exporting to Europe. The letter books of Baillie John Steuart (c.1722–5) indicate that he was regularly trading to Barcelona and Lisbon from Inverness. In one such venture his vessel the *Margaret* was sent to Le Harve with barrelled salmon and 25,000 cod (1722). Forth vessels were engaged in this direct trade from Aberdeen: NAS, HCAS, AC 9/1004, Whyte v Hill.

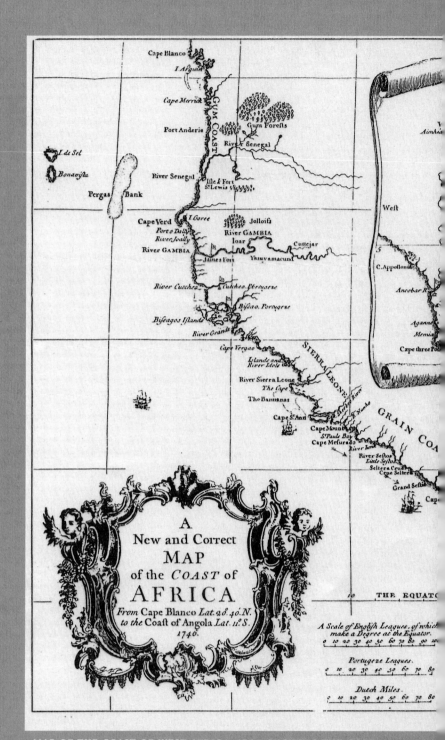

MAP OF THE COAST OF WEST AFRICA, 1746, SHOWING THE GOLD
COAST AS IT WAS DURING THE *HANOVER'S* SLAVING VOYAGE OF
1720 FROM RED CLIFFS (IVORY COAST) TO OLD CALABAR

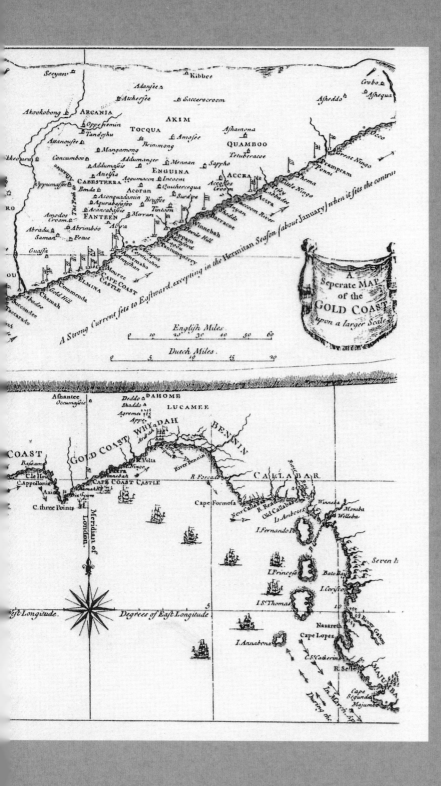

outgoing cargo – in this case biscuits – decided the first port-of-call rather than the superiority of dried Newfoundland cod over salted Scottish caught cod on the Iberian market.

What could go wrong when there was no kinship tie between the owners and the supercargo was dramatically demonstrated in the case of the gross mismanagement of the *Hanover* slaving venture. The owners – Robert Bogle junior and four other Glasgow merchants – had retained the trusted Claud Johnson to acquire the necessary cargo of 'Guinea goods' (Dutch beads and textiles, copper bars and trade guns) in London. These were shipped to Leith and carted to their Port Glasgow cellars. At the same time a ship's surgeon, previously unknown to the Glasgow owners but experienced in the Guinea trade, was recruited in London – presumably by Johnson. On his arrival at Port Glasgow he was also appointed supercargo, in the absence of a local candidate with the requisite knowledge of bartering on the Gold Coast. What happened after the *Hanover* sailed was a catalogue of mounting losses to the owners while the profits made by the supercargo's own trading in slaves soared.

Lured back to Port Glasgow from his bolthole in St Kitts, the supercargo was summarily arrested and imprisoned, at the behest of the betrayed owners, on stepping ashore. In court, however, his negligence and connivance could not be proved, such was the nature of the *carte blanche* commission he had received from the owners on departure. He was acquitted and awarded full costs. The implications of this high-profile, eight-year legal dispute before the High Court of Admiralty were, undoubtedly, not lost on the close-knit Glasgow merchant community, a considerable number of whom had been called as witnesses.[79]

Thereafter, the Clyde merchants, with their established links with the Scottish network in America, were to the fore in dispensing with the supercargo. For those engaged in the tobacco trade, the solution was to introduce 'store houses', staffed by kinsmen, in the creeks of the Chesapeake. This system had many advantages, including the ability to stockpile hogsheads in anticipation of the arrival of a company vessel. With a rapid turn-round now available to the master, the utilisation rate of the specialist transatlantic vessels increased in the following decades, with many completing two (a few three) transatlantic passages in any one year.[80]

---

79   NAS, HCAS, AC 9/1042, Horseburgh v Bogle.
80   This is the main thrust of Dell's analysis of the Naval Officer Accounts for the Chesapeake; see R.F. Dell, 'The operational record of the Clyde tobacco fleets', *Scottish Economic and Social History* (1982), II, pp. 1–17.

On the European side of the business, a trusted resident factor (usually Scottish) received the tobacco at the entrepôt port. The smaller companies engaged in general round-about trading to Europe in mixed cargoes shared a number of Scottish factors or established a business relationship with a reputable English or foreign firm. Under this system the factor, with his intimate knowledge of the local market, decided the disposal and acquisition of cargoes. He was also empowered to instruct the master as to his next best course of action if there were problems or a poor market.[81]

By the 1740s, the general acceptance of the 'Bill of Exchange' as an instrument of international settlement effectively sealed the fate of the supercargo model of trading with most trading houses. At the smaller east-coast ports, however, the employment of a locally recruited supercargo for an occasional venture abroad lingered on.

THE CLYDE'S LOCATIONAL ADVANTAGE

While the state of security in Northern European and Mediterranean waters remained volatile, the shippers of the Firth of Clyde benefited from their north-westerly location. Daniel Defoe, writing around the same time as the passage of the *Christian*, summed up this advantage:

> If it be calculated, how much sooner the voyage is made from Glasgow to the capes of Virginia, than from London, the difference will be made up in the freight, and in expense of the ships, especially in time of war, when the channel is thronged with privateers, and ships wait to go in fleets for fear of enemies, the Glasgow vessels are no sooner out of the Firth of Clyde, but they stretch away to the north-west, are out of the road of the privateers immediately, and are often at the capes of Virginia before the London ships get clear of the channel. Nay, even in times of peace, there must always be allowed, one time with another, at least fourteen or twenty days difference in the voyage, both going out and coming in, which, taken together, is a month or six weeks … and, considering the wear and tear, victuals and wages, this makes a considerable difference.[82]

---

81   The use of English factors at Bordeaux is mentioned in McAloon, 'A Minor Merchant,' pp. 17–27.
82   D. Defoe, 'A tour through Great Britain' (1727), as quoted by McUre, *Glasgow*, p. 313.

Table 5.5. Vessels belonging to the Clyde ports, 1735

Vessel	Owners	Masters	Destination
Show	James Corbet	Archibald Douglas	Virginia
Thistle	James Corbet & Co.	Colin Dunlop	Virginia
Nelly	Iames Corbet & Co.	Ninian Bryce	Virginia
America	Robert Donald & Co.	James Scott	Virginia
Albany	Robert Bogle & Co.	William Gemmil	Virginia
Glasgow	Buchanan & Co.	Andrew Gray	Virginia
Scipio	Robert Bogle & Co.	John Clark	Virginia
Martha	Oswald & Co.	James Gregory	Virginia
Betty	Sam McCall & Co.	William Dunlop	Virginia
Sophia	John Stark & Co.	Samual Bowman	Virginia
Diamond	Fogos & Co.	Robert Arthur	Virginia
Hardicanute	Scotts & Co.	Robert Rogers	Virginia
Jean	John Dickson	Patrick Jack	Virginia
Margaret	Robert Dreghorn	Hugh Crawford	Virginia
Port Glasgow	John Lyon & Co.	David Blair	Virginia
Restoration	Arthur Tran & Co.	John Shannon	Boston
Liberty	John Watt & Co.	Robert Hamilton	Jamaica
Amity	Oswald & Co.	George Blair	Jamaica
Speedwell	Oswald & Co	James Colhoun	Jamaica
Prince William	Buchanan & Co	James Peadie	Jamaica
Argyle	Buchanan & Co.	William Watson	Antigna
Bee (sloop)	John Watt & Co.	Robert Hasty	Antigna
Industry	James Milliken & Co.	William Houston	St. Kitts
John & Robert	[John] Scott & Co.	Thomas Clark	St. Kitts
Triton	John Stirling & Co	Walter Stirling	Barbados
Buchanan	Buchanan & Co.	Robert Rae	London
Virginia Merchant	Buchanan & Co.	James Montgomery	London
Friendship	Henry McCall & Co.	James Beanie	London
Fame	Henry McCall & Co.	James Hume	London
Caledon	John Stirling & Co.	John Stevenson	London
McDougal	James Milliken & Co.	Thomas Milliken	London
Britannia	Robert Robinson & Co.	William Fleming	Straits
Little Page	John Blackburn & Co.	Robert Wilson	Straits
Butterfly	Dinwiddie & Co.	Matthew Crawford	Straits
Friendship	Sommerville & Co.	Thomas Younger	Straits
Thomas	James Watt	William Watt	Gibraltar
McKenzie	John Blackburn & Co.	Alexr Woddrop	Holland
St. Andrew	John Brown & Co.	John Brown	Holland
Renfrew	Sommerville & Co.	Peter Sommerville	Stockholm
Susanna	Sommerville & Co.	John Ritchie	Stockholm
Thomas & John	John Lyon & Co.	Robert Ker	Stockholm
James	William Gemmil & Co.	William Chalmers	Stockholm
Spiers	James Spiers & Co.	John Stewart	Stockholm
May	James Hastie & Co.	James Hastie	Stockholm
Greenock	James McCunn & Co.		Stockholm

Vessel	Owners	Masters	Destination
Diligence	Arthur Tran & Co.	James Boucher	coastal
Glasgow Packet	Arthur Tran & Co.	Archibald Rainney	coastal
Welcome	Robert Donald & Co.	John Andrew	coastal
Euphemia	John Lyon & Co.	Andrew Crawford	coastal
James	John Lyon & Co.	John Orr	coastal
Jean	Sommerville & Co.	Robert Sommerville	coastal
Princess Mary	Sommerville & Co.	Alexr Campbell	coastal
Graham	Robert Dreghorn	Alexr Dunsmoor	coastal
Drummond	John Craig	William Eccles	coastal
Montgomery	Thomas Clark & Co.		coastal
Happy Return	Thomas Clark & Co.	Robert Crighton	coastal
Dalrymple	John Park & Co.	Robert Crighton	coastal
Stewart	Robert Paterson & Co.	James Orr	coastal
Dove	Robert Paterson & Co.	James Crawford	coastal
Jean & Elizabeth	John Scott & Co.	John Forrest	coastal
Alexander	John Scott & Co.		coastal
Mary & Jean	John McCunn & Co.		coastal
James & Thomas	John Lyon & Co	John Shearer	coastal
Prince of Orange	John Murdoch & Co.	James Crawford	coastal
Margaret	William Bryce & Co.	Thomas Young	coastal

Source: Gibson, History of Glasgow.

Defoe's emphasis on the Clyde's locational advantage in wartime has recently been reappraised in favour of emphasising the peacetime operational advantages.[83] To do so, however, is to make light of the fact that these peacetime advantages over London also held good for all the west-coast ports of Britain – from Bideford northwards. Indeed, the contemporary 'shipping intelligence' upholds Defoe's emphasis on the primacy of the wartime advantages as essentially correct for that particular time.

In wartime the Clyde offered the most northerly sheltered deepwater ports and anchorages on the western seaboard for vessels going north-about or running the Atlantic via the North Channel, far removed from the hotly contested St. George's and English Channels to the south.

Having acquired a greater market share in the Atlantic trades through this advantage, the Clyde's merchants consolidated their market share in peacetime by tight networking and cost-cutting. This latter objective was met by replacing chartered English vessels with Clyde-owned ocean-going

---

83   Dell laid great emphasis on the Clyde's geographic position in peacetime as 'Glasgow's first advantage' in the Atlantic trade. He considered, without elaboration, that its distance from the cruising grounds of enemy privateers was 'an added bonus': Dell, 'Clyde tobacco fleets', p. 3.

vessels.[84] It is, therefore, of little surprise that those English ports most involved in chartering – Whitehaven, Lancaster and Liverpool – were to the fore in the series of parliamentary campaigns and charges laid before the Treasury against the Scots in the tobacco trade during the period 1717–35.

By the latter date the Atlantic economy was again buoyant and, for the first time in a decade, relatively stable. The acquisition of the necessary shipping stock to capitalise on the upturn was by then well in hand at the Clyde ports. In that year the local commentator Gibson compiled his *List of ships, brigantines and sloops belonging to the Clyde* – which he considered to be 'pretty near the truth'.[85] This list catalogued sixty-seven vessels whose combined tonnage did not exceed 5,600 tons. He took a broad view of the shipping working out of the upper Clyde ports, a small number of which can be identified as belonging to the lower Firth harbours (Ayr, Irvine and Saltcoats). Likewise, those listed sailing for Virginia cannot always be assumed to have returned only to Port Glasgow or Greenock – for example the *Diamond* that sailed back directly to Fort William with tobacco for the Oban Company.[86]

Even so, it is clear from the trades he apportions to each of the foreign-going vessels that the upper Clyde ports had made their move in the conveyance of colonial commodities. Their Atlantic fleet numbered twenty-seven traders – eighteen to America and nine to the West Indies. A further nine were destined for Northern Europe and five for Southern Europe, leaving six to serve London.

With such resources the Glasgow merchants took over the lion's share of the re-export trade through the Scottish ports as well as handling the bulk of the domestic demand for tobacco. With the latter, hogsheads destined for the east coast of Scotland were usually landed first at the Clyde ports and then carted overland by the Kilsyth road to Bo'ness and Alloa. If the client was outside the Forth area, then the tobacco was delivered directly to his port from Virginia by a Clyde vessel.[87]

---

84   Examples of deeds of ownership of Port Glasgow Atlantic-going vessels are available: GCA, Dunlop of Shawfield MSS B10/15/ 2478,4528,4508, 4532 and 4842.
85   J. Gibson, *The History of Glasgow* (Glasgow, 1777), pp. 210–11.
86   Her captain was the twenty-year-old Robert Arthur of Crawfordsdyke. Not listed by Gibson was the Fort William-owned *Charming Molly* sent to America from the Clyde in 1736: NAS Lorn MacIntyre MSS 1279, p. 3.
87   An example of this was the arrival of the *Concord* of Port Glasgow at Dundee from Virginia with 249 hogsheads in 1730: Dundee Archive and Record Centre, CE 70/1, Collector of Dundee to the Board, 18 June 1730.

THE PORT OF LEITH, 1734-5

The rise of the Clyde tobacco trade has tended to obscure the fact that Leith, as the port of Edinburgh, remained the busiest Scottish harbour throughout the era. Although much of the incoming tonnage was locally shipped coal and foodstuffs, Leith also had a thriving foreign-going trade. In the year that Gibson compiled his view of activity on the Clyde, the 'shipping intelligence' for the Forth reported some fifty-five foreign-going voyages – involving around forty individual vessels entering or leaving Leith's chronically congested basin.[88] The Spanish and Biscay trades dominated the list with a number of masters undertaking two voyages to the same destination in one year.

Of the solitary arrivals, that of the galley *Edinburgh* in late August 1734 was of great significance. She had returned directly from St. Petersburg with a cargo of hemp and lint in flagrant breach of the English Russia Company's monopoly of access to this relatively new entrepôt port. Her safe arrival represents, therefore, the first blow of a well-orchestrated assault – led by the Edinburgh merchant William Hogg – on the English chartered companies' exclusive access to key markets. Hogg and his supporters openly rejected the English Attorney General's earlier ruling (1711) that upheld the English monopolists' right to continue to deny Scottish traders access to their preserve – despite Article XVIII of the Act of Union. The Russia Company had earlier retorted to their challenge with threats of seizing any Scottish vessels found at St. Petersburg and/or levying compensatory import duties at those Scottish ports found to be countenancing the breach.[89]

The following May (1735), however, this potential threat to the Union was removed by the Treaty of Navigation and Commerce concluded by Empress Anne of Russia. This trade agreement effectively threw open the Russian trade carried through St. Petersburg to all vessels of reciprocating nations – one of the first signatories was Britain – and hence nullified the monopoly of the Russia Company.

THE PRESSGANG IN SCOTTISH WATERS

There can be little doubt that the first three decades of the new century were a watershed in European affairs. Spain remained unappeased over

---

88   *Edinburgh Evening Courant,* successive reports January 1734 – January 1735
89   Macmillan, 'The 'New Men', p. 47.

Gibraltar but stopped short of declaring war in 1726. After the Treaty of Paris (1733) the Anglo–French accord was effectively dead as commercial and colonial rivalries gathered momentum. As a result the peacetime estab-lishment of the Royal Navy was enlarged in anticipation of hostilities. To support this move the first bounty system designed to stimulate the whaling industry – seen as a training ground for seamen – was introduced in that year. The bounty does not appear to have generated interest in the North, as earlier whaling ventures have proved unsuccessful. In the meantime the Navy required men and looked to Scotland to provide its quota despite the ruling – dating from William and Mary – that Scottish seamen were exempt from the press.

Prior to 1734 this understanding had been honoured by the British Admiralty and serving naval officers in Scottish waters. In the spring of that year, however, the press tender to HMS *Terrible* made a precedent-making tour of all vessels entering the Forth. Their first attempt to board a Scottish vessel – the *Happy Janet* in from Rotterdam – in search of men was stoutly repulsed. Greater resolve and force were brought to bear in the months that followed, and the crews of the *Mary* of Bo'ness and *Tartar* of Leith were secured for the King's Service.[90] Despite a local outcry, nothing seems to have done by the Scottish Admiralty or civil authorities to secure the release of their seamen. Little, of course, could be done without a Scots Navy as this pressgang was careful to seize its victims offshore and not from the quayside or harbour streets.

THE FIRST TRADE WARS, 1739–48

The first 'trade wars' (known collectively in America as 'King George's War') broke out in 1739, despite Walpole's determined opposition. The initial contest – the War of Jenkin's Ear (1739–44) – was a contrived affair to legitimise an assault on the Spanish colonial trade. The supposed mutilation of Captain Jenkin – master of the brig *Rebecca* of Port Glasgow – at the hands of the Spanish *Guarda Costa* in the Caribbean a number of years earlier provided the opportunity for a dramatic accusation of barbarism with which to mobilise public support for the war.

But the Spanish were not the soft target presumed by the war party

90   *Edinburgh Evening Chronicle,* 5 May, 12 June 1734 and 26 February 1735. One of their victims was David Burd who wrote his will (1734) while on board HMS *Terrible*. NAS, RH 15/54/39.

and the press of the day. By February 1740 Spanish privateers were operating in the southern approaches to within forty leagues of Cork, catching the chronically run-down Navy ill-prepared.[91] Indeed, by that summer their threat to shipping in the English Channel was such as to have the annual sailing of the East India Company fleet diverted north-about via Leith.[92] To meet the crisis the Government was forced to impose a temporary embargo on all outgoing vessels in order to meet the shortfall in men for the Navy.[93]

After the embargo was lifted, Leith's regular trade in southern European waters remained hard hit. After 1 September 1740 all trade to Spain and the Canaries was suspended as formal hostilities were declared in these sea areas.

The Baltic was beyond the European war zone in southern waters and so the northern trades were virtually unaffected, even though the Swedes technically joined the conflict in September and threatened to take British vessels as prize. The number of Scottish passages through the Baltic was, by and large, maintained by the protection offered by Anglo–Dutch convoys and was encouraged by the continuation of the export bounty on grain.

Much more damaging to Scottish interests was the state of security on the other side of the Atlantic. By 1741 the Clyde tobacco fleet ran the risk of capture by Spanish privateers cruising off the Capes of Virginia and the Newfoundland Banks. These raiders worked out from Spanish West Indian bases and their activities were largely unchecked because of the absence of an effective convoy system or naval presence in the Chesapeake region.[94]

In home waters, however, the security of the Clyde and the North Channel remained unchallenged. The *Glasgow Journal* for the three years prior to the French entry into the war (1741–3) makes no reference to any Spanish privateers or naval activity in or around the Clyde area.[95] During those years around 400 foreign-going passages (inwards and outwards) were reported from Greenock and Port Glasgow.[96] Overall the Clyde's

91   Due to Walpole's neglect, only thirty-five ships-of-the-line were serviceable in 1739.
92   *Lloyd's List*, 4 August 1741.
93   The embargo was imposed by 'full order' of the Privy Council, 25 February 1739.
94   The first Scottish casualties were reported from this region in July of the following year when two Port Glasgow vessels – *America* and *Argyle* – were taken off the Capes; *Lloyd's List*, 14 and 21 July 1741.
95   The only acknowledgement of the war was the departure of six transports under escort from HMS *Dolphin: Ibid.*, 1 October 1741.
96   *Glasgow Journal*, successive entries, August 1741 – July 1743. One-quarter of all passages were made by vessels from the lower Clyde ports.

Table 5. 6. Number of passages made by Scottish masters through the Danish Sound, 1725–49
Source:*Danish Sound Tolls*.

shipping activity was, apart from the conspicuous absence of sailings to Spain and the Mediterranean, largely unchanged by the war. Cushioning this loss was the suspension of the ban on importing Irish victuals (April 1741), the control of which was now at the discretion of the Scottish Court of Session and Exchequer. This decision allowed greater control of both the overseas and coastal trade in grain from then onwards.[97]

By then the import and export of tobacco dominated the foreign trade of the upper Clyde ports. Imports for the year 29 September 1743–4 numbered eighty-four cargoes of tobacco into Port Glasgow and Greenock (45 and 39 respectively), totalling 22,140 hogsheads (13,647 and 8,493 hogsheads respectively) weighing almost 18.5 million pounds.[98] Despite this high volume of tobacco, very few vessels were in fact involved in the Atlantic leg. Their numbers never exceeded twenty-six (c.5,000 tons) in any one year during this period. They were, with one exception (the *Christian* of Virginia), all owned by and based at the Clyde ports, the chartered vessels from Whitehaven and Lancaster having long since been discarded.[99]

Around double this number of Clyde vessels were directly involved in the re-exported trade in tobacco to Europe. This is not to say that they constituted a separate fleet since a substantial number of the transatlantic vessels were then often used on the secondary legs. This was particularly the case when delivering large whole cargo consignments to the French State Monopoly. The majority of the other vessels in this re-export trade at this time were, however, smaller vessels (under 100 tons) which were well suited to trading in small consignments to the ports of Northern Europe.[100]

By then there was already a discernible degree of geographic specialisation between the upper Clyde ports. Port Glasgow, the dominant port in the trade, looked more to the established French and Low Country markets, whereas Greenock found its niche in serving a wide range of ports of Guernsey, Norway and the Baltic.[101] Greenock depended more heavily therefore on the lower Clyde ports (notably Saltcoats) for the additional smaller vessels needed to serve this diverse range of markets. This symbiotic relationship is evident from the *Glasgow Journal*'s reports for the

---

97   Formal notice of a suspension was displayed at the Customs House of Leith. For the price of a shilling a copy was made available for any other interested port to display.
98   NAS, E504/ 28 and 15/ 1–2, Port Books Port Glasgow and Greenock.
99   *Glasgow Journal* successive entries, August 1741 – July 1743.
100   NAS, E504/ 15/ 1–2, Port Books Port Glasgow and Greenock.
101   Guernsey then served the same function as the Isle of Man – a smugglers' storehouse.

months of March and April where small groups of these vessels can be traced entering Greenock in ballast – after the winter lay-up at their home port – and then departing with tobacco.[102]

THE ENTRY OF FRANCE INTO THE WAR, 1744

This situation at the Clyde ports dramatically changed when France joined Spain (April 1744) in what has become known as the War of Austrian Succession (1744–48). Virtually the whole of Europe and every sea area was embroiled as Britain, Holland and Austria aligned against France, Spain and Prussia. The French entry had been eagerly awaited by her Dunkirk-based privateers who were quick off the mark. Within days the English Channel was untenable for unescorted vessels. By the end of the month French privateers were roaming the North Sea, mainly off the approaches to Norwegian and Dutch ports.[103]

The closure of French ports greatly inhibited the activity of those Leith merchants in the wine trade who had yet to establish an alternative supply. Even the Clyde masters who had switched to Lisbon and Bilbao found the risk of capture by St. Malo and Bayonne privateers very high in the Bay of Biscay.[104] Likewise, in the Baltic trades the greatly increased risk of capture out of convoy effectively halved the number of passages made by Scottish masters through the Danish Sound for the next two years.

With the approaches to the southern ports of Britain badly infested, the London insurance market panicked. In May 1744 the war was formally extended to the Caribbean, and as a result marine insurance quadrupled to between twelve and fifteen per cent outwards and between twenty and twenty-five per cent homewards. In September of that year a Chesapeake-bound vessel out of London was refused insurance. Bristol brokers were then asking up to fifty per cent of the agreed value of the hull and its cargo per passage via St.George's Channel. Their worst fears were realised in June the following year when an entire convoy of twenty-two merchantmen –

---

102   An example was the departure of *Providence, Cunningham, Margaret & Jean, Concord* (all of Saltcoats) and *Mayflower* of Irvine for Norway: *Glasgow Journal*, 10 April 1742.
103   The first reported losses were the sloop *John* taken into Dunkirk on her passage from Campvere to Scotland. The *John & Christian* of Montrose was taken soon afterwards while attempting a run to Rotterdam: *Lloyd's List*, 27 April and May 1744 respectively.
104   The first reported loss was the *Robert* from Greenock to Oporto: *Ibid.*, 19 June 1744.

with two naval escorts – heading for the Chesapeake, was taken in the English Channel by the Brest fleet.[105]

The Clyde's wartime locational advantage for her Atlantic traders should have immediately come into play as Clyde vessels carrying tobacco to the French designated ports were – in theory – immune from capture under the terms of the 'contract of 1744'. This contract had been concluded between a consortium of west-coast tobacco merchants and the *Les Fermiers Généraux* – the farmers of the French state monopoly. This was a highly astute and hard-won contract that anticipated the dislocation of the French trade by war and guaranteed delivery in return for safe passage for Clyde vessels delivering tobacco over the next six years. The proviso was that they did not engage in any other trading activity with France.

For reasons that are not fully understood, Clyde masters do not appear to have taken up this option of acquiring a French pass under the contract during this war. In all probability they were prudently waiting to see if such guarantees of immunity from capture were respected by Spanish as well as French privateers. A more immediate reason was, undoubtedly, the internal chaos generated by the 'Forty-Five Rebellion which severely blighted two sailing seasons.

During the first difficult years of the enlarged war, the danger of capture for those vessels that sailed across the Atlantic was greatest off the Capes of Virginia. French privateers from the Cape Breton ports, principally Louisbourg, were then cruising unopposed. Outgoing vessels using the North Channel had no regular escort beyond Ireland and so provided easy pickings as they approached the American seaboard independently.[106] By 1745, however, this privateering menace from French Acadia was greatly reduced by the daring capture of their fortress at Louisbourg.[107]

French and Spanish privateers working out of Caribbean bases were, however, still able to reach the Capes of Virginia for the next two years. Their work was greatly aided by the erratic sailing time and wholly inadequate levels of protection afforded by the annual Chesapeake convoy, which was grossly mismanaged during this particular war.[108] Adding to the

---

105 Middleton, *Tobacco Coast*, pp. 324–5.
106 Three Clyde vessels were taken while attempting to reach the Chesapeake: *Lloyd's List,* 7 May 1744. In the same month a Saltcoats vessel was looted and sunk *en route* from Dumfries to Newfoundland: *Ibid.*, 10 August 1744.
107 This was restored to the French after the war.
108 Middleton, *Tobacco Coast*, p. 323.

uncertainty and personal suffering was the fact that news of a Scottish vessel being taken off the Capes was late in filtering home as her crew was taken back to the privateer's Caribbean base.[109]

THE DISRUPTION IN HOME WATERS, 1744–8

In home waters the North-East coast of Scotland once again bore the brunt as enemy privateers worked deep into the North Sea within weeks of the French entry into the war (April 1744). The Calais privateer – the snow *Susannah* (100 tons/8 carriage guns/18 swivels/210 men) – led the way. Her two cruises serve to illustrate the mode of operation of an inshore hunting privateer and the extent of the counter-measures available at the start and end of this conflict.

She arrived off Orkney and Shetland in May 1744, ransoming a prize (her seventh) less than six miles off Shetland.[110] By July she had moved south to the Cromarty and Moray Firths where she ransomed two small Scottish coasters and was probably the unnamed privateer that took the brig *Indian Queen* of Aberdeen (80 tons) on her passage to Hamburg. [111] During her seven-week cruise she was never challenged, and by the time HMS *Aldborough* was finally sent north from Leith (September), she had already slipped away.[112]

By way of contrast her second cruise, during the last months of the war, demonstrated the much greater deployment of guard ships on the exposed east coast. The *Susannah* made her reappearance off St Abb's Head in early February 1748, taking the *Blessing* of Aberdeen returning from Rotterdam. Her French master – styling himself 'Captain Antoine L'Amie' – refused to offer ransom and sent her north-about to Brest with a prize crew.[113] The *Susannah* then cruised north, dropping off the *Blessing*'s crew at Slains Castle before rendezvousing with another Dunkirk privateering brig off Peterhead. Their intention was to cruise the Scottish coast in company

---

109 An example was the capture of the snow *Eliza* of Port Glasgow (60 tons) by a Spanish privateer. News of this loss was only confirmed many months, later when her crew were exchanged at Jamaica: *Aberdeen Journal*, 12 April 1748.

110 *Ibid.*, 29 May and 10 July 1744. The last prize was the *Helen & Margaret* from Norway to Inverness.

111 On this occasion the brig was dispatched to Dunkirk with a prize crew: *Lloyd's List*, 17 July 1744.

112 *Ibid.*, 18 September 1744.

113 *Ibid.*, 3 February 1748.

for the next five weeks, sending any prizes taken to Norway to minimise the risk of recapture. In March they appeared unopposed off Montrose, placing that whole stretch of coastline in a state of alarm. They abandoned this plan and parted company, with the *Susannah* heading south. Appearing off the Isle of May, she sent the Forth into a state of panic before continuing southwards, taking two Scottish vessels off Holy Isle and driving others ashore. Off Flamborough Head she ransomed her last prize – an Aberdeen-bound vessel – before being taken by HMS *Hastings*.[114]

The capture of the *Susannah* was probably inevitable, for she had stayed too long in Scottish waters after the alert had gone out. On receiving the first intelligence of her presence, Commodore Laurie – the Naval Commander of Scotland – sent orders north to the convoy escorts at Orkney. HMS *Experiment* was to make a sweep of the North Sea coast as far south as Leith for the intruder, while her consort – HMS *Fox* – was instructed to escort away from Scapa Flow and the danger zone those vessels heading for the west coast and Ireland.[115] In addition, one of the two Dutch warships sent to the Forth on convoy duties was detached to patrol the Moray Firth area as directed by the Provost of Aberdeen.[116] Finally, HMS *Hastings* was ordered out from Newcastle to cruise northwards as part of a pincer movement.

The scale of this hunt for the *Susannah* was only possible in the closing stages of the war. Between her two cruises the naval defence of the North-East coast remained piecemeal. At the time of her first cruise at least five other vessels were taken by small privateers operating along the east coast – without any response from the guard ships to the south.[117]

In March 1745, a French privateer lay off Aberdeen harbour at its leisure, seizing all fishing boats encountered and occasionally venturing into the harbour to cut out vessels at anchor. Pleas sent south for the two armed sloops at Leith – the *Hazard* and *Happy Return* – to be sent up fell on deaf ears.[118] The naval commander chose instead to reinstitute the convoy system, which did little to prevent individual vessels being picked off on their way to the convoy rendezvous.[119] Between the passing of the convoys

114 *Aberdeen Journal*, 8, 23 March and 12 April 1748.
115 *Ibid.*, 16 March 1748.
116 *Ibid.*, 1 April 1748. Their presence was by arrangement of the Staple Contract with the State of Zeeland.
117 *Lloyd's List,* April 1748 onwards.
118 Clark, *Aberdeen*, p.116.
119 The capture of the *Nelly* of Leith as she sailed to join convoy within the Forth by a small privateering schooner demonstrates just how close inshore these raiders were prepared to work.

whole stretches of the North-East coast remained open to attack. In August 1747 two large French privateers could afford to linger for a week off Aberdeen before HMS *Mercury* arrived and chased them off.[120] The overall result of this recurring disruption was that the trade and shipping of the North-East ports was, yet again, adversely affected by the war.

It was only in the last months of the war (January 1748 onwards), when a series of naval victories swung the balance of power at sea heavily in Britain's favour, that naval units were released from fleet duties to cruise the coasts and bolster the convoy system.[121] The immediate success of this enhanced cruiser and convoy strategy inspired one boastful contributor to the *Aberdeen Journal* to calculate that in the twelve months up to April 1748, sixty-one privateers had been taken and a further twenty-six sunk or burned. This was in addition to twenty-two French warships lost in fleet actions.[122]

While the war with France officially ended the following month, such self-congratulation was premature for the communities of Orkney. French privateers, 'acting under Spanish commissions', continued to raid the Scapa Flow area until the war with Spain ended two months later (12 July).[123]

In American waters the fast-sailing Spanish privateers that infested the Capes of Virginia during those final months of the war virtually halted the Scottish tobacco trade. By penetrating into the Hampton Roads, they stopped all unescorted movement at the entrance to the Chesapeake. Only after HMS *Loo* used a captured privateer as a decoy to take two of their number were they finally dislodged from this prime location.[124]

THE LOSSES AND WINDFALLS OF THE WAR

At the end of nine years of warfare the reports of the capture and recapture of Scottish vessels in the Atlantic and Caribbean were still being received in Scotland months after all hostilities had officially ceased.[125] At least one

---

120   The larger of the two – *Marshal Saxe* – carried thirty-four guns: *Lloyd's List*, 24 August 1747.

121   An example of this new deployment was the arrival at Leith, in January, of HMS *Launceston* (40 guns) with the Riga convoy of some twenty-six vessels . The same report mentions 'hundred vessel' Baltic and Scandinavian escorted convoys still at sea: *Ibid.*, 5 January 1748.

122   *Ibid.*, 19 April 1748.

123   HMS *Granada Bomb* took the last raider after escorting the Iceland cod fleet north of Shetland: *Ibid.*, 16 August 1748.

124   *Ibid.*, 10 May 1748.

125   Irvine lost two vessels – *Mayflower* and *John & Anne* – in the last weeks, taken 200 leagues off Cape Clear while *en route* to Barbados by a Bayonne privateer. The *Montrose* of Glasgow was also attacked but beat off the privateer: *Glasgow Courant*, 25 July 1748.

Scottish company took legal action through the Spanish courts to recover, or to extract compensation for, their vessel, taken after hostilities had ceased, an interesting demonstration of how universally accepted the Law of Nations was in European courts.[126]

For a few Scottish entrepreneurs the peace came too soon. Simon Dunbar, then residing at Newport, Rhode Island, informed his father, John Dunbar of Burgie: 'the accounts of a peace disconcert my measures a good deal as I am concerned in privateering'.[127] His venture was just one of thousands that had fitted out in the colonies under a Vice-Admiralty letter of marque to join the c.1500 commissions issued to English and Irish vessels by the London Admiralty.

In direct contrast, only nine Scottish traders took out letters during these wars due a combination of factors – primarily the restriction imposed by the '1744 Contract' and the distraction of the 'Forty-Five Rebellion.[128] The details of crew size and armaments given in their declarations indicate that they were all Clyde tobacco traders engaged as 'running ships' across the Atlantic.[129] This indicates the higher profit to be made in running tobacco independent of convoy than gambling on a long-distance privateering cruise. Indeed, only one letter of marque vessel – *Lily* of Glasgow – appears to have captured a prize. This was a well-laden French West Indiamen out from Havana. Such was the Frenchman's value (£7,000) that Captain Wallace (or Wallis) chose to escort his prize back to Port Glasgow rather than entrust it to a prize crew.[130]

With the return to peace, trade was resumed and advanced. By 1750 Leith's Iberian trade had fully recovered, along with the sugar trade from the West Indies. In such a climate of optimism Thomas Douglas and Company of Montrose chartered four snows – *St. George, Neptune, Montrose* and *Potomac Merchant* – for slaving expeditions to West Africa and on to the West Indies and the Chesapeake.[131] Only the *Potomac Merchant* is known to

---

126 A case in question was the *Sally* of Port Glasgow whose owners – William Wallace & Co.- hotly contested the privateer's declared date of capture: GCA, Shawfield MSS B10/12/1.

127 NAS, Ross of Pitcalnie MSS GD 199/99.

128 PRO HCA 26–32.

129 Running ships characteristically carried a larger than peacetime crew for their own defence and smart handling, but were of insufficient size to provide prize crews.

130 The prize – *Happy Lady* of La Rochelle – was retained by her new owners, granted her own letters of marque and sent out to Virginia as *Lily's Prize* in the tobacco trade: *Lloyd's List* 29 June 1744 and PRO, HCA 26, letter 28 January 1744.

131 D.G. Adams, 'Trade in the Eighteenth and Nineteenth Centuries', in G. Jackson and S.G.E. Lythe (eds.), *The Port of Montrose* (Tayport, 1993), p. 126.

have completed the circuit successfully.[132] It is interesting that – twenty years on from the *Hanover* slaving venture – the 'Guinea goods' for these ventures still had to be acquired in Holland as there were no locally produced alternatives. The rumblings of yet another war, in 1754, probably killed off this high-risk enterprise out of Montrose.

THE REBELLION OF 1745

During the nine years of general warfare came the second great Jacobite Rebellion (1745–6). As in the earlier uprising, the British Navy had mastery of the seas around Britain. The first incident at sea was the celebrated engagement off the Lizard between HMS *Lyon* and the French frigate *Elizabeth* (60 guns) and escort. Although the 'Young Pretender' escaped north on board the accompanying privateer *Du Teillay*, the loss of the *Elizabeth* denied the prince his principal supply of arms. More importantly, he lost the psychological advantage of a French warship in Scottish waters to encourage waiverers to his cause.[133]

The Young Pretender had embarked on his mission with only promises of Swedish intervention and French naval support. The first never materialised, while the only French naval unit of consequence to enter Scottish waters was the frigate *Le Fine* (32 guns) which landed Lord Drummond's regiment at Montrose harbour. There she was almost captured by HMS *Milford* (40 guns), which, however, had to retreat to Leith after running aground on Annat Bank, leaving Montrose, the wrecked *Le Fine* and the visiting sloop-of-war HMS *Hazard* to the Jacobites.[134]

On the west coast the sea ports in the Firth of Clyde held out for the Hanoverian cause. The mounted detachment of Jacobites sent west after their entry into Glasgow was quickly turned back by cannon fire from a line of British warships moored along the estuary – from Greenock to

132 In September 1752 a Glasgow merchant reported (to the *Aberdeen Journal*) that 'we have advice that one of the Montrose Guineamen is arrived in the Potomac River, Virginia, consigned to Mr. William Black. The sale of Negro males at £32 and for women £30 sterling'. By Christmas of the year she was back safely in Montrose with 118 elephants' tusks on top of barrel staves and hoops.
133 A further shipment of arms, conveyed by Sir John Hall on an unnamed French vessel, was taken by a Bristol privateer: NAS, GD 206 Hall of Douglas MSS 2/289.
134 D.G. Adams, 'Defence of the Harbour' in G. Jackson and S.G.E. Lythe (Eds.), *The Port of Montrose* (Tayport, 1993), pp.78–9. The *Hazard* had been captured by local Jacobites and renamed *Prince Charles*.

above Port Glasgow.[135] But the dislocation of seaborne trade was almost complete as shipping activity on the west coast came to a virtual standstill until the Jacobite host marched south. In November 1745 a morbid Provost Cochrane of Glasgow wrote to his associate Patrick Crawford:

> Our case in this place and country is deplorable. For eight
> weeks there has been no business, our Customshouse is shut up,
> though we have 4,000 hogsheads lying in the river undis-
> charged, our manufacture at a stand for want of sales and
> money, no payments of any kind, no execution, our country
> robbed, plundered and harrassed by partys.[136]

His observations were borne out by the nil return for duty paid on imported tobacco recorded by the Collector of Port Glasgow and Greenock for the trading year 1745-6, as well as the absence of any incoming vessels from the Chesapeake during the rebellion. The re-export trade in tobacco from the Clyde was, however, quickly resumed as soon as the Jacobites started their long retreat up the east coast. The upper Clyde ports Customs records for that year listed 135 outgoing voyages carrying tobacco to fourteen European ports.[137] As only three were incoming cargoes, this level of business could only have been sustained by the stock of the hogsheads held on board laid-up vessels.

Table 5.7. Vessels entering the upper Clyde from the Chesapeake. 1742-50

Year	1742	1743	1744	1745	1746	1747	1748	1749	1750
Voyages	9	18	11	0	3	36	44	49	45
Vessels	9	18	11	0	3	32	42	41	41
Incidence of double passages	0	0	0	0	0	4	2	8	4

Source: Port Books of Port Glasgow and Greenock, NAS, E. 504/28/1-5 and 15/1-15.

As the Jacobite army marched north, after its last victory at Falkirk, elements of the Royal Navy outflanked them. HMS *Glasgow* (24 guns) arrived in the Cromarty Firth (January 1746) to support the isolated and hard-pressed

135   Weir, *Greenock*, p.38.
136   J. Dennistoun (ed.), *Cochrane Consep* (Glasgow, Maitland Club, 1836), p. 31.
137   William King (Principal Collector), *Tobacco Duties 1729-49*, table dated 13 February
1749-50. I am grateful to R.F. Dell for access to this contemporary printed source.

Government troops under Lord Loudon. In the days leading up to the final reckoning at Culloden Moor, she was joined by three shallow-draft sloops – *Shark*, *Vulture* and *Speedwell* – detached from Byng's flotilla of eleven warships in the Forth to help evacuate the loyalist following from Inverness. On arrival they were deployed to blockade the Moray and Cromarty Firths. While doing so they intercepted three French merchantmen attempting to carry arms, men and intelligence to the Jacobites at this critical moment.[138]

In the aftermath of Culloden (April 1746), naval units patrolled both coastlines of Scotland while the prince remained a fugitive at large. HMS *Glasgow* remained on the North-East coast station until September while a naval flotilla of assorted small vessels (10–14 guns) – *Raven*, *Baltimore*, *Trial*, *Furnace* and *Trident* – patrolled the west coast and Isles. Their presence was more than sufficient to thwart the two expeditions fitted out from the neutral Swedish ports of Gothenburg and Uddevalla to rescue the prince.[139] They were also responsible for enforcing the government embargo on the sailing of all herring boats beyond August 1746, which particularly hit Campbeltown.[140]

After that date the west-coast ports were reopened to incoming foreign trade producing immediate resurgence of the tobacco trade. The east-coast ports' recovery would seem to have been sluggish by comparison. The number of passages made by Scottish domiciled masters in the Baltic trade (most from the east coast) had halved during the emergency and took five years to return to the 1744 level of activity.[141]

POST-REBELLION LEGISLATION

The principal effect of the Rebellion on Scottish maritime affairs was its impact on central government's attitude to North Britain. After Cumberland's bloody retribution had run its course, government policies turned to the long-term pacification of the Highlands by means other than military occupation. The old policy of isolating and containing the Jacobite areas north of the Great Glen was abandoned. In its place was the drive to rehabilitate and integrate the North-West – both politically and economically – into the rest of North Britain.

138   M. Ash, *This Noble Harbour* (Edinburgh, 1991), pp. 176–7.
139   G. Behre, 'Two Swedish expeditions to rescue Prince Charles', *Scottish Historical Review* (1980), LIX, 2, pp. 140–153.
140   A.R. Bigwood, 'The Campbeltown Buss Fishery, 1750–1800' (unpublished M.Litt. dissertation, Aberdeen University, 1987), p. 8.
141   See Table 5.3.

The first moves were, understandably, motivated by the need for security. As part of the dismantling of feudal military service, a new Disarming Act (1746) was rigorously enforced. This, however, left the coastal population at the mercy of every armed party sent ashore in future wars. The raising of Fort George (commenced 1747) to command the narrow entrance to the Moray Firth guaranteed the security of the town of Inverness and ensured military access to the Great Glen. Thereafter, the cannon of this major fortification offered protection ,from seaborne raiders to vessels frequenting the Cromarty and Moray Firths in wartime. Around the same time the Admiralty finally funded the charting of the Western Isles and Highlands, to reduce the Navy's dependence on local men as pilots.

The curbing of the unacceptable levels of lawlessness and disaffection in the Scottish coastal communities, by enforcing the writ of central government, was high on the agenda. A succession of legislative measures followed that sought to empower the preventive officers holding the Treasury's warrant at each Scottish head port and out-station against the smuggler. In the months that followed Culloden, the personnel of both the Customs and Excise services were again purged of Jacobite sympathisers.[142] Thereafter, preferment in recruitment was given to ex-soldiers who had served with regiments on the government side. This was especially the case in those Customs precincts in Jacobite areas, such as Campbeltown, where the service was expected to provide intelligence on and detain fugitives.

THE TOBACCO ACT OF 1751

From the Clyde shippers' point of view the most influential legislation of this period was the Tobacco Act of 1751. This laid down stricter rules to curtail the much-denounced abuses and frauds at the quayside. During the parliamentary debate considerable public discussion had focused on an alternative plan to create a separate certification system for tobacco traded through ports north of the Carlisle–Newcastle line.[143] This proposal tacitly recognised that the rise of the Clyde ports in the re-export trade in tobacco had been underpinned by widespread abuse of drawback of import duty.

---

142   As late as 1751, Captain Hay – the commander of the Customs sloop *Princess Ann* – was investigated for failing to raise his flag or fire a salute on the King's birthday: GCA, CE 82/1, Collector of Campbeltown to the Board, 21 October and 19 November 1751.
143   *Glasgow Journal*, 20 May 1751.

The solution was, therefore, to dispense with the payment of domestic duty on incoming hogsheads destined for the Continent and so deny the fraudulent dealer the option of claiming drawback on what was later illegally relanded. Without a bonded warehouse system in place this proposal was discarded as unworkable.

The 1751 Act concentrated, therefore, on tackling sharp practice within the existing drawback system. The Act introduced new procedures and stringent rules based on the London practice for the weighing, marking and release of hogsheads by Customs. One major fraudulent practice was stopped immediately – claiming draw-back of duty on tobacco deemed to be unsaleable due to damage but, in fact, sold into the domestic market. After 1751 drawback was recoverable only on damaged tobacco given up to the Customs officers of the port for disposal. The burning of this tobacco had to be independently witnessed and residual ash weighed to prevent collusion.

In the same year halving the weight of ground wheat or oatmeal (to 224 lb.) as the unit that attracted payment enhanced the export bounty on grains. Malt for brewing was also added to the export bounty list at this time.[144]

MOVES TO CURB SMUGGLING

To deny the small smuggling wherry the pretence of legitimate trade in tobacco, all vessels conveying tobacco overseas or coastwise now had to measure seventy tons or over. Further legislation passed at this time required surety for any vessel under one hundred tons voyaging to the colonies. The 'hovering' clause, first introduced in George I's time to stop smugglers choosing their moment to land goods, was extended to four leagues off the coast on all vessels carrying an array of enumerated goods – mainly, tobacco, tea, coffee and spirits. The transportation of brandy (later also applied to rum) had now to be in sixty-gallon casks if found on board a vessel anchored within two leagues of the shore; or four leagues if transferring goods at sea.[145]

Such stringent measures had the negative effect of consolidating 'the trade' in the hands of a network of well-armed smuggling gangs operating out from the islands off the west coast or running directly onto the east

---

144 Payment was out of Customs revenue, failing which a certificate of debenture was issued bearing interest until redeemed.

145 This Act, passed in June 1736, allowed a small anker (barrel) for the use of the crew.

coast from the Continent. The Isle of Man, whose fiscal rights belonged to the Duke of Atholl, rose to pre-eminence as the storehouse of commodities smuggled into Scotland during this period. The 'petty sovereignty' of the island was a matter of public concern. In May 1751 the *Gentleman's Magazine* published an article entitled 'Reasons for the annexing of the Isle of Man to the Crown of Great Britain' which outlined the vast compendium of goods that regularly left the island for Ireland and the British mainland despite the presence of Customs cruisers in the Irish Sea and North Channel.[146]

GOVERNMENT PROMOTION OF THE FISHERIES

Two years earlier the public debate had, yet again, turned to a closely related issue: the active promotion of the fisheries as the alternative employment to smuggling within the Scottish maritime communities. This panacea for Scotland's economic and social ailments was the cherished project of the *Mare Clausum* school of British mercantilism but it had consistently failed to take root.

During Queen Anne's time the monopoly company model of development was abandoned in favour of competing patented companies encouraged by a bounty payment on every 'last' of herring exported. This system was the outcome of a rationalisation, undertaken in 1704, of the hotchpotch of English legislation concerning herring fishing. Under Article XV of the Act of Union this concept of direct subsidies was extended to Scotland. The first subsidy was in the form of a bounty of £10-4/- on every 'last' of herring exported.

After the Union the only British rival to the Dutch and Danish companies in the offshore grand fisheries was a London-financed 'Orkney and Shetland Fishing Company'. This company existed for a short time around 1713 under the management of Christopher Jackson and Thomas Brown but seems to have achieved little. In 1719 an Act of Parliament set aside £20,000 from the Scottish Customs revenue to promote any Scottish company that would engage in the fisheries (or manufacture).[147] This coincided with the signing of a convention with Hamburg that allowed for the first time British-caught and British-barrelled herring to be imported at

---

146   As quoted by F. Wilkins, *The Isle of Man Smuggling History* (1992), Preface.
147   *Act of Parliament*, 5 Geo. I c.20. The bounty had been slightly raised the year before to little effect.

the same rate charged on Dutch imports. The only takers were another 'Orkney Company' formed the following year by 121 'gentlemen and merchants' mainly from Southwold (Norfolk). This company remained exclusively an English venture until it crashed in 1772. At the height of the speculation mania in the 1720s its shares commanded a price of £25 which encouraged other English-based flotations – Cawood's 'North Sea Company' and the 'British Fisheries Company'.[148]

Scottish enterprise and capital were also drawn in by this wave of speculation and opportunism. In 1722 the 'Co-partners of the Fisheries established by the Royal Burrows' held their first annual general meeting in Edinburgh to report on the progress of the deputation sent to London to secure a patent at a cost of £2,000.[149] Like the English schemes, this too fell victim to the general aversion to joint-stock ventures in the aftermath of the 'South Sea Bubble' scandal. In 1726 the Convention of Royal Burghs were relieved of their immediate control of the Scottish fisheries, and it passed to the 'Commissioners and Trustees for Improving Fisherys and Manufactures in Scotland'. The new body appears to have been the first to introduce the new concept of 'premium' payments to encourage those fitting out for the herring fisheries. The sum of £2,650 was set aside to reward the earliest arrivals or best performers in a targeted sector of the fisheries or manufacture.[150]

Nature also conspired against the promotion of grand fishery schemes. During the early 1730s great shoals of herring appeared in the Firth of Clyde and off Londonderry.[151] These inshore shoals could be readily caught and delivered to the quays of the Clyde ports by the indigenous four- to six-handed open boats, known as 'cobles'. There was therefore little incentive to invest local capital in building and fitting out an expensive decked 'buss' for the more dangerous offshore fisheries.

In 1749 the King's speech to Parliament recommended new efforts be made to establish the fisheries. By the following year a committee oversaw the creation of the London-based 'Society of the Free British Fishery'. By Act of Parliament this Society was authorised to raise £200,000, by the issue of half a million shares, of which £100,000 could be spent during the first eighteen months. As a result the Society built, at great expense,

---

148   The original capital target was £500,000 at 3% interest: J. Dyson, *Business in Great Waters* (London, 1977), p. 56.
149   *Edinburgh Evening Courant*, 2 March 1722.
150   Macpherson, *Commerce*, III, p. 159.
151   Bigwood, 'Campbeltown Buss', p. 13.

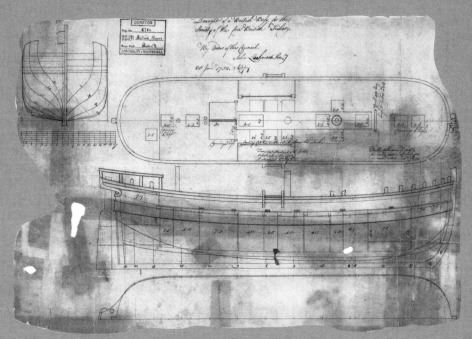

PROFILE AND PLAN OF A HERRING BUSS, c.1750.
(NATIONAL MARITIME MUSEUM, LONDON)

THE FREE BRITISH FISHERY OFF SHETLAND

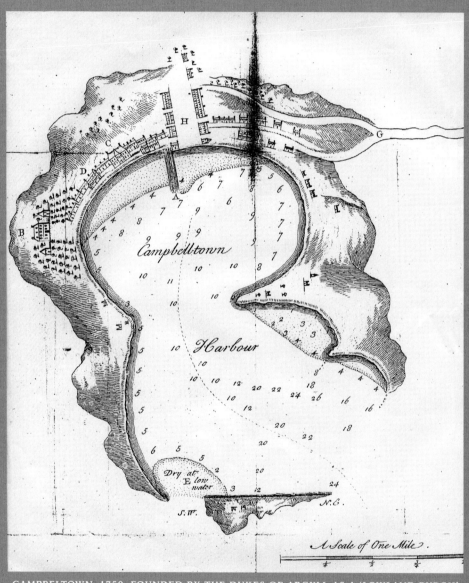

CAMPBELTOWN, 1750, FOUNDED BY THE DUKES OF ARGYLL AS A 'LOWLAND BURGH'
AND SETTLED MAINLY BY TENANTS FROM THE CUMBRAES AND BUTE ON CONDITION
THAT THEY DID NOT SUB-LET TO ANYONE NAMED MACCONNELL, MACDONALD,
MACLEAN, MACALLASTER OR MACNEILL (NATIONAL LIBRARY OF SCOTLAND)

four busses copied from a Dutch buss hired for the purpose. The first two busses – *Pelham* and *Cartaret* – were launched in time to sail for Bressay Sound with Danish crews in June 1750 and claim the new thirty shilling bounty; they were guarded by the armed sloop *Spy* to 'answer insults'. Their entire mode of operation, with its elaborate system of managers, superintendents and onshore stations, proved ruinously expensive. By the time the Society went bankrupt in 1753, they had managed to outfit only eight busses (819 tons) claiming a total bounty of £1,228 10/-.[152]

In that year, however, the first Campbeltown buss – *Farquharson* (48 tons) – was launched.[153] Nature again dealt a blow to the growth of the indigenous buss industry with the reappearance of great shoals of herring in and around the Firth of Clyde during the first half of the decade. Their appearance diverted all local interest towards inshore fishing from cobles centred on Campbeltown. Indeed, by 1755 only one Scottish buss (77 tons) claimed the bounty while the number of barrels of herring exported from Campbeltown alone leapt from 6,933 to 24,436.[154] This situation prompted the Government to change tactics to recruit local entrepreneurs to the buss industry.

THE RISE OF THE WHALING INDUSTRY

The number of Scottish-owned vessels engaged in Greenland whaling followed a similar pattern. Earlier joint-stock ventures, in the 1680s and 1720s, had been short-lived and incurred heavy losses.[155] Thereafter, the initial capital outlay required proved as prohibitive as the shortage of local mariners skilled in the art of whaling. It was, therefore, not until 1750 – when the whaling tonnage bounty was doubled from the original 1733 rate of twenty shillings per ton to forty shillings per ton – that the industry was finally established in the North.[156] This new era in Scotland's long

152 Dyson, *Great Waters*, p. 56. The other two – *Argyle* and *Chesterfield* – were launched in July at Southampton. Dutch busses (60–150 tons) were specifically designed for over-the-side fishing with a low freeboard and bow roller over which the nets were managed. The typical buss was a round-sterned, two-masted doggar.

153 Bigwood, 'Campbeltown Buss', p. 17.

154 J.Knox, *View of the British Empire*, Vol. II, as quoted by Bigwood, *op. cit.*, Table 2a.

155 In 1686 the *Dragon* of Queensferry returned with the master and four seamen from the *Jean* of Leith, which had been lost off Greenland: *RPC*, XII, p. 482.

156 Analysis of the progress of the early Scottish bounty whaling industry is available in G. Jackson. 'Government Bounties and the Establishment of the Scottish Whaling Trade', in J. Butt and J.T. Ward (eds.), *Scottish Themes* (Edinburgh, 1976), pp. 46–66.

involvement in northern whaling opened with the departure of the *Tryall* (333 tons) of the recently formed 'Edinburgh Whale Fishery Company' for the Spitzbergen and Greenland hunting grounds in 1750.

By then the British mercantilist system was approaching its most complex state. Although there would be future adaptations to the existing tariff and regulatory structure, the introduction of bounty and premium payments raised the final tier in the protective wall built around the home shipping industry.

CHAPTER 6
WAR AND PEACE
1756–75

The years 1756–75 were the high period of British mercantilism. Abroad the aggressive and expansionist trade policies instigated in the late 1730s reached a climax with a new trade war with France and her allies, the territorial gains from which consolidated Britain's first great overseas trading empire. In home waters the policy of exclusion of rivals in the fisheries was actively promoted by the bounty system. In doing so the administrative system developed to oversee and enforce the mass of prohibitive legislation, tariffs, bounties and premiums – from the working practices at the head port to the production of annual national accounts at Edinburgh.

Furthermore, by the mid-1750s Scotland's internal political conditions were, for once, stable. Jacobitism was a spent force and the administration, sitting in London, was actively seeking ways to promote the stability and prosperity of North Britain.

THE SEVEN YEARS WAR, 1756–60

The Scottish maritime experience of the Seven Years War falls into two distinct phases divided by the great security scares in northern waters during the winter of 1759–60. The war had long been expected, and so safeguards to protect the shipping stock had been in hand for sometime. Indeed, a full year before the formal declaration of hostilities, the Dutch warship *Hopende* arrived in Leith Roads with sixty-four Jutland whalers to escort the waiting Scottish contingent. The four Bo'ness whalers that joined those from Leith and Dunbar at the rendezvous were described as 'ready for war'.[1]

---

1   *Edinburgh Chronicle,* 17 and 31 March 1755.

By the following sailing season an Order in Council (2 March 1756) imposed an immediate embargo on vessels leaving Scottish harbours, as a prelude to declaring formal hostilities. This was to allow the Navy Board to procure the necessary transports to prosecute the war in America and the West Indies. In the Clyde this decree was widely ignored by the long-haul masters who gambled that the embargo would be withdrawn and forgotten by the time they returned.[2] Their guess was correct as the embargo was, to all intents and purposes, defunct by the time war was formally declared (18 May).

For the next three years the Clyde traders enjoyed relatively unfettered access to the Atlantic via the North Channel. During this time the St. Malo and Bayonne privateers were restricted to the waters immediately south of Ireland by the presence of convoy escorts and the guard ships at Kinsale, and numerous small English privateers in the English Channel.[3] Consequently, vessels from Bristol and the West Country ports suffered heavy losses running the gauntlet of enemy privateers that infested St. George's Channel and the Southern Approaches. The only alternative was to accept long periods of confinement in port between naval escorts.[4]

The Scottish masters trading across the North Sea were also well protected at the start of the conflict as eight naval sloops were allocated to that area. When not out cruising, these warships acted, along with their Dutch counterparts, as additional escorts to the regular convoy system out of Leith to Russia, Scandinavia and the Baltic.[5] With such a naval screen in position the Admiralty deemed it sufficient to renew only the Forth-Thames leg of the northern coastal convoy system.[6]

This deployment of naval power did little, however, to protect the North-East ports of Scotland from cut-and-run raids by small French

---

2   The 'regular' transatlantic master William Semple set the example in the first week of the embargo by clearing out of Greenock in the *Cochrane* (240 tons) for the Isle of May (Cape Verde Isles), ignoring the dire warnings of retribution on his return from the local Customs officers: GCA, CE 60 1/1, Collector of Port Glasgow and Greenock to Board, 13 March 1756.

3   To curb their excesses the 'rule of 1756' was introduced, placing a lower limit of one hundred ton-burthen on British privateers. This restriction was not, however, implemented until 1758.

4   Felix Farley's *Bristol Journal* reported that 113 Atlantic traders from that port were taken during the Seven Years War.

5   St. Malo was greater than Dunkirk as a centre for privateers during this war.

6   The arrival and departure of the Leith – Newcastle – London convoy was regularly reported, e.g., *Edinburgh Chronicle,* 23 February 1760.

privateers that slipped across from the Norwegian coast. As in previous
conflicts, the disruption was out of all proportion to the size of the threat.
In April 1757 the town council of Peterhead was compelled to write to the
Convention of Royal Burghs to enlist their help in securing protection
from a small enemy privateer which had brought all ship movements and
fishing to a halt along their stretch of the coast.[7] The temporary solution
to this recurring problem was to contract an Aberdeen whaler – *St. Anne* –
as the guard ship for the North-East seaboard. She was a fast New
England-built 'frigate' design hull, pierced to carry twenty cannon and
therefore well suited for her new role. After being fitted out at Leith with
ordnance and stores, she sailed in company with the captured French
privateer *La Fortune* as a decoy. Their only report of a capture was of a
Boulogne dogger found hovering off Aberdeen Bay.[8]

THUROT'S RAIDS

The raids of the great French privateering Commodore Thurot into
Scottish waters were of quite a different magnitude. In many ways his
method of waging war was the model that others would follow. He had
first established his reputation as a skilful and dogged opponent with a
highly successful cruise off the Irish coast and in North Sea in 1757–8 in
the ex-naval frigate *Maréchal de Belleisle* (44 guns/500 men).[9] During that
time he took over seventy prizes and survived two engagements with
British frigates. His last skirmish (26 May) was off Red Head, south of
Montrose, where he received a four-hour mauling from HMS *Dolphin* and
Solebay. He managed to escape, however, by virtue of the superior sailing
qualities of his frigate in light airs.[10]

---

7   Buchan, *Peterhead*, p. 27.
8   V.E. Clark, *Aberdeen* (Aberdeen, 1893), pp. 81 and 119. They had the benefit of the
French private codes found on the *La Fortune*: B. Lubbock, *The Arctic Whalers* (Glasgow,
1937), p. 90.
9   Thurot's intimate knowledge of the Irish and Scottish coasts, together with his sworn
intent to do harm to the Irish Customs service, gave rise to speculation in the contemporary
newspapers that he was either the Scottish renegade 'John Brand' or an Irish smuggler.
Lubbock states that this frigate was built at a cost of £20,000 to the owner – rumoured to be
Madame de Pompadour – and fitted out at the expense of her ladies at court. *Ibid.*, pp. 95–6.
10   Captain Marlow of the *Dolphin* described Thurot's frigate as 'the finest ship I ever
saw swim on the water': *Aberdeen Journal*, 6 June 1758. I am indebted to Michael Dun for
calling my attention to this incident.

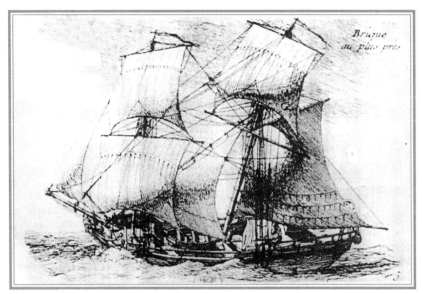

TRADING BRIG, c.1750

Thurot's hallmark was to do the unexpected. He did not wait off the Scottish coast for his opponents to reappear after their refit at Leith. He chose, instead, to cross the North Sea to join up with two other French privateers working the entrance to the Kattegat. During July this flotilla captured eleven British ships off Gothenburg. One prize was, almost certainly, the *Lothian* of Leith *en route* to St. Petersburg for hemp for the newly opened 'Edinburgh Roperie Company'.[11] Thurot's next move was to switch coasts, appearing off Liverpool in early September, thereby catching the whole region off guard. His cruise created widespread consternation on shore and paralysed shipping movements in the Irish Sea and St. George's Channel for weeks before he finally passed on through the North Channel, heading north-about to Bergen with his prizes. By the end of November he was back off the Scottish east coast, taking four prizes off St Abb's Head before the guard ships had wind of him.[12] After this chain of successes he was commissioned as an officer in the French navy.

Thurot's second cruise (October 1759 – February 1760) took on the proportions of an invading naval force. His mission in northern waters was

---

11   A.J. Durie, 'Gentlemen pretty much strangers to the Baltic trade: the Edinburgh Roperie and the Sailcloth Company, 1750–1802', *Scottish Industrial History*, XIV–XV, p. 29.

12   One of his last prizes, a Scottish snow taken off Whitby laden with flax, hemp and iron, was recaptured and taken into Scarborough. His cruise ended with his return to Ostend in early December 1758: Lubbock, *Arctic Whalers*, pp. 95–8.

twofold – to avenge the destruction of Cherbourg while creating a military diversion. The latter was intended to draw British naval units away from the English Channel at the critical moment when the blockaded Brest fleet broke out to join other French squadrons converging on Brittany. Once at sea, their primary mission was to seize and control the English Channel while the transports with Duc d'Aiguillon's army crossed to invade England.

To this end Thurot's original orders were to land troops on the west coast of Ireland or the Clyde before rounding Scotland to pick up a further company of soldiers waiting at Ostend to support the grand invasion. His formidable squadron comprised three heavily armed frigates and two corvettes, led by the *Maréchal de Belleisle* (now described as 44 guns/545 men). On board were 1,300 soldiers, under the independent command of an army officer, and a cache of 'musquets', the latter to be distributed to any local Jacobite support that they encountered.[13]

Thurot's lengthy preparations at Dunkirk were widely reported by the Scottish newspapers of the day. Fully alarmed, the Scottish Royal Burghs petitioned the Admiralty for warships to protect their coasts and for a stand of 200 muskets to be allocated to each port to arm a local militia.[14] On receiving the news of his sailing (30 September), the military in the Forth area were put on alert and additional munitions were hurriedly brought up from London to Leith and Aberdeen. At the same time Fort George, guarding the Moray Firth and access to the Great Glen, was again garrisoned. The convoy of transports also delivered cannon for transit to Fort William.[15]

Thurot's mission was partly achieved when Commodore Boyes' squadron, which had been blockading him in Dunkirk since August, was dispatched north from the English Channel to intercept him. There was a great sense of urgency, and to ensure its safe navigation of Scottish waters, eight Leith pilots were dispatched to Eyemouth to rendezvous with the approaching fleet.[16]

Thurot's expedition was, from the outset, plagued by internal divisions

13   An eye witness reported that her armament had been greatly increased. Her original four-pounders were now replaced with thirty eighteen-pounders on the main deck, twelve twenty-four-pounders on the lower deck and six six-pounders on the quarter deck: *Edinburgh Chronicle,* 6 September 1759 .

14   *Ibid.,* 9 August 1759.

15   *Ibid.,* 4 September 1759. The convoy consisted of six or seven transports.

16   *Ibid.,* 22 October 1759.

and an acute shortage of provisions and experienced seamen. Even before the squadron sailed, the military aspects of his mission had been substantially altered and scaled down. The second phase – returning to Ostend to transport troops in support of the grand invasion – was dropped. He was now commanded to stay in close support of the diversionary landing on the west coast. Thurot exploited the new situation to indulge his privateering instincts. His new plan now included a cruise off the Norwegian coast before rounding Scotland to make the landing. This was in the hope of intercepting the incoming Muscovy and Baltic convoys – an attractive proposition that served both his personal interest and that of his backers.

His opportunity came when Boyes was blown off station in a gale. Slipping out of Dunkirk, Thurot ran north to Gothenburg to provision. Once there, however, he received 'no succour' as the local Swedish authorities were determined not to incur British hostility by anything that might be construed as a 'national act' of support. Weeks of inactivity followed, during which time Thurot was reported to be 'impatient to put to sea to execute his enterprise, which is certainly designed against the coasts of Scotland'.[17] When, in November, the squadron finally sailed for Bergen, the sailing season was all but gone. Caught off the Norwegian coast in heavy weather, he missed his prey and lost one of his frigates – *Began* (40 guns) – with all 600 men on board.[18]

THE DEFENCE OF THE SCOTTISH COAST

During that month the French grand invasion scheme unravelled completely. The critical event was Admiral Hawke's desperate gamble in Quiberon Bay that succeeded in decimating the combined Brest and Martinique squadrons under Admiral de Conflan. This left the army transports waiting at Morbihan without the naval protection necessary to cross the Channel.

With the southern flank now secure, British naval forces gathered off the North-East coast of Scotland in December 1759 in anticipation of Thurot's next move. The main squadron under Boyes lay in wait off Peterhead while Captain Carkette on HMS *Hussar* was ordered to cruise between Orkney and Aberdeen. Carkette's orders were to rendezvous with

17   *Ibid.*, 28 November 1759.
18   *Ibid.*, 28 February 1760.

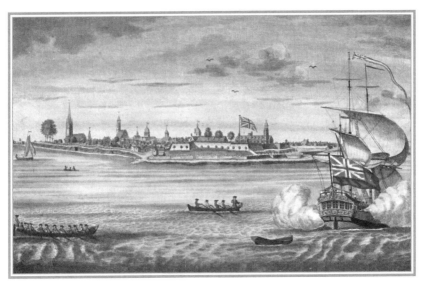

FORT GEORGE, NEW YORK, c.1750

the sloop-of-war *Dispatch*, returning from Iceland with the fishing fleet, to form a picket line. Boyes also had on call HMS *Surprise* at Stromness and HMS *Rye* in the Moray Firth.[19]

Thurot's reputation for doing the unexpected, and his willingness to take on guard ships, called for strong counter-measures elsewhere on the east coast. To the south, the Leith–London convoy escorts were greatly strengthened with the arrival at Leith of HMS *Portmahon* (20 guns) to join HMS *Prince Edward* (44 guns). They replaced the lightly armed sloop of war *Swan* which was reassigned to escort the Hudson Bay fleet as far north as the Shetlands.[20] The government's aversion to local port defences and militias meant that the civic officials responsible for their defence were left to rely on bluff. The Provost of Aberdeen primed his offshore fishermen to say – if boarded and questioned – that the town and harbour were well fortified and supplied with ample munitions.[21]

While the North-East braced itself, Thurot finally crossed the North Sea in late December. By rounding the Faroes in the face of bad weather he managed to avoid detection by the pickets to the south and entanglement with Boyes' squadron. Thurot kept his squadron well out to sea

19   The latter was conveying arms and baggage for Lord Sutherland's regiment then mustering at Inverness.
20   *Edinburgh Chronicle,* 28 April, 28 June and 7 July 1759.
21   Clark, *Aberdeen,* p. 120.

until making landfall at Islay in February. Once in Lochindaal Bay, discovery by government agents was unlikely. Only the lightly armed Customs sloop *Prince of Wales*, stationed at Campbeltown, was likely to be in these waters – but only when chasing smugglers.[22] The price Thurot had to pay to regain the initiative in this way was high. Three months at sea and a terrible winter passage had taken their full toll on old hulls and starving men. At Islay he was forced to hole up with the whole squadron while the badly leaking *Belleisle* was careened. As his men worked to recaulk the hull, parties were sent ashore to scavenge what meagre provisions could be had from the local inhabitants.

After the *Belleisle* was refloated, the squadron resumed their mission and made for the entrance to Lough Foyle. The intention was to force a landing at Londonderry but this was thwarted by a storm that swept them across the North Channel and into the Firth of Clyde.[23]

The first news to reach Edinburgh of their presence in Scottish waters came with reports from the village of Ballantrae on the Carrick shore of gunfire off Ailsa Craig. This was Thurot's first action as he fired on an incoming Virginiaman – the *Ingram* of Port Glasgow – to ensure her surrender. Thurot's privateering instincts came to the fore again as he put a prize crew on board for a high-risk north-about passage to Bergen – despite his chronic shortage of able seamen.[24] He was equally foolhardy in setting ablaze a small Belfast-bound coaster – after looting her cargo of fifty hogsheads of sugar and ten hogsheads of tobacco.[25]

The telltale pall of smoke on the horizon galvanised the unprotected Clyde coast ports into a frenzy of activity to meet the expected invasion. Riders were immediately dispatched to the ports of the Clyde with orders to suspend all further sailings. At the same time, a wherry was hired by the Greenock magistrates to go out into the North Channel to ascertain the whereabouts of the intruders. On shore, seven hundred regular soldiers and five hundred men from the Argyllshire militia were hurriedly moved from their quarters at Glasgow to Greenock to repel the expected landings.[26]

---

22 *Ibid.*, 2 August 1759. The *Ingram* (200 tons) was a relatively new plantation-built hull carrying wine and salt on the final leg of a triangular voyage (Clyde–Newfoundland–Lisbon) for John Glassford, John Munro & Company.

23 J.R.H. Greeves, 'Captain Thurot's Expedient', *Transactions of the Dumfries and Galloway Natural History and Antiquarian Society* (1961), XXXVII, pp. 147–156.

24 *Ibid.*, 3 March 1760.

25 *Ibid.*, 26 February 1760.

26 *Ibid.*, 5 March 1760. This militia, comprising mostly Campbells, was one of the few permitted by the government after the '45 Rebellion.

Under the command of Colonel Parr, they were set to constructing a cannon emplacement that would deny the enemy access to the port and the estuary beyond. Built at the end of the old ropework quay at Greenock, this 'Beauclerk battery' – as it was known – mounted twelve cannon. The Clyde lighthouse trustees acquired this ordnance in great haste from the small stock of the newly opened Carron Ironworks.[27] As it happened, Thurot had already taken the fateful decision to quit the Clyde and land his troops at Carrickfergus.

That decision was influenced by the report that a large number of French prisoners were held in the town. On arrival, six hundred French troops secured the town only to find that their comrades held prisoners had earlier been marched off into the countryside. Thereafter, the landing turned into a fiasco as squabbling factions within his own military command frustrated Thurot's plan for an immediate march on Belfast. Only there could he lay hands on the amount of stores desperately needed to revictual his squadron. With a large number of militia gathering to expel him, the Belfast authorities spurned his dire threats of fire and sword if stores were not forthcoming.[28] As the moment had gone and the way forward was blocked, Thurot resorted to looting the immediate area around Carrickfergus before re-embarking his troops.

Once out into the Irish Sea, he contemplated a landing at Whitehaven or Liverpool. Such plans were immediately discarded at the sighting of three British men-of-war working up from Kinsale. All his seamanship and cunning were to no avail as a strong nor'westerly denied him the escape route through the North Channel. Brought to action off the Galloway coast, more than his luck deserted him. Captain Crawford on the incoming Virginiaman – the *Cumberland* of Port Glasgow – witnessed at close hand the flight of his frigate escorts – *Blonde* and *Terpsichore*. Their desertion left only the *Belleisle* to make a stand while the transports dispersed.

The ensuing bloody engagement with HMS *Aeolus* lasted just over half an hour. In that short space of time the French flagship was reduced to a shattered hulk with 160 men, including Thurot, dead.[29] Soon afterwards,

---

27   G. Blake, *Clyde Lighthouses* (Glasgow, 1950), p. 13. They paid £100 for materials and £828 for the cannon. The Glasgow historian Eyre-Todd has, confusingly, the American John Paul Jones sailing in company with Thurot during this raid: G. Eyre-Todd, *History of Glasgow* (Glasgow, 1931), III, p. 290.

28   *Edinburgh Chronicle,* 1 March 1760.

29   Thurot's body, wrapped in a silk shroud, was later washed up on the Kirkcudbrightshire coast.

the two fleeing French frigates were caught in Kirkcudbright Bay by HMS *Pallas* and *Brilliant* and, along with the transports, carried into Ramsay Bay on the Isle of Man.[30] The annihilation of the expedition was completed with the capture of the prize crew – after wrecking the *Ingram* on the west coast of Scotland.[31]

THUROT'S LEGACY

The extended absence of the Kinsale guard ships during the Thurot emergency and its aftermath emboldened French privateers to cruise further north. That winter they made their first forays of the war deep into the Irish Sea and off the Atlantic coast of Northern Ireland. The Irvine merchant Robert Arthur had the great misfortune to have four vessels, in which he held an interest, ransomed in Irish waters in the space of six months.[32] His experience does not seem to have been unique. Indeed, the Glasgow marine insurance market remained jittery for the remainder of the spring, even though the first wave of raiders had move further north.

In June, insurance rates on local voyages to and from the Clyde again soared for a few weeks when two French privateers reappeared in the North Channel. This panic came on top of the general despondency generated by the leap in the number of Scottish vessels reported captured in West Indian waters. Insurance terms for the North Sea traders fared little better. Edinburgh and London underwriters reacted quickly to the report of a large number of enemy privateers cruising off the North-East and Norwegian coasts around at that time.[33]

The scare was, however, short-lived and largely over by July. With the west coast clear again, Arthur was able to secure a two per cent discount from his Edinburgh insurers of the *Katty* for her direct passage to New York

---

30   *Edinburgh Chronicle*, 8 March 1760, reprinting the *Belfast Newsletter* of the week before.

31   *Ibid.*, 2 April 1760, report of eight French crewmen under escort from Duart Castle to Edinburgh.

32   The largest was the *Kingston* of Greenock, which was taken just a few days out from Stranraer *en route* to Virginia by the *Chevalier Barte* of Bayonne. Arthur comments that the insurance rate between Greenock and Cork was 'extreamly high' owing to the presence of two enemy privateers in the North Channel: CL, Robert Arthur Letterbook, 8 May 1760.

33   One vessel reported was Arthur's *Peggy & Nelly* taken into Martinique: *Lloyd's List,* 7 July 1760. Arthur used the captain's report to contest the legality of the capture through his London insurer John Buchanan.

– provided she used the North Channel and did not touch Cape Breton.[34] On the east coast, security had been steadily improving since April when HMS *Tartar* was sent out from the Forth to clear out a nest of small privateers off Stonehaven. She was later joined by HMS *Cumberland* and *Prince Edward* which formed a flotilla of sufficient force to deter most raiders. At the same time HMS *Solebay* was assigned to escort the annual sailing of the Dutch and east-coast whalers gathered at Leith.[35]

Despite this greater naval presence, minor raids by small privateers continued off Aberdeen and Orkney, causing disturbance to local shipping for weeks at a time during that summer. But the tide had turned in the war against the French privateers in Scottish waters. This came with the capture of two of the larger raiders by the escort ships. HMS *Solebay* took the *Chevalier Barte* after a thirty-six-hour chase from the Forth to the Tyne, while in Orcadian waters the veteran Captain Allen on HMS *Grampus* cornered the most persistent North Sea raider – the Dunkirker *Duc d'Aumount* (12 guns).[36] The only major breach in what was otherwise an effective security screen was the appearance off St. Abb's Head of two French privateers during the spring of 1761. They succeeded in ransoming three Leith vessels before being chased off.[37]

THE PRESSGANGS

Perhaps more damaging to the general level of shipping activity in Scottish ports was the loss of seamen to the pressgang tenders that toured the Firths of Clyde and Forth and Aberdeen harbour. In 1755 Scottish immunity to the press was formally set aside by Admiralty order and the local provosts and magistrates were commanded to aid the pressgangs in their area.

For some officials this was an opportunity to display their ardour in pursuit of the King's service. In April, the fishing port of Rothesay was thrown into utter disarray when the commander of the revenue wherrie took it upon himself to round up local men for the Navy. He was

---

34   Arthur was quoted £300 on the hull and £100 on the cargo: CL, Robert Arthur Letterbook, 10 June 1760.

35   *Edinburgh Chronicle,* successive reports during that month.

36   In that engagement four of the privateer's crew were killed and the remaining one hundred survivors were taken as prisoners and landed at Kirkwall and Aberdeen: Lubbock, *Arctic Whalers,* pp. 89 and 91.

37   Grant, *Edinburgh,* III, p. 280.

GREENOCK, 1768 (NATIONAL MARITIME MUSEUM)

confronted by a mob of angry women who blocked his way until the able-bodied men of the town had escaped to the hills. He then vented his frustration by touring the boats in the harbour, pressing three old fishermen (the youngest over sixty), a cripple and the ship's boy from a visiting meal boat.[38] The local factor to the Earl of Bute complained, in the strongest terms, that this incident was a precedent-making threat to the inshore fishing industry and must not go unchallenged. He went so far as to petition his employer to intercede with the Admiralty to secure a comprehensive protection for the local fishing communities at Rothesay and the Great Cumbrae from further visitations.[39]

While the displeasure of a peer of the realm might have deterred a local Customs officer, the effect on the naval press was short-lived – if not negligible. By November, the tender to HMS *Glencairn* had taken up station at Gourock with instructions to intercept and apprehend 'straggling seamen' for the navy.[40] At first they respected the exemption of certain categories of seamen from the press, namely the captain, first mate, surgeon, carpenter, harpooners, line coilers, boy apprentices, Customs officers and their boatmen – none of which covered local fishermen.

By 1757, however, even these protected professions were fair game for commanders desperate for men.[41] As the war at sea reached its climax in 1759, only twenty-one (out of forty-one) of the Navy's ships-of-the-line were manned to adequate levels. Consequently, the general press was reintroduced and all pretence of selection was discarded. In June alone some fifty men were taken off outgoing vessels from Greenock and Port Glasgow irrespective of their professions. By the following month two press tenders moved down channel to work in unison off the tip of the Mull of Kintyre. From this location all vessels in the North Channel were intercepted and boarded, and four or five men were taken from each.

It was not only seafarers who went in fear of the press. In the

---

38 Letter from Hugh McBride to John Stuart, 3rd Earl of Bute: BU/162/2/12.

39 List intended for James Stuart Mackenzie or (in his absence) his brother John Stuart, 3rd Earl of Bute; BU/152/34.

40 GCA ,CE 60/1/1, Collector of Port Glasgow and Greenock to Board, 11 November 1755. The previous year a Scottish Admiralty judge had imprisoned Captain Palliser of HMS *Seahorse* for five weeks for contempt after he ignored a Scottish warrant to release an apprentice pressed from the *Cumberland* of Thurso while in Leith Roads: Grant, *Edinburgh*, III, p. 277.

41 An example was the seizure of a seaman from a Customs cruiser – the wherry *Cumbrae* – while delivering dispatches to the sloop-of-war HMS *Porcupine* off Tory Island: GCA, CE 60/1/1 Collector of Port Glasgow and Greenock to Board, 29 November 1757.

immediate hinterland of the Clyde ports, farm labourers were seized while working in the fields by a particularly 'hot' press, whereupon many others absconded to the hills, leaving the harvest to rot in the ground.[42]

The degree of force needed by the press officer to secure his quota reflects the determination of the average seaman to escape the horrors of life below decks on a British man-of-war. During a scuffle on board the merchantman *Grizy*, then in the Clyde, one seaman was shot dead and another wounded.[43] Casualties were sustained on both sides. As a later report from Stranraer noted: 'On Wednesday night last a tender endeavoured to board the *Rappahannock*, in order to impress her hands, but the crew standing to their defence, several shots were fired from both ships by which the master of the tender and one of the *Rap*'s people were killed.'[44] Soon after this incident one hundred pressed men were crammed on board the tender *Alexander & Anne* for a fateful passage to Plymouth.[45]

The hot press continued unabated well into the following spring, creating a dire shortage of seamen. Robert Arthur had the greatest difficulty in finding a crew for the large ship *Greenock* (400 tons), recently careened at Crawsfordsdyke: 'Hands are so scarce there was no getting hands to engage ... we have not, in fact, been able to get six able seamen engaged. I have now people out throu all the country looking for men ... as to carry her off by the next spring tide.'[46] A few weeks later, however, his extensive local network mustered the twenty men allowed under the 'normal' certificate of protection. As she was bound on transatlantic voyage to Quebec via Cork, Arthur sought to emulate the Earl of Bute and secure 'special protection' for a larger crew. All his string-pulling proved futile and so he reverted to underhand methods which meant the skeleton crew sailed her down to the Fairlie Patch anchorage where more hands were waiting to slip aboard.

In the Forth, the press was equally ruthless, and the departure of vessels from Leith was delayed for up to two months for want of men.

42   *Selections from the Judicial Records of Renfrewshire* (Paisley, 1876) as quoted by M.K. Barritt, 'The Navy and the Clyde in the American War, 1775–1783', *Mariner's Mirror* (1969), LV, p. 37.

43   *Edinburgh Chronicle*, 28 June, 12 July and 16 August 1759.

44   *Ibid.*, 2 May 1760.

45   The tender, under the command of Lieutenant Gentile, called in at Carrickfergus *en route* and was immediately captured by Thurot: *Ibid.*, 23 and 25 February 1760.

46   CL, Robert Arthur Letterbook, correspondence with Coutts and Bros, London, 26 April and 19 May 1760.

ABERDEEN FROM THE SOUTH IN 1750, BY WILLIAM MOSMAN. BLOCKHOUSE ON THE
SPIT IS ON EXTREME RIGHT. SALMON NETTING FROM SMALL BOATS IS IN PROGRESS
UPRIVER (ABERDEEN CITY ART GALLERY AND MUSEUM)

Attempts by the tenders to board the outgoing armed whalers invariably met with stout resistance.[47]

Aberdeen's seafaring community appears to have suffered the highest rate of attrition. This was primarily due to the zeal of Lieutenant Hay, commander of the press tender to HMS *Eagle*. In fifteen months (1756–7) he sent south seven hundred pressed seaman, despite direct Admiralty orders to suspend his activities. With his departure, Aberdeen enjoyed a short respite before the new Admiralty order (1759) reinstated the press, whereupon the tender to the HMS *Hussar* arrived in Aberdeen Bay. The town baillies went as far as to wine and dine Captain Carkette in the hope that he might exchange the recently pressed local whaling men for felons held in the town jail.[48] Fortunately, as the war at sea began to wind down after 1760 so did the activities of the pressgang tenders.

The lasting effect of the pressgangs and wartime demands elsewhere was to push up seamen's wages. By the time time the *Greenock* sailed from Fairlie Patch, wages had already jumped from £2 to £3 per month for those men who could be enticed from the safety of the inland towns such as Beith.

THE SECURITY FACTOR
AND THE TOBACCO TRADE

The numbers of incoming vessels carrying tobacco to the Clyde from the Chesapeake were always affected by the state of security.[49] During the first year of the conflict, when the sailing embargo compounded the initial shock of war, the number of incoming vessels fell to thirty-three. The Glasgow merchant John Buchanan led a deputation of tobacco merchants to appeal to Pitt to reintroduce the Chesapeake convoy system.[50] They were

---

47 *Edinburgh Chronicle*, 4 and 9 August 1759.
48 Clark, *Aberdeen*, pp. 118–9. At first the local authorities had co-operated with the pressgang to round up 'dissolute' seamen. In 1756 the *Aberdeen Journal* reported a combined operation with the local military, executed 'with great secrecy, vigilance and activity', which sealed off all streets leading away from the port. This operation netted around a hundred men of whom around forty were held for the press, including nineteen whaler men, a local pilot, a cooper and a shipwright's apprentice.
49 See Table 6.1.
50 Crowhurst, *Defence of British Trade*, p. 154. Escorts only operated one hundred leagues offshore.

successful and, with the Clyde's own security assured, the number of incoming vessels recovered strongly to eighty (1758). However, as the uncertainty surrounding Thurot's invasion (1759) mounted, so this number dropped back to forty-four. The following year, when security was regained on all fronts, the number of voyages leaped to ninety-seven. Thereafter, the general trend in the number of incoming vessels carrying Chesapeake tobacco was upwards for the remainder of the 'tobacco era.

The triumph of the Glasgow tobacco lords in securing their dominant position within the British Empire for the tobacco import and re-export trade after 1760 has since been recorded on both sides of the Atlantic.[51] Their elaborate credit-granting store system along the shores of the rivers and creeks of the Chesapeake guaranteed full and immediate return cargoes for the Clyde vessels. This, in turn, allowed for the 'clockwork' management of the Glasgow-owned company vessels producing an increasing rate of utilisation.[52]

The volume of tobacco reaching Scotland was, of course, also dependent on supply factors beyond the control of man. Availability fluctuated greatly with the variations in weather in the growing regions. During the early war years the crop yields were highly erratic: 1756 was a short crop followed by a bumper harvest; then followed two more poor harvests in succession.[53] The Glasgow merchants, with their warehoused stock, were able to exploit the erratic supply situation and so ride out both the security and credit crises of 1760-1. Their domination was secured immediately after the war when demand on the Continent for tobacco dropped – and hence prices – squeezing out their smaller competitors.

ADMINISTRATIVE CHANGES

Raising the legal size of hull permitted to carry tobacco to France (1760) to one hundred tons was a further blow to the continuing participation of the smaller estuary ports in the lower Clyde in the trade.[54] Their exit from the re-export trade was, however, a lingering one as a number of their 'casual' traders were retained to deliver small consignments of tobacco to

---

51 Notably the studies undertaken by Professors Devine and Price.
52 Dell, 'Clyde tobacco fleets', pp. 1–15.
53 1758 was down by one quarter and 1759 down by one eighth on average yields.
54 The lowest tonnage limit was first set by the 1751 Tobacco Act at seventy tons so as to exclude smugglers. The rule used 'tonnage measured' as opposed to 'tons burthen'; see Appendix A for explanation.

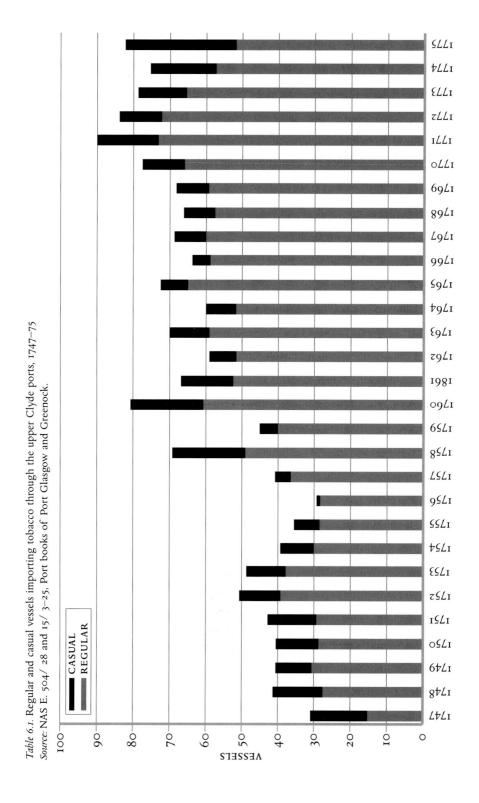

Table 6.1. Regular and casual vessels importing tobacco through the upper Clyde ports, 1747–75
Source: NAS E. 504/ 28 and 15/ 3–25, Port books of Port Glasgow and Greenock.

ports in northern Europe and Ireland. By then, the collection of the outgoing cargo of tobacco was almost exclusively from the 'legal quays' of Greenock and Port Glasgow. As a consequence ports such as Ayr allowed their status as a nominated entrepot in this commodity to lapse.[55]

By the mid-1760s, trading in tobacco was being rapidly consolidated in the hands of the great merchant partnerships of Glasgow. Their 'regular' vessels ran the Atlantic leg from Port Glasgow and Greenock to prearranged schedules.[56]

It was not until the early 1770s – when tobacco was being stockpiled in anticipation of the rupture with the American colonies – that they again resorted to the employment of a substantial number of 'casual' vessels to supplement the capacity of their own fleets.

THE WINDFALLS OF WAR

The war, however, created alternative business opportunities that percolated up through all levels of business activity. From 1756 onwards the Victualling Board commissioned local merchants to set up stores of provisions – including rum – for the Navy- and the Army-contracted transports that visited the major Scottish ports. To secure an adequate supply of foodstuffs, a strict embargo was immediately placed on the export of victuals.[57]

The Navy Board also needed to find vessels to supply General Amherst's forces in Newfoundland. In this capacity at least two vessels from the Clyde tobacco fleet were contracted for a short time. They were, however, released from government service soon after the fall of Quebec.[58] Arthur's charge – the *Greenock* – was more fortunate, undoubtedly because of her larger size. She was taken into government service within two days

---

55   By 1789 only Greenock, Port Glasgow and Leith remained listed as legal entrepôts in the tobacco trade.

56   Devine has sampled the 'shipping plans' of William Cunninghame & Co.;:T.M. Devine, *The Tobacco Lords* (Edinburgh, 1975).

57   The embargo came into effect in December 1756 and was renewed yearly until March 1759. The penalties were: fines of 20/- per bushel of cargo; the forfeiture of the vessel; and three months' imprisonment (without bail) for the offending master: Act 30 Geo.II, c.1. Thereafter, coastally conveyed cargoes of grain required a 'coast cocquet' on departure from Customs.

58   The *Argyle* (199 tons) and the *Mally* (180 tons), both of Port Glasgow: *Edinburgh Chronicle*, 7 January 1760.

Table: 6.2. Scottish letter-of-marque vessels, 1756–63

Vessel	Description	Master(s)	Owner(s)
Montrose of Aberdeen	160 tons/20 men/16 guns	Archibald Greig	Captain & Alexander Livingstone
Grand Tully of Dundee	260 tons/120 men/16 guns	Robert Mawer	John Halliburton & Co.
Alexander of Leith	200 tons/40 men/16 guns	Robert Munro	William Alexander & Co.
Little William of Leith	300 tons/50 men/16 guns	John Murray	-do-
Chistian (snow) of Leith	150 tons/25 men/10 guns	George Watt	-do-
Thistle (snow) of Leith	200 tons/30 men/14 guns	John Murray	-do-
Edinburgh of Leith	220 tons/35 men/6 guns	Thomas Murray	Jas Montgomerie, Alex Cunninghame
		James Hamilton	Andrew Ronaldson, Michael Angram
			John McLean (Jamaica)
Elizabeth & Mary of Leith	210 tons/40 men/24 guns	?	?
Achilles of Port Glasgow	160 tons/37 men/10 guns	Robert Watson	Richard & Alexander Oswald
		Daniel Graham	Thos Dunmore, Jas Denistoun
			John Stephenson
Betty of Port Glasgow	180 tons/30 men/6 guns	James Malcolm	John Coats or Couts
Binning of Port Glasgow	150 tons/25 men/10 guns	James Colhoun	George Buchanan, David Dalzell
			James Simpson
Bolling of Port Glasgow	190 tons/40 men/8 guns	Robert Douglas	Andrew Ramsay, James Baird Jnr
Buchanan of Port Glasgow	200 tons/25 men/10 guns	Robert Steel	Andrew & George Buchanan
			Daniel Dalzell, James Simpson
Cochran of Port Glasgow	200 tons/32 men/8 guns	William Semple	Andrew Dreghorn, John Murdoch
			Andrew Cochran
Duke of Cumberland of Port Glasgow	250 tons/40 men/10 guns	Allan Stevenson	Archie Buchanan, Alex Seddis
		Hugh Brown, John Bowman	
Elizabeth of Port Glasgow	200 tons/30 men/14 guns	William Noble	Hugh Wylie, James Dunlop

Vessel	Description	Master(s)	Owner(s)
George of Port Glasgow	150 tons/24 men/10 guns	John McLean	George Kippen, Archibald Ingram John Glassford, Arthur Connell
Glassford of Port Glasgow	150 tons/40 men/6 guns	William Hume	John Glassford, John Munro John Davidson (of Carolina)
Hope of Port Glasgow	150 tons/26 men/10 guns	Alex Hutcheson	John Wallace
Hyndman of Port Glasgow	150 tons/40 men/14 guns	Neil Gillies	Alexander Houston
Ingram of Port Glasgow	200 tons/40 men/12 guns	Charles Grieg	John Glassford John Ritchie & Alex Campbell
Jenny of Port Glasgow	130 tons/40 men/6 guns	Arthur Tran	John Glassford
Loudoun of Port Glasgow	120 tons/30 men/4 guns	James King	James Denistoun, John Pagan John Stevenson
Mars of Port Glasgow	140 tons/30 men/12 guns	James Weir	James Angus, George Brown
Matty of Port Glasgow	210 tons/30 men/10 guns	John Douglas	Andrew Buchanan & Son Colin Campbell, Patrick Carrick (St. Kitts)
Nancy & Kitty of Port Glasgow	160 tons/30 men/8 guns	John Tran	John Michael
Royal Widow of Port Glasgow	220 tons/30 mem/8 guns	Alex Hutchenson	Thomas Wallace Wm Cunninghame
St. Andrew of Port Glasgow	200 tons/50 men/14 guns	Hugh Wylie	James Dunlop, James Douglas George Anderson
Spencer of Port Glasgow	200 tons	? Riddell	
Three Sisters of Port Glasgow	90 tons/26 men/10 guns	Robert Hill	John Baird Jnr, Alex & Wm Walker John Weir (Antigua)

Source: PRO HCA 26.

of arriving at Quebec (1760) and employed as a cartel ship to carry exchanged French prisoners-of-war to La Rochelle.[59] Later in the war, a number of east-coast shippers were similarly engaged to convey the newly raised Scottish regiments to the Nore for onward passage to America.[60]

Scottish owners were not content to remain only on the receiving end of privateering. During the course of the war twenty-nine vessels were granted letters of marque to cruise against the French and Spanish marines.[61] They were an assortment of whalers, Virginiamen and West Indiamen.[62] But only the Dundee whaler *Grand Tully* displayed the level of manning characteristic of a determined privateer. This alternative deployment at the start of a war was a fairly common occurrence as whalers were built along 'frigot' design lines and so were easily armed with cannon,[63] but it was usually a one-off speculative venture prompted by the prospect of the first windfalls of a new war. The prime targets were rival whalers and lightly armed incoming long-haul merchantmen rounding Scotland to avoid the risk of capture in the English Channel. In the case of the *Grand Tully* she does not appear to have been successful in her new role and returned to whaling for the 1759 season.[64]

The remainder of the letter-of-marque vessels were armed 'running ships', a speciality afforded the Scots traders in wartime by their northern location. As in the previous war, once clear of the American coast these vessels invariably left the slow-moving Chesapeake convoy and so reached the market first. The Clyde's letter-of-marque vessels were (with one exception) tobacco traders in the 120–250 ton range.[65] Small as their

59   The Admiralty accepted her tonnage as 450 tons for hiring purpose at a rate of thirteen shillings per ton (see Appendix A): CL, Robert Arthur MSS, letter from Captain Thomas Lang to Robert Arthur, 6 December 1760. A prisoner cartel involved the exchange of matched prisoners (by rank) on parole not to take up arms.

60   Five transports were reported gathered at Leith: *Edinburgh Chronicle,* 14 April 1760.

61   Letters against the Spanish commissions were issued after January 1762.

62   Table 6.3.

63   Lubbock, *Arctic Whalers,* p. 100; he reports that the Liverpool whaler *Leviathan,* turned privateer, rescued the *Wolfe* of Leith (for Newfoundland with baled goods) from the clutches of the *Malice,* privateer of Boulogne, and carried her into Stromness (1761).

64   *Edinburgh Chronicle,* 9 August 1759. She was not a very successful whaler either, catching only one large whale (producing 46 butts) in that season.

65   The exception was the *Mars* of Port Glasgow which advertised for emigrating tradesmen and goods for St. Kitts (December 1759). She was 'well fortified' for her run from Greenock with fourteen carriage guns, two of which were multi-barrelled 'organ guns' (used at close quarters): *Edinburgh Chronicle,* 26 December 1759.

number was, they accounted for around two-thirds of the regular transatlantic fleet during the early years of the war.

Of the five Leith vessels, four belonged to William Alexander, Provost of Edinburgh, and were well-armed West Indiamen that ran north-about from their home port.[66] Caribbean waters were highly dangerous and so their defences were often tested, as demonstrated by the voyage of the *Edinburgh* (eighteen four-pounders, plus swivels). In the summer of 1760 she was engaged off Barbados by a large French privateer 'full of men' and exchanged shot for 'five glasses' during the chase. Having almost exhausted his powder and shot in standing-off his pursuer, her captain used the high-risk strategy of shutting his gun ports to tempt the Frenchman to close for boarding. Once she was alongside, he gave the privateer his last full broadside, forcing her to sheer off.[67] Such resolute masters were invariably well rewarded by their grateful insurers and owners. In the latter's view the risks and high rates of insurance were readily justified by the profits to be made from landing high-value cargoes ahead of convoys.

CHANGES TO TRADING

After the Thurot scare, the widely held apprehensions over the war were quickly dispelled by a series of spectacular victories abroad that opened whole new markets to Scottish traders. Typical of this root-and-branch conversion to the benefits of aggression was the Convention of Royal Burghs' open letter of gratitude, sent in July 1760, to the dying King George II.[68] The address listed the military successes in the West Indies and Canada, culminating in the capture of Quebec, the key to which were the crushing naval defeats suffered by the French fleets in Quiberon Bay and off Cape Lagos.[69]

---

66   The *Little William* was armed with six- four-pounders and was described as suitable for either the America or the West Indies trades when put up for sale: *Ibid.*, 27 February 1760.

67   The *Edinburgh* eventually made the safety of Barbados with her wounded and refitted for the voyage home: Grant, *Edinburgh*, III, p. 279.

68   H. & J. Pillan & Wilson (eds.), *Extracts from Records of the Convention of Royal Burghs, 1759–79* (Edinburgh, 1918), p. vi.

69   As early as October 1759, the Edinburgh publishers Gavin Hamilton and John Balfour of the Exchange, were selling maps of Guadeloupe, Louisburg, Quebec and Montreal – as well as coastal charts of France – printed by J. Jeffrey of Charing Cross, London: advertisement,.*Edinburgh Chronicle*, 15 October 1759.

PORT GLASGOW FROM THE SOUTH-EAST, 1760S, BY ROBERT PAUL. ROPE
WALK IN FOREGROUND, DRY DOCK WITH HORSE-POWERED PUMP IN THE
CENTRE (MITCHELL LIBRARY, GLASGOW)

As a consequence the opportunities to trade in colonial commodities were greatly enhanced. The European market for grain, rice, molasses, rum, sugar and indigo held firm as Holland remained neutral during this war. With greater access, security and the high wartime prices Scottish merchants were encouraged to speculate on 'round-about' trading, particularly in the Caribbean. The addition of the 'ceded isles' – Grenada, Tobago, Dominica and St.Vincent – and Florida generated great interest for decades to come. Without an established English presence to compete with, they offered new markets for Scottish exports (primarily salt herrings, textiles and household goods) and generous land-grant opportunitities to Scots settlers. Even the trade to Guadaloupe – restored to the French crown with the peace settlement – remained, albeit unofficially, within the Scots network after the war.

It was during this war that Caribbean rum (legally and illegally landed) rapidly displaced Spanish brandy on the home market. Boosting this trade were the large quantities required by the local agents for the Victualling Office of the armed forces. In such a demand-led wartime market, profits could be very high. Robert Arthur's accounts make it quite clear that, after 1760, acquiring rum was his prime activity, so much so that he ordered his masters to avail themselves of any opportunity to freight between the sugar islands and the American mainland until rum became available at the right price and quality.[70]

The direct import of indigo – an essential dyestuff to the growing textile industry – was a new venture created by the war.[71] Previously, small amounts (chests) of West Indian indigo had been imported via France. In 1751, to break the French monopoly, a premium of six pence per pound was introduced on British plantation-grown indigo produced in the Carolinas, but it was not until August 1756, when the French supply was cut off, that the first directly imported cargo (1440 pounds) of South Carolina indigo was landed at Port Glasgow from the *Rebecca*. The bewildered Collector wrote to Edinburgh for advice on how best to verify the quality against the French benchmark before paying the premium.[72] Almost a year later he was still haggling with the owners when a second

70   CL, Robert Arthur Letterbooks.

71   The root gave up a powerful blue dye, small amounts of which were added to starch to whiten textiles and garments.

72   On the account of John Glassford, John Stevenson and William Laird: GCA, CE 60/1/1, Collector at Port Glasgow and Greenock to Edinburgh, 14 August 1756.

delivery arrived on the *Glassford*.[73] The inspection and premium issues were resolved soon after, allowing the trade through the Clyde ports to became well established.

Colonial rice was another commodity in which Scottish participation was stirred by the dramatic improvement in security after the victories of 1760. Prior to the war the Government had encouraged an export trade in rice grown in South Carolina and Georgia. This was achieved in two ways: by exempting rice destined for the European markets south of Cape Finisterre from British duty; and by waiving the Navigation Act requirement to clear through a British port *en route*.[74] The only documentation necessary – other than registration as a British vessel – was a 'rice certificate' issued at Charleston or Edinburgh via the local head port Collector.[75]

Vessels carrying colonial rice for the northern European markets, on the other hand, remained under the terms of the Navigation Acts. During the war years they often called at Orkney, the first nominated British Customs precinct on the north-about route to Europe. The open anchorage of Stromness provided the most convenient entry and exit and hence quickest (less than five days) clearance time. Such was the passing trade that, in the absence of a 'legal quay', an old, moored hulk was used to facilitate the unloading and weighing of hogsheads in transit. The spin-off for the local economy in victualling and repairing these incoming vessels incurred the envy of Kirkwall – the head port for the precinct – which acquired its own hulk to get in on this trade.

Most of this passing trade was, however, lost after the peace. With the risk of capture in the English Channel removed, Atlantic traders in rice, as well as tobacco and sugar, switched to Cowes (Isle of Wight) as the port conveniently *en route* to Holland and the Low Countries.[76] The Government, anxious to promote stability in the North, acknowledged the effect of this

73   Matters were aggravated by the fact that the *Glassford* was a French prize, condemned at the Vice-Admiralty Court in America, carried no evidence of her hull ever being reregistered as 'British', nor of a certificate of duty having been paid on the foreign canvas of her sails: *Ibid.*, 4 June and 4 August 1757.

74   By statute renewed every seven years from 1730.

75   In 1759 a rice licence cost 5/-, a Mediterranean pass £1-15/6; and a plantation certificate 5/6. The vessel's register had to be produced on application. Only the small amount of rice shipped directly to Scotland for the home market was recorded in the official Scottish 'ballance of trade'.

76   The last two rice traders passed through Orkney in 1771: *OSA*, Parishes of Sandwick and Stromness, xvi, p. 440.

development on the fragile Orcadian economy. By way of compensation Kirkwall and Stromness were granted the unique right to export local 'big' barley – as horsefeed to Portugal – duty free.[77] This was at a time when the other Scottish ports had to put up with the reintroduction of the seasonal embargoes on the export of victuals for most of the 1766–75 period.[78]

THE CANADIAN TRADES

Undoubtedly the greatest long-term opportunities for Scottish shippers resulted from the conquest of Canada. Dried British Newfoundland fish had always been deemed a 'free good' under the Navigation Acts but safe access had previously been compromised while the French threatened the fishing stations from the fortress of Louisbourg on Cape Breton. Likewise, their control of the Gulf of St. Lawrence curtailed general trading with the interior.

Following on the capture of Quebec, the Treaty of Fontainebleau (1763) ceded Canada to Britain, thus unifying the eastern seaboard market of North America for the round-about trader. Imaginative moves were immediately made to placate what had been French Canada and assimilate it into the British mercantilist system. In the first year of peace (January 1764) Quebec was granted free access to cargoes originating from any port in Europe provided it was carried in a British hull. This presented the Scottish merchants with a new solution to the eternal problem of finding a saleable cargo on the outgoing transatlantic leg. This was to carry the greatly preferred French or Iberian 'clean' sea salt direct to the Newfoundland fisheries.[79] On the return run, dried cod and timber now joined the list of paying cargoes that attracted a government premium or bounty. The bounty on timber was specially designed to ease the chronic shortage of shipbuilding materials created by the war.[80]

---

77 The yearly amount was limited to 5,000 quarters: Act. 9 Geo. III, c.61.

78 By 1774 the embargo was extended to peas[e], beans and malt.

79 Scottish salt was extracted from sea water by boiling in open pans over which oxblood was poured. The congealing scum took with it the impurities that had floated to the surface. Salt purified in this way was considered too tainted for salting cod fish. English rock salt, on the other hand, discoloured the fish.

80 The bounty was 20/- per ton on Canadian fir timber: CL, Robert Arthur Letterbook, note to Robert Findlay, Glasgow, 17 October 1764.

Table 6.3. The marine owned by the ports of Scotland, 1759-75

Year	Number	Tonnage	Crew	aver t/n	aver t/c
1759	909	47751	5398	52.53	8.85
1760	999	53912	5943	53.97	9.07
1761	1043	55821	6327	53.52	8.82
1762	1029	54766	6205	53.22	8.83
1763	1120	60253	6764	53.80	8.91
1764	1246	67005	7673	53.78	8.73
1765	1332	75750	8419	56.87	9.00
1766	1294	72807	8456	56.27	8.61
1767	1385	78375	8862	56.59	8.84
1768	1478	85066	9412	57.55	9.04
1769	1475	86369	9752	58.56	8.86
1770	1509	88846	9460	58.88	9.39
1771	1501	88452	9207	58.93	9.61
1772	1560	91470	9552	58.63	9.58
1773	1578	91721	9823	58.12	9.34
1774	1646	93341	9907	56.71	9.42
1775	1559	91330	10048	58.58	9.09

Source: GUL MSS 1075, hereafter referred to as 'Register of Shipping'.

For Scotland's middle-ranking merchants, many of whom were based at a lesser port and owned small ocean-going vessels, these commodities provided good paying cargoes in round-about trading between the colonies and the Iberian market.[81]

SHIPPING RETURNS

After 1758, the shipping owned by the Scottish ports was once again closely monitored, this time by the Inspector-General of Customs at Edinburgh. Unlike the one-off survey undertaken by Paul's team of inspectors in 1725, he instigated an annual return that would serve as an ongoing non-monteraised prime indicator of trade and prosperity. Henceforth, every local Collector was required to extract from his port books a yearly return of the total number of vessels, their tonnage and

---

81   A glimpse of some of these owners and their trading interests is available in fragmentary victualling bills for 1760 and the *Lloyd's Register* for 1764 –6, the earliest complete register to survive. The latter lists some 140 vessels with a Scottish connection.

crews owned by the ports within his precinct. These were then listed under the headings foreign-going, coastal and fisheries.[82]

Their returns plot the rise of the Scottish marine in all three areas of seafaring, as nurtured by the mercantilist system at its highest state of development. In the fifteen years leading up to the American War of Independence the actively employed tonnage owned by the Scottish ports doubled.[83] The tons-to-man utilisation rates, which usually dipped during the war years as more crew were required for defensive capability, remained unchanged: a clear indication that the improved security during the last three years of the war had allowed an early return to near-normal trading conditions.

That the manning ratio did not improve during the peacetime years (1763–75) points to the lack of incentive to be competitive while mercantilism protected British trade from rivals. Likewise, the average hull size barely increased, mainly owing to the shallow depths of the estuary harbours and creeks frequented – both at home and abroad.

A COMPARISON OF THE SCOTTISH FLEET OF 1759 WITH THAT OF 1712

The ongoing shift in the concentration of the Scottish fleet from the east to the west coast becomes apparent when the 1759 shipping returns are compared with the last survey of the nation's fleets catalogued by Paul's 1725 Review.[84] Despite an overall increase of almost a quarter in national tonnage since 1712, the tonnage owned by the ports of the Firth of Forth had shrunk by a third while that of the Firth of Clyde ports had nearly tripled. The Galloway and Solway Firth area, previously the least developed on the lowland coastline, experienced the biggest increase in its shipping stock as Portpatrick, Dumfries and Stranraer benefited from the rising Irish cattle and passenger trades. Increases were also evident at those precincts involved in the bounty fisheries, the coal trades or serving a large agricultural hinterland.

The other notable shift was in the numbers and tonnage allocated to

---

82 A worked example is available in E.J. Graham, *The Port of Ayr, 1727–80* (Ayrshire Archaeological and Natural History Society, 1995), Monograph 15, pp. 28–29.

83 See Table 6.3.

84 See also Table 6.4.

the components of the Scottish fleet – foreign going, coastal and fisheries.[85] In both counts the fisheries out-stripped the advances made by the other two categories. The expansion of the labour-intensive herring buss industry accounted for most of the increase in numbers.

THE FISHERIES

The fisheries schemes were the prime instruments for promoting the mercantilist doctrine of exclusion. Consequently, they were the most regulated of all the maritime activities and received the full attention of the statistical compilers and commentators. In Customs returns the fisheries category refers to two distinct groups receiving a subsidy – Greenland whalers (harpoon) and herring busses (nets).[86] Not included were the small inshore open boats that caught white fish (ling, cod and haddock) by 'hook, line and sinker'.

THE WHALING INDUSTRY, 1750–1775

A primary aim of the 'ballance of payments' school of government intervention was to replace imports with a domestic supply. A clear case in question was the supply of essential whale oil and bone. Promoting the home industry at the expense of rivals fitted perfectly with the wider mercantilist view of the balance of power as it also created a reserve of prime seamen and vessels for the Royal Navy.[87] Indeed, such was the importance of the Greenland whalers to strategic planning that they received a naval escort to and from the hunting grounds off Spitzbergen and the Greenland ice-shelf in wartime.

Government intervention took the form of a bounty on vessels of 200 tons and above that fitted out as whalers and stayed north of the Artic circle for the season. Payment was calculated by the vessel's tonnage, not the size

---

85 These were crude divisions based on use of vessel whereby a transatlantic 200-ton Virginiaman is placed with a 40-ton Irish-bound collier under 'foreign-going'; and a 300-ton whaler with a 20-ton herring buss under 'fisheries'. Even so, the general increases in number and tonnage in all sectors over this period are incontestable: Table 6.5.

86 Table 6.6. The data do not match those of the 'fisheries' category of the annual Customs shipping returns due to the deployment of many of the herring busses in the coastal trade in the same year.

87 Although the skilled crew of a whaler were exempt from the press.

Table 6.4. A comparison of the Scottish fleet by region, 1712 and 1759

	Port	1712 Tonnage	1759 Tonnage	% 1712
9	**Dunbar**	640	1100	172%
25	**Prestonpans**	2082	393	19%
17	**Leith**	8202	6044	74%
5	**Bo'ness**	6913	4316	62%
3	**Alloa**	1976	1530	77%
15	**Kirkcaldy**	3867	3794	98%
4	**Anstruther**	2173	795	37%
	Total Forth Area	*25853*	*17177*	*66%*
10	**Dundee**	2922	2500	86%
21	**Perth**	140	608	434%
18	**Montrose**	2669	1535	58%
1	**Aberdeen**	3408	4404	129%
12	**Inverness**	1136	280	25%
6	**Caithness/Thurso**	298	1146	385%
	Total East Coast	*10573*	*10473*	*99%*
20	**Kirkwall**	265	545	206%
32	**Zetland**	118	0	0%
11	**Ft.William**	0	455	n/a
19	**Oban**	10	0	0%
	Total Highland & Isles	*393*	*1000*	*254%*
22	**Upper Clyde***	5384	19425	361%
14	**Irvine**	2325	3543	152%
2	**Ayr**	372	635	171%
26	**Rothesay**	199	0	0%
7	**Campbeltown**	395	1378	349%
	Total Clyde	*8675*	*24981*	*288%*
28	**Stranraer**	207	100	48%
29	**Portpatrick**	154	51	33%
31	**Wigton**	104	181	174%
16	**Kirkcudbright**	25	173	692%
8	**Dumfries**	132	166	126%
	Total Galloway	*622*	*671*	*108%*
	Total	43394	53604	124%

* Port Glasgow & Greenock
Source: Register of Shipping.

Table 6.5. A comparison of the Scottish fleet by sector, 1759 and 1775

	Number		Tonnage		Crew	Aver t/n	Aver t/c
Foreign							
1759	380		29137		3015	76.60	9.60
1775	635		51448		4302	81.02	11.96
		167%		177%			
Coastal							
1759	431		14829		1685	34.41	8.80
1775	606		23979		2355	39.57	10.18
		141%		162%			
Fisheries							
1759	98		3785		698	38.62	5.42
1775	318		15903		3391	50.01	4.69
		324%		420%			

Source: Register of Shipping.

of the catch, so as to guarantee a return to the investors.[88] The bounty had first been offered in 1730 but it was not until 1750 – when it was raised to forty shillings per ton – that the whaling industry finally took hold in the North. In the space of only two years, ten whalers were fitted out from Scottish ports. Thereafter, the annual number of Scottish whalers ranged between fourteen and sixteen for the next ten years.[89] Small though this fleet was (not exceeding c.5,000 tons), it consisted of the largest vessels then in Scottish ownership. They also represented the prime assets of the few Scottish joint-stock companies – other than the Carron Ironworks and the Banks – formed at this time. The recent acceptance of the concept of limited liability into Scots law was, undoubtedly, a major factor in encouraging a cross-section of Scottish society to invest in whaling ventures.

Despite the high level of the bounty, the west-coast companies did not stay long in the industry. The distance of their ports from the onshore boiling houses and naval escorts was compounded by a lack of business acumen. The mismanagement of the bounty claim for the two Campbeltown whalers – Argyle (443 tons) and Campbeltown (299 tons) – illustrates the latter problem. Both whalers returned safely from their first year's season in the Arctic (1751)

88   The whaling bounty was paid only on vessels between 200 and 400 tons – 'measured' by the tonnage formula of 1720. Vessels exceeding this ceiling received the maximum permissible bounty, i.e. on 400 tons.
89   See Table 6.7.

Table 6.6. Numbers and tonnage of Scottish whalers and herring busses, 1750-75. War years in bold.

| | Whalers | | | Herring Busses | | | Combined | |
	Number	Tonnage	Average Tons	Numbers	Tonnage	Average Tons	Number	Tonnage
1750	1	333	333	0	0	0	1	333
1751	6	1933	322	2	148	74	8	2081
1752	10	3137	314	4	301	75	14	3438
1753	14	4294	307	8	519	65	22	4813
1754	15	4680	312	6	403	67	21	5083
1755	16	4964	310	1	77	77	17	5041
1756	**16**	**4964**	**310**	**1**	**77**	**77**	**17**	**5041**
1757	**15**	**4531**	**302**	**2**	**103**	**52**	**17**	**4634**
1758	**15**	**4500**	**300**	**3**	**181**	**60**	**18**	**4681**
1759	**15**	**4480**	**299**	**3**	**181**	**60**	**18**	**4661**
1760	**14**	**4239**	**303**	**13**	**554**	**43**	**27**	**4793**
1761	**14**	**4239**	**303**	**17**	**745**	**44**	**31**	**4984**
1762	**14**	**4239**	**303**	**49**	**2056**	**42**	**63**	**6295**
1763	**10**	**3110**	**311**	**7**	**3691**	**42**	**97**	**6801**
1764	10	3114	311	119	5131	43	129	8245
1765	8	2560	320	157	7056	45	165	9616
1766	9	2798	311	261	12476	48	270	15274
1767	9	2798	311	263	12556	43	272	15354
1768	9	2798	311	202	9553	47	211	12351
1769	9	2798	311	85	3868	46	94	6666
1770	9	2798	311	19	861	45	28	3659
1771	9	2798	311	29	1249	43	38	4047
1772	9	2798	311	165	7251	44	174	10049
1773	10	3017	302	190	8340	44	200	11357
1774	9	2774	308	249	11350	46	258	14124
1775	9	2774	308	281	13073	47	290	15847

Sources. Whalers – Board of Trade Papers 6/93/98, 126 & 6/230, 76 (Jackson) Herring busses – J. Knox, *View of the British Empire*, Vol. 1, 'Report on the Herring Fisheries, 1798' (Bigwood).

having killed three whales between them. Their inexperienced owners, however, made fundamental errors in completing the necessary affidavits and securities required by the Receiver General of Customs. The bounty payment was consequently withheld. It took a direct appeal to the Treasury before it was reinstated more than a year later.[90] In the interim the impoverished owners had put both vessels up for sale (November 1751). They were subsequently acquired by the Edinburgh Whale Fishery Company and relocated at Leith in time for the following season.

---

90   The Treasury Bill release of payment to Philip Howe and partners: 26 Geo.II, c.11.

Table 6.7. Scottish whalers, 1750–75

Vessel	First season	Known details
Peggy of Glasgow and Bo'ness	1751	238 tons Captains Gray/Hamilton/Reid
Thistle of Glasgow	1751	Captain Sands
Glasgow Fisher of Glasgow and Bo'ness	1751	Captain Ker
Bo'ness of Bo'ness		Lost in the ice, 1758
Tryall of Leith	1750	333 tons/46 men Plantation-built Edinburgh Whale Fishery Co.
Leith of Leith		335tons/44 men Plantation-built Captain Al Cheyne & Ballantyne, owners D. Loch & Co.
Edinburgh of Leith	1751	285 tons/43 men Plantation-built Lost in the ice, 1763
Royal Bounty of Leith		330 tons/41 men Plantation-built Captain William Kerr Edinburgh Whale Fishery Co.
Royal Endeavour of Leith		331 tons
Campbeltown of Campbeltown and Leith	1751	333 tons/40 men River-built Captains Spencer & George Provane. Acquired by the Edinburgh Whale Fishery Co. 1751
Argyll of Campbeltown and Leith	1751	299 tons/acquired by the Edinburgh Whale Fishery Co. 1751
St Anne of Aberdeen	c.1756	Aberdeen Whale Fishery Co. Captain Bretony
City of Aberdeen of Aberdeen	1753	343 tons/44 men Aberdeen Whale Fishery Co. Ex-Whitby whaler
Diana of Aberdeen	1773	243 tons
Grand Tully of Dundee	1757	244 tons/36 men
Dundee of Dundee	1752	352 tons/48 men Newcastle-built 1739 Dundee Whale Fishery Co. Captains William Logan & Thomas Robson Lost in the ice 1782
Princess of Wales of Dunbar	1755	344 tons East Lothian & Merse Whale Fish Co.
Blessed Endeavour of Dunbar	1755	316 tons East Lothian & Merse Whale Fish Co.
North Star of Dunbar	1755	295 tons East Lothian & Merse Whale Fish Co.

Source: SRO RH2/4 500-553, Victualling Bills; *Shipping Intelligence; Lloyd's Registers;* Jackson; 'Scottish Whaling'.

As the Seven Years War loomed, the two remaining whalers on the west coast – *Peggy* and *Glasgow Fisher* – were relocated to Bo'ness where there was an onshore boiling house. The hazardous and unescorted route around the Western Isles to rendezvous with the Greenland fleet escorts at Bressay Sound was thus avoided.

The ensuing war gave a distinct advantage to those east-coast ports that remained in the industry. The government's co-opting of London's

GREENLAND WHALERS, c.1760

whaling fleet as armed transports (1757 onwards) and the absence of the Dutch fleet curtailed supply and drove up prices for whale oil and bone. The combination of high prices and high bounty effectively maintained Scottish whaling at a high level throughout the war.

The conclusion of the war, however, released the London whalers to join the returning Dutch fleet to swell the number of whalers off the ice-shelf. This was at a time when American sperm whalers were beginning to flood the market with superior oil. The consequence was a sharp fall in the price of whale oil and bone immediately followed by a contraction in the number of Scottish whalers back to a core of nine or ten vessels.[91]

CREWING, OUTFITTING
AND MAINTENANCE OF WHALERS

The bounty requirements set the minimum number and composition of crew as well as the levels of victualling and whaling equipment. The average British whaler was reported (in 1771) as 300 tons in size, manned by fifty-

---

91   G. Jackson, *British Whaling Trade* (London, 1978), pp 63–4 and Lubbock, *Arctic Whalers*, pp. 101–2.

four men and six apprentices.[92] While the Scottish whalers conformed in average hull size, they do not appear to have confirmed to the average crew size and often departed from their home port with smaller crews. This practice was tolerated by the Customs officials charged with policing the bounty, as the additional hands required to fulfill the conditions of the bounty were recruited in Orkney or Shetland on the voyage north.

The accounts of the first whaler of the 1750s boom – Tryall's (333 tons and valued at £1612–13/4) – give details of her fitting-out and hence her mode of operation. On her first voyage (1750) for the Edinburgh Whale Fishery Company she carried six whaling boats and 272 empty blubber butts in her hold.[93] There was no attempt at boiling on board, and so the blubber stripped from the carcass had to barrelled in an un-reduced state. The crew numbered forty-six – a first mate, second mate, surgeon, five harpooners, six boat-steers and line-coilers, nineteen sailors, two carpenters, coopers and cooks. Their wages for the voyage amounted to £382-7/4, a figure that would double if the prescribed provisions, replacement of whaling equipment and basic maintenance to the hull and rigging were also included. Set against this outlay was the income from the tonnage bounty (£666) and the sale of the blubber from four walruses. By this simple tally the venture broke even on running costs if nothing else.[94]

This level of government support encouraged the flotation of other companies: the East Lothian and Merse Whale Fish Company of Dunbar; the Aberdeen Whale Fishing Company (both 1752); and the short-lived Anstruther Whale Fishing Company (1756). As Sir John Anstruther of Elie (the chief promoter of the latter) remarked to the Earl of Leven, 'I am assured that there can be but a trifle lost were the ship unsuccessful, the bounty given by the government being so considerable'.[95]

Sir John was referring to the prospect of returning 'clean' for a season, having failed to kill a 'fish'. This was a very real prospect, as the first generation of Scottish whalers lacked the basic skills to kill and retain whales. Their owners were also too pennypinching to hire experienced harpooners from elsewhere. As a result the early expeditions usually came home 'clean' (having remaining in Arctic waters until 10 August to meet the bounty requirements) or with small amounts of blubber from a few walruses and

---

92   Macpherson, *Commerce*, III, p. 512.

93   All blubber was barrelled for delivery to the onshore boiling houses which appear to have been then situated at Leith, Bo'ness and Dunbar.

94   I am indebted to S. Mowat for a transcript of this account.

95   NAS, Leven and Meville MSS, GD 26/13/648/1, letter 29 November 1756.

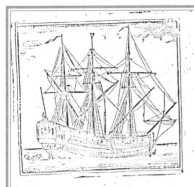

FOR
SALE
BY THE
CANDLE,

ON *Wednesday* the 22d of *November* 1752, at *Lloyd's* Coffee-house in *Lombard-street*, at Twelve o'Clock at Noon,

The Good Ship *Campbeltoun*,

Lately Arrived from GREENLAND, with all her Fishing Stores,

An exceeding fine Sailer, Square Stern'd, *River* built by Mr. *Henry Bird* sen.

Burthen 300 Tons more or less, and extremely well found, now lying at the *Red-house*, MARK M'CALLUM Commander.

SALE POSTER OF THE *CAMPBELTOWN*, 1752 (PRIVATE COLLECTION)

seals caught on the ice-flows. Over that decade three-quarters of all Scottish whaling voyages would have been loss-making without the bounty.[96]

The vessels of the first Scottish whaling fleet were either English- or American-built. The sale of Campbeltown's two London-built whalers gives full details of the outfit and furniture of Scottish whalers of this period. The exhaustive printed inventory for each sale indicates that they were square-sterned vessels, ship-rigged, carrying top-gallants and a flying-jib. Neither inventory lists carriage guns. That of the *Campbeltown* included light armaments – two swivel guns (used mainly for signalling) and four muskets.[97] Their reliance on their naval escorts for defence is also evident in the fact that no Scottish whaler took out a letter of marque while sailing under the bounty scheme during the Seven Years War.[98]

---

96 Jackson, 'Scottish whaling', p. 55.

97 I am grateful to A.R. Bigwood and Mary Petrie for sight of the original printed advertisements. The *Argyll*, lying at Port Glasgow quay, was auctioned at the Old Coffee House, Glasgow. The *Campbeltown*, in the Thames, was put up for 'sale by the candle' at Lloyd's Coffee House, London.

98 It is quite likely that it was not permitted as this would be, in effect, subsidising privateering.

THE HERRING BUSS INDUSTRY, 1757–75

The establishment of the herring buss industry in Scotland got off to a slow and faltering start, even after the existing bounty was raised to fifty shillings per ton of British-built buss in 1757. At the same time the outfitting requirements were eased, which had a profound influence on the future direction of the industry. Consequently all attempts at replicating the large Dutch busses and their over-the-side offshore fishing techniques were abandoned in favour of the locally tried and tested inshore small boat method. The average Scottish buss was, therefore, a mother vessel to between one to three open boats from which all fishing was done.[99] The first bounty imposed no specific design requirements for the buss other than that she should be fully decked, between twenty and eighty tons and built after 1750.[100] The result was that the Scottish buss fleet was made up of an assortment of mainly small, square-sterned sloops and a few larger brigs.[101]

The raising of the bounty did not have an immediate effect as Scottish busses numbered only three by 1759.[102] The security factor probably played a major part in deterring investors as the Seven Years War was well under way and there was then no regular naval protection on the west coast. The first discernible rise in the number of Scottish busses is in 1760 – after the Thurot raid and recovery of British naval supremacy. Even so, by 1761 there were only seventeen busses (745 tons/174 men) of British origin compared with 152 Dutch busses fishing off Scotland (with a further 122 off Ireland).

Other factors explain the slow response to the higher bounty. Firstly, unlike whalers which were bought secondhand, busses had to be built after the introduction of the scheme to qualify for the bounty. There was therefore an extensive time lapse between ordering, launching and outfitting a new British-built buss. At first the local shipbuilding capacity on the west coast simply could not meet the demand, and so many busses had to be constructed elsewhere in Britain, mainly Leith. There was also the problem of raising the necessary capital locally, though it would appear that the windfall of prize money from the *annus mirabilis* of 1760 may have

99   The number and lengths of nets were regulated, as were the number of crew and apprentices in proportion to the tonnage – five men for the first twenty tons and one extra for every five tons thereafter.

100   The height of the internal decks of the large busses was to allow for the stacking of the statutory size of herring barrel.

101   Campbeltown Registry of Shipping (1763–78): GCA, CE 82/11/1.

102   Appendix C, Table 6. 7.

played a significant part in financing local partnerships in the Campbeltown area.[103] By the following year, however, these initial constraints would appear to have been dissipated as British busses outnumbered the war-ravaged Dutch in Scottish waters for the first time.

THE FIRST BOOM AND BUST
IN THE HERRING BUSS INDUSTRY, 1763–71

With the peace (1763) the Scottish herring buss industry gathered momentum. At first the rise in numbers was overshadowed by that of its Irish and English counterparts who benefited from a lower duty on English salt and reliable payment of their bounty out of all English tax revenue. The Scottish bounty, on the other hand, was met exclusively out of Scottish Customs receipts which only just managed to keep pace with bounty voucher claims until 1767. During that year the first boom reached its height as 263 Scottish busses, employing over 12,500 men and boys, were outfitted for the season. After 1767, however, irregular payment of the bounty to owners of the Scottish busses, leading eventually to complete default in 1770, effectively killed off the home industry.[104]

THE NEW BOUNTY SCHEME OF 1771

As only nineteen Scottish busses claimed the bounty in 1770, the scheme had to be revamped for the 1771 season, in ways not wholly advantageous to the buss promoter.[105] While redemption of bounty vouchers was henceforth guaranteed against all government sources of revenue, in line with English practice, the bounty was reduced to thirty shillings and the

---

103   Macpherson notes that a vast amount of prize money resulting from the taking of Havana was in local circulation by 1762, as 'some of the petty officers – each receiving £1804 – (crewmen £485) – by retiring to their native places, and entering the herring fishery, became men of consequence, and chief magistrates of their towns': *Commerce*, III, footnote to p.357.

104   Bounty payments were honoured years later, but by then many of the original holders of receipts had gone bankrupt or sold off their receipt at a high discount to a third party.

105   In the same year the pressgang in Larne Lough seized 'a great number of sailors' from Campbeltown herring busses: CE 82 /1 Collector at Campbeltown to the Board, 20 July 1773.

higher salt duties imposed in Scotland remained. Further practical inducements were a relaxation of the regulations concerning the out-fitting of a buss and the introduction of a dual rendezvous system: the summer rendezvous (on or before 22 June) at Bressay Sound in the Shetlands; and the winter rendezvous (on or before 1 October) at Campbeltown on the Mull of Kintyre. This latter arrangement allowed busses to miss one rendezvous in order to engage in other trades without losing their bounty status.

This flexibility in deployment, coupled with the guarantee of bounty payment and the lower wages and costs of peacetime, was sufficient to spark a revival in buss ventures which peaked in 1776 with 294 busses making at least one bounty voyage. As a consequence Campbeltown grew over the 1750–77 period from a town of c.3,000 inhabitants (owning four small vessels) to c.7,000 inhabitants (owning sixty-two busses, manned by 750 men), second only to Greenock as an exporter of barrelled herring.

THE WHITE FISH INDUSTRY

Fishing for cod, ling and haddock by line from an open boat required considerable expertise and local knowledge. In the mid-'50s Campbeltown wherries attempted to emulate the Dutch technique of fishing over-the-side from larger decked vessels off the Shetlands but lacked the necessary skill. Thereafter most line fishing was conducted from oared open boats, some of which were up to fifteen tons and capable of raising a sail in the right conditions. By the mid-eighteenth century, however, the inshore stocks along the North-East coast, the traditional centre of the industry, had been heavily over-fished.

The pressgangs of the Seven Years War inadvertently helped establish the white fish industry in the Firth of Clyde. Local tradition has it that a large number of pressed Aberdonian fishermen were paid off at the end of the war at Ayr and chose to settle on the Clyde coast. Their news of unfished stocks quickly spread back and others, notably from Elgin and Pitsligo, made the trek south-westwards.[106] By the early 1770s the Government sought to intervene to encourage both the relocation and the deployment of larger vessels on the relatively unexploited offshore banks of the Western Isles by offering premiums on the first boats on station.[107]

---

106 Graham, *Shipping Trade of Ayrshire*, pp. 26–7.
107 Stornoway was the centre of the white fish trade on the North-West coast.

Such incentives were the final tier in the interventionist fisheries schemes that mark the mercantilist system in its most developed state prior to restructuring in the late 1780s.

CHAPTER 7
WAR AND PEACE
1776–90

The American War of Independence breached the elaborate interlocking Atlantic trading system that had evolved under the constraints of the British Navigation Acts. In doing so it brought to an abrupt end the 'tobacco era' in Scottish history. It also cancelled out many of the overseas territories and colonial markets accumulated from the Seven Years War. Another, less obvious, casualty of this war was the illusion of a favourable 'ballance of trade' generated by the flawed national accountancy techniques.[1]

In the aftermath, William Pitt circulated an open letter to the Commissioners of Customs 'concerning navigation and commerce to the revenues of the Empire' as a precursor to a radical overhaul of the existing British mercantilist system,[2] the tangible outcomes of which were the Act of Registry (1786) and the Consolidation Act (1787). The former tightened the control of shipping carrying the trade of what was left of the first empire; while the latter rationalised the complex system of duties and regulations that had caused the breach and nurtured the all-pervading black economy.[3]

WARTIME SHIPPING LOSSES

The American War was undoubtedly a traumatic episode in the history of the eighteenth-century British marine. The exact number of losses sustained by the Scottish ports is unclear. The Customs returns indicate that the numbers of vessels owned by the Scottish ports fell by around 200 vessels during the six consecutive years (1776–82) of the active war. The pre-war fleet tonnage level of around 91,000 tons was only regained in the

---

1   Appendix B.
2   Preface to Commissioners' returns: PRO Customs 17 /12 series.
3   The Act of Registry was primarily aimed at excluding American vessels from British trade after the war: R.C. Jarvis, 'Ship Registry – 1786', *Mariner's Mirror*, 4. 1, pp. 12–30.

first year of peace.[4] Hidden within these overall totals are an unknown number of vessels that had been absent from the home port for over a year on government contract (not included in the local Customs returns) and – of equal significance – the replacements for vessels lost during the war.[5]

Losses reported to Lloyd's of London indicate that around one-third of Britain's seagoing fleet (3,386 vessels) was taken by the enemy.[6] Using that ratio, the Scottish merchant marine – then seventeen per cent of the British marine by number at the start of the war – could be expected to have lost around 580 vessels. This, of course, begs the question: was the Scottish marine's war experience typical of the British marine as a whole?

Opinions vary greatly. On the one hand, the contemporary commentator Knox reckoned that 'the American War almost annihilated' the shipping stock of the Clyde and asserted that '313 vessels of various sizes were captured.[7] On the other hand, a modern reappraisal of the impact of the war on the Clyde's tobacco trade considered his latter statement to be 'almost certainly exaggerated.'[8] Supporting this verdict are the Customs shipping returns for the upper Clyde ports which, if taken at face value, appear wholly to discredit Knox. Far from being 'annihilated', they indicate that the number of upper Clyde vessels was relatively unaffected until 1778, after which time there was a small drop (c.10 per cent) before it stabilises again after 1781.

A reconciliation of the two views requires a return to the Lloyd's of London loss reports to isolate Scottish-owned vessels.[9] This reveals that there had, indeed, been a dramatic cull of the Clyde's pre-1776 stock of oceangoing vessels in American and West Indies trades (less than one

---

4   See Table 7.4.
5   Scottish vessels retaken by British warships or privateers became prize to the new captor if found to have been in the hands of the enemy for more than twenty-four hours. They were not usually returned to their original owners.
6   C. Wright and C.E. Fayle, *History of Lloyd's List* (London, 1928), p. 156.
7   Knox, *View of the Empire*, II, pp. 533–534. The Clyde ports owned virtually half the 1775 tonnage of Scotland.
8   T.M. Devine, 'Glasgow Merchants in Colonial Trade, 1770–1815' (unpublished Ph.D. thesis, University of Strathclyde, 1972), p. 268.
9   This generates a core population of around 713 Scottish-owned vessels (c.95,500 tons). A further 164 vessels can be added to this database from other contemporary sources: the Liverpool Plantation Registers, letter-of-marque commissions, Greenock Register of Shipping, Victualling Bills, bounty receipts and advertisements and reports in newspapers. The criterion used to validate the existence of a new vessel has been a minimum of three matching features. Using this system, five separate vessels can be identified bearing the name *Blandford* c.1750–84, the last four vessels sailing under the same master (Andrew Troop), which demonstrates the degree of loyalty Scottish masters had to a successful name.

CARTOON: THE HORSE 'AMERICA' THROWING HIS MASTER, 1779

hundred in number), so much so that very few identifiable hulls were still in Scottish ownership after 1781. Reported losses were particularly high amongst the larger vessels hired to the Government as transports or sent out as running ships during the early years of the conflict.

Why such losses are not reflected in the Customs shipping returns for the upper Clyde ports can be explained by the very high rate of replacement. During this war there were both the motivation and means to stay in the shipping business. On the side of the business equation, freight rates – hence profits – soared as the wartime shortage of larger hulls bit hard. On the other side, there was little real business risk to the owners of vessels on contract to one or other of the government agencies. If their vessel was lost or captured, they received full and reasonably prompt compensation. Likewise, non-contracted vessels were invariably covered by marine insurance available from underwriters at Glasgow, Edinburgh and London – albeit at a price.[10]

To accept Knox's much-quoted number of captured Clyde vessels requires putting due emphasis on his accompanying phrase – 'of various sizes'. This widens the scope to include the smaller vessels engaged in trading to Europe or coasting or fishing in home waters. The lower Firth of Clyde precincts – Ayr, Irvine and Campbeltown – were heavily involved in such trades. Their Customs returns indicate that the number of vessels owned fell by half (a loss of c.160 vessels) during the years when American

---

10   By 1775 Lloyd's of London had appointed agents at Greenock, Port Glasgow and Leith to survey vessels for insurance purposes.

raids on the west coast were at their height (1776–1781). Without knowing their replacement rate, it can never be ascertained whether this drop, when added to the Clyde's Atlantic fleet losses, accounts for Knox's exact and dramatic figure of 313 vessels. But it would seem plausible, given the length and nature of this conflict.

THE PHASES OF THE WAR AT SEA

The wartime experience of the Scottish marine moved through three distinct phases. During the first phase (1775–77) the war at sea was fought mainly in American and West Indian waters. The second phase (1777–80) commenced with the French ports hosting American privateers determined to carry the war back into British waters, a situation which inevitably led to the entry of France and her ally Spain into the war. The third and final phase (1780–3) was triggered by the entry of the Dutch, which greatly enlarged the scope of the conflict. During this latter period Britain stood in isolation from the rest of Europe as the other major maritime powers took up a stance of armed neutrality. By then the Scottish marine, in common with the rest of the British merchant marine and Navy, was close to exhaustion: another year of war would have seen virtually the entire overseas trade of the nation carried in neutral bottoms.

THE FIRST PHASE

The rebellion had been fomenting for a number of years, and many Scottish merchants had been quietly liquidating their American assets and calling in debts in anticipation of the breach. The descent into full-scale war, however, happened at an unexpected rate. The shock of war was, therefore, severe but short-lived. Indeed, it is only during the first months of the war that the image of laid-up Virginiamen and hundreds of unruly idle hands roaming the ports of the upper Clyde conforms to the hyperbole of contemporary reporters.[11]

---

11   T.M. Devine, 'Glasgow merchants and the collapse of the tobacco trade, 1775–1783', *Scottish Historical Review* (1973), 52, pp. 50–74; and 'Transport problems of Glasgow West Indies merchants during the American War of Independence, 1775–83', *Transport History* (1971), IV, pp. 266–304.

The war effort soon took up any slack. Scottish-owned vessels and masters became directly involved shortly after the opening skirmishes when the American rebels besieged British forces in Boston. The ship *Glasgow* of Port Glasgow (270 tons), then in Boston harbour, was pressed into government service without consultation with the master, local agents or owners.[12] In September of that year a further unnamed vessel was hired in the Clyde to carry to Boston

> … plaids Tartans, Shoes, Bonnets, Belts and shorts for One
> thousand private men, Sixty serjants, Sixty corporals, and Forty
> Drums, with other necessaries for the said Regiment, called the
> Royal Highland Emigrants together with Officers, their Servants
> and non-commissioned Officers with their personal arms to the
> number of twenty.[13]

From such small beginnings, the logistics of carrying and supplying, across the expanse of the Atlantic ocean, an army capable of crushing the rebellion in a single campaign rapidly escalated beyond all previous experience, so much so that the achievements of the transport services have been described as 'the greatest military and administrative feats of the eighteenth century'.[14]

The chartering of transports was in the hands of four separate government departments – Treasury, Victualling Office, Ordnance and Navy Boards.[15] The Navy Board were responsible for contracting troop carriers and surveyed the shipping stock of the upper Clyde ports early in 1776. There they found only thirty-two (poorly seasoned, American-built) square-rigged vessels of the desired size (above 200 tons). Most were lying with their undischarged cargoes of tobacco imported before the closure of the Chesapeake. Such was the Board's urgent need that the majority were immediately contracted.[16] By February 1776, the Navy Board had 101

---

12   It was not until late 1776 that the Glasgow owners (John and George Buchanan) secured the release of their vessel and were awarded £500 in lieu of lost freight charges: D. Syrett, *Shipping in the American War, 1775–83* (London, 1970), pp. 14–15.

13   GCA, CE 61/1/9, Collector of Port Glasgow to Edinburgh, 11 September 1775.

14   Syrett, *Shipping in the American War*, p. 248.

15   Only one Scottish vessel was contracted by the Treasury prior to 1780 – the *Jameson & Peggy* of Kinghorn (200 tons) – enlisted while at Exeter: PRO HCA 26/60 letter 14 May 1777. I am grateful to Michael Dun for calling my attention to this entry.

16   A. Brown, *History of Glasgow*, III, p. 380. The number of Scottish vessels is deduced from the contractor's size requirement of 200 tons and above.

HALIFAX, NOVA SCOTIA, 1764

transports totalling 38,996 tons assembled at ports around Britain – of which 7,000 tons (*c*.35 vessels) were gathered at Greenock.[17] Eight of these were immediately employed to convey an advance element of the 31st Regiment from the Clyde to Cork and on to Quebec.[18]

The second Navy Board convoy was a major undertaking consisting of thirty-three transports with 3,466 officers and men of the 42nd and 71st Highlanders on board, under the escort of HMS *Flora* (32 guns). At least fifteen of these vessels belonged to Port Glasgow. After much delay, because of American raider scares, this convoy sailed from Greenock on 29 April 1776. They departed unaware that Lord Howe had already evacuated

17   These vessels generated an income of over £4000 per month in freight rates to their owners. In addition 56,000 gallons of warehoused rum was purchased by Robert Grant of Glasgow – the Victualling Office agent – for the transports: Syrett, *American War,* pp. 41 and 251.

18   Devine, Glasgow West Indies Merchants', pp. 280–281.

Boston and transferred his headquarters to Halifax.[19] Such poor communications were, of course, typical of the era and would probably have been rectified in time had not a storm scattered the convoy off the Scilly Isles. Thereafter, over two-thirds of the transports lost sight of the escorting frigate and made for Boston of their own accord.

The front-runners, arriving in ones and twos in Massachusetts Bay, fell easy prey to General Washington's four armed schooners working out of Marblehead. The first in – the ship *Anne* of Port Glasgow (230 tons) – was taken without a fight despite carrying carriage guns and 110 armed Highlanders. Three of her sister ships arrived during the next ten days – the *George* (220 tons), *Annabella* (180 tons) and *Lord Howe* (200 tons) – and were all captured after a running fight.[20]

The credit for averting a total disaster must be shared between Captain Brisbane, on HMS *Flora,* and the highly experienced Clyde master, Humphery Taylor, on the transport *Bowman.* While Brisbane marshalled nine transports back into convoy after the storm, Taylor gathered up six other stragglers off the American seaboard and held them together long enough to fall in with HMS *Merlin.* Once the true state of affairs at Boston was known, this flotilla of transports made for Halifax under Taylor's command. Thereafter, warships were put on station to divert incoming vessels.

In the final tally five transports from the Clyde convoy were lost to Washington's privateers, and with them their companies of Highlanders and war supplies.[21] Congress did not delay in utilising their windfall to prosecute the war. The *Anne, Lord Howe* and *George* were quickly repaired and dispatched as armed running ships between Virginia and France.[22] Early in the following year, the *Annabella* was renamed the *Rising States* and sent out as a privateer for a short-lived cruise to the West Indies.[23]

By then the theatre of war had rapidly extended. As soon as Congress formally authorised the issuing of letters of marque (3 April 1776),

---

19   The warning came too late for the *Jane* of Port Glasgow, taken off Boston (May) with a cargo worth £6,000 mostly insured in Glasgow.

20   C. Hearn, *Washington's Schooners* (Maryland, 1995), pp. 174–188.

21   By the end of the year sixty-six British vessels were listed as taken in Massachusetts Bay: *Lloyd's List,* 27 December 1776.

22   W.J. Morgan (ed.), *Naval Documents of the American Revolution* (Washington, 1976), VII, p. 300.

23   She was sent out in February but was retaken by HMS *Terrible* off Belle Isle in April 1777: Syrett, *American War,* p. 85.

American privateers sailed south to raid the West Indies convoys. As fate would have it, slave insurrections had delayed the sailing of the Jamaica convoy long enough for the Americans to congregate. Thereafter, survival out of convoy was virtually impossible. As one master warned, 'The seas [off Florida] are swarming with privateers, you will be taken before you are forty-eight hours older'.[24]

The scale of early Scottish losses to these American predators is evident from the exchange of prisoners that followed. In mid-November the brig *Triton* departed from Rhode Island for a British port carrying the paroled seamen and passengers from twenty-six British prizes – of which five were Scottish-owned.[25] All, with the exception of the army transport straggler – the *Oxford* of Port Glasgow (taken heading for Halifax) – had been seized in Caribbean waters.[26] Not all captured vessels, however, remained in rebel hands as there was a high rate of recapture during this early phase.[27]

Around the time the *Triton* sailed for Europe, hopes of a reconciliation of the mother country and her colonists had evaporated. Congress now actively sought to carry the war back into British home waters with the aid of the French.[28] In retaliation the British government finally unleashed British privateers (11 April 1777) on the shipping of 'His Majesty's rebellious American subjects' with the aim of reducing their capacity to wage war before France entered the conflict.[29]

---

24   *Lloyd's List,* 25 October 1776.
25   Council of War Papers, Exchange of Prisoners, Rhodes Island Archives, 15 November 1776 as listed by Morgan, *Naval Documents,* VII, pp. 165–8.
26   This cartel should have included the master of the Irvine brig *Countess of Eglinton* (160 tons), taken heading for Antigua from Port Glasgow with a cargo of linens, hosiery, shoes and provisions (worth c.£4,500): Revolutionary War Prizes Cases No.9, Court of Appeal as listed by Morgan, *Naval Documents,* VI, p. 639.
27   An example was the ex-Virginiaman *Speirs* of Port Glasgow (180 tons), taken homeward-bound from the Bay of Honduras and retaken by her own men, led by the mate. She reached Port Glasgow on 3 October 1776, three months ahead of her paroled captain: *Public Advertiser,* 23 October 1776 and *Whitehall Evening Post,* 24/26 December 1776, as cited by Morgan, *Naval Documents,* VII, pp. 300–1.
28   The first Scottish loss to an American privateer in European waters was the brig *Isabella* from Bo'ness to Minorca: *Lloyd's List,* 7 November 1776.
29   A full review of naval policy is available in: D. Syrett, 'Home waters or America? The dilemma of British Naval Strategy in 1778', *Mariner's Mirror,* 77, 4, pp. 365–377.

AMERICAN PRIVATEERS IN SCOTTISH WATERS

This second phase of the war commenced in British waters in that month when the American brigs *Massachusetts* and *Tyrannicide* (both 20 guns/120 men) appeared off Cork. This port was the major departure point for military supplies and soldiers crossing the Atlantic.[30] Four more joined that spring – *Commodore* (18 guns/130 men), *Reprisal* (18 guns/130 men), *Lexington* (16 guns/120 men) and *Dolphin* (10 guns/64 men). By the end of May, the last three had twice circumnavigated Ireland, netting fourteen prizes. The fate of their five Scottish captures bears witness to their commerce-destroying mission: no ransom was offered; two vessels in ballast were sunk; two vessels with cargoes were sent to France; while the fifth was released with the captured crews packed on board.[31]

Benjamin Franklin, newly arrived in Paris, immediately saw the potential of extending this mode of warfare against Britain's commerce in home waters. On 26 May 1777, he wrote to Congress:

> I have not the least doubt but that two or three Continental
> frigates sent into the German Ocean [North Sea], with some
> lesser swift-sailing craft, might intercept and seize a great part
> of the Baltic and Northern trade. One frigate would be
> sufficient to destroy the whole Greenland fisheries and take the
> Hudson Bay ships returning.[32]

The most obvious points for interception were off Orkney and Shetland.

The first American privateer to appear at the entrance to the Firth of Clyde was the *Mufflin* (20 guns) early in July. From the outset there were elements of psychological warfare involved in these 'visits', designed to maximise the disruption. As the master of the captured sloop *James* of Greenock (looted of her rigging and sunk off the Mull of Kintyre) reported his captors had deliberately let slip that they had left Boston a month earlier in company with ten others intent on raiding in British waters.[33] The *Mufflin* – flying a white pennant with a pine tree emblem and

---

30   Report by Captain James Grayson of the *Lonsdale* of Whitehaven as listed in K. G. Davis (ed.), *Documents of the American Revolution, 1770–83* (Dublin, 1976), item xxxi, p. 73.

31   *Lloyd's List*, 1 June 1777.

32   H. Malo, 'American privateers at Dunkerque', *Proceedings of the United States Naval Institute*, XXXVII, 3, p. 913.

33   Affidavit of Abram Russell: Davis, *Documents of the American Revolution*, item lxxvi. pp. 130–131.

the melodramatic motto 'Appeal to Heaven' – took two more prizes in the North Channel in as many days. As before, their crews were put on board a passing brig heading for Ballyshannon while the prizes were sent off to Bordeaux.

Captures so close to the unprotected Clyde ports had the desired effect of spreading intense consternation. On 30 June the Customs Comptroller at Port Glasgow sent a night express to Robert Donald, Provost of Glasgow, concerning the dire security situation in the North Channel. In turn, the despairing Provost wrote (at four o'clock in the morning) to the Secretary of State for the Colonies, Lord George Germain:

> These rascally privateers have been within a few hours sail of
> this place … it is extremely hard, that although we have made
> repeated applications, that the Lords of the Admiralty will not
> spare us one frigate to protect above three hundred sail that are
> continually coming and going and lying in the ports of
> Greenock and Port Glasgow, besides from seven to eight
> thousand hogsheads of tobacco and great quantities of rum,
> sugar and other valuable commodities.[34]

In his lengthy communication he related that, pending a response from central government, the Duke of Argyll had been approached to organise the defence of the Clyde coast. On the Duke's orders, two companies of the 70th Regiment had already been sent to Greenock and Port Glasgow, and four companies of the Royal Scots (at Edinburgh) and one of dragoons (at Hamilton) put on alert. The Provost concluded:

> But alas, this will not save our shipping and warehouses, and
> indeed the two towns [Port Glasgow and Greenock] should
> these rascals come in. Nothing can be of immediate service but
> a frigate of war which we have the greatest right to expect.

In the meantime shipping activity in the Clyde and the North Channel came to a standstill.

The campaign to have a naval frigate as guard ship for the Clyde was immediately taken up by the local Member of Parliament – the energetic Lord Frederick Campbell – in unison with the Convention of Royal

---

34   *Ibid.*, item lxv, p. 124.

Burghs.[35] The Admiralty, however, were not in a position to respond, having then only ten frigates in home waters. It was not until late July, after another nine vessels had been captured in the North Channel, that an old fifth-rater – *Arethusa* (32 guns) – was finally sent to cruise between the Mull of Kintyre and Belfast Lough.[36] The local magistrates of the highly exposed Campbeltown were not placated by this belated gesture and minuted that they were '… taking into serious consideration the present alarming situation of the Burrow from the American Privateers now hovering upon the coasts and in the Irish Channel'.[37]

The upper Clyde ports' response was to raise a local subscription of £3,000 (filled in two hours) to arm three local vessels for the defence of their coast and shipping – *Charming Fanny, Katie* and *Ulysses*. Despite their warlike departure and the zealousness of their crews, the eight-day cruise of the Irish Sea by the latter two vessels ended in farce.[38] Their quasi-naval appearance simply heightened the local hysteria, causing local masters to run their vessels onshore or dispose of their registers overboard. Calling at Belfast Lough, the guard ships were arrested as suspected American raiders. After their release, they endured the further humiliation of being rough-handled by a pro-American mob.[39]

As the conflict at sea was certain to escalate in European waters, it was conceded that such amateurish defence was wholly inadequate to meet the threat in home waters. By December 1777 the First Lord of the Admiralty, Lord Sandwich, informed the Prime Minister, Lord North, that a switch to a naval defensive posture was unavoidable. Twenty frigates had to be recalled, mainly from the Mediterranean, to defend home waters. Most of the markets in that sea area were subsequently lost to Scottish traders for the rest of the war.

In the meantime losses, in what had become a war of attrition, mounted on both sides. In February 1778, a committee of the House of Lords assessed that 173 American cruisers (2,556 guns/ 14,000 men) had taken 733 British vessels – of which 47 were released and 127 were retaken. The African trade was all but wiped out and the insurance to North

---

35 Lord Frederick was the third son of the Duke of Argyll.

36 Barritt, 'The Navy and the Clyde ', p. 33. Captures 5–14 July: *Edinburgh Evening Courant*, 12 and 19 July 1777.

37 Campbeltown Town Council Minutes, 10 July 1777, as quoted by Bigwood, 'Campbeltown Busses', p. 88.

38 The crews took large sweeps onboard to oar their ships up to the enemy in light airs.

39 Devine, 'Glasgow West Indies merchants', p. 271.

America and the West Indies had doubled to five per cent if in convoy and fifteen per cent if running independently. On the credit side they reckoned that the colonies in rebellion had lost 904 vessels and had been expelled from both the whaling and cod fisheries.[40]

Such crude numbers imply that the Royal Navy, with the help of British privateers, was then winning this war of attrition in West Indies and American waters. But this largely illusory advantage was already being seriously eroded by the diversionary actions of American raiders in British waters. It only required the entry of a European maritime power on the rebels' side to raise this fratricidal war into a major international conflict.

The entry of France into the war was assumed to be only a matter of time. In the same month as the committee reported on shipping losses, intelligence received in London made it clear that both France and Spain were – after the British army's defeat at Saratoga – making preparations to recognise an independent United States of America. As yet the French preparations for war were incomplete, and so they made an appeasing gesture towards British remonstrations that American privateers were being allowed to operate from French bases. This took the form of an edict – widely ignored – ordering all American cruisers and their prizes out of French ports. This pretence of neutrality was soon dropped as Article XVII of the Franco-American Alliance explicitly gave American privateers full liberty to use French ports with effect from 17 July of that year.[41]

With the formal declaration of war imminent, a belated attempt was made to plug the holes in the coastal defence and convoy systems. In lieu of frigates, the Admiralty hired eight armed vessels. By March two were allocated to the Clyde – *Three Brothers* (30 guns) and *Satisfaction* (20 guns) under naval commanders. At the same time moves were made to activate the Leith – London convoy system.[42]

THE FIRST CRUISE OF JOHN PAUL JONES
IN SCOTTISH WATERS

It was during this period that the Dumfriesshire-born American, John Paul Jones, sailed from Brest (April 1778) in the *Ranger* (315 tons/18 x 9

---

40 Macpherson, *Commerce*, p. 617.
41 F.R. Stark, *The Abolition of Privateering and the Declaration of Paris* (New York , 1897), p. 125.
42 Leith does not appear to have been allocated armed guard ships until 1779.

pounders) to raid in the Irish Sea.[43] By then attitudes as to how the war should be conducted had hardened. Killing off any hope of a belated reconciliation was the Admiralty order to burn the American seaports whenever the opportunity arose. The war of attrition had also left large numbers of American seamen in British hands. Paul Jones's declared objectives were, therefore, 'to put an end to burnings in America by making a good fire in England of shipping' and secure prisoners for exchange.[44] His exploits in the Irish Sea – the landings at Whitehaven and Kirkcudbright and the capture of the naval sloop *Drake* (20 guns) off Carrickfergus – are now enshrined in American naval history.

His landing made from the *Ranger*'s cutter on St Mary's Isle, Kirkcudbright had a profound psychological impact north of the Border. Though he only managed to take the plate from Lord Selkirk's house and not the man himself for exchange, his actions demonstrated just how defenceless the Scottish coastal communities were – stripped of the simplest means of self-defence by the Disarming Act of 1746.

Furthermore, his overwhelming of a sloop-of-war proved the case for the stationing of a 'permanent' frigate on the west coast. John Murdoch of Kirkcudbright summarised the situation in his indignant open letter to the Provost of Dumfries, published within days of the landing:

> Surely the administration will now extend its attention to the northern part of the [British] Island, will give us armed vessels for the protection of our trade, and if no part of the regular forces can be spared, will at least permit us to provide for the defence by a well regulated militia.[45]

That Paul Jones did not sail on to raid the Clyde ports can be put down to military expediency. In the Clyde at that time there was – in addition to the armed vessel *Satisfaction* – the naval frigate *Thetis* (32 guns). She had been sent north to escort a new convoy that was slowly gathering to transport a further five regiments of Highlanders (6,500 men) to Halifax. Paul Jones probably

---

43 Paul Jones – as captain of the *Alfred* (30 guns) of the newly created Continental Navy – had previously taken the *Molly* of Port Glasgow off the Grand Banks of Newfoundland and, rather naively, entrusted her crew to sail her to an American port. They made for Londonderry instead: *Lloyd's List,* 1 February 1777.
44 S.E. Morison, *John Paul Jones* (Boston, 1959), p. 135.
45 *Cumberland Pacquet* as quoted by J. Gordon, 'A chronicle of press reports relating to John Paul Jones', *Scottish Genealogist*, XX, 2, p. 45.

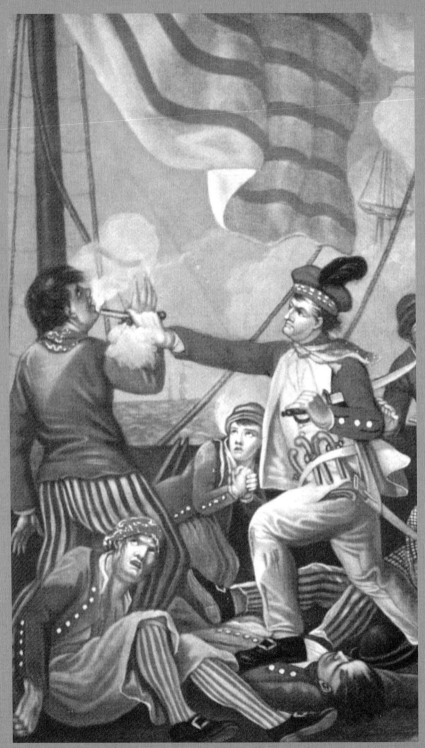

JOHN PAUL JONES – A BRITISH VIEW – RENEGADE AND MURDERER, 1779

JOHN PAUL JONES – THE AMERICAN VIEW: NAVAL HERO

knew of her presence from the master of the Irvine schooner which he had previously sunk in the Irish Sea, and so he kept away.

The guard ship and frigate were, on the other hand, quite unaware of his presence, even though he had chased a small cutter into the lower firth as far as Ailsa Craig. The first to bring them news of his whereabouts was the Clyde's Customs wherry *Cumbrae*, which raced to inform the visiting frigate lying at anchor in Lamlash Bay. Officials in Glasgow received the news by an overland express from Whitehaven around the same time. Their immediate response was to dispatch a small craft to Ayr and Irvine to stop all further sailings until such time as the armed vessel *Doctor* could be brought up to guard the coast. In the meantime, the sailing of the Navy Board convoy was postponed while the hunt for John Paul Jones and his prize got under way.[46]

The force sent out to find him was substantial. In the North Channel the frigate HMS *Thetis* (32 guns) met up with the frigate *Boston* (28 guns) from Waterford and the armed vessel the *Heart of Oak* (20 guns) of Liverpool. They were later joined by the armed ship *Satisfaction* and the frigate *Stag* (32 guns) out from Belfast, in what proved to be a fruitless sweep of the Irish Sea.[47] By the time the Navy Board convoy – 'the finest fleet ever seen' – finally sailed from the Clyde at the end of May, Paul Jones was already back in Brest. It was generally assumed in government circles that he had been after the army transports.

Local officials on the west coast, on the other hand, were much more concerned with his precedent-making landings which were bound to be emulated by others. Campbeltown was highly vulnerable to a 'visit' by virtue of its exposed location and so did not wait for Government approval to set up its own early warning system. This took the form of a fast local vessel which cruised the immediate coastline of the Mull of Kintyre. She was guided by intelligence passed on by three signal stations, each manned by three men, at Corvin and on the islands of Sanda and Davaar. In the town, a night watch of twenty men was instituted and two hundred men were enlisted in a local defence militia to counter any landings.[48] Across the firth at Ayr a guard of thirteen men was appointed to raise the alarm while the local gentry took the precaution of removing their furniture inland.[49]

46   Barrett lays most of the blame for the delay on inter-departmental mismanagement – not the raid: Barrett, 'The Navy and the Clyde', p. 40.
47   Morison, *John Paul Jones*, p. 161.
48   C. McTaggart, 'Campbeltown in the 18th century', lecture delivered 1923 and reprinted in the *Campbeltown Courier*, pp. 64–7.
49   Dunlop, *Ayr*, p. 202.

In the upper Clyde, Lord Frederick Campbell was the prime mover in having a 'permanent battery' raised at Greenock – known as Fort Jervis – to command the anchorage and entrance to the Clyde estuary. The Cumbrae Lighthouse Trustees once again funded the new structure and acquired twelve cannons from Carron Ironworks in September 1778, almost all of the costs of which were eventually recovered from the government.[50]

The Clyde's defences were never tested. By the summer of 1778 the first wave of American privateers in European waters were on their way home to refit, naval stores at the French ports having been virtually exhausted. Even in departing, they continued to inflict damage on Britain's ability to wage war overseas. A case in question was the *General Mifflin* (ex-*Isaac* of Liverpool/20 x 6 pounders/20 swivels/170 men) which intercepted seven unescorted Archangel traders off Shetland (28 June–11 July). The dearth of naval stores is evident from the fact that the smaller vessels were looted for anchors, masts, sails and rigging before being scuttled. A larger vessel was retained as a store ship for this plunder while the two major prizes (carrying 1,600 and 1,000 masts respectively) were sent off to France with prize crews.[51]

Shortly afterwards Britain chose its moment and seized two French warships in British waters which instantly brought a declaration of war. Consequently, from August 1778 onwards, letters of marque were issued against the French marine.

PAUL JONES'S SECOND RAID

A year later the west coast was again in turmoil over the reports of a new flotilla being fitted out at L'Orient by Paul Jones. The Duke of Argyll sent warning – prematurely as it happened – to the magistrates of Campbeltown that Paul Jones was out with six other vessels with the avowed intention of burning the West Highland herring buss fleet and the town itself. In this charged climate major defences were raised to repel any such 'visits'. At the Duke's personal intervention, Captain Mar of the Royal Engineers was sent to advise the town council on the building of two battery platforms on which eighteen-pounders were mounted to command the entrance to Campbeltown Loch.[52]

---

50 £100 was discounted for commissions and charges: Renwick, *Extracts from the Records of the Burgh of Glasgow*, VIII, p. 4.

51 Lubbock, *Arctic Whalers*, p. 117.

52 These cannons were in position by early 1780: McTaggart, 'Life in Campbeltown', p. 65.

The Government's aversion to established militias in Scotland was set aside around this time as companies of fencibles were raised in the maritime counties. In the West, two companies were dispatched to the Kirkcudbright coast while others were raised in Ayrshire and Argyllshire. A small recruiting party for Lord Frederick Campbell's West Fencibles scored a remarkable success in February 1779 when they came upon and boarded the Continental ship – the *Monmouth* – lying in Lochindaal anchorage, Islay.[53]

The threat was real enough as Paul Jones's second cruise into Scottish waters (August–September 1779) was on the *Bonhomme Richard* (ex-*Duras* 40 guns) with three consorts – the frigates *Alliance* and *Pallas* and the corvette *Vengeance*, a force that had the potential to devastate Scottish ports and shipping.

His north-about cruise had all the hallmarks of a Thurot planned raid. He was probably aware, or surmised, that there would be increased naval patrols in the Irish Sea and new defences in the Clyde since his last visit. Consequently he stood his flotilla well out to sea, passing west of Ireland and the Hebrides on his way north. It was not until he had rounded Lewis that he took his first prizes in Scottish waters. These were dispatched to Bergen once they had been safely shepherded clear of the Pentland Firth, after which his commanders bickered over objectives and parted company.[54]

Sailing on alone, the *Bonhomme Richard* made her next landfall south of Dunbar (18 September 1779). There she was rejoined by the *Pallas*, which had been cruising independently off the North-East coast of England. The first news of their presence to reach Edinburgh was an overland report from Dunbar of a 'french squadron' taking two Riga-bound colliers. The ensuing panic galvanised the ports of the Forth into action. In the space of a single day three batteries were raised – two at the old citadel of Leith and one at Newhaven comprising; 'thirty guns, besides carronades and howitzers, one hundred stands of small arms from the castle … and a guard … mounted all night'.[55]

---

53   She was outward bound from Casco Bay, America, with a cargo of masts, yards and booms for the French Navy: GCA, CE 82/1/5, Collector of Campbeltown to the Board, 20 February 1779.

54   They were released a few months later by the Admiralty Court of Denmark and escorted back to Leith by the guard ship *Alfred*: *Glasgow Mercury*, 13 April 1780.

55   *Glasgow Mercury*, 19 September 1779. Thereafter, an officer with eighteen to twenty artillerymen was permanently stationed at the Leith battery: *OSA*, Edinburgh, VI, p. 574. The east coast was already in a state of alarm before Paul Jones arrival, following the cruise of the *Comtesse de la Brionne* of Dunkirk (frigate built 26 x nine pounders/ 150 men) off the Forth a few weeks earlier. She ransomed three vessels which caused the local underwriters to refuse insurance on London-bound vessels. This may explain Paul Jones's slim pickings: *Glasgow Mercury*, 26 August 1779.

Tacking up the Forth in search of prizes, Paul Jones took the Kirkcaldy collier *Friendship* – detaining her master as a pilot – and Sir John Anstruther's private yacht the *Royal Charlotte*.[56] His primary objective was to land a party at Leith who would demand a minimum ransom of £50,000 under threat of close bombardment. But a violent gale blew him out of the Forth and carried him south to his engagement with HMS *Serapis* and immortality.[57]

His capture of this man-of-war in British home waters (taking 500 prisoners) was a tremendous propaganda coup for the American cause in Europe. Not only was Franklin, in Paris, greatly impressed but also the heads of state of the neutral powers – notably Catherine of Russia.

Paul Jones never raided Scottish waters again but the spectre of his return haunted the civil authorities for the duration of the war. With such a threat hanging over their heads, George Chalmers – then a lobbyist for the Convention of Royal Burghs – exploited their anxieties to raise a further £7,000 to complete the Forth & Clyde Canal from Glasgow to the sea at Bowling: a cost, he claimed, that 'would be more than compensated in one year of war'.[58]

FRANKLIN'S PRIVATEERS IN
SCOTTISH WATERS, 1779–80

The next wave of raiders in Scottish waters followed immediately on the heels of Paul Jones. They were led by the 'renegado' commanders – Patrick Dowlin, Edward Macatter and Luke Ryan. The privateering activities of these disaffected Irish-born masters were legitimised by Congressional commissions issued in Paris by Franklin – now the plenipotentiary American ambassador to the French court. Franklin's compelling need was to acquire British prisoners to exchange for Americans languishing in British jails and prison hulks.[59]

Dunkirk was their chosen base as it was exempt from the press of the French Navy and held its own Vice Admiralty Prize Court. Of the one

---

56 Morison, *John Paul Jones,* p. 216. The *Friendship* was probably 'of Wemyss'. The *Royal Charlotte* had come along side the *Bonhomme Richard,* mistaking her for HMS *Romney.*
57 During the night he passed the frigate *Emerald* and the armed ships *London* and *Content* heading for Leith.
58 Macpherson, *Commerce,* III, p. 641.
59 W. M. Clark, *Ben Franklin's Privateers* (Baton Rouge, 1956), p. 9.

hundred and fifty privateers registered with the 'Admiralty of Dunkerque', seventy-eight were under the command of Americans (six under letters issued by Congress via Franklin). Few, if any, however, placed capturing British seaman for exchange above prize money in their decision-making.

These masters, having learned from their earlier engagements with resolute British masters, armed their fast cutters in a markedly different manner from that previously employed by the French. As a privateering prospectus for the *Jeunne Dunkerquoise* (*c*.120 tons/60 men) concluded:

> The war in which the Americans are engaged against their
> metropole has forced them to seek the means of resisting
> English force … instead of equipping the privateer after the
> European manner with 12 or 14 three-pound guns, it will be
> armed with 5 six-pounders and 5 one-pound swivels, which can
> be put in action from either side of the vessel and with a
> rapidity twice as great as cannon mounted in the accustomed
> way. For this reason the 5 six-pound guns will do the work of
> ten. In addition to this remarkable advantage, the crew will
> remain invisible.[60]

This combination of speed, weight of broadside and large crew proved a highly successful formula against lightly armed merchantmen, packets and rival privateers. So much so that Macatter, Dowlin, Fall and Ryan were ranked amongst the top privateering masters in terms of value of prizes brought into French ports.[61] These particular masters had a great advantage over their French counterparts in that they were one-time smugglers with an intimate knowledge of inshore Scottish waters.

LUKE RYAN'S DESCENTS

The five cruises of ex-Portrush smuggler Luke Ryan illustrate the blend of personal profit mixed with anti-British sentiment that had been harnessed to Franklin's cause. They also serve to demonstrate how effective raids on remote anchorages and villages were – thereafter the mention of his name

---

60 Malo, 'American Privateers', p. 953.
61 Macatter was ranked first, capturing prizes to the value of 1,820,280 livres, Dowling fourth (1,539,045 livres), Fall sixth (793,669 livres) and Ryan seventh (675,521 livres): *Ibid.*, p. 952. The franc replaced the livre in 1795.

was sufficient to disrupt shipping of a major firth and have the guard ships and local militia patrolling the coastline.

Ryan – on the *Black Prince* – was the first of Franklin's privateers to run the North Channel to foray 'among the herring busses' and anchorages of the west coast.[62] He arrived in September 1779 just as Paul Jones was departing from the Forth, thereby refuelling the general state of anxiety. He announced his presence by bombarding a village on Lismore Island (Argyll) until provisions were forthcoming. He also set fire to two brigs found in the anchorage before turning south for Dunkirk.[63]

On 24 March 1780 he set sail again as master of a new privateer – the *Fearnought* (150 tons/14 six pounders/12 swivels) – under a new Franklin commission. His international crew numbered ninety-six 'of whom forty-five were Irish or American and the rest French, Spanish, Italian and Portuguese', all of whom were motivated by the prospect of prize money and shared their captain's lack of interest in Franklin's primary concern – that they should take prisoners for exchange.[64] During this cruise Ryan, unlike Paul Jones, does not seem to have been politically motivated. He avoided detection by the guard ships by standing off the east coast until he reached the Pentland Firth. Only then did he reveal his presence by taking a Newcastle whaler as his first prize.

This tactic was repeated on his third raid into Scottish waters – departing from Dunkirk 8 July. By then Ryan was not the only raider working in Scottish waters. As the unlucky master of a Saltcoats brig, *en route* from Christiansund to the Clyde with deals, later attested:

> On the 9th July we fell in with the *Rising Sun* privateer of
> Dunkirk, 20 guns of 9 pounders, off Buchanness, and after
> long consideration with the captain of the privateer at last
> ransomed the vessel for 120 guineas and took one of the
> seamen as a ransomer. On the 12th we unluckily fell in with the
> *Fearnought* of Dunkirk, Luke Ryan Commander, and as the crew

---

62   He was the *de facto* commander of the cutter *Black Prince* (ex-*Friendship* of Portrush). Already in the Western Isles was the cutter *Commandant* of Dunkirk sailing under British colours, which recaptured a large Spanish vessel from the prize crew of a Scottish privateer, took a Liverpool brig and ransomed a Saltcoats brig in Lowlander's Bay, Jura: GCA CE 82/1/5, Collector of Campbeltown to Edinburgh, 20 September 1779.
63   One Continental officer declared, 'I have sailed with many brave men, Com. John Paul Jones & Co., yet none of them equal to this Capt. Luke Ryan for skill and bravery', as quoted by Clark, *Franklin's Privateers*, p. 125.
64   *Glasgow Mercury*, 14 April 1780.

found that the vessel was already ransomed a few days before they plundered her of everything that [they] could belonging to master and men. On the 15th we fell in with John Paul Jones as Commodore of three frigates when the vessel was plundered a second time and all the clothes, liquors and 10/- in silver taken from the crew.[65]

His third captor was probably Macatter – in the *Black Princess* – on his way home from terrorising the North Channel. Posing as Paul Jones had then become the means of leaving a state of tension behind.

The unchallenged freedom of action to be found in the waters of the Western Isles brought out the cavalier side of Ryan's nature. On the afternoon of 24 July he took time off his hunt for prizes to turn his hand to extortion on land. He sailed the *Fearnought* into Stornoway harbour, where 'the crew landed … and after plundering the town they carried off some of the principal inhabitants as hostage for ransom of houses'.[66] Fifteen miles further down the coast at Loch Shiel he made a local farmer a prisoner and dallied with a group of Londonderry gentlemen 'pleasuring to the Highlands', before extracting a small ransom. He then made for Portree on the Isle of Skye where he may have had old smuggling friends as he did not threaten the town, choosing instead to pay for his provisions. Sailing up Loch Duich, he landed at Kintail and robbed the local public house of eighty guineas.

By then Stornoway had partially recovered from the 'terrible panick' of his first visit and had gathered some eight or nine armed English merchantmen in the harbour to resist any further landings: '… but it is really hard that we do not [have] solid defence against these plundering vermin'.[67] Ryan did not, however, attempt any further visits on his return passage back through the Minches to France.

During these first three visits to Scottish waters Ryan had taken twelve prizes and, yet again, demonstrated the potential for large-scale disruption by armed descents on the unprotected stretches of the Scottish coast. As an Inverness gentlemen wrote in a letter to the *London Chronicle*, 'On the west coast the *Fearnought*, American privateer, Luke Ryan commander, reigns

---

65   *Ibid.*, 27 July 1780.
66   *Ibid.*, 10 August 1780, letter from Portree, Isle of Skye.
67   NAS, GD 427/218/8, John Downie of Stornoway to George Gillander of Highfield, 26 July and 12 August 1780.

LUKE RYAN, AT THE TIME OF HIS TRIAL, 1782 (*HIBERNIAN MAGAZINE*)

uncontrolled'.[68] His unopposed landings also drew bitter responses from the isolated west-coast communities, still forced to live under the thirty-year-old proscriptive legislation of the Jacobite era. For them the quandary was quite simple: 'If they should now aim to prevent privateers [by arming themselves] they are liable to the penalties inflicted by statute [the Disarming Act]. If they remain unarmed then they are at the mercy of every boat crew the enemy may choose to send ashore'.[69]

The political cost of allowing Irish commanders to sail under American Letters from French ports had, however, been mounting during Ryan's latest cruise. This put Franklin under great pressure to cancel their commissions. Consequently, Ryan's next foray into the North Sea (8–22 August), on the *Maréchal* of Dunkirk, was undertaken with a regular French commission. This short, strictly profit-driven cruise netted him fourteen prizes.

His declared ambition – to return to Scottish waters with a more powerful vessel capable of tackling the Forth's guard ships – was realised when he was given command of the two-year-old *Calonne* (ex-*Tartar* 32 guns/250 men) in 1781. Emboldened by the firepower of his new charge, he changed his cruising pattern and, with it, his luck. Cruising the inshore shipping lane off the Forth, he was captured off St Abb's Head (3 May) by HMS *Berwick* and *Belle Poule,* having mistaken the latter for a merchantman.

Macatter was captured in October and joined Ryan in the dock of the Old Bailey the following year. Their charge was 'felony and piracy on the high seas'. Both were found guilty and sentenced to death by hanging. But with peace in the offing and the intervention of the French crown, they were pardoned.[70]

THE SECURITY NEUROSIS OF 1780–1

Rumours of imminent 'visits' and reports of phantom landings by Paul Jones and Luke Ryan were at their height during the summer of 1780. The state of anticipation in the Clyde can be surmised from the *Childers* incident. This sloop-of-war and her escort, the cutter *Pilotte,* had been sent up from Liverpool specifically to guard the exposed townships of the outer Firth of Clyde from the likes of Ryan. By way of preparation their commander – the zealous Right Honourable Lieutenant Chetwynd – had

68   *London Chronicle,* 19–22 August 1780.
69   *Glasgow Mercury,* 10 August 1780, letter from Portree, Isle of Skye.
70   D.A. Petrie, 'The Piracy Trial of Luke Ryan', *American Neptune,* 55, 3, pp. 185–204.

them sallied out from Loch Ryan into the expanse of the lower Firth to practise in a mock skirmish. Their firing of cannon put the whole coast in a state of alarm and brought out the guard ship *Satisfaction* from Greenock, along with the visiting warships *Boston, Stag* and *Ranger* from Campbeltown. The fiasco ended in the *Childers* being holed and boarded 'after a good deal of difficulty'.[71]

With better communication the armed vessels, along with the Customs cutters 'double mann'd and gun'd', were fairly effective in reducing losses to inshore enemy privateers. In April 1780 the Clyde's latest armed escort, *Three Sisters* (20 guns), supported by the sloop *Ranger* and the cutter *Expedition,* fought off two French 'frigates' (32 and 20 guns), saving their convoy of sixty sail from capture.[72] In August of that year the Customs cutter *Lairn* engaged a large French privateer (22 guns) off Ailsa Craig long enough for the becalmed frigate *Boston* to work up close enough to secure her with a broadside.[73]

Beyond the guarded firths, however, the numerous Dunkirk cruisers in Scottish waters enjoyed virtually a free hand that summer.[74] Most involved hit-and-run raiders swooping in from the North Sea. The notable exception was the Dunkirker *Duc de Estissac* (20 guns), which ransomed at least eight Scottish vessels during her extended cruise off the east coast. Across the North Sea, the approaches to the Norwegian and Danish coasts were well patrolled by French and American cruisers which took a sizeable number of Scottish vessels.

On the west coast, sailing was again temporarily suspended by the cruise of two large privateers, *Madame Adrum* (40 guns) and the *Duc de Chartres* (24 guns), in the North Channel. News of their arrival sent local marine insurance rates soaring. Later that month, the Glasgow insurance market was again in turmoil over the news of the loss of three Atlantic-bound Clyde vessels – *Catherine, Loudon,* and *Margaret* – taken off Cape Clear by a sixty-four gun French man-of-war.[75]

Communication with the Western Isles was cut in late October when another Irish renegade, calling himself Kane, took the *Islay Packet* out from West Loch Tarbet. She was carried off northward along with the twenty

---

71   *Glasgow Mercury,* 17 August 1780.
72   *Ibid.,* 14 April 1780.
73   *Ibid.,* 10 August 1780.
74   *Ibid.,* successive reports May to October 1780.
75   *Ibid.* This news followed closely on the report of the capture of the *Venus* of Port Glasgow, taken *en route* to Savannah.

passengers onboard. Mimicking Macatter, Kane also put out misinformation by informing his victims that his privateer was Ryan's *Fearnought*. A day later in the Sound of Mull he ransomed a large brig, posing this time as the master of Macatter's *Black Prince*.[76] Invoking such names had the desired effect and the frigate *Seaford* and her cutter – then on fisheries protection duty – were sent to chase him out of Scottish waters.[77]

THE STATIONING OF A
'PERMANENT' FRIGATE IN THE CLYDE

After Kane's departure (in December) the exasperated Provost of Glasgow demanded the permanent stationing of the *Seaford* in the Clyde:

> For these last two years our Coast has been very much infested and our trade distressed, by a set of Piratical Smugglers and yet from the unfitness of the *Satisfaction*, they have all escaped with impunity ... We must entreat of their Lordships, Seriously to Consider the Naked and defenceless state of our Coast & be pleased to order a frigate of 24 guns, if she sails fast, will effect.[78]

In response the *Seaforth*, a fast-sailing, copper-bottomed frigate, was formally allocated to the Clyde station that month. This did not end complaints to the Admiralty, as her high-handed captain – Brabazon Christian – failed to return to the Clyde after his cruise off the Western Isles in search of Kane. Christian had unilaterally decided that the Clyde's coastal trade was less important that the east-coast fisheries, and so he rounded Scotland in search of his quarry, arriving in Leith in January 1781. He was not back in the Clyde until early April, an absence of more than two months that brought upon him the full wrath of Glasgow's city fathers.

To curb his scope for future independent action they demanded that in future the city magistrates should direct his movements. These were to

---

76   GCA, CE 82/1/5, Collector of Campbeltown to Edinburgh, 23 October 1780.
77   Bad weather stopped them rounding the Mull of Kintyre, during which time Kane ran south to Loch Ryan where he attempted to take the incoming *Glasgow* of Port Glasgow: *Ibid.*, referring to letter from Hugh Wylie, Provost of Glasgow, to Captain Samber, 14 November 1780.
78   *Ibid.*, letter from Hugh Wylie to J. Crawford, M.P., 15 December 1780.

be restricted to no further than Cork, when convoying south, or one hundred leagues west of Tory Island, when patrolling the North Channel. The matter was never resolved as Christian remained aloof and the Admiralty were reluctant to intervene. As it happened, neither Ryan nor Paul Jones (nor their imitators) returned to exploit the frigate's long absences from her station or test the coastal defences at Campbeltown and Greenock.

In the Forth the neglected state of security was addressed after Paul Jones's visit. Three armed vessels – *Content* (22 guns), *Leith* (20 guns) and *Alfred* (20 guns) – were hired by the Admiralty as guard ships and convoy escorts. While they deterred small privateers, it would seem certain that they would have been overpowered had Ryan succeeded in reaching the Forth in the much more powerful *Calonne*.

On land a new battery of four twenty-pounders was raised on Inchgarvie island and supplied with one hundred rounds to support the shore batteries at Leith. To cover the anchorage at Inverkeithing and deny the enemy access to the upper Firth, a further battery of eight twenty-pounders and a number of field pieces were assembled on raised ground east of North Queensferry.[79]

WILLIAM FALL'S DESCENT, 1781

The last 'American' commander to harass the Scottish coast stayed well away from these batteries. William Fall was a war-hardened and ruthless master who had previously sunk, after a bloody three-and-a-half hour engagement, the Leith letter-of-marque vessel *Eagle* (140 tons/16 guns/40 men) on her run to Portugal in February 1781.[80]

On his second cruise (late May-early June) in the cutter *Sans Peur* of Dunkirk (120 tons/19 guns/12 swivels/85 men) he fully exploited the vulnerability of the east-coast ports outside the Forth's defensive cordon.[81] His presence in Scottish waters was first reported on 21 May when he chased a brig in the mouth of Dunbar harbour. Fortunately for the town's inhabitants, an armed cutter was in the harbour and was able to assist the brig in fending him off, whereupon he vented his frustration by

79   *OSA*, Parish of Inverkeithing, X, p. 514.
80   The Leith master reported from captivity in Ostend that had Fall known that he was a privateer, he would have left his crew to drown: *Glasgow Mercury*, 27 February 1781.
81   He sailed under a French commission for Porean & Co., of Dunkirk.

bombarding the town.[82] The following day he made a landing on the Isle of May where he respected international convention and demanded only water from the light keepers. He did, however, leave them with fourteen prisoners from his cruise to feed.

Getting rid of them was essential to his grand plan to ransom a town. The very next day he appeared off Arbroath where he demanded no less that £30,000, the payment of which was to be guaranteed by taking six notaries hostage: 'Be speedy, or I shoot your town away directly, and I [will] set fire to it.' The local magistrates fobbed him off until armed reinforcements arrived from Montrose. On receiving their final refusal, he fired a heated shot into the town, 'knocking down some chimney tops, and burning the fingers of those who took up his balls', before sailing off in pursuit of a passing sloop.[83]

Moving north, he stopped and ransomed two more sloops and chased a cutter into Aberdeen harbour, despite volleys being fired at him from the blockhouse and the new shore battery at Torry. In the harbour he cut out two letter-of-marque vessels abandoned by the crews. One was stripped of her provisions and rigging before being set alight while he placed the other – the cutter *Liberty* of Leith (150 tons/14 guns/12 swivels) *en route* to Lisbon – under the command of his lieutenant and renamed her *La Liberté*.[84] She was lost days later when she ran aground at Flushing during an attempted raid on British shipping in the estuary, after which Fall gave up that scheme and returned to plague the North-East (11 June), ransoming three more sloops off Aberdeen and bombarding Peterhead's south harbour, before being chased out to sea by a frigate.

Fall's descent with a small cutter prompted further additions to Scotland's coastal defences, at considerable cost to the Government. A substantial fortified battery of twelve cannon (nine-, twelve- and eighteen-pounders) was raised on the 'island' of Dunbar harbour within months of his first visit.[85] At Peterhead, a small fort and guardhouse was constructed on Keith Inch to cover the south harbour. After the poor performance of the Torry battery at Aberdeen, this new fort received four twelve- and eighteen-pounders.[86] Although Fall had not raided in the extreme North, the vulnerability of the Shetlands was acknowledged with the dispatch of

82   Malo, 'American Privateers', p. 968.
83   *OSA*, Parish of Arbroath, VII, p. 345.
84   PRO HCA 26, letters 27 January 1781.
85   *OSA*, Parish of Dunbar, V, p. 471.
86   *Ibid.*, Parish of Peterhead, XVI, p. 596.

Captain Fraser, Chief Engineer for Scotland, to repair Fort Charlotte, which was subsequently garrisoned for the reminder of the war.[87]

Reports from the outlying areas of landings from enemy privateers continued up until July of the last year of hostilities (1782).[88] In May of that year, the whole east coast was put on alert and the Forth–London convoy prevented from sailing by the departure of the Dutch fleet from the Texel.[89] The eventual clash of the two navies on Dogger Bank was a slugging match that failed to produce a victor.

THE SCOTTISH LETTER-OF-MARQUE FLEET

Beyond home waters the Scottish marine was embroiled in a war of attrition against the marines of the major maritime European nations, with the notable exception of Portugal. British letters of marque were first issued against Spain in June 1779 and Holland in December 1780. By then Russia had led Sweden and the Baltic States into forming the 'League of Armed Neutrality' (August 1780). Given such an array of enemies, it is understandable that the number of Scottish vessels sailing under letters of marque greatly exceeded those of previous wars. Over the entire war period the Scottish ports sent out 234 letter-of-marque running ships and privateers (40,146 tons).

The great majority (33,861 tons) were from the two upper Clyde ports.[90] Shortly after the entry of France into the war, the Board of the Carron Company enthused over the purchase of 2,000 cannons – 'many of them large calibre'.[91] By 1780 virtually every large hull, whether contracted

---

87   *Ibid.,* Parish of Lerwick, III, p. 420.

88   In January a landing party looted a few houses on Kintyre before being rounded up by the local militia. In late April, a large American schooner stopped all sailing off Peterhead. A month later, a French privateer made a descent on South Ronaldsay, stripping the local inhabitants of their possessions, clothes and bedding. Two or three enemy privateers were also reported in the North Channel that month, bringing the usual complaints about lack of protection: *Glasgow Mercury,* 3–10 January, 2 May, 4 June and 21 June 1782.

89   *Ibid.,* 16 May 1782. HMS *Winchelsea* took a Dunkirk privateer (12 guns) off Aberdeen Bay while shadowing the Dutch fleet.

90   PRO HCA 26, Port Glasgow – 117 vessels (20,947 tons): Greenock – 78 vessels (12,914 tons).

91   Pamphlet, 'Carronades', published by the Carron Company in December 1778, as quoted by R.H. Campbell, *The Carron Company* (Edinburgh, 1961), preface. Scottish vessels had been allowed to defensively arm themselves as for January 1776 – which attracted a premium from the Navy Board.

as a transport or victualler or deployed as a running ship in the Atlantic, had joined the few dedicated smaller privateers in the hunt for prizes.

The entry of the Dutch into the war that year (December) inspired a short but intense bout of privateering ventures at the Scottish ports: 'Never was the spirit of privateering at such a pitch as at present, all Lloyd's coffee-house is in a foment and every vessel that can swim upon the water for twenty-four hours is expedited for a cruise.'[92] The mania swept through a number of the outlying ports – Ayr, Irvine, Aberdeen, Perth, Kincardine, Carronshore and Dunbar – luring a diverse range of local merchants and professionals to speculate on the potentially dazzling returns from raiding the Dutch marine.[93] But the mania was short-lived, as evident from the dramatic reduction in advertisements selling cutters and 'sharp' vessels 'suitable as a privateer' by early summer 1781.

The numbers of prizes taken by Scottish vessels during this war can never be satisfactorily ascertained, as most (prior to 1781) were taken in American and Caribbean waters and condemned by the Vice Admiralty courts at Halifax, New York, Barbados and Jamaica.[94] Reports of prize-taking in British newspapers are also unreliable as the recapture rate was high. The impression given, however, is that the number of prizes safely brought into harbour fell well short of the number of Scottish vessels lost to enemy cruisers.[95] This is not, of course, a matter of like-for-like in this crude comparison by tally. Some prizes taken by Scottish privateers were large and very valuable, while many Scottish losses were small coasters and herring busses.[96]

Towards the end of the war the British navy regained much of its superiority. Government sought to exploit the high rate of recapture by naval units to prohibit British masters from accepting ransom (1 June 1782)

---

92   *Glasgow Mercury,* 25 December 1780.

93   At Dunbar a £25 pounds per shareholder subscription was opened to fit-out two privateers – *Thistle* (60 tons/35 men), sent to West Indies and New York, and *Prince of Wales* (325 tons/45 men), Greenland whaler: *Glasgow Mercury,*30 December 1780; and PRO HCA 26, letters 8 February and 17 March 1781.

94   Little documentation has survived from these courts. Occasionally a vessel captured off North America was brought home. An example is the sale at Greenock of the *Achilles* (200 tons), formerly an 'American cruiser': *Glasgow Mercury,* 28 June 1781.

95   Barritt's study of the newspapers found forty-four prize reports, 'but I cannot claim the least accuracy for this figure: 'The navy and the Clyde', p. 35.

96   As late as 1790 thirty-nine ex-prizes – mostly in the larger hull ranges – were registered to Scottish owners: PRO Customs 17, Scottish fleet as of September 1790. This is not to say that any or all of these vessels were taken by Scottish privateers.

– on pain of a £500 fine and the nullification of the ransom bill.[97] This was intended to weaken the effectiveness of enemy cruisers by forcing them to reduce their complements on prize crews.[98]

THE PRESSGANG

The general press was introduced in June 1777, and by the spring of the following year an exceedingly 'hot' press was operating in the Clyde. This prompted all but exempted professions to flee to the safety of the hinterland. By March 1778 the Glasgow magistrates were forced to offer a bounty payment to any seaman who voluntarily presented himself to the Regulating Officer at Port Glasgow or Greenock to serve on the, once popular, guard ships. Although regularly readvertised throughout the war, such inducements rapidly lost their appeal in the face of generous signing-on gratuities and high wages offered by Clyde masters or the privateering promoter's lure of prize money.[99] The magistrates' bounty offer of 30 June 1779 failed to entice a single man to come forward, whereupon they doubled the bounty to three guineas for seamen and two for landsmen that September – with little effect.[100]

In December 1780, when the privateering mania was at its height, the Government was forced to compete for able-bodied men by promising that the allocation of naval prize money would, in future, match that of a privateer.[101] By whatever means – inducement or pressgang – the numbers of men taken by the Navy were high enough to drive up seamen's wages fourfold.[102]

---

97   Act 22 Geo. III, c.25, as reported in *Glasgow Mercury,* 16 May 1782.

98   By accepting a ransom bill, the captured vessel had a forty-day immunity in which to make for a friendly harbour. The practice was resumed in the war against Revolutionary France.

99   Devine, 'Transport Problems', pp. 289–91.

100   The bounty was usually on offer over a three-month period: 12 March 1778, 30 June and 7 July 1779, 5 April and 19 October 1781 and 11 July 1782: *Glasgow Records,* VII, pp. 521, 556–7 and VIII, pp. 6, 27 and 51.

101   *Glasgow Mercury,* 30 December 1780.

102   The west-coast fisheries were particularly vulnerable as Campbeltown lost 900 men to the navy, the island of Tiree 120 youths and Saltcoats 200 men: *OSA,* Parishes of Campbeltown, X, p. 59: Tiree, X, p.405: and Stevenston, VI, p. 614,

THE CARRON COMPANY
FLEET AND THE CARRONADE

The most readily identifiable fleet of letter-of-marque vessels under a common ownership was that serving the Carron Ironworks – Scotland's only international manufacturer of consequence in the eighteenth century. The formation of this fleet was a direct response to the first appearance of American cruisers in northern waters (1777). The Government – mindful of the previous year's losses of military equipment to the enemy – commanded the company to stop the hire of poorly armed local vessels when shipping their cannons abroad. In complying with this order, the company purchased an old Thames-built ship (250 tons) which they renamed the *King of Spain*, of Bo'ness. She was subsequently heavily armed with eighteen eighteen-pounder carriage guns and six swivels.[103] Her substantial crew of thirty-six men was considered sufficient to deter most privateers on her regular run to the Spanish arsenal at Ferrol. She was a prize worth having as she normally delivered up to three hundred iron cannon – ranging from three to twenty-four pounders – per passage.

With the entry of Spain into the war (June 1779) she was renamed the *Earl of Dunmore* – after the company's benefactor in London – and switched to running to St. Petersburg and New York. On these highly dangerous voyages she was mounting an additional six cannons served by a further fourteen crewmen.[104]

While this company ship continued to sail to the overseas markets, an additional fleet of armed vessels was required to convey ordnance and munitions to Carron Wharf, London. The domestic market for Carron's array of lightweight cannons (bored by the Wilkinson method) had soared after January 1776 when the Navy Board introduced a premium on armed vessels and British privateers were unleashed (August 1778). This latter event coincided with the Ordnance Board acceptance of the 'carronade' for the Navy. By December 1778 the company could boast that they had sold 5,000 cannon since 1776.[105]

---

103 PRO, HCA 26, letters 29 April, 4 July 1777 and 18 June 1779. Her owners were : James, Samuel and Francis Garbett: Benjamin Roebuck: John Adam of Edinburgh: John Minyer of Gray's Inn: and Charles Gascoigne, the manager of Carron.
104 She was later sold and renamed the *William* for a voyage from London to New York: *Lloyd's Registers* of 1778–81.
105 Campbell, *The Carron Company*, p. 91.

At CARRON for LONDON,
To SAIL April 9th, 1782,

THE Carron Shipping Company's veſſel, The Ship PAISLEY, JOHN GARDINER, Maſter, mounting twenty 18 pounders, and men anſwerable. For freight or paſſage, apply to Mr. G. Hamilton, Glaſgow; Mr. John Brown, Leith; or to the Carron Shipping Company, at Carron-Wharf.

N. B. The Carron veſſels are fitted out in the moſt complete manner for defence, at a very conſiderable expence, and are well provided with ſmall arms. Able-bodied landmen, who are deſirous to ſerve on board thoſe veſſels for three years certain, will meet with the beſt encouragement, and be protected; and all mariners, recruiting parties, ſoldiers upon furlough, and all other ſteerage paſſengers, who have been accuſtomed to the uſe of firearms, and will engage to aſſiſt in defending themſelves, ſhall be accommodated with their paſſage to or from London, upon ſatisfying the maſters for their proviſions, which in no inſtance ſhall exceed ten ſhillings and ſixpence ſterling.

✝ The Carron veſſels ſail regularly as uſual, without waiting for convoy.

The Carron Shipping Company employ in the carrying trade to, and from London the following veſſels, viz. Ship Lady Charlotte, Frigate built, 20 carronades, 18 pounders.

Ship Paiſley, Frigate Built,	20 carronades,	18 pounders.
Brig Carron.	20 ditto,	18 ditto.
Brig Paiſly,	20 ditto,	18 ditto.
Ketch Stirling,	16 ditto,	12 ditto.
Ketch Glaſgow,	16 ditto,	12 ditto.
Ketch Forth,	14 ditto,	12 ditto.

These veſſels will afford the public an opportunity of a conveyance to and from London once every ten days through the year.

THE CARRON IRONWORKS FLEET, 1782
(*GLASGOW MERCURY*)

To supply the rapidly expanding domestic market, the semi-autonomous 'Carron Shipping Company' of Carronshore was founded by the Right Honourable Captain William Elphinstone – a kinsman of Gascoigne. The first of his small fleet of five – *Carron* (200 tons) – was equipped with the prototype eighteen-pounder carronade (autumn 1778) prior to its general release. Over the next two years he acquired and armed, in a like manner, a further four vessels – *Stirling, Paisley, Glasgow* and *Forth*. These company vessels ran, singly or in pairs, independent of convoy every ten days (weather permitting) from Carronshore to London via Leith. Well-armed and with a large crew, not one of these vessels was lost to the enemy. Their shipping agents at Glasgow, Leith and London capitalised on their aura of security by advertising passage on reduced terms for 'all mariners, recruiting parties, soldiers on furlow and all other steerage passengers who have been accustomed to the use of fire arms'.[106] This sort of marketing in wartime apparently proved successful as a smaller independent firm – the 'Sea Lock Shipping Company' – was formed in 1781 and ran a packet service on the same route and on similar terms.[107]

Early in 1782 Elphinstone sold out to the Ironworks Company in order to pursue his privateering interests which had been inspired by the successes of his brig *Paisley* (200 tons).[108] His five vessels thereafter joined the *Lady Charlotte* (20 eighteen-pounders) – the replacement for the *Earl of Dunmore* – to create a Carron Company fleet.[109]

Carron Ironworks made a range of cannons but it is its innovative carronade that commands attention. Its lightweight construction propelled a heavy shot at relatively low velocity. Highly destructive at close range, this weapon effectively put paid to the 'close-and-board' tactic previously preferred by the more aggressive privateers. The master of the Greenock privateer *Hawke* (140 tons/ 70 men) gleefully testified that '… we sent our twelve- and eighteen-pounder carronades [balls] through both sides [of

---

106 The reduced single passage charge was 10/6d: *Glasgow Mercury*, 5 March 1779.
107 *Ibid.*, advertisement for the sailing of their packet *Sea Lock* (18 six-pounders), 27 December 1781.
108 *Ibid.*, successive reports: prizes were *Frederica* bound for Bordeaux with hemp and cordage (January 1780): a 500-ton naval stores Dutchman (taken December 1780): and a Russian ship (February 1781). She also had a brush with the American privateer *Arlington* (April 1781), which rescued a number of coasters from certain capture.
109 Anonymous, *Carron Company* (Falkirk, 1959), p. 27. By then the Navy had 429 vessels carrying carronades.

their hulls]' during a three-hour engagement with two French privateers in July 1779.[110]

Thereafter, reports of a successful defence by carronades alone quickly dry up as the enemy privateers learned to stand-off from a potential prize until its defences were known. This, in turn, caused the masters of Scottish running ships – particularly those heading for West Indian waters – to re-equip with a mixture of short-range carronades and a few stand-off 'long' six- or nine-pounders during the following year.[111]

AMERICAN RAIDERS AND REGIONAL SHIPPING ACTIVITY

Under the combined assault of American and French raiders in foreign and home waters after August 1778, the level of shipping activity at the Scottish ports had slumped by a half.[112] Regional experiences, however, varied greatly, with those heavily engaged in the coastal trades to the south and enjoying the protection of shore batteries or guard ships faring best.

On the much-troubled west coast only the Irvine precinct – the centre of the Ayrshire coal trade to Ireland – maintained its level of shipping activity throughout the war. On the east coast the high-volume ports of the inner Firths of Forth and Tay – Alloa, Bo'ness (which included Carronshore), Dundee and Perth – positively flourished. Leith, as the seaport for the centre of administration, also sustained, by and large, its level of activity during the war years. By way of contrast the tonnage passing in and out of the ports of the outer firths and an undefended stretch of the coastline contracted further after 1778 – by as much as half again in the case of Ayr, Montrose, Dunbar, the Solway and Western Isles ports.[113]

---

110   *Ibid.*, 26 August 1779. She had up-gunned since her first letter of marque (18 six- and three-pounders, six cohorns (four-pound shot), six swivels). On this cruise she took the large snow *La Nymphe* from Cape Francois to Bordeaux with sugar and cotton valued at £10,000. On her next cruise she took the *Lively* of Newbury heading for Guadaloupe and the *Jolly Tar* bound from Piscataqua to St. Martins with lumber. The *Hawke* was subsequently wrecked off Bermuda: NAS E504/15/03–1; *Glasgow Mercury,* 28 October 1779, 25 August 1780; and *Lloyd's Lists,* 15 June 1781.

111   This change is evident in the armament details given in new letter-of-marque declarations against the Dutch: PRO HCA 26, December 1780 onwards.

112   In 1774 incoming foreign trade amounted to 103,078 tons and from Ireland 42,163 tons: PRO T64/251.

113   Port book of Ayr as quoted by Graham, *Port of Ayr,* p. 30.

THE CUSTOMS CRUISER *ROYAL GEORGE*, 1780. FROM AN 1881
PHOTOGRAPH OF A WATERCOLOUR (NORTH AYRSHIRE LIBRARIES,
MUSEUM OF THE CUMBRAES)

Table 7.1. Inward and outward tonnage through the Scottish ports, 1778-84

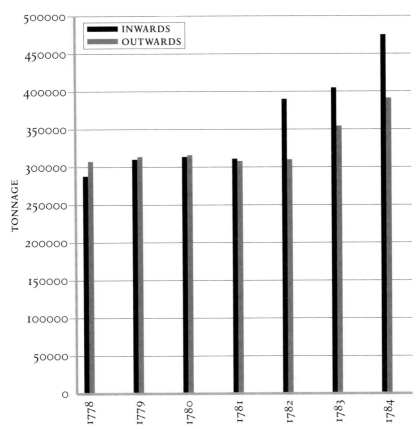

Source: GUL MSS GEN 1075.

The slow recovery of shipping activity in and out of the Scottish ports suffered a reversal in 1781 – the year of Fall's raid. The Western Isles and Highlands, being without adequate defence or the legal right to carry arms, suffered the most. The Edinburgh merchant John Inglis reported it was 'difficult to get shipping on any terms in these hazardous times' and struggled to hire a vessel to run from Lewis to Liverpool with the product of the island's kelping for that year – seventy-four tons of ash.[114] The few masters who could be contracted, he lamented, were unreliable, as 'their dread of falling in the hands of privateers makes them skulk along the shoar and backward in sailing except when the winds are very favourable'. Their caution was not unfounded, as the vessel he finally secured – the

114 NAS, GD 427/134/1, John Inglis to George Gillander of Highfield, 6 June 1781.

Industry of Wick (44 tons) – was promptly captured and ransomed on her departure from the Birkin Isles with her first load of kelp.[115]

THE CLYDE'S FOREIGN TRADERS

A windfall of the war was the rapid escalation of colonial commodity prices. It has been estimated that the Glasgow merchants had made £5,000,000 from selling off their stockpile of tobacco to the Continent during the early years of the war when prices soared.[116] The conveyance of this stock to France before August 1778 was a boon to the larger vessels left on the Clyde. An example was the privateer *Cochrane* of Port Glasgow (240 tons) which delivered a cargo of tobacco to Bordeaux for William Cunninghame & Co., in September 1777, before crossing the Atlantic to cruise for American prizes.[117] By 1780, however, prices had dropped and the re-export trade to Holland had been lost to British shipping. The Americans were then eluding British cruisers to deliver tobacco directly to Europe '... in small fleets of ten to thirty ships generally armed and well manned ... and it is remarkable that only two have been captured in the year 1780'.[118]

The high wartime prices initially commanded by West Indies sugar and its products also dropped by 1778. By then refineries had taken to retaining their own stockpile as a buffer against wartime fluctuations in supply.[119] Over the next three years much of the carrying trade to and from the West Indies was lost as the French captured the British sugar isles –

---

115   *Ibid.*, items 8,9 and 11. She was taken by the *Fly* of Dunkirk, commanded by yet another 'Captain Fall'.

116   In August 1776 the Collector of Customs concluded that between the two ports, forty-one companies held a stockpile in excess of fourteen million pounds of tobacco. The price had doubled from 3d to 6d in a matter of days and would reach 3/6d a short time later: GCA, CE60/1/9, Collector of Port Glasgow and Greenock to the Board, 10 August 1776.

117   PRO HCA 26, letters 23 September 1777. She took three American vessels in the following months, including one with a cargo valued at £100,000: *Edinburgh Evening Courant*, 7 November 1778.

118   *Glasgow Mercury,* 14 September 1780.

119   In December 1777 the leading West Indies merchant Alexander Houston wrote to his factor in St. Vincent telling him not to over-commit as 'sugars have been almost unsaleable these six weeks': National Library of Scotland, Letter books of Alexander Houston & Co., Foreign Letter Book E, p. 336.

with the exception of Jamaica and Antigua.[120] Under the favourable terms of surrender British property on the captured isles had been left untouched and free to export, but only in neutral bottoms.

Furthermore, the British capture of the Dutch isle of St. Eustatius (February 1781) struck at Scotland's illegal trade to the West Indies. This six-mile-long 'nest of villains' had long served as a conduit to the French West Indies for smuggled Scottish goods. Consequently Rodney's sequestration of the island – along with over one hundred and fifty vessels found in the harbour – caused the greatest chagrin to the West Indies merchants.[121]

As overseas markets closed, the tonnage entering and leaving the Atlantic-oriented upper Clyde ports responded – dipping by one-sixth between 1779 and 1781.[122] A contributory factor was the continuing drain on the remaining stock of larger vessels from the Scottish ports to the war effort: 'This day [April 1780] orders arrived at Edinburgh [to] immediately engage in the service of the government all ships of 200 tons and upwards. Various are the conjectures as to the reason for these orders.'[123] One certain reason was the increasingly unfavourable terms of contracting with the Navy Board. Indeed, the Board was forced to promise to reimburse a month's wages for the crew of any vessel sailing south to London or Plymouth for contractual measurement.[124] The months following the entry of the Dutch into the war (December 1780) marked the lowest point in shipping activity as the last swarm of privateers departed for West Indian and Iberian waters in search of Dutch merchantmen.

THE BALTIC TRADES

The number of passages made by Scottish masters through the Baltic Sound had halved with the arrival of American cruisers in the North Sea

---

120   Dominica (1778), St. Lucia (1778), Grenada and St. Vincent (1779), St. Kitts, Monserrat and Nevis (1780). Scottish transports were heavily committed in supplying the garrisons on these isles. The defeat of the French fleet at the 'Battle of the Saints' (February 1782) saved Jamaica and Antigua.

121   3182 vessels visited that island in the space of thirteen months during the war: T. A. Bailey, *A Diplomatic History of the American People* (New York, 1964), p. 41.

122   Greenock was then handling twice the tonnage of Port Glasgow.

123   *Glasgow Mercury,* 24 April 1780. A number of the whalers were contracted at this time, e.g. the whaler *Leith* leaving Leith as a transport: *Lloyd's Register* 1780.

124   All vessels contracted by the Navy Board had to be inspected at a royal dockyard: Syrett, *Shipping in the American War,* pp. 107-8.

(1776). Any recovery was forestalled, firstly, by the entry of France (1778) and, secondly, by the formation of the League of Armed Neutrality (1780–83). British naval supremacy, however, kept the Baltic open to British convoys, virtually wiping out the Dutch presence in the area in the process. This situation ensured that the League was little more than an 'armed nullity'. Indeed, it is notable that it was during the war that the centre of the timber trade to Scotland markedly switched from Norway to the eastern Baltic ports of Prussia and Russia.[125]

Table 7.2. Passages made by Scottish-domiciled masters through the Danish Sound, 1776-83

Source: Danish Sound Tolls

125   The accessible prime standings of timber suitable for shipbuilding on the Norwegian coast had been steadily depleted since the 1750s. There was a ban on the export of baulk timber from the Finnish forests which were under Russian control.

THE END OF HOSTILITIES

The war on the American mainland had been effectively lost in September 1781 when De Grasse's fleet slipped into the Chesapeake, cutting the supply line to Cornwallis at Yorktown. In April 1782 the Prime Minister-in-waiting, Lord Shelborne, dispatched the Scottish merchant Richard Oswald to Paris to open the negotiations with his old acquaintance Benjamin Franklin. His mission was to extract Britain from her position of being 'foolishly involved in four wars'. After much posturing, a 'preliminary' peace treaty was signed on 30 November 1782. By then a quarter of all foreign-going tonnage inwards and a fifth outwards from the Scottish ports was being carried by foreign bottoms.

The independence of the American colonies was formally recognised by the Treaty of Versailles the following year (3 September 1783). In the interim, the recovery of Scotland's overseas trade got underway – albeit with a switch of emphasis in European trading from France and the Low Countries to Northern Europe, the Baltic states and Russia. The reinstatement of the Navigation Acts hastened the pace as the number of foreign vessels passing through Scottish ports fell back dramatically towards pre-war levels of under ten per cent. This recovery combined with a surge in coastal trading to double the tonnage passing through the Scottish ports between 1782 and 1784.[126]

THE FISHERIES DURING
AND AFTER THE WAR

The progress of the herring buss industry on the west coast during the war had been highly sensitive to the compound effect of security scares, pressgangs and wage inflation. During the war years the number of Scottish herring busses claiming the bounty dropped by over a half – bottoming in 1781.

After the war new moves were made to attract new promoters to the fisheries. To facilitate business Leith, Inverness, Stranraer and Oban were added to the list of ports at which bounty vouchers were validated. Finally, in 1787, the old restrictions on hull size and fitting-out requirements were dropped to allow any size of vessel to claim the herring bounty. At the

126 PRO TD64/251.

same time half the bounty was transferred to the catch – 'barrel bounty' – to link payment with productivity.

The fortunes of the Scottish whaling industry revived with the restoration of the tonnage bounty to forty shillings in 1782 and the release of whalers from Government contract. This financial incentive, along with the absence of the American whaling fleet during the war and high oil prices, maintained the Greenland whaling interest in the northern ports. Though many American whalers transferred to the British flag after the war, rising domestic demand allowed their absorption into the British whaling fleets with little adverse effect.

In 1788, at the height of this second wave of bounty whaling ventures, thirty-one Scottish whalers were fitted out, in spite of the drop in the bounty to thirty shillings per ton the previous year. But this boom was over by 1789 as the increasing availability of cheaper oil from the South Atlantic seas reduced the importance of the Arctic whalers in the eyes of the Board of Trade. Cuts in the tonnage bounty to twenty-five shillings in 1793 and to twenty shillings in 1796, coupled with the uncertainties of a new war, hastened the decline in the number of Scottish whalers for the remainder of the century.

THE RISE OF THE
SHIPBUILDING INDUSTRY

The beneficial effect of the loss of America on the British shipbuilding industry was a major theme with contemporary commentators, anxious to quantify the full economic implications of the American War.[127] Macpherson calculated that two-thirds by number (half by tonnage) of the pre-war British marine was American-built.[128] By the end of the war this element – including prizes and vessels brought across by American loyalists to reflag as British – had been reduced to a third on both counts. [129]

The composition of the Scottish marine would appear to have

---

127   Examples are: Lord Sheffield's *Observations on the commerce of the American States* and George Chalmers' *Opinions on interesting subjects of public law and commercial policy arising from American Independence*, both published c.1783.

128   Macpherson's survey was based on the *Lloyd's Registers* of 1773–5 that have since been lost to fire: *Commerce*, III, p. 11. It is, therefore, not possible to emulate his survey to isolate the American component in the Scottish marine for the same period.

129   Since the Prize Act (1747) vessels condemned in a British Vice-Admiralty Court were deemed to be 'British' for the purposes of the Navigation Acts.

mirrored Macpherson's findings as half the Scottish tonnage prior to 1783 (*c*.43,400 tons) was American-built.[130] They numbered some 263 vessels (one-third of the marine) and constituted the vast majority of over-150 tons vessels in the 'foreign-going' category.[131] The remaining half of Scotland's tonnage (two-thirds by number) consisted mainly of locally built busses, sloops and brigs serving the fisheries and coastal trades.

At the start of the war Scotland was a minor shipbuilding region. The Scottish-built vessels listed in *Lloyd's Register* for 1776 accounted for slightly under ten per cent by number (323 vessels), or just over five per cent by tonnage (26,195 tons), of the total British-built marine.[132] Leith was still the centre of the industry, a position sustained by the construction of two small dry docks by the master shipbuilders John Sime Senior and Robert Dryburgh in the early to mid-1770s. The range of building skills available at the Leith yards extended from herring busses to the occasional 200-ton brig for the mercantile interest. Dryburgh's yard even succeeded in meeting the rigorous requirements of the Customs service to build their cutters. Naval repair work had been undertaken for the Admiralty since the time of the 'Old Scots navy' but the first contract to build a warship was not won until 1778 – the sloop HMS *Fury* (launched 1780).[133]

During the American War, however, virtually every Scottish port of consequence supported a yard capable of repairing, lengthening and occasionally building fishing boats and small traders. The port of Saltcoats demonstrates this dynamic effect of the war on a local economy:

> The Saltcoats people finding an increasing demand for ships,
> which they could not build in America, nor buy at the time in
> Britain but at a high price, were naturally led to attempt to build
> them themselves, their harbour being remarkably convenient for
> launching them ... in a place where scarce a boat had been built

---

130 Tonnage in this case is a high variation of 'tons burthen'; see Appendix A. The problems in attempting to isolate every Scottish vessel listed in *Lloyd's Register* beyond 1782 are the rapid turn-over in ownership (which effectively creates a new population of vessels) and the dispersal of Scottish-owned hulls to other British ports (principally Liverpool and London) after this date.

131 A rare example was the Virginiaman *Paxutent*, built originally for William Cunninghame & Co., later described as 'Scottish built' at change of owner from Glassford & Co., to Hogg & Co.: *Lloyd's Register*, 1780.

132 J.A. Goldenberg, 'An analysis of shipbuilding sites in *Lloyd's Register* of 1776', *Mariner's Mirror*, Vol.59 (1973), pp. 419–433.

133 The contract was awarded to John Sime the younger after he acquired the Sandport yard from Dryburgh: Mowat, *Leith* pp. 238–241.

before three carpenter's yards were set up one after the other, which have gone on successfully ever since. [134]

Between 1775 and 1790, the seventy-odd carpenters at the Saltcoats yards produced sixty-four vessels (7095 tons) comprising six ships from 160 to 220 tons (1155 tons); thirty-seven brigs from 55 to 180 tons (4630 tons); eighteen sloops from 20 to 85 tons (1085 tons); and three smaller vessels on the stocks (225 tons). The larger hulls required a spring tide to be slipped. [135]

The raw materials were imported by an annual cargo of hemp from St. Petersburg or Riga, a consignment of bar iron from Gothenburg, three cargoes of spar and mast timber from Memel and as many deliveries of oak planking as required from South Wales.

The year 1778 appears to have triggered new ventures in shipbuilding activity in the Forth. Kirkcaldy opened its first yard that year, eventually building thirty-eight hulls (3000 tons) by 1791. [136] At Dysart an additional yard opened in 1778 employing around forty-five men. By 1791 the combined output of the two Dysart yards had surpassed Saltcoats' tonnage – as seventy-four vessels (8634 tons) were launched. [137] Charges for such hulls were between half to two-thirds of the total cost of a rigged vessel outfitted for sea and were around one-third cheaper than a comparable 'river' [Thames]-built hull. [138]

After the war, the search to replace American shipbuilding timber continued. To the fore in the exploitation of accessible Scottish forests was a substantial operation spearheaded in 1785 by the 'English Company of Garmouth' at the mouth of the River Spey. At this site a sawmill supplied cut timber for the local shipbuilders at Aberdeen and the North as far as Skye, while another prepared timber for dispatch to Hull and the naval dockyard at Deptford. The residual timber was used by twenty-eight shipwrights and blockmakers on site to build twenty-three vessels (c.4000 tons) over seven years. A few of their larger vessels were subsequently sent out to the Bay of Campechy region of Honduras to fetch logwood. [139]

---

134   OSA, Parish of Stevenston, VI, pp. 598–9.

135   The principal shipyard of Saltcoats harbour is sketched in the Eglinton Plan Book (1789) lodged with the NAS. A gated wall enclosed the immediate tidal stretch of the beach. Reproduced in Graham, *The Shipping Trade of Ayrshire*, p. 9.

136   OSA, Parish of Kirkcaldy, XVIII, p. 540.

137   *Ibid.*, Parish of Dysart, XII, p. 513.

138   Kirkcaldy vessels were sold at £4-5/- to £6 per ton depending on size and requirements. At Saltcoats the average charge was £5 per ton.

139   The founders were two merchants – Dodsworth of York and Osbourne of Hull: OSA, Parish of Speymouth, XIV, pp. 391–5.

Table 7.3. Numbers of Scottish herring busses claiming the bounty, 1776–91

Source: J. Knox, *View of the British Empire*, Vol.I; 'Report on the Herring Fisheries', 1798 (Bigwood).

By 1790 the building of larger hulls at the lesser Scottish ports had peaked. The principal cause of their decline was the rapid increase in the demand for much larger vessels – partly driven by changes in legislation. After the Act of Registration (1786) the growing demand was for deeper-draught hulls that exploited the inherent flaw in the tonnage 'formula of 1775' used in the Act to measure vessels for duty purposes. In the following four years the Greenock and Port Glasgow yards, with their direct access to a deep channel, launched double the tonnage of their Leith competitors.[140] A milestone was reached in 1791 with the launching of the 1100-ton ship *Brunswick* at Greenock which marked the step-up to building large ocean-going square-riggers on the upper Clyde.[141]

The master shipwrights responsible for this leap in technology were part of a general drift of skills and talent from the lesser to the deepwater ports. The most notable arrivals at Greenock were the Saltcoats master-shipwrights, Robert Steele and his partner John Carswell, in 1796.[142]

While such men looked to the future, the smaller decked vessels of the buss class (twenty to eighty tons) remained the mainstay of the Scottish shipbuilding industry. During the last years of the bounty system in the herring fisheries and the rapid expansion of the coastal trades, particularly in coal, demand for the smaller hull remained buoyant. In the year before the launch of the *Brunswick*, the Scottish yards built 106 vessels (7,206 tons), of which sixty-six were in the buss class – with only two in the 220–240 tons class. Even so, in comparative terms, the Scottish yards accounted for one in every five vessels (just over one in every eight by tons) launched in mainland Britain in that year.

The majority of the larger hulls were sold on an increasingly international market. Saltcoats brigs were sold to buyers in England, Ireland and Spain as well as to owners at the upper Clyde ports. Over the four years 1787–90 Scottish shipbuilders had launched vessels worth something in the region of £210,000 – double when fully rigged and canvassed – on the open market: a major industry and employer by Scottish standards.

By 1790 shipbuilding dominated North Leith where the five yards

---

140 PRO Customs 17/82.

141 J. Wilson, *General View of the Agriculture of Renfrewshire* (Paisley, 1812), p. 237. The *Brunswick* was built for a naval contract – won by a consortium of Greenock merchants – to ship masts from Nova Scotia to Deptford dockyard.

142 Between 1796–1816 the company of Steele and Carswell launched twelve full-rigged ships from their new premises and were considered the finest builders on the Clyde. Another Saltcoats shipwright relocated at Belfast.

of the master builders employed 152 skilled carpenters at 1/10d per day. In crude terms each Leith carpenter turned out around eight tons of shipping per year which, if applied to the whole tonnage built in Scotland that year, would suggest that the nation supported around 900 ship's carpenters onshore around this time.[143] This figure would probably double if those employed in the related industries – anchor smiths, coopers, sail-, rope-, blockmakers, and victuallers – are added.

The shipping industry was, by 1790, a mainstay employer of men and women around the Scottish coast. The manning of seagoing traders, whalers and herring busses above fifteen tons employed just under 13,000 seamen that year. If those employed in open boats under fifteen tons (engaged in the inshore fisheries or as ferries) were also considered, then the final tally of those directly engaged in or serving maritime activities would probably approach 20,000.[144]

THE CHANGES TO THE MERCANTILIST SYSTEM

The most profound long-term legacy of the American War was the restructuring of the mercantilist system – commencing with Pitt's Consolidation Act of 1787. The loss of much of the re-export trade in colonial commodities to Europe had undermined the basic rationale behind the elaborate high tariffs of the old regime. Smuggling, nurtured by that system, had become rampant under the cover of war, and many of the letters of marque taken out by small cutters at the outlying ports were simply a cover for a heavily armed smuggler.[145] By 1789 new legislation – containing 173 sections – had been passed with the intention of removing the prime incentives for the smuggling trade.[146] The duty on imported spirits was dramatically reduced – the revenue made up by an increase in the excise duty on whisky distilling. The bonded warehousing of goods immediately on import was finally introduced at the three remaining

---

143 OSA, Parish of North Leith (Edinburgh) , VI, p.14.

144 PRO Customs 17. The inshore estimate is based on the OSA reports which indicate that at least 1,000 men were deployed in the Firth of Clyde fisheries while other coastal communities list open boats used in herring and white fishing as the major employer of men after agriculture.

145 An example was the cutter Greyhound of Ayr (50 tons/4 guns/35 men) owned by the Ayr branch of the Breckenbridge family of smugglers: PRO HCA 26, letter 13 January 1781.

146 Act 13 Geo. III, c.68.

Table 7.4 Tonnage owned by the Scottish ports, 1759–91

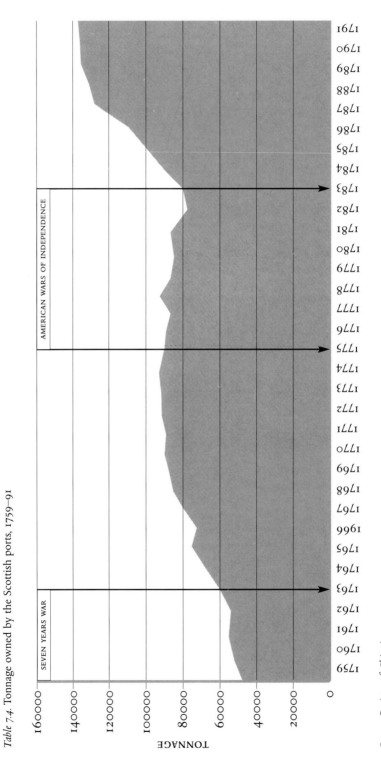

Source: *Register of Shipping*

nominated ports – Leith, Port Glasgow and Greenock, killing off the endemic drawback frauds. To deter sharp practice the minimum size of vessel allowed to carry tobacco was raised to 120 tons. The shipping of tobacco off-cuts such as stalks and its derivative, snuff, was prohibited while the minimum weight of parcel of compressed leaf legally imported was set at 450lb.

Firm action was also taken to prevent American vessels and masters passing themselves off as British so as to engage in the Empire's carrying trade. The central device was the Act of Registry (1786) which reinforced the Navigation Acts by making it a legal requirement that all vessels over fifteen tons be formally certified as 'British' and registered at their home port.

Far removed from international trade politics but of equal significance to the general progress and direction of the Scottish economy was the growth of her coastal trade, which doubled between 1776 and 1791.[147] Technological advances in mining and haulage in the Ayrshire coalfields allowed the coal trade to Ireland to lead the way. A further contributory factor was the abolition of the British duty on coal shipped coastwise beyond the precinct boundaries,[148] which had a beneficial effect on Scotland's emerging manufacturing and brewing industries and on agriculture (lime burning). Indeed, a number of farmers are listed in the first Greenock Registry (1786) as part-owners of small sloops.[149]

By 1790 the composition of the Scottish marine reflected an economy still heavily dependent on: the coastal conveyance of bulk goods and commodities, and subsidised fisheries, and had yet to venture beyond the North Atlantic in foreign trade. In that year the marine consisted of: c.1,500 busses, coasters and North Sea traders under 100 tons; c.400 of the oceangoing class (100–300 ton); and the twenty-three vessels of the Scottish whaling fleet (300 tons and above). In all, 142,029 tons of shipping compared to England's 1,072,363 tons.[150]

---

147   From 660 vessels (25,140 tons) to 1,058 vessels (51,998 tons): GUL MSS 1075 coastal category.

148   A review of technological developments at the Stevenston colliery is available in E.J. Graham, *Robert Reid Cunninghame of Seabank House*, Ayrshire Archaeological and Natural History Society (1997), Monogram 17.

149   Greenock was, by then, the greatest (owning 27,484 tons) and most diverse of the Scottish ports.

150   PRO Customs 17, Scottish Fleet as of September 1790.

CHAPTER 8
AIDS TO NAVIGATION
AND PORT DEVELOPMENT

The pursuit of mercantilist goals required the Government and its agencies to consider the best means by which the nation's maritime assets could be safeguarded and advanced where possible. National security was the prime motivation for direct Government intervention in the promotion of aids to safer navigation and port development. But it was also well understood that the nation's prosperity lay in the safe passage and docking of vessels in home waters – in both peace and war.

STATE-SPONSORED CHARTING
OF THE SCOTTISH COASTLINE

Symptomatic of Scotland's backwardness as a maritime nation was the absence of reliable coastal charts. The home market was initially too small to support an indigenous cartography industry, and so it was left to interested foreign nations to provide the first useful charts of Scotland.

The most comprehensive chart of the Scottish mainland in general circulation at the onset of the mercantilist era was by the French royal cartographer, Nicolas de Nicolay. First published in Paris (1583), it used rutters (compass rosettes) to give bearings. The sailing directions were based on the account of King James V's voyage round Scotland (1540). Thereafter, regional maps were occasionally produced by French, Dutch or German engravers that focused on the 'grand fisheries' sea areas – principally Orkney and Shetland.

The first indigenous mapping was undertaken sometime between 1583 and 1610 when the Rev. Timothy Pont of Dunnet undertook an arduous series of regional surveys on foot. These were used, together with Robert Gordon of Straloch's notes and observations of Orkney and Shetland, by Joannis Blaeu to complete his *Atlas of Scotland* (1654) which greatly improved on fixing the position of the isles relative to the mainland.

In 1681, as part of the general assault on the nation's deplorable trading position, the Scottish Privy Council appointed the mathematician John Adair to survey Scotland. His initial two-year commission gave priority to surveying the coastal areas. Adair was, however, distracted by financial and legal wrangles and disheartened by the commissioning of a rival – Sir Robert Sibbald, the Geographer Royal. To appease his paymasters he resorted to modifying older maps, notably those of Nicolay and Pont. As a consequence his first set of published charts, *Mappe of Orkney* (1682), *Hydrographicall Mappe of Forth* (1683) and *Firth of Clyde and Solway* (1686), were poorly received. In his defence he complained to the Privy Council about his lack of finance and authority. The immediate outcome of this dialogue was the imposition of a levy in 1686 of twelve shillings Scots, on all indigenous vessels (double on foreign vessels) entering Scottish ports, to finance the completion of his coastal surveys. Reassured, Adair hired the *Mary* of Leith and a Highland pilot for an expedition to the Western Isles (1698), closely followed by a cruise on the Firth of Clyde.

By then he had another rival for his funding from John Slezer, a German artillery officer. Slezer had spent some twenty years touring Scotland depicting royal burghs, castles, harbours and sea views – which were engraved and published in London as *Theatrum Scotiae* in 1693. After that he successfully petitioned the Committee of Trade to recommend to the Scottish Parliament that he should receive a retrospective payment – out of general taxation – for his efforts on behalf of the nation. Their response was to add his name to that of Adair's as beneficiaries of the new Tunnage Act of 1695, which sparked an acrimonious propaganda war between the two claimants.

Under even greater pressure to produce results, Adair cobbled together *A Hydrographical Description of the Sea Coast and Isles of Scotland*. This was engraved in Edinburgh in 1703 by a Dutchman specifically recruited by him for the task. It was, yet again, a re-work of his old surveys accompanied by the sailing instructions from King James V's voyage and did little to advance the safer navigation of vessels in Scottish waters.[1]

Raising his levy to one shilling sterling per ton in 1704 only served to distract Adair further as he spent more of his time at the Scottish ports

---

1   A fuller account is available in D.G. Moir, *The Early Maps of Scotland* (Edinburgh,1973), I, pp. 65–78 and A.H.W. Robinson, 'The charting of the Scottish coast', *Scottish Geographic Magazine* (1958), 74, pp. 116–127.

enforcing its collection. Furthermore, in 1706, his remit – as the 'Geographer of Scotland' – was extended to include policing Scottish maritime jurisdiction. His new powers allowed him to seize 'all foreign vessels found fishing in the lochs, creeks, bays and rivers of Scotland, or within sight of the shore, and secure them in safe harbours'.[2] The few seizures he did make involved prolonged and costly legal wrangles that kept him in Edinburgh and away from his primary mission.

After the Act of Union English masters refused to pay the tonnage levy, and as a consequence he died in penury (1718) without completing his commission. His widow eventually extracted a pension from the Treasury (1723) in return for surrendering his portfolio of manuscript charts and journals of thirty years' surveying the coast of Scotland. They were never published and were probably lost in the Exchequer fire of 1811.

While the Scottish Parliament's experiment in sponsoring cartography had failed to provide the required detailed coastal charts – based on updated soundings and sight-lines – a separate royal initiative was partly successful. This was the survey undertaken by Greenvill[e] Collins, 'hydro-grapher to King James II', during his cruises from Harwich to the Shetlands (1684–5). The results were published in 1689 under the misleading title *Great Britain's Coasting Pilot*. In fact his work had been interrupted by his recall to command one of the Stuart frigates dispatched to contest William's landing at Torbay (1688). In a footnote to his *Pilot* he stated his 'hearty wish that the west part of Ireland and Scotland may hereafter be surveyed'.[3]

Collins' pilotage remained the only practical inshore chart of Shetland, Orkney and the east coast for almost a century. Engraved prints were generally available in Scotland by the early 1700s and were regularly reprinted throughout the eighteenth century.[4] The durability of his work owed much to the quality of his sailing directions and inshore soundings, often acquired from local masters.[5]

---

2   Commission dated 26 July 1706: HCAS. AC 13, I, p.51. He was cited in a legal action involving a detained Spanish vessel shortly afterwards: *Ibid.*, AC9 / 380.
3   G. Collins, *Great Britain's Coasting Pilot* (London, 1693).
4   His charts were reprinted by a succession of London publishers in 1723, 1738, 1756 and 1785. They were also reprinted in Dutch by Gerard Van Keulen c. 1727.
5   A caption in the Fife Ness to Montrose chart acknowledged the help of 'Mr Mar, an injenious marriner of Dundee'. Mar was a leading figure in Leith Trinity House at this time.

NATIONAL SECURITY AND
CHARTING THE WEST COAST

The recurring Jacobite threat to national security prompted the Admiralty to make provision for proper charts for the navy of the remote and complex Western Isles and the West Highland coastline omitted by Collins.[6] In 1741 an Act of Parliament gave authorisation but their Lordships failed to appoint an 'Admiralty Surveyor of the North' until the crisis of the '45 Rebellion was over.

This commission was finally given, in 1749, to the Scottish mathematician and experienced surveyor, Murdoch McKenzie the Elder. By then, the opening up of the western fisheries was an integral part of the Government's pacification programme, and so McKenzie's remit included locating and noting the inshore fishing grounds, channels, races, shoals and rocks. Delays in funding, however, deferred his embarkation on the newly built and suitably named naval sloop – *Culloden* (35 tons/2 guns) – until 1751. After three years in the field, his commission was extended (1753–7) to include the south-west coast of Scotland and Ireland, the result of which was nineteen maps covering the area from Lewis to the Solway.

His methodology was a major step forward for cartography as a science, as he perfected the use of triangulation to map a rugged coastline. By using a theodolite, plane table and chain (loaned by the Admiralty) he pinpointed the position of specially raised beacons on the surrounding hilltops relative to a measured base line (usually a beach).[7]

In 1776, as the first American raiders appeared off the Firth of Clyde, a highly concerned Parliament voted him a grant of £2,145 to cover the cost of engraving these charts, which were quickly published in two volumes that year as *A maritim survey of Ireland and west coast of Great Britain.*[8] They did not, however, include the offshore fishing banks that had been reported by incoming Virginiamen as they plumblined their approach to landfall. To remedy this omission Captain James Huddart was instructed by

6   The hiring a pilot for the western seas was not only an additional security risk, but also costly. The commander of HMS *Mermaid* was charged £5 sterling pilotage from Leith to Bute, £2 between Bute and Ayr and a further £5 for his detached cruise from Argyll to Orkney in 1685: *RPC*, XI, p. xxvii.

7   This technique formed the basis for his *Treatise on Marin Surveying* (1776): Macpherson, *Annals*, III, p. 577. The accuracy of his later maps was, unfortunately, poor in comparison with his earlier private surveys. His greatest error was to calculate the length of the Isle of Arran as fourteen not twenty miles.

8   Act of Parliament, 15 Geo. III, c. 42.

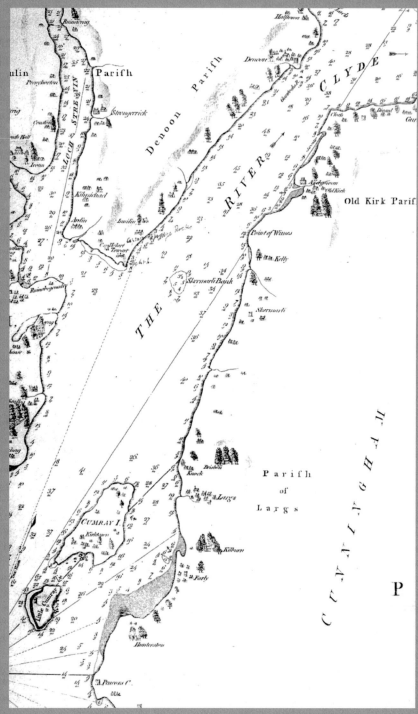

MCKENZIE'S CHART OF THE NORTH AYRSHIRE/RENFREW COAST. THE
FAIRLIE PATCH ANCHORAGE IS OPPOSITE THE GREAT CUMBRAE
(NATIONAL LIBRARY OF SCOTLAND)

the Admiralty, in 1777, to take soundings to the west of Islay. In 1781 and 1789 his remit was extended to survey the banks off the other western isles. The preliminary results of which were passed to the 'Commissioners and Trustees for Improving the Fisherys & Manufactures in Scotland'.[9]

Captain Murdo Downie took up the challenge to update Collins' old pilotage of the eastern seaboard in 1783. As the new commander of HMS *Champion* on the Leith station he found 'no chart published of the east coast of Scotland that could in any degree be relied on'. He therefore sought and received Admiralty approval to embark on his own survey. This work was eventually published in 1792 as *The New Pilot for the east coast of Scotland* and was well received by the Master of Trinity House of Leith.

The chart in Downie's pilotage was the last significant advance in coastal cartography until 1825 when the Admiralty ordered a complete recharting of Scottish waters, starting with the Western Isles.[10] This review included the Shetland Isles for the first time, having been previously ignored by eighteenth-century British naval strategists and cartographers.

PRIVATELY FUNDED MAPS AND CHARTS

Government schemes to promote seaborne trade and the fisheries were aided by the increase in the number and quality of local maps privately commissioned during the eighteenth century. Inshore tidal races, shelving and obstructions are evident in such early examples as those of Bruce's *Loch Sunart* (1730) and Jaffray's *Peterhead* (1739). The plotting of the main anchorages of the upper Firth of Clyde by John Watt Senior in 1734 was, on the other hand, basic and lacking in detail.[11] Dumfries Town Council were more careful in their recruitment of Thomas Winter, the estate surveyor of Monymusk, who used 'a machine' (probably a quadrant) for his survey (1742) of the great sandbanks in the middle stretch of the Solway Firth.[12]

Murdoch McKenzie the Elder privately surveyed Orkney (1746 or 1747), producing an eight-map collection entitled *Orcades, or a Geographic*

---

9   Eventually published as *Coasting Pilot for Great Britain and Ireland* (1804).
10   Robinson, 'Charting ', pp. 122–4.
11   John Watt was a mathematician and uncle of the more famous James. Prints of his survey do not appear to have been generally available until 1759.
12   J.N. Moore, 'Thomas Winter's Chart of the Solway Firth', *Transactions of the Dumfries and Galloway Natural History and Antiquarian Society* (1984), LIX, pp.57–63.

and Hydrographic Survey of the Orkney and Lewis Islands (1750). This set a new standard as the true location and outline of the isles was finally fixed to within working tolerances. Indeed, his work was still held in high regard by Orcadians fifty years later: 'It may be presumed ... that his map is as near the truth ... as any idea we can form.'[13]

After 1760 details of the shoreline were regularly included in the new generation of county maps funded by private subscribers. These were mostly landed gentry who had an interest in developing seaborne access to their mineral and agricultural investments. The accuracy of maps such as Ainslie's of *Fife, Kinross and the Firths of Forth and Tay* and the Armstrong's of the *County of Ayrshire* (both published in 1775), owed much to Murdoch McKenzie's earlier advances in field surveying.

LIGHTHOUSES

Documentary evidence points to the existence from medieval times of a light at Aberdeen, and tradition has it that there were ecclesiastically maintained lights (peat fires) at Portpatrick and possibly on Fair Isle, north of Orkney.[14] By 1707, however, there was only one permanent illumination in the waters of North Britain. That was the privately owned fire tower on the Isle of May situated at the crossroads of the eastern seaboard coastal traffic and the entrance to the Firth of Forth. Built in 1636, by James Maxwell of Innerwick and John Cunninghame of Barnes, its fire was frequently obscured in low cloud and was more detectable by its smoke than by its glow when clear.[15] In stormy conditions its chauffer (firebox) could consume four tons of Fife coal a day, but the cost was more than recovered through the light duty levied on passing vessels (£1 for a typical 160-ton British trader – double for a foreign vessel).[16]

By the early 1780s the poor service and high cost of this privately maintained light were the subject of public debate. Prompted by a series of

13   *OSA*, Parish of Sandwick and Stromness, XVI, p. 412. He is also mentioned in four other Orcadian parish returns.

14   D.B. Hague and R. Christie, *Lighthouses: their architecture, history and archaeology* (Llandysul, 1975), pp. 15–19.

15   They held the patent from Charles I – granted in 1635: *APS*, V, pp. 494–5.

16   Collection of the May light money was farmed out. The principal tacksman was at Leith after 1707 who commissioned others at the headports around Britain. Some of whom were, apparently, reluctant to pass on their collection, e.g.: HCAS AC 8/83 Allan - v- Gardner. By 1799 annual duties amounted to £1,600.

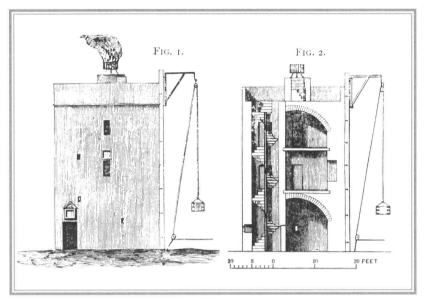

ELEVATION AND SECTION OF THE ISLE OF MAY COAL-FIRED LIGHTHOUSE,
FROM AN 1893 PAMPHLET BY DAVID A. STEVENSON

wrecks incurring loss of life in the Forth, the Master of Trinity House of Leith recommended in 1786 that the Edinburgh Chamber of Commerce should intervene and pay to have the 'grossly neglected' coal brazier replaced by a 'moving oil light of reflective glass'.[17] He also suggested that the tower be raised to a height of sixty feet. These proposals were rejected on the grounds that they did not address the basic flaw of having an elevated light liable to be obscured by low cloud. The newly created Commissioners for the Northern Lights did, however, provide a horse-powered hoist to speed up the delivery of coal to the chauffer which was then three feet square – twice that of any other in Britain.

It was not until 1810 and the loss of HMS *Nymphen* and *Pallas* off Dundee with their entire crews (600 men) that the Government intervened with a compulsory purchase order.[18] It took, however, an Act of Parliament

17   The 'Incorporation of the Master and Assistants of Trinity House of Leith' had grown from its medieval role – as a group dedicated to the welfare of local seamen and their families – to that of a highly influential organisation. After 1650 it oversaw the examination and appointment of pilots and advised on all matters of maritime safety on the east coast, and beyond.

18   The tragedy occurred when their pilots mistook the glow from an open door of a limekiln on the Haddingtonshire shore for the feeble illumination of the May Light: PRO ADM 1/ 5121, Miscellanea, 'Correspondence with the Commissioners for the Northern Lights and others about fires inshore being mistaken for the May Light' (1811). Its owner – the Duke of Portland – received £60,000 in compensation as part of the compulsory purchase.

to effect its purchase (1814), after which it was placed under the control of Trinity House of Leith who dispatched Robert Stevenson to raise a new light at a lower elevation on the Isle (lit 1816).[19]

The Clyde masters sought similar aids to marking the channels on either side of the Little Cumbrae island that gave access to the upper Firth ports and the prime foul weather anchorage of Fairlie Roads. Their initial petition of 1743 eventually secured, in April 1756, an *Act for erecting, maintaining and supporting a lighthouse* on the island.[20] Its chauffer was mounted on a round tower and burned Saltcoats coal when first lit in December 1757.[21] The trustees appointed to operate the light were required by the Act to use all surplus 'Light Money' to fund the removal of the shoals and mudflats in the upper reaches of the Firth of Clyde. The original levy was one penny per ton burthen for British hulls, double for foreign vessels, and half for coasters over thirty tons.[22]

The Cumbrae light (standing at 122 metres above sea level) suffered from the same locational defect as that on the Isle of May and was regularly obscured by low clouds.[23] In 1785 it was proposed that the coal fire should be replaced by candlepower but this was rejected as not providing the final solution. Eventually the fire tower was abandoned and a new light (mounting thirty-two oil lamps with silvered glass reflectors) was built in 1793 on the western end of the island at a much lower height of 35 metres.[24]

George Dempster of Dunnichen, Provost of Forfar and Member of Parliament, championed the awesome task of illuminating the rest of the Scottish coastline. He was motivated by the destruction of vessels driven ashore for want of knowing their position during the severe storms of 1782. This cause he raised in the Convention of Royal Burghs and, subsequently, in the House of Commons. As a result of his emotive campaign the government established the Commission of Northern Lights in 1786. Sitting at Edinburgh, this influential body was empowered to levy duties,

19   The old tower was reduced to half its original height in the process so as not to obscure the new illumination: Hague, *Lighthouses*, p.40.
20   A beacon fire had been lit from the height since 1750: J. Lamb, *Annuals of an Ayrshire Parish: West Kilbride* (Glasgow, 1896), p. 128.
21   Graham, *Saltcoats*, p. 17.
22   Act of Parliament, 29 Geo. II, c.20.
23   Hague, *Lighthouses*, p. 40.
24   Lamb, *Ayrshire Parish*, p. 130. The wider management role of the Trustees is discussed in G. Blake, *Clyde Lighthouses* (Glasgow, 1950).

borrow funds and purchase land without further recourse to Parliament.[25]

They, in turn, appointed an English-trained lampmaker of renown – Thomas Smith – to execute their initial remit to raise four new lights.[26] The first was at Kinnaird Head, near Fraserburgh, which he illuminated in December 1787 with twenty oil lights raised on top of an existing four-storey castle.[27] The three other lights were raised on towers at the Mull of Kintyre (lit 1788); Scalpay (Eilean Glas) on the southern tip of Lewis (lit 1789); and on the Pentland Skerries (lit 1794).

In making the case for the Kintyre light, the Collector of Customs for Campbeltown stressed:

> Unspeakable advantages would ensue from the light … for ships coming in from America and the West Indies come frequently between the coast of Ireland and the Island of Islay [where] the Mull of Islay (the Mull of Oa) is often mistaken for the Mull of Kintyre by which frequent shipwrecks happen.[28]

The position of this light proved, however, to be inadequate for vessels approaching from the south. The remedy was to build an additional light on the island of Pladda at the southern tip of Arran (lit 1790).[29] One contemporary commentator concluded that the new light – together with those already lit at Cumbrae, Portpatrick and Donaghadee – formed a chain of illuminations that was 'of singular use to the towns of Air, Irvine and Saltcoats, which carry on a considerable trade with Ireland and the towns of the west of England'.[30]

---

25   The nineteen members of the Commission of Northern Lights were men of power and influence: the Lord Advocate; the Solicitor General; the Lord Provosts of Edinburgh, Glasgow, and Aberdeen; the Provosts of Campbeltown and Inverness; the senior Baillies of Glasgow and Edinburgh; and the Sheriffs of the maritime counties.

26   Smith was trained at King's Lynn by Ezekiel Walker at the expense of the Commissioners for the Northern Lights. It is highly probable that the design of the lighthouse structures was left to others in this tight-knit fraternity, namely, Robert Stevenson and Robert Kay. The latter, the architect of South Bridge in Edinburgh, submitted plans for lighthouses to Smith during the years 1787–8.

27   When raised, this lighthouse was found to be masked by Rattray Head from vessels approaching from the south: *OSA*, Parish of Fraserburgh, VI, p.13.

28   Collector Campbeltown to the Board, CE 82 1/1, 8 March 1786.

29   Act of Parliament, 26 Geo. III. c. 52. The Commissioners' powers had been extended by Acts in 1788 and 1789.

30   *OSA*, Parish of Ballantrae, VI, p. 46.

LIGHT MONEY

'Light money' was charged to all vessels with the exception of open boats, whalers and Archangel traders. It was calculated on the basis of the tonnage burthen of the vessel and the number of lights passed. It was normally collected at the port of arrival. The variations in the cost of light money had a considerable effect on the route taken by masters and the attractiveness of some harbours as ports-of-call. This was particularly the case after 1788 when, to meet a shortfall in revenue, the Commissioners for the Northern Lights invoked their powers to raise the duty levied on British vessels passing the new lights to one and a half pence per ton (three pence on foreign vessels).

The east-coast traders made the greatest saving on light money by going north-about when heading for Southern Europe or the Atlantic, rather than south-about through the English Channel.[31] So much so that by the early 1790s more than 2,000 vessels were passing through the Pentland Firth annually.[32] Similarly, west-coast traders working the Atlantic or Southern Europe made savings on light money by using the North Channel rather than St. George's Channel.[33] Costs could be further reduced for those in transit by using the anchorages of the lower Firth of Clyde (Lamlash Bay, Campbeltown, Loch Ryan), thereby avoiding having to pass the Cumbrae light.[34]

Coastal trading was encouraged between and within the Firths of Forth and Tay by waiving up to a fifth of light dues charged by the May Light and one quarter of the Tay light. The sea area as far north as Red Head (south of Montrose) was also declared free from the 'British Duty' for the coastal movement of Fife coal. This was in order to protect the market for local coal from cheaper Tyneside imports.[35]

31 A 160-ton vessel out from Leith would save round £10 by going north-about – the equivalent of three months' wages for an able seaman: GUL MSS.GEN 1057, 3 March 1790, Custom House Report, Edinburgh.
32 *OSA*, Parish of Canisbay, VIII, p. 167. While going north-about to Leith and the Baltic was commonplace for west-coast vessels, they invariable went south-about when heading for London. This is evident in the reply given by the Collectors at the Clyde to the general enquiry made by the tacksman for the Spurn Head Light (Hull). His question was whether it would be appropriate or not to appoint agents at the Clyde ports. Their answer was that he would be wasting his time as few vessels took such a route.
33 A 160-ton vessel clearing for the Atlantic from Port Glasgow via the North Channel saved the master £4 -13/8d per passage: GUL MSS GEN 1057.
34 The Cumbrae light money was by then 2d per ton plus 3d for improvements to the River Clyde: *Ibid.*
35 This situation was denounced by commentators as highly detrimental to the growth of industry in the towns north of this headland.

No such dispensations were allowed elsewhere in Scotland, much to the indignation of local commentators. Indeed, after 1772, the Trustees of the Cumbrae Light imposed an additional three pence per ton levy on all passing vessels to pay for the dredging of the River Clyde. This, along with the imposition of the iniquitous 'British duty' on coal shipped along the Clyde coast, meant that most coal extracted from the leading Ayrshire fields went to Ireland rather than to the Scottish lowland market.

SEAMARKS AND LOCAL LIGHTS

One of the most important changes in eighteenth-century maritime activity was the rapid growth in the number of winter voyages undertaken by Scottish masters, particularly on the west coast. In the vanguard were the tobacco fleets that often returned in the depths of winter with the new crop from America.[36] They were joined by an increasing number of coastal traders and herring busses, the former tempted by the high prices fetched by Ayrshire coal in the expanding Irish markets and the latter sailing to claim the second bounty payment (after 1771). Consequently, the traditional lay-up period (end of December to early April) becomes decreasingly less evident in the port books of the major ports as the century progresses.[37] The cost of this change in seasonal activity was a sharp rise in the loss of vessels and seamen, which prompted the maritime communities to seek the authority and funding to raise seamarks and local lights at key harbours and anchorages.[38]

In the expanse of the lower Firth of Clyde the risk of embayment (being caught on the lee shore) was greatly increased by winter gales. In a strong nor'westerly the shoaled bays of the Ayrshire coast trapped the average square-rigged brig unable to point sufficiently to windward to beat round Portencross headland to gain the safety of Fairlie Roads. During the infamous winter of 1789 fourteen vessels were caught in this way and eventually driven up on the rock-strewn shores of the Kyle and Carrick districts of South Ayrshire.[39]

36   Entries of dockings in December and January are commonplace in the Port Books of Greenock and Port Glasgow (1742 onwards). The degree of attrition sustained by the transatlantic hulls is evident from the fact that only a handful made more than ten crossings in their working lives.

37   Graham, *Ayr*, p. 30.

38   Seamarks were unlit perches or cairns or tall structures raised to act as channel marks or sight lines in approaching an anchorage. At Ayr the old tower of St. John's church was left standing for the benefit of mariners.

39   *OSA*, Parish of Stevenston, VI, p.681.

Vessels under 200 tons had the option of attempting to cross the sandbar at the mouth of the two estuary ports on that coast (Ayr or Irvine). For this to be successful, the entrance had first to be located in time to coincide with a high tide and a reasonable sea-state. When wind and tide were against the embattled master, the fate of his vessel and crew was at the mercy of the elements. In one tempestuous night, twelve vessels were stranded on the bar at Ayr, and one of them broke up with great loss of life. As a result, a local subscription was raised to install a twin set of suspended coal-burning lights (later replaced by reflecting lights) to indicate the approach line to the harbour channel and, by their vertical position, the depth over the bar.[40]

The other option was to seek what shelter was available in the bays. In an earlier effort to increase the survival rate of their investments in the lower Clyde, the Glasgow merchants had raised two seamarks on the small, flat Lady Isle, just off Troon Point, to direct their embayed masters to the last possible deepwater offshore anchorage. The Rev. Dr. McGill of Ayr considered their investment futile as 'nothing ... but extreme necessity, can induce any ship to attempt anchoring there, be the [holding] ground ever so good, because there be no shelter above'.[41]

In south-westerlies this anchorage became untenable. The last hope of avoiding a wrecking was to run the vessel up on the sands behind Troon promontory. This desperate manoeuvre was successfully executed by a number of masters. During another long-remembered great storm (19 January 1739) Captain Denholm on the galley *Anne* (200 tons) 'drove from Lamlash roads over to Troon where [he] ran her upon the same sands and was, with the whole crew, preserved'.[42]

The search for a suitable storm haven on the lower Clyde coast was a matter of much concern throughout the century. A consortium of Glasgow merchants tried, unsuccessfully, to acquire the Troon headland prior to their decision to build Port Glasgow.[43] Another scheme mooted was that a 'New Port Irvine' should be built in Millport Bay on the Great Cumbrae.

Robert Reid Cunninghame, owner of the coal port of Saltcoats,

40 *OSA*, Parish of Newton-on-Ayr, VI, p. 494.
41 *Ibid.*, Parish of Ayr, VI, p. 36.
42 North Ayrshire Libraries, Auchenharvie MSS [CA], box 22, bundle 3, handwritten commentary. Other reports of this practice include that of Captain Andrew Troop, *Blandford* of Port Glasgow (110 tons), which was later salvaged from the sands along with its cargo of tobacco in 1774.
43 *OSA*, Parish of Dundonald, VI, p. 179. Troon Point came under the precinct of Irvine which sought to levy a charge for vessels using the anchorage as early as 1609.

widely circulated a pamphlet addressed *To the Shipping Interest of the Clyde* that extolled the virtues of his small port as a storm haven.[44] This harbour had been built in 1700 on a volcanic dyke that jutted out into the lower Firth and so was free of sandbars. In order to fully exploit its locational advantage he proposed an ambitious plan to double its sheltered anchorage by enclosing the northern shore of Saltcoats Bay (owned by the Earl of Eglinton) behind a new northern pier.[45] This scheme fell foul of the personal animosity between the two men, and Reid Cunninghame's final contribution to maritime safety was a coal-burning brazier at the end of the pier extension built in 1797.[46]

Lesser schemes sought to improve access to the existing estuary ports. Ayr expended considerable time and effort attempting to dredge a channel through the bar by dragging a sunken tree between two boats. This crude effort was abandoned in favour of channel fencing, using triangular boxes filled with stones, to increase the scurry effect of the river. At Irvine, in addition to fencing, it was proposed that a new channel should be cut across the last great meander of the River Irvine to increase its force at the harbour bar.[47]

The maritime development of the Solway Firth was greatly retarded by its notorious shifting sandbanks, strong currents and wide tidal range (twenty-five feet on a spring tide at Annan). In 1741 Dumfries Town Council embarked on major harbour improvements at Glencaple and Kingholm on the River Nith to secure their continued presence in the Atlantic and European trades. Part of this initiative involved anchoring buoys at the entrance to the river and in the main offshore channel between the great Dumreef and Robin Rigg sandbanks. The technology apparently did not exist in Scotland at this time to construct the three buoys needed, which had to be purchased and shipped from Rotterdam.[48] To compensate

---

44   North Ayrshire Libraries, Auchenharvie MSS Box 22, bundle 3. He claimed that his pamphlet was prompted by 'the recent unfortunate stranding of the ships *Montezuma* and *Minerva* of Charleston, in the Bay of Ayr and Irvine'.

45   *OSA*, Parish of Stevenston, VI, p.7.

46   The iron fire cage suspended from a derrick at the pier end is evident in a drawing of the harbour (1818) now displayed in the North Ayrshire Museum, Saltcoats.

47   McJannet, *Irvine*, p. 249. There are indications that the physical union of the rivers Garnock and Irvine close to the harbour mouth is a fairly recent topographical event. Pont's survey (c.1608) would appear to represent the Garnock meeting the sea a few miles further north at the Stevenston side of the Ardeer sands. If this was so, then the harbour at Irvine, without the additional force of the Garnock, would have been much shallower prior to 1650.

48   Moore, 'Thomas Winter's Chart', p. 58.

for the lack of notable landward features from which to identify the entrance to the Nith, a seamark tower was raised at Southerness (1749). The widow of Richard Oswald subsequently increased its height, sometime after 1784, as part of a plan to promote a coal exporting trade from the area. This structure was finally illuminated in the late 1790s.[49]

West of the great sandbanks there was no natural storm haven on the Scottish side of the Solway. Little Ross Isle in Kirkcudbright Bay was the only anchorage with good holding ground but offered limited shelter from the prevailing south-westerlies. It also served as 'the roads' for vessels waiting to negotiate the sandbar across the mouth of the River Dee that lay two miles across the bay. Such was the importance of this anchorage during the eighteenth century that the Rev. Robert Muter proposed that a lighthouse should be raised on the isle to guide ships in distress to the anchorage, as 'many fatal accidents happen by ships missing the harbour, and being driven; either into Wigton Bay; or on to the banks of the Solway'.[50]

The Government's ongoing obsession with its strategic communication links with Ireland ensured that the funds were forthcoming to raise a forty-six-foot-high light with a reflecting lamp at the pier end of Portpatrick harbour in 1779. This beacon compensated for the lack of natural landmarks when attempting to locate the harbour entrance – flanked by two submerged reefs – in poor visibility.

On the east coast, Aberdeen was the only estuary port, north of the Forth, to undertake major works to improve its estuary channel prior to 1790. In 1770, Smeaton was retained by the town council to deflect the creep of sand along the coast and to funnel the force of the River Dee to scurry the bar. The outcome was the construction of the North Pier and a new 1,200 feet bulwark on the south shore (1775–80). The scoured channel was marked by an unlit seamark until the 1790s when a signal tower was raised. This displayed a red flag during the day and a reflector light at night when there was nine feet or more depth of water over the bar.[51] The Montrose shippers floated equally ambitious schemes, but the only tangible

49   G. Stell, 'Southerness Lighthouse', *Transactions of the Dumfriesshires and Galloway Antiquarian and Natural History Society*, LIX, p. 67.
50   *Ibid.*, p, 13. A case in question was the loss of the *Neptune* of Dumfries, overset in Kirkcudbright Bay *en route* for Dieppe with tobacco from James Guthrie of Dumfries, in 1750; Act 24 Geo. II, c.35.
51   The original Parliamentary Act (1773) permitted fixed moorings to be laid in the roadstead and regularised the pilotage service: *OSA*, Parish of Aberdeen, XIX, pp. 153–5.

result was a twenty-foot-high seamark raised on Scurdieness Bank in 1770.[52]

The earliest channel lights in Scotland (1687) were the two coal-fired beacons at the mouth of the Tay on Buddonness sandspit. When aligned, these lights set the course to enter the Firth's narrow channel between the Averte and Goa sandbanks and clear of the treacherous Cross Sand shoal.[53]

In the Forth the highly influential Fraternity of Leith had seamarks raised on the islets of Inverkeith and Cramond, the tidal-washed Black Rocks, and on a rocky patch at the extreme edge of the tidal bank off Leith. In 1709, at the behest of the Admiralty, they surveyed the tidal harbour that served the administrative capital of Scotland.[54] By then the old windmill at the landward end of the main pier had been converted into a signal tower which indicated the depth in the harbour and answered requests for pilots.[55] At the seaward end of the great wooden curved north pier, which flanked the tidal course of the Water of Leith, was a small roundhouse. This was later illuminated by a coal-fire basket in bad weather and was replaced (1789) by a more efficient reflecting oil lamp: 'Its effect at sea is surprising, and the expense of maintaining it does not exceed that of the former one.'[56]

GOVERNMENT INTERVENTION
IN PORT DEVELOPMENT

Considerations of national security were prime movers in the development of a number of Scottish ports. During Cromwell's subjugation of Scotland military imperatives dictated that almost all the major investment at the ports of Leith, Ayr, Inverness, Inverlochy and Lerwick was channelled into building giant 'star' citadels, with very limited improvements to quays or piers.[57] After the Jacobite Rebellion of 1715, however, the inadequate quay

---

52   For a fuller review of proposed harbour improvements, see D.G. Adams, 'The Harbour, its early history', in *The Port of Montrose* (G. Jackson and S.G.E. Lythe (eds.), Tayport 1993), pp. 27–41.

53   Claims that the beacons date from 1660 are probably referring to earlier unlit seamarks. The illuminated beacons were authorised by the Privy Council in February 1687: *RPC*, XVI, p. 616.

54   The mud floor of the main tidal basin was considered good for either 'flat or sharp' hulls: Mason, *Trinity*, p. 45.

55   A light was displayed as long as there was nine feet of water in the main basin.

56   Grant, *Edinburgh*, III, p. 273.

57   Cromwell had a small pier built at Belhaven, East Lothian, but this was abandoned by the time of the Restoration.

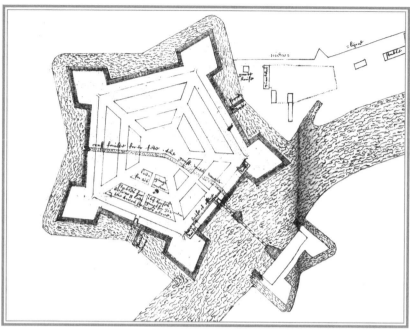

THE CITADEL AT INVERNESS
(PROVOST AND FELLOWS OF WORCESTER COLLEGE, OXFORD)

at Inverness – then the headport for northern mainland Scotland including the Isle of Skye – received the attention of government planners. The existing town quay on the southern bank of the River Ness (built in 1675) was only capable of receiving vessels of *c*.80 tons. This excluded the admission of the average contracted vessel (*c*. 150 tons) when loaded with supplies and ordnance for the line of new forts along the Great Glen. As a consequence the new 'Citadel Harbour' was built (1725–32) further downstream at a cost of £2,750.[58]

Portpatrick on the Mull of Galloway is the most outstanding example of later direct government intervention in port development. The administration's security-driven obsession with the shortest possible line of communication to Ireland dictated the choice of site for this strategic link.[59] This exposed anchorage had been used as a ferry point for the twenty-mile crossing since the Middle Ages but was still 'almost in a state of nature' when Smeaton surveyed the haven in 1768, at the behest of the Post Office

58   'The Harbour of Inverness', *The Inverness Courier*, 30 September 1910; and Pollitt, *Historic Inverness*, p. 113.
59   In 1715 Adair had recommended the diminutive Port Logan, some ten miles south and marginally closer to Ireland, as the site for the Irish packet service: I. Donnachie, *The Industrial Archaeology of Galloway* (Newton Abbot, 1971), p. 180.

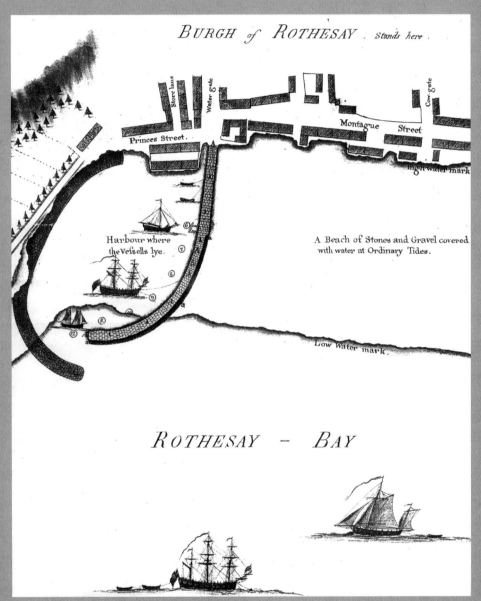

BURGH of ROTHESAY. Stands here.

Store lane

Water gate

Cow gate

Princes Street.

Montague Street

High water mark

Harbour where
the Vessells lye.

A Beach of Stones and Gravel covered
with water at Ordinary Tides.

Low Water mark.

ROTHESAY - BAY

PROPOSED IMPROVEMENTS AT ROTHESAY, 1779
(NATIONAL ARCHIVES OF SCOTLAND)

General. The anchorage at that time was open to the full force of the Irish Sea and had no landing pier. The open-decked, flat-bottomed wherries that acted as ferries normally resorted to a primitive 'over-the-side' mode of landing passengers and animals. In rough weather this could not be safely done, and so an incoming wherry was met by 'the whole inhabitants, men and women, [who] ran down, and by main force, dragged her up the beach, out of the reach of the waves, which would otherwise have dashed her to pieces'.[60]

The spur to the port's development was the completion in 1764 of the military road from Carlisle to Portpatrick at the end of the Seven Years War. By 1770 traffic had increased to such an extent that a dozen or so new dispatch boats (20–60 tons), hired on a first-come-first-served basis, were in operation.[61] In 1774 Smeaton was awarded the contract to build two piers to create a harbour that would be protected from the force of the fetch. It was a major project, as 'the finest quays in Britain' cost the government double the original estimate of £6,000 by the time they were completed in 1778. This outlay was considered justified, as the following year the volume of the passenger trade leapt again when a post-coach service from Carlisle to Portpatrick via Dumfries was inaugurated.[62]

Maintaining Portpatrick harbour was a costly business as sections of the North Pier were regularly demolished by the winter seas. By 1786 part of the pier was so undermined that a supporting bulwark had to be erected behind it at a further cost of £1,200. This bulwark required rebuilding in 1792 and was completely demolished nine years later by a storm that threw its breastwork into the harbour mouth. After that natural disaster Thomas Telford surveyed the harbour and expressed serious reservations as to the suitability of the site for its purpose.[63] Nevertheless, the administration (supported by Trinity House of Leith) came down in favour of maintaining the packet service at Portpatrick and supported John Rennie's new scheme (begun in 1820) to rebuild and expand the harbour.

A spin-off of this major development was the construction of a pier at Millport on the Great Cumbrae in the Firth of Clyde to facilitate the shipment of quarrystone to Portpatrick.[64] The remarkable Captain

---

60   OSA, Parish of Portpatrick, I, p. 39. Cattle boats, after the embargo on Irish livestock imports was lifted in the 1750s, ran mainly in the summer months.

61   *Ibid.*, pp. 40–1.

62   R.R. Cunninghame, *Portpatrick through the ages* (Stranraer, 1985), pp. 8–11.

63   Donnachie, *Archaeology*, pp. 181–2.

64   Stone shipped from Dumbarton was also used.

Crawford – commander of the *Cumbrae* Customs wherry – secured the contract and had the quarry rubble dumped in the tidal way between the shoreline and the islet of Craiglee to create 'a good working free stone quay' for the island by 1772. This pier guaranteed the use of Millport as the home station for the principal Customs cruiser of the Firth of Clyde, which by 1790 was a very large cutter – the *Royal George* (200 tons) – crewed by sixty local men.[65]

To be overlooked by the government agencies was often the deathknell for the older ports, such as Burntisland in the Forth. Its promoters had sought to regain its former prosperity by advocating its suitability as the watering and naval station of the Forth: 'In the opinion of professional men, docks ought to be established here, capable of receiving the largest ships of war. This is surely an object, well deserving the attention of government.'[66] As with Alloa, such proposals got nowhere as the Admiralty continued to use Leith, despite its shortcomings, as its principal base in the Forth.

THE DEEPWATER PORTS
ON THE UPPER CLYDE

While Scotland was geographically well placed to benefit from both the general expansion in European trade and the rise of the Atlantic economy, the retarded state of her estuary harbours hampered the pace of her maritime development. For example, vessels waiting for a high tide to cross the harbour bar at Ayr or Irvine had to anchor in Lamlash Bay (Arran) some eighteen miles across the Firth. Even with the tide, a fully laden Virginiaman could only enter once it had been lightened – a high-risk operation as the vessel had to ride to anchor in Ayr Bay while lighters took off part of the cargo.[67] In the Forth, Inverkeithing Bay – eight miles from Leith – served as the inshore anchorage for vessels waiting for the tide or

65   The entire local population then numbered 509. Crawford also managed to lease his privately owned vessel – the *Mary* – to the Customs service as an additional cruiser out of Stranraer.

66   The recent careening of the frigate HMS *Champion* was quoted as proof of its suitability: *OSA*, Parish of Burntisland, X, p. 93.

67   The owners of the *Hope* of Ayr (140 tons) – anchored 'a good distance' out in Ayr Bay – appealed unsuccessfully to the Collector to have her unstamped documentation accepted so that the transshipment of her cargo of 235 hogsheads of tobacco to lighters could commence: GCA, CE 76?, Collector of Ayr to Edinburgh, 26 February 1766.

doing quarantine.[68] In the Tay estuary larger vessels had to be loaded and unloaded in mid-channel as there was insufficient depth, even with a full tide, at Dundee's town quay.[69]

The larger traders and whalers required accessible deepwater harbours, preferably with drydock facilities, for the maintenance and repair of hulls. The Government's promotion of commercial docks was restricted to the passing of Acts permitting an appropriate body to raise a local tax – invariably on malt or the sale of ales – to refund the initial outlay.[70]

The first deepwater Scottish harbour built to give quayside access in all tides was 'New Port' Glasgow.[71] It was raised on a virgin sight in Newark Bay acquired by the magistrates and Council of Glasgow as an alternative to developing Irvine or Dumbarton. Construction of the west quay was commenced in the late 1660s when the windfalls of the Dutch Wars and Charles's policy of neutrality led to a general recovery in west-coast foreigngoing trade. It was, however, a staged development as the breastwork of the inner harbour was only finally completed in 1675. The east quay was built some fifty years later (1732) and the mid-quay in 1773.[72]

The catalyst for the development of a rival deepwater port at Greenock – next to the Crawfordsdyke anchorage – was the ongoing dispute between the shippers of the 'unfree' burgh of Greenock and those of the 'free' New Port Glasgow in the early 1690s. The Atlantic trade, albeit illegal, was then taking off, but the aspirations of the Greenock fraternity were frustrated by the high harbour dues and partisan allocation of warehousing at New Port Glasgow. In addition, the site of Greenock harbour had the distinct advantage of immediate access to open deep water and a substantial holding ground – the 'Tail o' the Bank' – off Kempock Point. On the latter, large numbers of ocean-going vessels rode to their anchors in moderate weather awaiting a berth or change in the wind direction. Port Glasgow, by contrast, required a pilot to negotiate the estuary channel. This operational disadvantage, in both time and cost, undoubtedly made a significant contribution to the diverging growth rates

68 An old Dutch hulk was moored there as a 'lazaretto' (quarantine station): *OSA*, Parish of Inverkeithing, X, pp. 805–6.
69 An example was the mid-channel loading of the *Amelia* of Perth (150 tons) with corn for Leghorn which the Collector allowed as 'the harbour cannot afford water [at high tide] to a ship of that burden laden ... to go aboard in lighters without it were shipt at the Key': Archive and Records Centre, Dundee, CE 70 1/1, Collector of Dundee to Edinburgh, 6 March 1735.
70 The cost of the Citadel Quay at Inverness was recouped by this method.
71 The 'New' prefix was retained until 1774.
72 Marwick, *River Clyde*, p. 178.

of the two ports during the eighteenth century.[73]

The development of the port of Greenock can be attributed to one man – Sir John Shaw – whose determination and foresight cannot be overestimated. He was spurred into independent action by the opportunities created by the Act of Union, having previously failed to secure a grant for his 'unfree' port from the Scottish Parliament in 1696 and 1700. His new harbour cost £5,555 11/1d, recoverable over thirty years by a local tax on malt, and was the greatest capital project of its day in Scotland.[74] The harbour covered eight acres when completed in 1710, with eighteen feet of water at springs and eight feet at low tide, and provided the model for the final layout of New Port Glasgow. These two ports were, when completed, the only harbours north of Liverpool capable of receiving a fully loaded vessel of 250 tons burthen at the quayside in all tides.

QUAYSIDE OPERATIONS
AT THE UPPER CLYDE PORTS

The high levels of shipping activity at the upper Clyde ports placed an intolerable workload on the Customs officers charged with enforcing the Government's 'prohibitions, restrictions and regulations of trade' at the quayside. The lengthy and elaborate procedures prescribed by the Acts for the loading and unloading of 'customable' commodities greatly delayed the turn-round time of vessels.

Port Glasgow and Greenock was a unified Customs precinct until 1763 and covered the entire upper Firth of Clyde including the inner islands and Inveraray at the head of Loch Fyne.[75] To maintain control at the various legal quaysides, the Collector imposed a rigid queuing system for a berth, as it was 'not the custom to unload two ships at one port at the same time'.[76] The rate of unloading of tobacco was largely determined by access to the

---

73 The tonnage owned by Greenock first exceeded that of Port Glasgow in 1767.

74 A. Brown, *History of Glasgow*, III, p.377, as quoted by McArthur, *Port Glasgow*, p.72. The *Manie* (500 tons), built at Archangel for the East Indies trade, was advertised for sale by the local shipbuilders Scott and Frazer while in the dry dock: *Glasgow Mercury*, 19 September 1782.

75 Inveraray had been allocated to Port Glasgow, rather than Campbeltown, at the insistence of the Duke of Argyll.

76 The only exception to come to hand was the early admittance of the embargo-breaking *Cochrane* of Port Glasgow (240 tons) as she was 'in great danger of sinking and with much difficulty her pumps keeps her above water' after an arduous Atlantic crossing: *Glasgow Mercury*, 24 December 1757.

appropriate weighing beam and the availability of tidewaiters and landwaiters (and their porters). By mid-century Port Glasgow, as the main entrepôt for American tobacco, had two great 'triangles', each supporting two weighing beams. The weighing beams on the heavier triangle were normally assigned to incoming cargoes while those on the lighter triangle were for outgoing smaller consignments of tobacco.[77] Greenock, being more diverse in its trading interest, had a greater range of weighing beams. The single beam on the East Quay was used to weigh tobacco while the two on a great triangle on the Mid Quay were general purpose. A fourth smaller beam was situated in the warehouse for weighing salt used in the fisheries.

The opening of the Broomielaw legal quay in 1755 by the Corporation of Glasgow – due to 'want of cellar room' at the downriver seaports – placed an additional burden on the Port Glasgow Collector.[78] Henceforth, his officers were required to board vessels anchored off Port Glasgow to oversee the transshipment of their cargoes into gabbarts (sailing lighters) for the upriver journey.[79] Early in the following year a weighing triangle and two beams were acquired from Edinburgh to facilitate the inspection and collection of duty on enumerated goods landed at this new quay.[80] Thereafter, it was permissible for tobacco destined for domestic distribution or re-export (via land carriage to Bo'ness or Alloa) to be delivered directly from America to its owners in Glasgow.[81] By November 1757 the riverborne traffic was such that the Collector of Port Glasgow petitioned Edinburgh to have the city's Customhouse and warehouse relocated to the 'end of the Bridge, next to the Broomielaw'.[82]

EXTENDING THE UPPER CLYDE PORTS

The great enterprise of deepening the River Clyde to receive seagoing vessels at the Broomielaw quay has been told by many.[83] Smeaton proposed

---

77   GCA CE 60 1/1 Collector of Port Glasgow and Greenock to the Board, 28 September 1756.
78   The original quay was built in 1724 at a cost of £1833 sterling.
79   *Ibid.*, 27 March 1758.
80   *Ibid.*, 24 March 1757.
81   The first cargo processed in this way was 394 hogsheads of Maryland tobacco transshipped out of the hold of the *Scott* (130 tons) in March of that year: *Ibid.*, 16 March 1756 (arrived in November 1755).
82   *Ibid.*, 17 November 1757.
83   A technical account is available in J.F. Riddel, *Clyde Navigation* (Edinburgh, 1979), pp. 11–33.

to canalise the river along the twelve-mile stretch of tidal-washed shoals between Glasgow and Dumbuck Ford by erecting a series of locks. Fortunately for the future Clydeside shipbuilding industry, this scheme was dropped in favour of the creation of an unrestricted narrow channel by a series of 'Jettees, Banks, Walls, Works and Fences' and selective dredging (started in 1773).[84] The cost was to be borne by the users of the river who were, in turn, guaranteed a minimum of seven feet in the channel at neaps or the remission of duty.

By then serious silting problems threatened Port Glasgow's continuing role as Glasgow's deepwater port, so much so that a series of Acts (up to 1772) had been sought to impose heavier berthing charges to finance the necessary improvements.

Greenock, as a self-governing Town Council after 1751, had regularly voted to use its harbour dues for small improvements but in 1773 responded to Port Glasgow's lead and petitioned Parliament to match its neighbour's rise in harbour duties. This was in order to finance Watt's elaborate scheme to channel fresh water into the town from the surrounding hills and to erect new quays. In 1789 an Act of Improvement authorised the deepening and cleaning of the harbour floor. It also permitted Scott, the shipbuilder, to build a new 'Customhouse pier' to the east of the original harbour (completed 1791).[85] In 1801, as plans to build rival wet-docks were being made further down the Clyde coast, this piecemeal development of Greenock came to an end with the formation of a harbour trust to oversee the running of the port.

THE DEVELOPMENT OF PETERHEAD

On the North-East coast the only large-scale 'new port' built during the eighteenth century was the southern anchorage of Peterhead Bay. The strategic importance of Peterhead in wartime was emphasised by the Rev. Dr. Moir: '... in time of war, this being a head-land, is the place where privateers most frequently keep their station, and pick up ships which might find shelter here, but for want of access to a harbour, are obliged to beat against the wind for several days.'[86]

---

84 Act of Parliament, 10 Geo. III, c.104.
85 *OSA,* Parish of New Greenock, V, p. 577; and Dow, *Greenock,* p. 33.
86 *OSA,* Parish of Peterhead, XVI, p. 600.

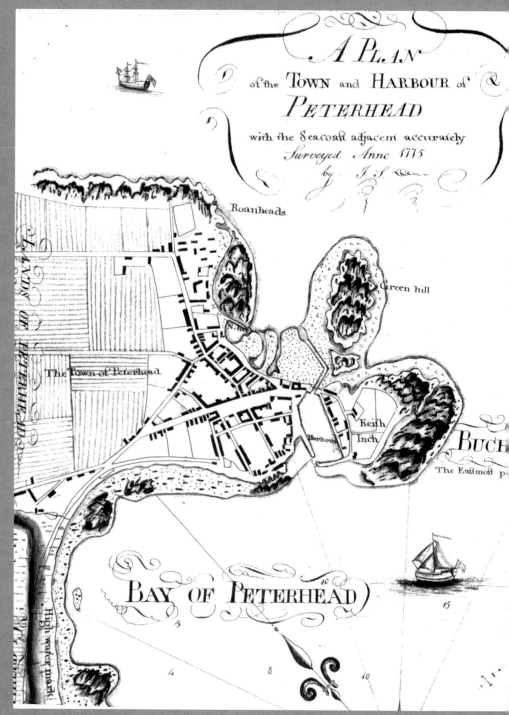

A PLAN

of the TOWN and HARBOUR of
PETERHEAD

with the Seacoast adjacent accurately
Surveyed Anno 1775
by   J. S. ....

Roanheads

Green hill

LANDS OF PETERHEAD

The Town of Peterhead

Keith
Inch

Harbour

BUCH

The Eastmost p...

LANDS OF PETERHEAD

BAY OF PETERHEAD

High water mark

15

5

4

8

10

PROPOSED IMPROVEMENTS AT PETERHEAD, 1775
(NATIONAL ARCHIVES OF SCOTLAND)

A hollow Channel

Part of the Greenhill

This is dry at low water and cover'd at high

D

C

Rocks

The proposed Cut

B

A Draught of the Harbour of Peterhead ith M.r Smeaton's proposed Projection of Piers, represented by the green colouring; a Draught of the intended Cut Quays surrounding the Harbour distinguished by the ton colouring ABCDEF

E

Harbour of Peterhead

Part of Keith-inch

West Pier

ESS

F

South Pier

Castle

Mew Craig

ow water mark

High water mark

Low water

After the failure of the Jacobite Rebellion of 1715, the Earl Marischal's town and lands of Peterhead were forfeited and sold to an English fishing company – in all probability the 'Orkney and Shetland Fishing Company'. When it went bankrupt in 1726, the Merchant Maiden Hospital of Edinburgh acquired the town. This organisation, with the aid of funds from the Fraternity of Leith and the Convention of Royal Burghs, developed the southern harbour from 1737 onwards as a haven.[87] Smeaton surveyed the port in 1772 and found that 'present pier … greatly decayed and shaken so that it will take two or three thousand pounds to put the harbour in good condition'.[88] Such was the importance of this anchorage that this large amount of capital was forthcoming. Thereafter, a new granite-clad pier and enclosing bulwark on the western shore, capable of withstanding the full force of the North Sea, were completed by 1777.

PORT DEVELOPMENT IN THE FORTH

Bo'ness and Alloa were the only tidal anchorages in the Forth to deepen their harbours. This investment largely accounts for their high ranking – by shipping activity – in eighteenth-century Customs accounts.

Bo'ness had developed rapidly as a port shortly after the Union when the long West Pier with an inner quayside was built out into the Firth. The East Pier was added sometime after 1744 when parliamentary permission was given to raise the necessary finance by the usual blend of higher docking dues and a levy on the local consumption of beer. The result was an enclosed two-acre harbour that was deepened in 1762 by a rather novel, but effective, scouring method developed by the local engineer, Robert McKell. His system consisted of a moveable double-walled barrier that could be lowered into place between the two existing piers to dam the water in the inner quarter of the harbour:

> During spring tides, these sluices are regularly opened, and shut
> at full sea, when a great body of water is retained. At low water,
> the sluices are opened; emptying [into] the bason with so rapid
> a current, that in the course of a few years from the erection, a

---

87   The Fraternity of Leith granted 25 guineas towards improvements: J. Mason, *The History of Trinity House, Leith* (Glasgow, undated), pp. 44–5.

88   Buchan, *Peterhead*, p. 31.

great increase to the depth of water in the harbour, was made, and continues to be maintained at a very small expense.[89]

The result was deep and safe berthing which attracted whalers and larger traders, including those that served the recently opened Carron Ironworks. The increase in activity was such that congestion at the quays had become a major problem by the winter of 1763. In that year the harbourmaster ordered the laid-up whalers of Charles Addison & Co. to move off the quaysides and anchor in the middle of the harbour.[90] In June 1772 the Carron Company opened a waggonway from the ironworks to the west pier, which became the main loading quay for the company fleet and those local contractors delivering ironstone from Dysart. This remained the situation until Grangemouth was developed twenty years later, causing a rapid decline in shipping activity at Bo'ness.[91]

Alloa — the head port for the tidal stretch of the River Forth — mimicked the Bo'ness system, though on a much reduced scale, by periodically releasing the retained head of water behind the local mill dams to scour the harbour basin. This, combined with her greater tidal range, allowed seagoing draft vessels to reach Alloa with the flood. Consequently, the port conducted a steady trade to the Continent throughout the century.[92]

The Water of the Leith did not have the force to scour the whole harbour floor at Leith and only deepened the basin along its immediate low-tide course by two feet. This narrow channel, however, permitted the deeper draft hulls to moor upstream and helped to ease the chronic congestion along the piers. A traveller's report of 1779 described Leith as 'a very poor place … the harbour is generally crowded with vessels from any parts and from here to Kinghorn, in Fifeshire, the passage boat passes every tide, except on Sundays.'[93] Clearance of the harbour bar required a full tide for most vessels of burthen. During nor'-easterly gales, the inrunning fetch threw up the bar to a level such that running aground

---

89   *OSA*, Parish of Borrowstounness, II, p. 705.

90   T.J. Salomon, *Borrowstounness and District* (Edinburgh, 1913), p. 239.

91   *Ibid.*, pp. 238–259.

92   The Alloa Customs records for the period 1742–1786 have been the subject of a local history group research project, the finds of which were published in 1978 by M. Haynes: 'Alloa Port, Customs and Excise Accounts', *Forth Naturalist and Historian*, III, pp. 113–127.

93   'A Modern Universal Traveller', published 1779 and quoted by J. Campbell, *Leith and its Antiquities* (Edinburgh, undated), p. 177.

became a common occurrence for months afterwards. Indeed, many London-bound passengers preferred to travel by road to Berwick-on-Tweed, there to board the fast cutters and smacks that regularly sailed for London with salmon.[94]

The dire financial straits of Edinburgh Corporation during the eighteenth century effectively checked the adoption of a 'Bo'ness solution' for the port of Leith. In 1753, an Act was passed to extensively develop the port but, without the powers to raise capital, the scheme was never implemented. In 1771 the entrepreneur and privateering promoter, Thomas Catanach, returned from Holland with a working model of his plans for improving the harbour. This was to be achieved by a system of tidal lock gates and a canal link to a small basin developed out of the North Loch in the centre of Edinburgh.[95] The city magistrates apparently dismissed his plans out of hand on grounds of cost. Instead, they ordered a small-scale programme of widening and deepening the existing basin, which included building a new 'Customs House' quay (1777).

In 1786, however, Whitworth was engaged to survey the North Shore and the low ground to the south of Leith Mills upriver from the existing harbour. At the former site he proposed excavating a twenty-acre wet dock area. On the latter site, he proposed damming the Water of Leith to create an enclosure reached via a lock at high tide. By the following year the necessary Act of Parliament was secured empowering the magistrates and councillors of Edinburgh to act on his proposals.[96] The outcome, however, was little more than some repairs to the existing quay and a drawbridge – similar to Catanach's model – over the river mouth.

Government intervention was required to solve Leith's chronic congestion and limited access. In 1800 the Court of Exchequer of Scotland authorised the diversion of £25,000 from the repayments of Government loans made to the Forth & Clyde Canal consortium to finance Rennie's plan. This scheme, first submitted in 1779, was for an entirely new wet-dock complex on reclaimed land.[97] This sum eventually reached £160,000 by the time the foundation stone for the new Queen's wet dock was laid in 1801.[98]

94   Ibid., p. 273.
95   Macpherson, Commerce, IV, p.175.
96   Act of Parliament 25 Geo. III. c.58.
97   Act of Parliament 39 Geo. III. c.76.
98   Work was not started, however, until 1810 and only completed in 1817: Grant, Edinburgh, III, Ch. xxxiii.

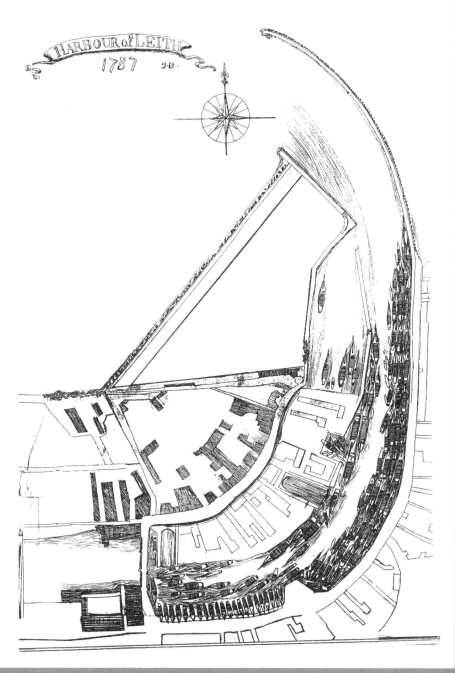

THE HARBOUR OF LEITH, 1787. BIRD'S EYE VIEW
BY WHITWORTH, SHOWING CONGESTION

The wet-dock solution was also embraced on the west coast at this time. The Dukes of Portland and Eglinton sunk their personal fortunes into similar grand schemes at the virgin sites of Troon and Ardrossan respectively.

DRY DOCKS

Prior to 1707 there were no drydocks (graving docks) in Scotland. Instead a 'hard standing' – a sloping mud shelf usually bolstered by bundles of bound heather – was usually set aside at the major ports on which to clean and repair hulls at low tide.[99] The first drydocks were built after the Union to serve the Navy in the Forth. Sometime shortly after 1710, after much wrangling and competition, the Admiralty finally commissioned the building of a dry dock at Leith. By all accounts it was badly built and too small to serve its intended purpose as it was only capable of admitting vessels under 150 tons. A drydock at Alloa, reputedly capable of receiving 'a forty-gun warship', was excavated with private funding sometime afterwards, but does not appear to have been patronised by the Navy.[100] Indeed, during the eighteenth century naval and Customs commanders in Scottish waters often chose to careen their vessels on local beaches – a dangerous and time-consuming operation – rather than make use of the dry-docks at Leith and Alloa.[101]

On the west coast the needs of a rapidly expanding Atlantic fleet dictated events. In 1762 the excavation of a major drydock was started at Port Glasgow and took three years to complete, because of the wartime shortage of oak beams. When completed, it was drained by a horse-driven pump designed by James Watt, who later improved the dock (1772) so as to accommodate two vessels of 500 tons at one time.[102] The problem of the lack of a drydock at Greenock was not addressed until the last year of the American War when a subscription was raised amongst the local shippers

99 Retarring the bottoms of smaller vessels required the careened hull to be cleaned by burning whinbush. The beach set aside for this essential operation was locally known as the 'tar-pot'.
100 *OSA*, Parish of Alloa, IX, p. 660.
101 The naval vessels in the Forth often used the shore at Burntisland while the Excise brigs used Elie.
102 GCA CE 60 1/1, Collector of Port Glasgow and Greenock to the Board, 28 October 1756.

and merchants. This dock was completed sometime before 1789 at a cost of £4,000. These docks were central to the subsequent rapid expansion of shipbuilding and repair at these ports.

THE FORTH & CLYDE CANAL

The hazards inherent in a circumnavigation of Scotland were a major consideration, along with national security, in the promotion of ship canals during the eighteenth century. Only the Forth–Clyde Canal, however, was completed prior to 1790.

This thirty-five-mile-long canal was opened in sections and so had a significant impact on shipping activity even before the final section to Bowling (completing the sea-to-sea route) was formally opened on 28 July 1790. The opening of the canal branch to Glasgow (1777) effectively ended the north-about seaborne conveyance of grain from the east coast to the west, and in doing so heralded an increasingly unified grain market. In other bulk trades, for example in Baltic timber, the raising of the height of the canal banks in 1787 (which deepened the canal by a foot) allowed larger barges of c.108 tons registered to pass its length at a charge rate of two pence per ton per mile. With the opening of the final Bowling section, the total cost was 5/10d per ton from coast to coast. Henceforth, much of the coastal bulk trade – such as West Highland slate previously carried north-about to Edinburgh – crossed the waist of lowland Scotland in the safety of a canal barge.[103]

The principal loser to these transport developments was the port of Bo'ness, eclipsed by Grangemouth. Port development at Grangemouth had commenced in the year of the opening of the canal cutting to Glasgow (1777) but had little impact on shipping patterns of the area until 1783. In that year a cut was made across the bends in the River Carron which greatly facilitated direct waterborne access to the Forth for the Carron Company. As the eastern saltwater terminal of the Forth–Clyde Canal, Grangemouth's monopoly of the transshipment trade was complete when the Bowling section was finally opened.[104]

---

103   *OSA*, Forth and Clyde Navigation, V, p. 591. On the 'north-about' Forth-Clyde sea route, light duties alone would account for one-fifth of the transportation cost by canal.
104   I. Bowman, 'The Grangemouth Dockyard Company', *Scottish Industrial History* (1977), I.2, XVIII, p. 4.

CONCLUSION

An impoverished Scotland located on the periphery of European trade and racked by internal religious and political strife was ill prepared for the imposition of aggressive mercantilism that followed on Cromwell's invasion. Thereafter, the prosperity – and ultimately the stability – of the Scottish nation became increasingly identified with the fluctuating state of maritime relations with her dominant neighbour. This was, in turn, largely predetermined by the English Navigation Acts and the course of the wars they fostered – the most tangible manifestations of the ascendant *clausum mare* school of political economy.

After the Restoration this relationship turned to confrontation when the English protectionist lobby succeeded in having the Scottish marine reassigned 'alien' status in a new series of English Navigation Acts, which effectively excluded Scottish traders from further participation in the English colonial and domestic trades. Completing their isolation was the royal promotion of patented English Merchant Adventurer monopolies and Fishery Companies.

Retaliation – in the form of a Scottish Navigation Act (1661), import embargoes, colonial and fishery schemes – failed to produce a workable homespun version of mercantilism. Such strikes for independence and parity all floundered on the dire lack of indigenous skills and capital and royal interference. Aiding and abetting in the general malaise, that kept the Scottish economy languishing for decades, was the internal feuding between the 'free' and 'unfree' burghs over the right to engage in foreign trade.

There were some, albeit unintentional, benefits from the restored regal union. One was the great windfall of prizes taken, mainly by Forth privateers, during the Second and Third Dutch Wars. Another was the right, secured by Lauderdale's 1668 Commission, to settle and conduct business in the English colonies. The 'Scots lots' conceded in the proprietary colonies served as the primary conduits for those enterprising Scots who later dispersed along the eastern seaboard of America. They were largely instrumental in nurturing a small but flourishing direct trade from Scottish ports, under a number of guises, to the English plantations – all of it in defiance of the English Navigation Acts.

Accelerating this shift in entrepreneurial focus to the Americas were recurrent warfare and security scares in Northern Europe and a resurgence of Barbary corsair activity in Southern and Mediterranean waters. These 'push-pull' factors combined to redirect Scottish overseas trading ventures westward – to the benefit of the Solway and Clyde ports.

Less dramatic but of equal significance in laying the foundations for her future participation in the expanding European and Atlantic trades was the convergence of Scottish maritime law with international practice. This was part of a great judicial review overseen by James, as High Lord Admiral of Scotland. Having restored the integrity of this once discredited office, and later as a Royal Commissioner, he sought to accommodate Scottish trading aspirations and so address the nation's chronic economic ailments. Under his *diktat*, however, Scottish maritime affairs came to be fully subordinate to the needs of the Crown. Commanders of the Stuart Navy in Scottish waters were henceforth expected to defend the realm without concern for local maritime jurisdiction or sensitivities.

The accession of the House of Orange to the British throne in 1688 abruptly ended this understanding and reopened the question of Scottish maritime sovereignty in all its aspects.

During the 1688-1705 period, against a backdrop of fratricidal warfare and failed colonial schemes, the outrages perpetrated by English captains and Scottish Jacobite commanders in Scottish waters fully exposed the fallacy of a 'United Kingdom'.

As full political schism seemed to be gathering its own momentum, wiser counsels prevailed. On the Scottish side, the recent harsh lessons of woefully inadequate maritime defences, the ill-fated Darien Scheme and the national backlash that led to the trial and execution of Captain Green, deeply influenced the position taken up by those Commissioners summoned south to negotiate a union. In their opinion, without a significant maritime 'force' at its disposal or England's 'assistance', an independent Scotland could never hope to sustain a presence in a world increasingly dominated by the major maritime powers.

On the English side, the paramount issue of state security dictated that the possibility of a disgruntled and independent Scotland forming an alternative trading alliance with or seeking the naval protection of a rival European maritime power was simply unacceptable.

To the pro-Unionists the inescapable conclusion was that *realpolitik* dictated that only a 'full incorporating' union would placate or satisfy the maritime interests either side of the Border. The alternative option of a Customs union had, by then, become untenable, the primary reason being that the trading regulations and agencies set up by the English Navigation Act of 1696 and Walpole's new high-tariff regime had so widened the gulf between the English and Scottish systems as to render them incompatible.

It was, therefore, imperative that the full rigour of the English mercantilist system be imposed on North Britain, immediately followed the 'covert annexation' of Scotland. As a result the Scottish Customs Service experienced the most extensive and immediate restructuring of any Government agency after May 1707. It was a rushed, ill-conceived, fraught and expensive business that permitted the operators of the black economy, which had taken root at every Scottish port during the interim period, to reorganise and consolidate their position.

Reports of widespread smuggling and sharp practice were adeptly exploited by English opponents of the terms of the Union to sway public opinion. While they did not succeed in their ultimate aims, their lobbying did result in series of purges and unique reviews undertaken by the Customs Inspectorate. From their surveys it is evident that there had been a boom in shipping activity in the North immediately following the Union. Scottish traders subsidised by Walpole's generous duty concessions and bounties (and smuggling) had broken away from bilateral trading in indigenous low-value bulk cargoes. Working within the protection of the Navigation Acts, many had taken up triangular and round-about multilateral trading with English and continental ports. This allowed them to 'trade-up' cargoes or contract to freight for a third party. In only a few years the critical stock of vessels and masters necessary to maintain a regular presence in all categories of maritime activity – foreign-going, coastal and fisheries – had been amassed at the Scottish ports.

This upturn in general trading did not, however, lead to an immediate expansion into the Atlantic trades. Security crises and the long depression of the 1720s – compounded by a general inexperience – prevented any such take-off. Indeed, the first attempts to break into African slaving, Greenland whaling and the Newfoundland sack trade directly from Scottish ports all proved costly failures.

Warfare continued to play its part in the slow but ongoing shift of the Atlantic traders to the Clyde as the east-coast ports bore the brunt of enemy incursions. Prior to 1750, trade slumps and the recurring threat of

Jacobitism restricted the Clyde's potential to exploit its wartime locational advantages over other major British ports.

After Culloden, however, the Government's moves to pacify the Highlands heralded a more stable era during which the Scottish shipping industry finally reaped the benefit of its membership of the British mercantilist system. The Seven Years War was a 'good war' for most Scottish west-coast traders. The short-lived disruptions in home waters were more than compensated for by the new trading opportunities in Canada and the West Indies. So much so that, after the restoration of the security of the North Channel (1760), the Clyde's Atlantic fleet established itself as the principal carrier of American tobacco for the next fifteen years. In such an atmosphere of business optimism – propped up by bounty increases – Scottish participation in the Greenland whaling and West Highland herring fisheries finally became established.

Security concerns also drove Government attempts to remedy the lack of reliable pilotage charts and navigational aids. On the other hand, harbour development – with the notable exception of Portpartick – was left to local interests to pursue. As a result only Port Glasgow and Greenock offered adequate wet and dry docks to the larger ocean-going hulls prior to 1790. Such facilities ensured their domination of the Atlantic trades in peace and war. Elsewhere, the limits imposed by nature set the numbers and depth of hulls at the estuary ports.

The 'high' period of mercantilism ended with the American War of Independence, which breached the system, dislocating Scotland's established overseas trading patterns in the process. For once the full psychological shock of war was brought into home waters by American raiders and their allies. So much so that the disruption and panic they created were wholly disproportionate to the damage they managed to inflict. In the long term, however, the war stimulated Scottish armaments manufacture and shipbuilding, laying the foundations of new staple industries.

The promotion and management of the various bounty schemes in the fisheries up to 1790 served to illustrate the contradictory forces inherent in the mercantilist system. The resort to tonnage bounties to nurture non-existent home industries may have laid the foundations but did little to promote an efficient and competitive industry, as Adam Smith put it, 'fishing for the bounty not the fish'. Likewise, the massive black economy in Scotland created by Walpole's high-tariff regime severely undermined the revenue received from Customs duties. This, in turn, led to irregular payments of bounty to the herring industry – with disastrous effects on the stability and growth of the fishing industry.

Without a bonded warehouse system to regulate the transit of re-exports, inordinate amounts of time and energy (and occasionally life) were expended by the Customs Service in curtailing the tax evasion endemic in the local coastal communities. Smith's *Wealth of Nations* (1776) was just one denunciation of this elaborate, often unenforceable, web of duties and bounty payments that stifled free enterprise.

In its defence, the protection afforded the Scottish marine by the British mercantilist system had the dynamic effect of nurturing virtually non-existent trades, skills and support industries. At the time of the Union, Scotland was an economic backwater without a manufacturing base of any consequence. By 1790 Scotland had caught up with her European rivals in seagoing trade, the fisheries, shipbuilding and armaments. Such skills and experience were invaluable in securing the place of the Scots in the great expansion of the trade of the British Empire in the following century. Likewise, the rise to pre-eminence of Scottish engineering with the new marine technologies was firmly based on the late eighteenth-century legacy: a world-class industry that owed as much to the introduction of the composite hull and new sail plans as to the more acclaimed iron hull and steam propulsion.

TONNAGE
MEASUREMENTS

Tonnage measurement was integral to the 'political arithmetick' of the mercantilist era. The co-existence of a number of differing tonnage measurements and descriptions, however, poses problems.

The prime calculation was 'registered' tonnage – the official description of the vessel's internal carrying capacity. This was first imposed on English vessels trading to the plantations and colonies by an appendix to the 1694 English Navigation Act and extended to Scottish vessels after 1707. The 'formula of 1694' calculated the internal measurements of the hull by: 'the length of the keel within the board, by the midships beam from plank to plank, multiplied by the depth of the hold from the plank below the keelson to the under part of the upper deck plank, divided by ninety-four':

$$\frac{\text{length x breadth x depth}}{94}$$

By 1720 the impracticality of regularly attempting to measure the true depth of a loaded and floating hull was conceded and a further Act of Parliament (6 George. I) dispensed with this. In its place was substituted an assumed depth derived by halving the breadth of the hull;

$$\frac{\text{length x breadth x ½ breadth}}{94}$$

This formula was extended to all seagoing vessels in the ports of Great Britain by an Act 13 George III c.14 (1773), as 'it is expedient that one certain Rule for this purpose should be settled and established in all cases'.

Soon afterwards the formula was revised (Act, 13 George III c.74) to simplify measuring of hulls by allowing all measurements to be taken externally. Length was the 'between the perpendiculars' dropped from the bow and the apex of the stern post with the deduction of 3/5th of the breadth to compensate for the rake of the hull. Breadth was measured at the extreme point of the hull on the outer side of the planking. The true depth of hold stayed out of the calculation:

$$\frac{(\text{length} - 3/5\text{th breadth}) \times \text{breadth} \times (\text{breadth} \; \frac{1}{2})}{94}$$

This formula has since become known as 'Builders' Old Measurement' (B.O.M.) or 'Old Law' measurement and was in force at the time of Act of Registry (1786). It was retained – with an adjustment to the size of the denominator – for the next fifty years.

The other common format of measurement – tonnage 'burthen' – was used in business transactions throughout the period. The modern concept of 'light displacement' tonnage (the weight of the empty vessel) did not then exist, nor, indeed, was it of interest to the owner or master during the mercantilist era. Their common concern was the carrying potential or 'burthen' of the vessel. This concept has its closest modern equivalent in 'net registered' tonnage (the income-yielding enclosed space).

The Scottish mariner William Falconer, in his *Universal Dictionary of the Marine* (1780), defined a vessel's burthen as 'the weight or measure of any species of merchandise that a ship will carry when fit for sea'. Such a flexible definition gave masters the scope to minimise their tonnage for duty purposes or maximise if claiming insurance or chartering to government agencies prior to 1786.

The relationship between the 'registered' and 'burthen' measurements changed with time and formulae. McCusker's research on tonnage measurements concluded that the pivotal point was the 1694 Navigation Act which presented the authorities with the opportunity to realign 'registered' (then over-estimated) with tonnage burthen.[1] After 1700 changes in hull design swung the drift between the two measurement the other way so that

---

1   J.J. McCusker, 'The tonnage of ships engaged in British Colonial trade during the Eighteenth Century', *Research in Economic History*, VI, pp. 73-106.

'registered' fell behind tonnage 'burthen'. This trend received a further boost with the '1720 formula' which dropped the true depth-of-hull element in the calculation. The database of Scottish vessels used here indicates that by the 1770s the ratio between 'registered' and 'burthen' measurements was in the region of 1:2 for the large bulk traders and 2:3 for the smaller 'sharp' hulls, such as cutters.

This was acknowledged by the authorities of the time. The Navy Board measured all hulls chartered during the war years by the formula but paid 'ton and tonnage' (up to an additional one-third over and above 'registered' tonnage) in acknowledgement of a vessel's true cargo-carrying potential.

The tonnage measurement(s) employed in the main sources prior to 1786 are as follows:

REGISTERED TONNAGE
('measured' or 'carpenter's'):

Plantation Registers; Naval Officers' Accounts; bounty vouchers, government contractors.

TONNAGE BURTHEN
('captain's' or 'cargo'):

Low variation: Port books – light duties – Greenwich Hospital (sailor's sixpence) – Danish Tolls – letters of marque declarations – Customs annual shipping returns.
High variation: Lloyd's Registers – newspaper advertisements for sale.

Even within a particular source, inconsistencies in reporting can cause the tonnage for the same vessel to fluctuate as much as 20% between entries prior to 1786.

THE 1725 REVIEW AND THE REGISTRATION OF VESSELS PRIOR TO THE ACT OF REGISTRY (1786)

The credibility of the Paul's 1725 Review is called into question by the existence of a second and fundamentally incompatible Customs review of Scottish shipping for the same period (1707-13). This second survey was ordered much later (1790) by the Committee of Trade. The anonymous Edinburgh Customs official charged with the task (almost certainly James Garrety) put forward 'after several attempts ... a guess' that the Scottish ports in 1707 had supported an impressive fleet of 528 vessels. Over the next five years this tally rose by a modest net gain of sixty-nine hulls.[1] His postscript expressed his concern for the accuracy of his report:

> It is observed that a very great proportion of the shipping
> belonging to Scotland both at the Union and in 1713 were not
> registered but owing to the want of materials it is hard to guess
> at this distance in time, what number of vessels and amount of
> tonnage and number of mariners might pertain to that part of
> the United Kingdom at either period.

From this admission it is plainly evident that he was unaware of the existence of the earlier 1725 Review and did not have access to its original source – the 'generall register'.[2] It would also seem fairly certain from his

---

1   GUL, MSS Gen 1057. Taken at face value, this second survey would imply that the Scottish fleet of 1707 had doubled in number since the Convention of Royal Burghs survey in 1692, which would contradict established opinion that the dire condition of the Scottish marine was only alleviated after 1707.

2   It was probably lost in the devastating fire that swept the London Customs House in 1742.

comment that few, if any, of the early Scottish port books and registers had survived by the time of his enquiry. All things considered, this second survey can be discarded as largely guesswork.

Of more concern is his assertion that 'a very great proportion' of Scottish masters had not registered their vessels immediately after 1707. If this comment is applied to the 1725 Review, that would imply that it cannot be taken as reporting the full Scottish marine at that time. His view may well reflect the deeply entrenched and jaundiced assumptions held by late eighteenth-century officialdom: which was that the earlier lawlessness and anti-establishment sentiment of the Scottish coastal communities engendered a wanton disregard for all statutory requirements – including the registration of foreign-going local vessels.

Logic, on the other hand, suggests that registration after December 1707 was one legal requirement that every Scottish trader and smuggler would adhere to. Failure to produce the vessel's register on demand was grounds for arrest at sea or at a colonial port and, ultimately, the confiscation of the vessel and its cargo. On the other hand the reward for conformity was the freedom to carry British and European manufactures to the British plantations and home market, including Ireland. There was, also, no significant financial incentive to avoid this requirement. After payment of the small registration fee no subsequent tax or duty was levied, other than the unavoidable harbour, wharfage and lights dues, on the vessel itself.

The physical act of registration, prior to the more rigorous system imposed by the Act of Registry (1786), was a relatively simple matter. One or more of the owners attested before the Collector of Customs at the home port as to their vessel's 'British' origin or produced a condemnation from a British Court of Vice-Admiralty if she was a foreign-built prize. Thereafter, all other essential documentation (Mediterranean passes and plantation certificates) was forthcoming via the local Collector.

It would therefore seem reasonable to assume that most, if not all, Scottish traders intent on a foreign-going venture registered their vessel in the six months following the Union or thereafter. This view finds strong support from Rupert Davis, one-time librarian to HM Customs and Excise and authority on eighteenth-century British shipping registers, who concluded his review of the 1707-86 period with the remark:

The Scots, perhaps out of naive Scottish pride, seem to have thought that the object of registry was to register as many vessels as possible to the Scottish ports ... [when] the real object of registry was precisely to register only those vessels that qualified [to engage in colonial trade under the requirements of the Navigation Acts] ... and hence to refuse to register those that did not.[3]

But there are two simpler explanations. Firstly, that Scottish owners and masters were more than canny, given their previous experiences, in protecting their new post-1707 legality when engaged in foreign-going and colonial trades or to the home market. Secondly, they were differentiating themselves from Irish vessels that were excluded from full trading rights to mainland Britain and the plantations until 1800.

It would seem, therefore, that the 1725 Review stands unchallenged as one of the most comprehensive maritime surveys to have survived from the early mercantilist era.

---

3   R.C. Davis, 'Ship Registry, 1707–1786' *Maritime History* (1972), 2.2, p.154.

APPENDIX C
INDEX OF VESSELS

Prior to the Act of Registry (1786) there was no formal or rigorous recording of a name change or replacement or change of home port or owners of a vessel. It must not, therefore, be assumed that all entries listed against a particular name refer to the same vessel.

343

344

BIBLIOGRAPHY

PRIMARY SOURCES

Ardrossan, Cunninghame District Council, Auchenharvie MSS, bundles 1, 15, 33 and 50.

Ayr, Burgh Records, B6/33.

Ayr, Carnegie Library, Balcombe private collection of Port Books of Ayr harbour (1774-80) and the letterbooks and accounts of Robert and Thomas Arthur, merchants of Irvine.

Dundee Archive and Record Centre, Customs Records Class I, Letter books Collector to the Board, CE 53, 70 and 80.

Glasgow City Archives, MSS TD/97, log book of John Dow, sailor from Saltcoats.

Dunlop of Garnkirk MSS 120 D12/11 family correspondence.

Shawfield MSS B10/15/6710, 1/82a; 1/42-43, 2/397, 332, 373 and 365, deeds and contracts registered with Glasgow Burgh Court.

Maxwell of Pollock MSS T/PM 107/7/20/4 correspondence concerning the fisheries.

Customs Records Class I, letter books Collector to the Board, CE 59, 60, 71, 73, 76 and 82.

Glasgow University Library, Hunterian Collection, MSS Gen 1057, annual extracts from the Customshouse Edinburgh to London.

Greenock, Her Majesty's Customs and Excise Office, Register of Shipping.

Inverness, Inverness Burgh Records MSS CTI/IB 36/1 and INV/M 11/1-8.

London, British Library, Harle: an MSS 6269 and 35126, customs survey and civil contracts.

London, National Maritime Museum, Admiralty A/1976/f.50.

London, Public Record Office, High Court of Admiralty 26/1-108 and 32/33, letter-of-marque declarations.

Treasury 1/146/13 and 1/94.

Admiralty 1/ 5121, Miscellanea, Correspondence.

Naval Officers Accounts (Chesapeake), CO5/1443, 1447 and 1450.

Edinburgh, National Archives of Scotland, Customs Records Class I, Collector to the Board, CE 51,54, 56, 57, 61, 63, 64, 65, 69, 77, 86, 87 and 93.

Exchequer, E. 504, 508 and E. 72-4.

Privy Council of Scotland, 1/49-58.

Clerk of Penicuik MSS GD 18 2476 and 6072.

Leven and Meville MSS GD 26 9/260.

Bruce of Kinross MSS GD 29 1962/23, 46/8 and 29/48.

Grant of Monymusk MSS GD 37 1/32 and 345.

Lothian MSS GD 40 5/24-5.

McPherson of Cluny MSS GD 80 568.

Douglas MSS GD 90 34/2.

Morton MSS GD 150 box 136.

Ross of Pitcalnie MSS GD 199 99.

Hall of Douglas MSS GD 206 2//206 and 289.

Lorn MacIntyre MSS 1279.

Auchenharvie MSS RH 15/106/801.

Court of Session processes 29/1752.

High Court of Admiralty Scotland, processes AC7-19.

Edinburgh, University of Edinburgh Library, Laing Manuscript, II, 490/1.

Mountstuart Archives, Bute family papers, BU/ 152 & 162

Saltcoats, North Ayrshire Museum, unlisted MSS; 'Account book of anchorage fees and harbour expenses 1738-40' and 'Accounts of Robert and James Kelso'.

Stirling, Central Regional Council Archives, Customs Records Class I, Letter books Collector to the Board, CE 67.

Orkney Library Archives, Kirkwall, Customs Records, Letter books Collector to the Board, CE 63.
Washington DC, Library of Congress, Neil Jamieson Papers, 4.

PRIMARY SOURCES PRINTED

Danish Sound Tolls database compiled by H.C. Johansen (Odense Universitet Denmark)
Liverpool Plantation Registers 1744-86 database compiled by D. Richardson, K. Beedham and M.M. Schofield
    (Economic and Social Research Council Data Archives)
Lloyds Registers 1764, 1776, 1778-82
The Commonwealth Sea Officers of the Royal Navy 1660-1815, I, compiled by the National Maritime Museum,
    London.
Ships into Leith 1624-1690, database compiled by S. Mowat.

PRINTED RECORDS

Accounts of the proceedings of the Estates in Scotland (1689-90), E.V.M. Balfour-Melville (ed), Scottish History
    Society (Edinburgh, 1954), I.
Acts of Parliament of England.
Acts of Parliament of Great Britian.
Acts of Parliament of Scotland.
Acts of Parliament and Ordinance of the Interregnum, 1.
Act of the Privy Council (Colonial), I.
Calendar of State Papers, Charles II, CXXXIII.
Documents of the American Revolution, K.G. Davies (ed.) (Dublin, 1976).
Extracts from the Customs House Reports of Campbeltown, B.R. Leftwich (ed.) compiled from the McEachran
    Collection, No. 146, Dunoon Library.
Extracts from the Records of the Convention of the Royal Burghs of Scotland, Pillan and Wilson (eds.) (Edinburgh,
    1918).
Extracts from the Records of the Burgh of Aberdeem, Scottish Burgh Records Society (Edinburgh, 1922).
Extracts from the Records of the Burgh of Edinburgh, M. Wood (ed.) (Edinburgh, 1940 & London 1950).
Extracts from the Records of the Burgh of Glasgow, R. Renwick (ed.) (Glasgow, 1912).
Records of the Privy Council of Scotland, P. Hume Brown (ed.) (Edinburgh, 1909), Series iii, 1-14.
Miscellany of the Scottish Burgh Records Society, J.D. Marwick (ed.) (Edinburgh, 1881).
Naval Documents of the American Revolution, W.J. Morgan (ed.) (Washington, 1976).
State Papers Domestic, 1658-1659.
State Papers America and West Indies, 1675-76.
State Papers (Scotland) Warrant Books, VXV and XIX.
The Statistical Account of Scotland 1791-99, Sir. J. Sinclair (ed.) the maritime parishes.
The Kirkcaldy Burgh Records. L. Macbean (ed.) (Kirkcaldy, 1908).
Vice-Admiralty Court of Argyll: processes 1711-1823, W.F.L Bigwood (ed.) No. 2. (private, 1999).

NEWSPAPERS AND JOURNALS

Aberdeen Journal	*Edinburgh Evening Chronicle*	*Lloyd's List*
Caledonian Mercury	*Edinburgh Flying Post*	*London Gazette*
Broadside	*Edinburgh Gazette*	*Scots Courant*
Edinburgh Courant	*Glasgow Journal*	*Scots Post Boy*
Edinburgh Chronicle	*Glasgow Mercury*	

CONTEMPORARY PRINTED

Anonymous, *A letter from a Gentleman in the Country to His Friend at Edinburgh: Wherein it is clearly Proved, That
    the Scottish African and Indian Company is Exactly Calculated for the Interest of Scotland* (Edinburgh, 1696).
Brereton, W., *Travels in Holland, the United Provinces, England, Scotland and Ireland* (reprinted by the
    Chetham Society, 1844).
Chalmers, G., *Opinions of Eminent Lawyers* (London, 1814), I.
Chalmers, G., *Opinions on interesting subjects of public law and commercial policy arising from American Independence*
    (London, 1783).

Cunninghame, R.R., *A Concise statement of the coal process betwixt the Curators of Mr. Warner of Ardeer and Rob. R.. Cunninghame of Auchenharvie*, unsigned (Dalry, 1801).

Cunninghame, R.R., *To the Shipping Interest of the Clyde*, pamphlet North Ayrshire Museum, bundle 22, item 3.

Dalrymple of Stair, Sir James., *Institutions of the Law of Scotland* (Edinburgh, 1681).

Defoe, D., *The History of the Union of Great Britain* (Edinburgh, 1709).

Defoe, D., *A tour through Great Britain* (1727).

Falconer's *Maritime Dictionary* (1780).

Franck, R. 'Northern Memories', reprinted in P. Hume-Brown (ed.), *Early Travellers in Scotland* (Edinburgh, 1891).

Gee, *The Trade and Navigation of Great Britain* (London, 1729)

Gibson, J., *The History of Glasgow* (Glasgow, 1777).

Heron, R., *Observations made in a journey through the western counties of Scotland in the autumn of 1792* (Glasgow, 1799), I and II.

Knox, J., *A View of the Empire, more especially Scotland, with some proposals for the improvement of that country, the extension of its fisheries, and the relief of the people* (London, 1785), third edition, I and II.

Macpherson, D., *Annals of Commerce, Manufactures, Fisheries and Navigation* (Edinburgh, 1805).

McUre, J., *A View of the City of Glasgow and an acount of its origin, use and progress* (Glasgow, 1736, reprinted 1830).

Munn, T., *England's Treasure by Foraign Trade. Or, the ballance of our Foraign Trade is the Rule of our Treasure* (London, 1664).

Sheffield, Lord, *Observations on the commerce of the American States* (London, 1783)

Spruell, J., *An Accompt Current betwixt Scotland and England* (Edinburgh, 1705).

Wilson, J., *General View of the Argriculture of Renfrewshire* (Paisley, 1812).

SECONDARY PUBLICATIONS

Albion, R.G., *Forests and Sea Power*, (Harvard Economic Studies Cambridge, Massachusetts, 1926), No. 29.

Aldridge, D., 'Jacobites and the Scottish Seas, 1689-1719', in T.C. Smout (ed.), *Scotland and the Sea* (Edinburgh, 1992), pp. 76-93.

Anderson, M.S., *Europe in the eighteenth century 1713-1783* (London, 1961).

Anonymous, *Solway Ports and Shipping in the Past* (Craigie College, 1976), pamphlet No.13.

Anonymous, *Carron Company* (Falkirk, 1959).

Anonymous, 'Notes on the History of the Burgh Cess or Stent Tax, payable by the Town of Saltcoats and Parishes of Ardrossan and Stevenston, 1710-1896', in O. Kelly (ed.), *Quater Centenary – Burgh of Saltcoats* (Glasgow, 1928), pp.19-23.

Anonymous, *Two Centuries of shipbuilding – Scotts of Greenock* (London, 1906).

Arbuthnot, J., *An Historical Account of Peterhead* (Aberdeen, 1815).

Armitage, D., 'The Scottish vision of empire: intellectual origins of the Darien Scheme', in J. Robertson (ed.), *A Union for Empire: political thought on the British Union of 1707* (1995), pp. 97-118.

Ash, M., *This Noble Harbour* (Edinburgh, 1991).

Astrom, S-E., 'North European timber exports to Great Britain, 1760-1810', in P.L. Cottrell and D.H. Aldcroft (eds), *Shipping, Trade and Commerce. Essays in memory of Ralph Davis* (Leicester, 1981), pp. 81-97.

Balneaves, E., *The Windswept Isles* (London, 1677).

Ben Jones, R., *The Hanoverians* (Leicester, 1972).

Black, J., *A System of Ambition?* (London, 1991).

Blake, G., *Clyde Lighthouses* (Glasgow, 1950).

Boxer, C.R., *The Dutch Seaborne Empire* (London, 1965)

Brock, W.R. and C.H., *Scotus Americanus* (Edinburgh, 1982).

Bromley, J.S., 'Jacobite Privateers in the Nine Years War', in A. Whiteman, J.S. Bromley and P.G.M. Dickson (eds.), *Statesmen, Scholars and Merchants* (Oxford, 1973).

Bruijn, J.A., 'Dutch Privateering during the Second and Third Dutch Wars', *Course et Piraterie*, papers to the 15th Conference of the Commission Internationale d'Histoire Maritime (San Francisco,1975), II. pp. 397-417.

Buchan, A.R., *The Port of Peterhead* (Peterhead, 1980).

Cameron, A.D., 'The Hub of the Highlands', Inverness Field Club (Inverness, 1975).

Campbell. J., *Leith and its Antquities* (Edinburgh, undated).

Campbell, J.R.H., *Clyde Coast Smuggling* (Darvel, 1994).

Campbell, R.H., *Carron Company* (Edinburgh, 1961).

Campbell, R.H., *Scotland since 1707* (Oxford, 1971).

Carragher, P.C., *Saltcoats: Old and New* (Saltcoats, 1909).

Carson, E., *The Ancient and Rightful Customs* (London, 1972).

Chalmers, G., *Caledonia* (London, 1810).

Chalmers, G., *Opinions of Eminent Lawyers* (London, 1814), I.

Chapman, R., *Miscellanea Scotica* (Glasgow, 1820), III.

Chisholm, A., *Millport Pier Album* (Largs, 1992).

Clark, G., *The Later Stuarts 1660-1714* (Oxford, 1955).

Clark, V.E., *The Port of Aberdeen* (Aberdeen, 1921).

Clark, W.E., *Ben Franklin's Privateers* (Baton Rouge, 1956).

Cleland, J., *Annals of Glasgow* (Glasgow, 1816).

Cochran, L.E., *Scottish Trade with Ireland in the Eighteenth Century* (Edinburgh, 1985).

Cowes, W.L., *The Royal Navy* (New York, 1960).

Crighton, J., *Contributions to Scottish Maritime History* (Ayr, undated).

Crowhurst, P., *The Defence of British Trade* (London, 1977).

Cullen, L.M., *Anglo-Irish Trade Trade 1660-1800* (Manchester, 1968).

Cullen, L.M., *Smuggling and the Ayrshire Economic Boom of the 1760s and 1770s* (Ayrshire Archaeological and Natural History Society, 1994), Monograph No.14.

Cullen, L.M. and Smout, T.C., (eds), *Comparative Aspects of Scottish and Irish Economic and Social History* (Edinburgh, 1977).

Cunninghame, R.R., *Portpatrick through the ages* (Stranraer, 1985).

Davis, R., *The Rise of the English Shipping Industry in the 17th and 18th centuries* (Newton Abbot, 1962).

Davis, R., *The Rise of the Atlantic Economy* (London, 1973).

Dennistoun, J. (ed.), *Cochrane Consep* (Glasgow, Maitland Club, 1836).

Devine, T.M., *The Tobacco Lords* (Edinburgh, 1975).

Devine, T.M., 'The Cromwellian Union and the Scottish Burghs: The Case of Aberdeen and Glasgow, 1652-60', in J. Butt and J.T. Ward (eds.), *Scottish Themes* (Edinburgh, 1976), pp. 1-16.

Devine, T.M. and Dickson, D. (eds), *Ireland and Scotland* (Edinburgh, 1985).

Devine, T.M. and Jackson, G., (eds), *Glasgow* (Manchester, 1995), I.

Dickinson, W.C. and Pryde, G.S., *A New History of Scotland* (Edinburgh, 1962).

Dobson, D., *Scottish Maritime Records 1600-1850* (St. Andrews, 1997).

Dobson, D., *Ships from Scotland to America 1628-1828* (Baltimore, 1998).

Dobson, D., *The Mariners of the Clyde and Western Scotland* (St. Andrews, 1994).

Donaldson, G., *Scotland: James V – James VII* (Edinburgh, 1965).

Donnachie, I., *The Industrial Archaeology of Galloway* (Newton Abbot, 1971).

Donnachie, I. and McLeod, I., *Old Galloway* (Newton Abbot, 1974).

Dow, J.L., *Greenock* (Greenock, 1975).

Dunlop, A.I., *The Royal Burgh of Ayr* (Edinburgh, 1953).

Dunlop, J., *The British Fisheries Society* (Edinburgh, 1978).

Dyson, J., *Business in Great Waters* (London, 1977).

Ehrman, J., *The British Government and Commercial Negotiations with Europe 1783-1793* (Cambridge, 1961)

Ehrman, J.R.R., *The Navy in the War of William III* (Cambridge, 1953).

Eunson, J., *Shipwrecks of Fair Isle* (Stromness, undated).

Eyre-Todd, G., *History of Glasgow* (Glasgow, 1934), III.

Fereday, R.P., *The Longhope Battery and Towers* (Stromness, 1971).

Fergusson, J., 'A wine merchant's letter book', in R. Pares and A.J.P Taylor (eds.), *Essays Presented to Sir Lewis Namier* (reprinted in *Ayrshire Collections*, Ayrshire Archaeological and Natural History Society), IV, pp. 216-224.

Flinn, D., *Travellers in a Bygone Shetland: An anthology* (Edinburgh, 1989).

Fraser, D., *The Smugglers* (Montrose, 1971).

Fullarton, W., *General View of the Agriculture of the County of Ayr* (Edinburgh, 1793).

Gibson, J.S., *Playing the Scottish Card: the Franco-Jacobite Invasion of 1708* (Edinburgh, 1988).

Gradish, S.F., *The Manning of the British Navy during the Seven Years War* (London, 1980).

Graham, A., *Old Ayrshire Harbours* (Ayrshire Archaeological and Natural History Society, 1988), Monograph No.3.

Graham, E.J., *The shipping trade of Ayrshire 1689-1791* (Ayrshire Archaeological and Natural History Society, 1991), Monograph No.8.

Graham, E.J., *The Port of Ayr 1727-80* (Ayrshire Archaeological and Natural History Society, 1995), Monograph No.15.

Graham, E.J., *Robert Reid Cunninghame of Seabank House* (Ayrshire Archaeological and Natural History Society, 1997), Monograph No. 17.

Grant, J., *Old and New Edinburgh* (London, undated), III.

Grant, J., *The Old Scots Navy* (London, 1914).

Gray, M., *The Fishing Industries of Scotland 1790-1914* (Oxford, 1978).

Hague, D.B. and Christie, R., *Lighthouses: their architecture, history and archaeology* (Llandysul, 1975).

Hamilton, H., *An Economic History of Scotland in the eighteenth century* (Oxford, 1963).

Hancock, D., *Citizens of the World* (Cambridge, 1995) .

Harper, L.A., *The English Navigation Laws* (New York, 1973).

Hearn, C., *Washington's Schooners* (Maryland, 1995).

Hobsbawm, E.J., *The Age of Revolution* (London, 1973).

Holland, H.H., *The King's Customs* (London, 1910), ii, pp. 490-1.

Hoon, E.E., *The Organisation of the English Customs System 1696-1786* (1938, reprinted Newton Abbot, 1968).

Insh, G.P., *Papers relating to the ships and voyages of the Company of Scotland Trading to Africa and the Indies* (Scottish History Society, Edinburgh, 1924), No. 87.

Insh, G.P., *The Darien Scheme* (London, 1947).

Irvine, J.W., *Lerwick* (Lerwick, 1985).

Jackson, G., *The British Whaling Trade* (London, 1978).

Jackson, G., 'Scottish Shipping, 1775-1805', in P.L.Cottrell and D.H. Aldcroft (eds.), *Shipping, Trade and Commerce: Essays in memory of Ralph Davis* (Leicester, 1981), pp. 117-136.

Jackson, G., 'Government Bounties and the Establishment of the Scottish Whaling Trade, 1750-1800', in J. Butt and J.T. Ward (eds.), *Scottish Themes* (Edinburgh, 1976), pp. 45-66.

Jackson, G. with Kinnear., K., *The Trade and Shipping of Dundee 1780-1850* (Dundee, 1991).

Jackson, G. and Lythe, S.G.E. (eds.), *The Port of Montrose* (Tayport, 1993).

Jones, S.J., *Dundee and District* (Dundee, 1968).

Karras, A.L., *Sojourners in the Sun* (London, 1992).

Kent, H.S.K., *War and Trade In Northern Seas: Anglo-Scandavian Economic Relations in the Mid Eighteenth Century* (Cambridge, 1973).

Lamb, J., *The Annals of an Ayrshire Parish* (Glasgow, 1896).

Landsman, N.E., *Scotland and its First American Colony 1683-1765* (New Jersey, 1985).

Lenman, B., *From Esk to Tweed* (Glasgow, 1975).

Lipson, E., *The Economic History of England* (London, 1948).

Lockhart, J.Y., *Kirkcaldy Harbour, an historical outline* (Kirkcaldy, 1940).

Lounsbury, R.G., *The British Fishery at Newfoundland* (reprint, 1969).

Lubbock, B., *The Arctic Whalers* (Glasgow, 1937).

Lyon D.A., *Ayr in the Olden Times* (Ayr, 1928).

Lythe, S.G.E., 'Early modern trade', in G. Jackson and S.C.E. Lythe (eds.), *The Port of Montrose* (Tayport, 1993), pp. 87-101.

McAloon, T., 'A Minor Scottish Merchant in General Trade: the case of Edward Burd, 1728-39', in J. Butt and J.T. Ward (eds.), *Scottish Themes* (Edinburgh, 1976), pp. 17-27.

MacArthur, W.F., *History of Port Glasgow* (Glasgow, 1932).

McDowall, W., *The History of the Burgh of Dumfries* (Dumfries, 1972).

MacGregor, D.R., *Merchant Sailing Ships* (Watford, 1980).

MacInnes, C.M., *The Early English Tobacco Trade* (London, 1926).

Macintyre, D., *The Privateers* (London, 1975).

McJannet, A.F., *The Royal Burgh of Irvine* (Glasgow, 1938).

MacLagan, I. *Rothesay Harbour 1752-1975* (Buteshire Natural History Society), XIX.

MacMillan, D.S., 'The "New Men" in Action: Scottish Mercantile and Shipping Operations in the North American Colonies, 1760-1825', in D.S. MacMillan (ed.), *Canadian Business History* (Toronto, 1972), pp. 45-103.

Mason, J., *The History of the Trinity House of Leith* (Glasgow, undated).

Marwick, J., *The River Clyde and the Clyde Burghs* (Glasgow, 1909).

Middleton, A.P., *The Tobacco Coast* (Maryland, 1989).

Moir, D.G., *The Early Maps of Scotland* (Edinburgh, 1973).

Morison, S.E., *John Paul Jones* (Boston, 1959).

Morris, M.S., *Colonial Trade of Maryland* (Baltimore, 1914).

Mowat, S., *The Port of Leith* (Edinburgh, 1994).

Munro, J., *The Founding of Tobermory* (Hereward Press for the Society of West Highland and Island Research, 1976).

Nicholson, J.R., *Lerwick Harbour* (Lerwick, 1987).

Oakley, O.A., *The Second City* (Glasgow, 1946).
Pagan, J., *Sketches of the History of Glasgow* (Glasgow, 1847).
Pagan, T., *The Convention of the Royal Burghs* (Edinburgh, 1920).
Paterson, J., *History of the Counties of Ayr and Wigton* (Edinburgh, 1863), I.
Paxton J. and Wroughton, J., *Smuggling* (London, 1971).
Pares, R., *War and Trade in the West Indies* (New York, 1938)
Parry, J.H., *Trade and Dominion* (London, 1971)
Pollitt, A.G., *Historic Inverness* (Inverness, 1981).
Pryde, G.S., *The Treaty of the Union of Scotland and England 1707* (London, 1950)
Riddell, J.F., *Clyde Navigation* (Edinburgh, 1979).
Rodger, N.A.M., 'Britain', in J.B. Hattendorf (ed.), *The State of Naval and Maritime History* (Newport, 1994), pp. 45-58.
Salmon, T.T., *Borrowstoneness and District* (Edinburgh, 1913).
Smith, G., *King's Cutters* (London, 1983).
Smith, G., *Something to declare* (London, 1980).
Smith, H.C., *Shetland Life and Trade 1550-1914* (Edinburgh, 1984).
Smith, R.S., *The History of Greenock* (Greenock, 1921).
Smout, T.C., *Scottish Trade on the Eve of the Union* (Edinburgh, 1963).
Smout, T.C., 'Where had the Scottish economy got to by the third quarter of the eighteenth century', in I. Hont and M. Ignatieff (eds.), *Wealth and Virtue* (Cambridge, 1983), pp. 45-72.
Stark, F.R., *The Abolition of Privateering and the Declaration of Paris* (New York, 1897).
Stevenson, S., *Anstruther* (Edinburgh, 1989).
Strawhorn, J., *750 years of a Scottish School – Ayr Academy 1233-1983* (Ayr, 1983).
Strawhorn, J.,. *A History of Ayr* (Edinburgh, 1989).
Strawhorn, J., *A History of Irvine* (Edinburgh, 1985).
Syrett, D., *Shipping and the American War of Independence* (London, 1970).
Syrett, D, *The Royal Navy in American Waters 1775-1783* (Aldershot, 1989).
Szechi, D., 'The Hanoverians and Scotland', in M. Greengrass (ed.), *Conquest and Coalescence* (London, 1991), pp. 116-133.
Tyson, W., *Rope: a history of the Hard Fibre Cordage Industry in the United Kingdom* (London, 1966).
Ward A.W. and others (eds.), *The Cambridge Modern History* (Cambridge, 1909), VI.
Weir, D., *History of the Town of Greenock* (Glasgow, 1829).
Whatley, C.A., *The Finest Place for a lasting Colliery - Coal Mining Enterprise in Ayrshire* (Ayrshire Archaeological and Natural History Society, 1983), Monograph No.2.
Whatley, C.A., *Bought and sold for English gold'? Explaining the union of 1707* (2nd edition) (East Linton, 2001)
Whyte, I., 'All Kynds of Graine: the trade in victual circa 1680-1825', in G. Jackson and S.C.E. Lythe (eds.), *The Port of Montrose* (Tayport, 1993), pp.115-124.
Wilkins, F., *Strathclyde's Smuggling Story* (Blakedown, 1992).
Wilkins, F., *Dumfries and Galloway's Smuggling Story* (Blakedown, 1993).
Wilkins, F., *The Smuggling Story of the Two Firths* (Blakedown, 1993).
Wilkins, F., *The Smuggling Story of the Northern Shore* (Blakedown, 1995).
Wilkins, F., *George Moore and friends* (Blakedown, 1994).
Willan, T.S., *The English Coasting Trade 1600-1750* (Manchester, 1938 and 1967).

ARTICLES IN JOURNALS

Armstrong, J., 'The significance of Coastal Shipping in British Domestic Transport 1550-1830', *International Journal of Maritime History* (1991), III, No.2, pp. 63-94.
Barritt, M.K., 'The Navy and the Clyde in the American War 1777-1783', *Mariner's Mirror* (1969), LV, pp. 33-42.
Baty, T., 'The Judge Admiral of Scotland', *Juridical Review* (1954), pp. 144-154.
Behre, G., 'Sweden and the rising of 1745', *Scottish Historical Review* (1972), 51, No.152, pp. 148-171.
Behre, G., 'Two Swedish expeditions to rescue Prince Charles', *Scottish Historical Review* (1980), LIX, pp.140-153.
Bell, C.J.M., 'The *Dartmouth*, a British frigate wrecked off Mull 1690', *International Journal of Nautical Archaeology and Underwater Exploration* (1978), VII, pp. 29-58.
Bowman, I., 'The Grangemouth Dockyard Company', *Scottish Industrial History* (1977), 1.2, pp. 4-9.
Clissold, S., 'The Ransom Business', *History Today* (1976), XXVI, No.12 pp. 779-787.
Coull J.R., 'Fisheries in the North-East of Scotland before 1800', *Scottish Studies* (1969), No.13, pp. 17-32.

Crispin, B., 'Clyde Shipping and the American War', *Scottish Historical Review* (1926), 41, pp. 124-133.

Cullen, L.M., 'Smuggling in the North Channel in the eighteenth century', *Scottish Economic and Social History* (1987), 7, pp. 9-26.

Davis, R., 'The Rise of Protection in England 1689-1786', *Economic History Review* (1966), 2nd series, XIX, pp. 306-317.

Dell, R.F., 'The operational record of the Clyde tobacco fleets', *Scottish Economic and Social History* (1982), II, pp. 1-17.

Denholm, P., 'Captain Troop and Mister Sharp: a contrast in eighteenth century entrepreneurial trading styles', *Scottish Industrial History* (1990), XI-XIII, pp. 85-102.

Devine, T.M., 'Glasgow merchants and the collapse of the tobacco trade 1775-1783', *Scottish Historical Review* (1973), 52, pp. 50-74.

Devine, T.M., 'Transport Problems of Glasgow West India Merchants during the American War of Independence 1775-83', *Transport History* (1971), IV, pp. 266-304.

Duncan, W.R.H., 'Aberdeen and the early development of the whaling industry 1750-1800, *Northern Scotland*, 3.1, pp. 47-59.

Durie, A.J., 'Gentlemen pretty much strangers to the Baltic trade: the Edinburgh Roperie and the Sailcloth Company 1750-1802, *Scottish Industrial History* (1992), XIV-XV, pp. 27-34.

Farnell, J.E., 'The Navigation Act of 1651, the First Dutch War, and the London Merchant Community', *Economic History Review* (1964), XVI, pp. 439-452.

Farr, G., 'Custom House Ship Registers', *Mariner's Mirror* (1969), 55, pp. 3-15.

French, C.J., 'Seamen's Sixpences and Eighteenth-Century Shipping Records: An Exercise in Shipping Reconstruction', *International Journal of Maritime History* (1995), VII, No.1, pp. 57-81.

Fryer, L.G., 'The Covenanters' lost Colony in South Carolina', *Scottish Archives* (1996) 2, pp. 98-106.

Gavine, D., 'Navigation and Astronomy teachers in Scotland outside the Universities', *Mariner's Mirror* (1990), LXXVI, pp. 5-12.

Gibson, A.J.S. and T.C. Smout, 'Regional prices and market regions: the evolution of the early modern Scottish grain market', *Economic History Review*, XLVIII, 2 (1995), pp. 258-282.

Goldenberg, J.A., 'An analysis of shipbuilding sites in Lloyd's Register of 1776', *Mariner's Mirror* (1973), 59, pp. 419-433.

Gordon, J., 'A chronicle of press reports relating to John Paul Jones', *Scottish Genealogist* (1973), XX, No.2, pp. 39-50.

Gouldesburgh, P., 'An Attempted Scottish Voyage to New York in 1669', *Scottish Historical Review* (1961), 40, pp. 56-62.

Graham, A., 'Morison's Haven', *Proceedings of the Society of Antiquaries of Scotland* (Edinburgh, 1961-2), pp. 300-303.

Graham, A., 'Old harbours of Dunbar', *Proceedings of the Society of Antiquaries of Scotland* (Edinburgh, 1966-7), pp. 173-190.

Graham, E.J., 'The Scottish Marine in the Dutch Wars', *Scottish Historical Review* (1982), LXI, No. 171, pp. 67-74.

Graham, E.J., 'Saltcoats - a pre-railway coal port', *Scottish Industrial History* (1978), 2.1, pp. 14-33.

Greeves, J.R.H., 'Captain Thurot's Expedient', *Dumfriesshire and Galloway Natural History and Antiquarian Society* (1961), XXXVII, pp. 147-156.

Hannay, R.K., 'Gibraltar in 1727', *Scottish Historical Review* (1919), XVI, pp. 325-334.

Hamilton, H., 'The founding of the Carron Ironworks', *Scottish Historical Review* (1928), XXV, pp. 185-193.

Haynes, M., 'Alloa Port, Customs and Excise Accounts', *Forth Naturalist and Historian* (1976), III, pp. 113-127.

Harris, B., 'Scotland's Herring Fisheries and the Prosperity of the Nation, c.1660-1760' *Scottish Historical Review* (2000), LXXIX, 39-60.

Jarvis, R.C., 'Cumberland Shipping in the eighteenth century', *Transactions of the Cumberland and Westmoreland Antiquarian and Archaeological Society* (1955), 54, pp. 212-235.

Jarvis, R.C., 'Ship Registry to 1707', *Maritime History* (1971), 1.1, pp. 29-45.

Jarvis, R.C., 'Ship Registry 1707-1786', *Maritime History* (1972), 2.2, pp. 159-167.

Jarvis, R.C., 'The Register of Shipping – 1786', *Maritime History* (1974), 4.1, pp. 12-30.

Johansen, H. C., 'Scandinavian shipping in the late eighteenth century in a European perspective', *Economic History Review* (1992), XLV, 3, pp. 479-493.

Laing, W., and Urquhart, R.H.J., 'A seventeenth century description of herring fishing off the west coast of Scotland', *Scottish Archives* (1999), 5, pp.100-106.

Lindsay, J.M., 'Some aspects of the Timber Supply in the Highlands, 1700-1850', *Scottish Studies* (1975), XI, pp. 39-51.

Lythe, S.G.E., 'The Dundee Whale Fishery', *Scottish Journal of Political Economy* (1964) XI, pp. 158-69.

McCusker, J.J., 'The tonnage of ships engaged in British Colonial trade during the Eighteenth Century', *Research in Economic History* (1981), VI, pp. 73-106.

McCusker, J.J., 'The Current Value of English Exports 1697-1800', *William and Mary Quarterly* (1971), XXVIII, pp. 607-628.

MacDonald, S., 'Campbeltown's American trade in the eighteenth century', *The Kintyre Magazine* (Edinburgh, 1978), IV, pp. 3-6.

McMillan, A.R.G., 'The Admiral of Scotland', *Scottish Historical Review* (1922), 77, pp. 11-18.

McMillan, A.R.G., 'Admiralty Patronage in Scotland in 1702-1705', *Juridical Review* (1938), pp. 144-154.

Malo, H., 'American privateers at Dunkerque', *Proceedings of the United States Naval Institute* (1911), XXXVII, No.3, pp. 933-993.

Michie, R.C., 'North-east Scotland and the northern whale fishing 1752-1893', *Northern Scotland* (1966), IV, pp. 61-85.

Middleton, A.P., 'The Chesapeake Convoy System 1662-1763', *William and Mary Quarterly* (1946), III, pp. 182-207.

Mitchell, J.F., 'Englishmen in the Scottish Excise Department 1707-1823', *Scottish Geneaologist* (1966), XIII, pp.16-28.

Mitchison, R., 'Two Northern Ports', *Scottish Studies* (1963), 7, pp. 75-82.

Moore, J.N., 'Thomas Winter's Chart of the Solway Firth', *Transactions of the Dumfries and Galloway Natural History and Antiquarian Society* (1984), LIX, pp.57-63.

Morgan, K., 'Shipping Patterns and the Atlantic Trade of Bristol 1749-1770', *William and Mary Quarterly* (1983), 46, No.3, pp. 506-577.

Nash, R.C., 'The English and Scottish Tobacco Trades in the Seventeenth and Eighteenth Centuries: Legal and Illegal Trade', *Economic History Review* (1982), XXXV, pp. 354-371.

Norris, J.M., 'The Struggle for Carron', *Scottish Historical Review* (1928), XXV, pp. 185-193.

O'Brien, P., 'Did Europe's mercantilist empires pay?', *History Today* (1996), 46, p.32.

O'Connor, T.M., 'The Embargo on the Export of Irish provisions 1776-79', *Irish Historical Studies* (1940), 2, pp. 3-11.

Paille, M., 'The French privateer *Du Teillay* which carried Prince Charles Edward to the Highlands 1745', *Mariner's Mirror*, XIII, pp. 309-10.

Petrie, D.A., 'The Piracy Trial of Luke Ryan', *American Neptune* (1995), 55, No.3, pp.185-204.

Pincus, S.C.A., 'Popery, Trade and Universal Monarchy: The Ideological Context of the Outbreak of the Second Anglo-Dutch War', *English Historical Review* (1992), CCCCXXII, pp. 1-29.

Prevost, W.A.J., 'The Solway Smugglers and the Customs Port of Dumfries', *Transactions of the Dumfries and Galloway Natural History and Antiquarian Society* (1984), LIX,, pp. 59-67.

Price, J.M., 'The Rise of Glasgow in the Chesapeake Tobacco Trade', *William and Mary Quarterly* (1954), XI, pp.179-199.

Price, J.M., 'New Time Series of Scotland's and Britain's Trade with the Thirteen Colonies and States 1740 to 1791', *William and Mary Quarterly* (1975), pp. 307-325.

Price, J.M., 'Buchanan and Simson, 1759-1763: A Different Kind of Glasgow Firm Trading to the Chesapeake', *William and Mary Quarterly* (1983), XL, No.1, pp. 2-41.

Price, J.M., 'Glasgow, the Tobacco Trade and the Scottish Customs 1707-1730', *Scottish Historical Review* (1984), LXIII, pp. 1-36.

Robertson, M.L., 'Scottish Commerce and the American War of Independence', *Economic History Review* (1956-7), IX, pp. 123-131.

Robinson, A.H.W., 'The charting of the Scottish coast', *Scottish Geographic Magazine* (1958), 74, pp. 116-127.

Robinson, W.S., 'Richard Oswald the Peacemaker', *Ayrshire Archaeological and Natural History Society* (1950-4), 3, pp. 119-135.

Rothschild, E., 'Adam Smith and conservative economics', *Economic History Review* (1992), 2nd series, XLV, 1, pp. 74-96.

Sawyers, L., 'The Navigation Acts Revisited', *Economic History Review* (1992), 2nd series, XLV, 1, pp. 262-284.

Scott, W.R., 'The Trade of Orkney at the end of the eighteenth century', *Scottish Historical Review* (1912-3), 10, pp. 360-368.

Sée, H., and Cormack, A.A. 'Commercial Relations between France and Scotland in 1707', *Scottish Historical Reveiw* (1926), 23, pp. 275-9.

Smith, D.B., 'Glasgow in 1781', *Scottish Historical Review* (1918), XVI, pp. 212-234.

Smout, T.C., 'Scottish Commercial Factors in the Baltic at the end of the seventeenth century', *Scottish Historical Review* (1960), 128, pp. 122-128.

Smout, T.C., 'The Glasgow merchant community in the seventeenth century', *Scottish Historical Review* (1968), 47, pp. 53-71.

Smout, T.C., 'The Overseas Trade of Ayrshire', *Ayrshire Archaeological and Natural History Society* (1961), 2nd series, 6, pp. 56-80.

Smout, T.C., 'Customshouse Letters to the Officers at Dunbar 1765', *Transactions of the East Lothian Antiquarian and Natural History Society*, LXVI, pp.145-157.

Sperling, J., 'The International Payments Mechanism in the Seventeenth and Eighteenth Centuries', *Economic History Review* (1965), second series, XIV, pp. 446-468.

Stell, G., 'Southerness Lighthouse', *Transactions of the Dumfries and Galloway Natural History and Antiquarian Society* (1984), LIX, pp. 64-9.

Steuart, A.F., 'Sweden and the Jacobites 1719-20', *Scottish Historical Review* (1926), XXIII, pp. 111-127.

Syrett, D., 'Home waters or America? The Dilemma of British Naval Strategy in 1778', *Mariner's Mirror* (1991), 77, No.4, pp. 365-377.

Syrett, D., 'The procurement of shipping by the Board of Ordnance during the American War 1775-82', *Mariner's Mirror* (1995), pp. 409-416.

Thomson J.K.J., 'Scotland and Catalonia and the American market in the eighteenth century', *Scottish Economic and Social History* (1989), IX, pp. 5-20.

Tucker, D.G., 'The Slate Islands of Scotland: a History of the Scottish Slate Industry', *Business History* (1977), XIX, pp. 18-36.

Unger, R.W., 'The Tonnage of Europe's Merchant Fleets 1300-1800', *American Neptune* (1992), 52, No. 4, pp. 247-261.

Whatley, C.A., 'The Ayrshire Salt Industry c.1707-1879', *Scottish Industrial History* (1977), 1.3, pp. 13-30.

Whatley, C.A., 'Scottish Salt Making in the 18th century: a regional study', *Scottish Industrial History* (1982), 5.2, pp. 2-26.

Whatley, C.A., 'Salt, coal and the Union of 1707', *Scottish Historical Review* (1987), LXVI, 1, pp. 26-45.

Whatley, C.A., 'Economic causes and consequences of the Union of 1707: a survey', *Scottish Historical Review* (1989), LXVIII, pp. 150-181.

Whatley, C.A., 'The Union of 1707, Integration and the Scottish Burghs: The Case of the 1720 ood Riots', *Scottish Historical Review* (1999), LXXVIII, pp. 150-181.

Wilson, C., 'Treasure and Trade Balances: the Mercantilist Problem', *Economic History Review* (1949), pp. 152-61.

Woodward, D., 'Anglo-Scottish Trade and English commercial policy during the 1660s', *Scottish Historical Review* (1977), 56, no.162, pp.153-174.

Zupro, R.E., 'The weights and measures of Scotland before the the Union', *Scottish Historical Review* (1977), LVI pp.119-145.

THESES AND DISSERTATIONS

Blair J.R., 'Greenock Harbour Development to 1886' (unpublished honours dissertation, Strathclyde University, 1976).

Bigwood, A., 'The Campbeltown Busses Fisheries' (unpublished M.Litt. dissertation, Aberdeen University, 1987).

Cochran, L.E., 'Scottish Trade with Ireland in the Eighteenth Century' (unpublished Ph.D. thesis, University of Stirling, 1980).

Devine, T.M., 'Glasgow Merchants in Colonial Trade 1770-1815' (unpublished Ph.D. thesis, University of Strathclyde 1972).

Graham E.J., 'Privateering – the Scottish Experience' (unpublished M.A. dissertation, University of Exeter, 1979).

Monaghan, S.J., 'The Dundee Shipping lists as a Record of the Impact of the Union upon the Dundee Shipping Industry 1705-10' (unpublished M.A. dissertation, University of Dundee, 1988).

Macdonald. E.G., 'The Overseas Trade of Port Glasgow and Greenock 1743-44' (unpublished honours dissertation, University of Strathclyde, 1967).

McClain, N., 'Aspects of the Scottish Economy during the American War of Independence' (unpublished M.Litt. dissertation, University of Strathclyde 1968).

Whatley, C.A., 'The Process of Industrialisation in Ayrshire 1707-1871' (unpublished Ph.D. thesis, University of Strathclyde, 1975).

355

GENERAL INDEX

Aberdeen 13, 34, 44, 71, 91-2, 110-11, 123-4, 128-34, 156, 158-9, 175, 190-2, 207, 209-15, 220-2, 226, 238, 241, 247, 276-8, 292, 304, 307, 312
Aberdeen Whale Fishery Company 241-3
Acheson, John – master 24
Act of Consolidation (1787) 249, 295
Act of Registry (1786) 249, 293, 297, 339
Act of Security (1703) 7, 94
Act of Union (1707) 97-9, 100, 108-9, 122, 133, 159, 160, 183, 199, 319, 331-2
Adair, John – geographer 299-300, 314
Adam, John – of Edinburgh – shipowner Carron fleet 280
Addison, Charles & Co. – shipowners 325
Admiralty, Danish 266
Admiralty, English (British post-1707) 23, 34, 74, 95, 148, 197, 206, 209, 222, 259-61, 290, 301-3, 313, 317, 328
Admiralty, Scottish 21, 27, 35-36, 71-5, 84, 86, 92, 98-9, 151, 159, 178, 184
Africa 15, 30, 84, 88, 193-4, 259, 332
Ailsa Craig – actions around 212, 264, 273
Ainslie, John – estate surveyor 304
Ainsworth – London agent 95
Alberoni – Spanish Prime Minister 162
Alexander – shipowner & Provost of Edinburgh 226, 229
Alexander, Sir William 40
Algerine duty 31
Algiers 31, 36, 168-70
Alicante 170
Aliens Act (English) 96
All Saints, battle of (1782) 287
Allen, Captain HMS 215
Alloa 58, 101, 108-9, 117, 124, 128-32, 182, 238, 283, 317, 320, 324-5, 328
America 15, 36-51, 87, 125, 144, 149, 154, 182, 228-34, 283, 290, 297, 320, 330-3
American privateers & cruisers 249-78, 280, 282-3, 301, 333
American War of Independence (1775-83) 7, 9, 28, 236, 249-97, 333
American whalers 242
Amherst, J – General 225
Amsterdam 144
Anderson, George – shipowner 227
Anderson, William – of Dowhill & Provost of Glasgow 23, 65

Andrew, John – master 181
Anglo-Dutch Maritime Treaty (1674) 28
Anglo-Portuguese Accord (1703) 151
Angram, Michael – shipowner 226
Angus, James – shipowner 227
Annan 123, 311
Annat Bank – Montrose 194
Anne, Empress of Russia 183
Anne, Queen 29, 89, 100, 111, 160, 199
Anstruther – Easter & Wester 75, 108, 124-30, 137-8, 141-2, 238
Anstruther Whale Fishing Company 243
Anstruther, Sir John – of Elie 243, 267
Antigua 39, 134, 180, 256, 287
Ap-Rice, John – master with Company of Scotland 95
Arbroath 56, 151, 276
Arbuckle, William – Glasgow merchant 88
Arbuthnot, Rev. Dr. John 98
Archangel 24, 135, 143, 156, 174, 265, 308, 319
Ardeer sand dunes 311
Ardnamurchan Point 149
Ardrossan 140, 328
Argyll, Duke(s) of 73, 160, 258, 265, 319
Argyll's Rebellion 145-8
Argyllshire 109, 145-8, 212, 266
Armaments 22, 65, 86, 111, 137-9, 149, 194, 209, 213, 228-9, 244, 265-6, 268, 273, 275-7, 333-4
Armstrong, A & M – estate surveyors 304
Arran, Isle of 29, 301, 307
Arthur, Robert – master, owner & merchant 180, 182, 214, 219, 225-8, 232, 234
Asia 15
Atholl, Duke of 104, 198
Attorney General – 183
Austrian Succession, War of (1744-8) 188-94
Ayr 13, 29, 38-43, 49, 62, 138-40, 142, 182, 225, 238, 247, 251, 264, 277, 283, 295, 301, 307, 309-11, 317
Ayrshire 40, 150, 266, 297, 309-11

Baird, James of Saughtonhall 23
Baird, John junior – shipowner 227
Baird, Sir Robert – of Saughton Hall 46
Balfour, John – Edinburgh publisher 229
Balance of Trade school 2-3, 8, 29, 52, 233, 237
Ballantrae 125, 212
Ballantyne – whaling master 241